KNIGHTS OF THE GOLDEN RULE

KNIGHTS OF THE GOLDEN RULE

The Intellectual as Christian Social Reformer in the 1890s

Peter J. Frederick

THE UNIVERSITY PRESS OF KENTUCKY

ISBN: 0–8131–1345–8

Library of Congress Catalog Card Number: 76–9497

A statewide cooperative scholarly publishing agency
serving Berea College, Centre College of Kentucky,
Eastern Kentucky University, Georgetown College,
Kentucky Historical Society, Kentucky State University,
Morehead State University, Murray State University,
Northern Kentucky State College, Transylvania University,
University of Kentucky, University of Louisville, and
Western Kentucky University.

Editorial and Sales Offices: Lexington, Kentucky 40506

For Robert and Eleanor Frederick,
my father and mother

CONTENTS

Christian Socialism is but the holy water with which the priest consecrates the heart-burnings of the aristocrat.

KARL MARX *

Then there is what is called a too intellectual tendency. Can there be too much intellect? We have never met with any such excess. But the criticism which is leveled at the laws and manners, ends in thought, without causing a new method of life. The genius of the day does not incline to a deed, but to a beholding. It is not that men do not wish to act; they pine to be employed, but are paralyzed by the uncertainty what they should do. The inadequacy of the work to the faculties is the painful perception which keeps them still. This happens to the best. . . . But we must pay for being too intellectual.

RALPH WALDO EMERSON †

PREFACE

This is a book about intellectuals as social reformers and what happens to them when they are inspired to do battle for Christian socio-economic ideals in the arena of practical politics and life. This is, essentially, a story of failure. We begin with three anecdotes.

In the summer of 1894 Professor Richard T. Ely, director of the new School of Economics, Political Science, and History at the University of Wisconsin, was on trial by a special committee of the University Board of Regents for economic heresy. He was charged not only with the teaching of subversive principles of political economy but also with being too heavily engaged as an activist reformer. Part of Ely's defense, other than appealing to rights of academic freedom, was to deny all allegations, especially those concerning his participation in the labor reform movement. "Only twice in my life," he wrote shortly before the official hearings began, "have I even spoken to audiences of working men, and I had always held myself aloof from agitations as something not in my province—something for which I am not adapted." His publications, he went on to explain, were written for "men of wealth and culture," the natural leaders of reform. Although he was later exonerated, the experience of the charges and hearings caused Ely to withdraw from activist reform organizations, to terminate his association with the dangerous radicalism of Professor George Herron of Iowa College, to soften his economic theories, and to cloister himself more and more in the safe confines of academia.[1]

One year later, a small group of men, organized as the Brotherhood of the Kingdom, met at a spacious summer home overlooking the Hudson River at Marlborough-on-the-Hudson, north of New York City. The brotherhood was formed in 1892 by Walter Rauschenbusch and two other Baptist ministers in New York. Its fundamental aim was to reestablish the idea of the kingdom of God on earth in the church and "to assist in its practical realization in the world." Specific aims included keeping contact with the common man and issuing regular reports, few of which the common man ever saw. The Third Annual Conference of the Brotherhood of the

Kingdom, held August 5–9, 1895, was devoted, as Rauschenbusch wrote in the Marlborough Visitor's Book, to the bringing of God's kingdom. To this end, the participants read papers. W. D. P. Bliss, the tireless Christian socialist organizer and publicist, spoke on the various spiritual, personal, and social conceptions of the Christian kingdom of God. He concluded that Jesus' conception of the kingdom embraced remaking the social order as well as saving individual souls. Rauschenbusch's paper, "Ideals of Social Reformers," urged that the brotherhood's task was "to wed Christianity and the social movement, infusing the power of religion into social efforts, and helping religion to find its ethical outcome in the transformation of social conditions." He expressed sympathy for the humanitarian aims of socialism, but argued that extreme socialists were a threat to liberty, patriotism, and the centrality of the family. Worse yet, they were all too frequently violent and materialistic. After the paper was read, Bliss commented that the present competitive order damaged the family more than socialism would, and a good-natured discussion followed. During those August days at Marlborough, other papers were read on "The Unchristianized Portions of Life," by the Tolstoyan disciple Ernest Crosby and on "Lessons from the Life of Francis of Assisi," by the Reverend O. P. Gifford. The conference closed with the participants agreeing to meet again the following summer, as they continued to do for nearly twenty years.[2] In this way, the members of the Brotherhood of the Kingdom sought to effect "the transformation of social conditions."

The third anecdote is from literature. The poet Presley, in Frank Norris's *The Octopus*, published in 1899, endures with artistic neutrality the raging battle between the heroic ranchers of the San Joaquin Valley in California and the foul-playing Pacific & Southwestern Railroad. Finally, as tragedies mount, his outrage moves him, first, to write a poem about the noble farmers, modeled after Edwin Markham's "The Man with the Hoe," and second, at a meeting of the Farmers' League, to deliver a stirring speech full of pertinent biblical and historical references. But no sooner had he finished than he realized the futility of his effort. He had, as Norris wrote, "not once held the hearts of his audience. He had talked as he would have written . . . he had been literary. . . . For all his love of the people, [Presley] saw clearly . . . that he was an outsider to their minds. He had not helped them or their cause in the least; he never would."[3] Recognizing his ineffectiveness, he tried a different approach, secured a bomb from a local anarchist, and hurled it at the villain of the novel, a railroad agent—and missed! And so it goes.

What these three anecdotes seek to illustrate is the well-intentioned and noble, but ineffective and impractical, impact of middle-class reformers on the kinds of social change they endorse. As Emerson said, the intellectual's critical tendency "ends in thought" but not in "a new method of life." Intellectual reformers talk to one another, found societies and journals, write articles and poems, and give lectures and sermons, mostly for one another, attend conferences and caucuses together, organize unity meetings where they endlessly debate fine points of ideology and tactics, and contribute money and their names to worthy causes. And for all this, they accomplish little in the way of bringing about the new social order that is their common goal. The various causes of leftist reform are not furthered by National Conferences for New Politics, or by Centers for the Study of Democratic Institutions, or by caucuses of radical historians, or by the exchanges of letters in the *New York Review of Books*. Whether hurling verbal brickbats and indicting social commentaries or literal bombs at the reality and symbols of the established order, intellectual reformers, like the poet Presley, usually miss.

Reformers also miss in establishing harmonious and effective relationships with those who are the intended beneficiaries of their efforts, be they workers, farmers, immigrants, or ethnic minorities. Good intentions and noble ideals, however vigorously expressed and however often reiterated, are never enough to effect the institutional changes that provide bread, land, and relief from drudgery and oppression. This kind of significant change occurs as a result of economic pressures, direct action, the politics of guile and compromise, and highly organized (and possibly violent) expressions of power, means usually antithetical to the temperament of middle-class intellectuals. As Mr. Dooley observed, "a rayformer thries to get into office on a flyin' machine. He succeeds now an' thin, but th' odds are a hundherd to wan on th' la-ad that tunnels through." And the sage of Tammany Hall, George Washington Plunkitt, warned that most voters, at least those living in cities, resented an appeal to intellect. "Don't try to show how the situation is by quotin' Shakespeare," Plunkitt advised. "Shakespeare was all right in his way, but he didn't know anything about Fifteenth District politics."[4] These are lessons most intellectual reformers fail to learn.

Certainly the subjects of this study failed to learn them. Yet this is not entirely a story of failure. The ten Christian-motivated reformers at the turn of the twentieth century, who are the subjects of this book, were profoundly influenced by the elevated ideals of nineteenth-century social prophets. In turn, they extended that influence—and their own—to countless others. They made reform respectable, helping to prepare the middle class, especially other middle-class professionals like themselves, for the progressive labor reforms of the twentieth century. Yet even this achievement is questionable, for the reforms they may have indirectly inspired served to strengthen the very socioeconomic system they sought drastically to change. If their tangible accomplishments were meager, at best, it was not for lack of persistent effort or intensity of vision. Their primary means of achieving a reconstructed social order was educational; as such, they frequently suffered from self-doubts over their excess of words and deficiency of deeds. They paid the price, as Emerson said, of being "too intellectual." These ten Christian knights rode high on clouds of words, carrying swords of good intentions, tilting at windmills often of their own despair. This is a story, then, of what happens to men and women of good hope who are constantly thwarted in their efforts to apply the golden rule and the ethics of Jesus not only to the socioeconomic institutions of their society but to their own lives as well.

This was not an easy book to write, not just for the usual reasons of indolence and distraction, but because I have identified so closely with my subjects. The ten years I have spent thinking about and writing this book have been marked by the student revolt, the Vietnamese war and peace movement, the revolutions for Black, Chicano, Native American, and women's liberation, and the various overt or insidious attempts to suppress or deride these struggles for liberty and human dignity. Since the Free Speech movement at Berkeley in 1964 (of which I was a part), I have alternated between the study of intellectuals engaging in reform and occasional participation myself in that role. I have therefore identified with the enthusiasms and failures of the ten knights of the golden rule.

Their ideals and dreams are my own, which has been personally illuminating and inspiring. But their dilemmas, deficiencies, and defeats have also been my own, which has been personally distressing and discouraging. Despite my overidentification with these ten persons—or perhaps because of it—I have sought throughout to treat them with the fairness and respect that is their right and my obligation. Nevertheless, in a very real sense this is a book not just about the 1890s and some historical personalities but about the present and about me. Otherwise, there would have been no reason to write it.

The book is a much revised and recast version of a dissertation done at the University of California at Berkeley in the mid-1960s. Many persons have helped me along the way. Henry May's early and continuing wisdom, patience, and confidence have been essential. He understood how close I came to abandoning the whole thing and assumed a delicacy of approach that made me feel good about my decision to continue. Herbert Gutman offered needed encouragement and helpful suggestions in more recent stages of my work, as did Mary Young and other members of the Frederick Jackson Turner Award Committee of the Organization of American Historians. Among colleagues and friends, Dick and Eve Rice, Al Smith, Chuck Herndon, Bob Larsen, Dick Traina, Bert Stern, David Greene, and Norman Moore have provided the encouragement, substantive suggestions, and love, without which no project—whether writing a book or living a life—is possible. Many many undergraduate students have helped me as much to understand myself and my subject as I hope I have helped them to understand themselves and their subjects.

The staffs of more libraries than I like to remember visiting have been professionally helpful and efficient. These include the libraries of the University of California at Berkeley and the University of Southern California in Los Angeles, the Hoover Institute of War and Peace at Stanford University, Palo Alto, the Saint Louis Public Library, the University of Chicago and University of Chicago Theological School libraries, the New York State Education Library in Albany, the New York City Public Library, the Library of Congress, the Wellesley College Library, and Widener, Houghton, and the Divinity School libraries at Harvard. Specifically, I would like to thank the following individuals not only for their professional service but also for their personal attention during and after my visits: Josephine Harper, MSS Librarian of the State Historical Society of Wisconsin, Madison; Mary Klausner, Archivist, Burling Library, Grinnell College, Grinnell, Iowa; Edward Starr, Curator of the American Baptist Historical Society, Ambrose-Swasey Library, Colgate-Rochester Divinity School, Rochester, New York; Sophie K. Shields, Curator of the Edwin Markham Memorial Library, Wagner College, Staten Island, New York; Irene McCreery, Local History Head, Toledo Public Library, Toledo, Ohio; and James H. Rodabaugh, Department of History, Miami University, Oxford, Ohio. Roberta Barry, Nancy Foos, and Virginia Zachary helped with the typing. A grant from the National Endowment for the Humanities enabled me to finance a summer in Michigan for uninterrupted, quiet writing. I would like especially to thank the administration and the history and religion departments at Wabash College for their support and encouragement.

My wife, Kathy, has been most helpful of all, primarily for pushing me to understand those areas of my inner self (and of herself) separate from but closely related to the human aspirations and frailties of the subjects of this study. Observing from my desk the joys and crises of Jeffrey and Jennifer's childhood world these past few years has been an easy and rewarding distraction, reminding me of the persisting challenge, in Martin Duberman's words, to "live fully and well with others and at the same time 'produce.' "[5] The dedication attests to the original and enduring source of my commitment not only to a respect for the world of ideas but also to an appreciation for the specific values and ideals represented by the ten knights of the golden rule.

1

KNIGHTS AWAKENED AND INSPIRED

One thing that Jesus could not and would not tolerate, because it is the very spirit of false prophecy, was the condition of being uninspired. Inspiration will finally organize the economic justice which law has no power to utter; which custom is impotent to procure.

GEORGE HERRON *

IN THE 1880s and 1890s many American intellectuals were awakened to the increasing social evils of the new urban, industrial age. They took their cue from Henry George that "it is around the standard of duty rather than around the standard of self-interest that men must rally to win the rights of man."[1] Not since the abolition movement had educated Americans been so disturbed by the inequalities and injustices of their society. The new culprit, however, was not the slave owner but the industrial and financial entrepreneur, the Rockefellers, Goulds, and Morgans. The revered values of American society seemed to many to be turned around, stressing private avarice, inequality of opportunity and treatment, and competitive greed rather than public responsibility, equality, and cooperation. The building of transcontinental railroads, large cities, and monolithic corporations were notable achievements but had human costs: sordid slums, forbidding factories, municipal, state, and federal corruption, and the dehumanization of less fortunate Americans. The most distressing element of industrialism for many intellectuals—the destruction of the dignity of the individual by the industrial process and urban life—had been of peripheral interest to the antebellum reformers (except to intellectual giants like Theodore Parker) and had been generally ignored in the agitation and struggles over slavery and reconstruction. This loss of dignity, especially in factory workers, was magnified to alarming proportions by the post-Civil War industrial boom. No William Lloyd Garrison or Theodore Weld stirred human consciences. Only Wendell Phillips and Frederick Douglass, of the old abolitionists, were able to transfer their reform energies from the chattel to the wage slave. The emancipation of the chattel slave, such as it was, had been achieved at a terribly high cost, and no social question seemed worth risking another civil war. Civil service reform, as Henry Adams observed, was dangerous enough; here, certainly, was a cause appropriate for the intellectual's participation. To restore honesty and principle to politics was the proper domain of the educated public servant, not to tamper with orthodox economic theories or industrial conditions.

But beginning with Henry George's *Progress and Poverty* in 1879, the civic conscience awoke to the long-neglected problems and underlying causes of poverty, bad working conditions, and urban ills in America. The awakening occurred partly as a result of George's inspiring statement (and later of those by Edward Bellamy and others), and partly as a result of worsening socio-economic conditions. The depressions of the mid-1880s and mid-1890s, the growth of the labor movement with its conflicting socialist, trade unionist, single tax, and anarchist components, and the increasingly violent clashes between the forces of organized labor and capital created a climate of fear of social upheaval. These developments both repelled and attracted intellectuals, prompting some to condemn the threatening aspects of the labor movement and others to seek remedies to the growing crisis. The would-be reformers, however, were generally uneasy with the day-to-day tactical struggles of the worker, for which they were temperamentally ill prepared, and with the daily struggle for survival of the urban poor, for which they had no personal experience. They therefore retreated to vague declarations that the solution to the social evils of their day, in George's eloquent language, required "a higher conscience, a keener sense of justice, a warmer brotherhood, a wider, loftier, truer public spirit."[2] Such was the case with the ten intellectuals who are the subjects of this study.

These ten "knights of the golden rule" (actually, nine "knights" and one "lady") include the two genial elder statesmen of late nineteenth-century reform in America, William Dean Howells (1837–1920) and Henry Demarest Lloyd (1847–1903); two crusading editors of reformist journals, William Dwight Porter Bliss (1856–1926) and Benjamin Orange Flower (1858–1918); a professor of English literature at Wellesley College and founder of the college settlement house movement for women, Vida Scudder (1861–1954); two Christian socialist ministers and religious scholars, Walter Rauschenbusch (1861–1918) and George Herron (1862–1925); two poets of peace, brotherhood, and love, Edwin Markham (1852–1940) and Ernest Howard Crosby (1856–1907); and a factory owner and mayor of Toledo, Ohio, Samuel "Golden Rule" Jones (1846–1904). These nine men and one woman were awakened to the seriousness of the social crisis in America within a few years of one another and shared common ideological sources of their commitment to reform. They were similar in background and belief, in the directions and manifestations of their social concern, and in the idealistic solutions they posed for social questions, an idealism that brought them both comfort and distress.

They were intellectuals, in the broadest sense, by virtue of their occupations and because they were concerned with "the core values of society." In the tradition of the sacred prophets, they castigated "the men of power for the wickedness of their ways." As writers, professors, ministers, and journalists, detached from seats of power in politics and industry, their livelihood was earned by questioning things as they were and "by invoking the 'impractical ought.'"[3] Only Samuel Jones, although also a writer and social critic, earned his living from entrepreneurship and elected office. In his *New Radicalism in America*, Christopher Lasch argues that intellectuals emerged around 1900 as a distinctive social type, conscious of themselves as a unique class sharing common goals and dissatisfactions. As intellectuals, they "understood the end of social and political reform to be the improvement of the quality of American culture as a whole, rather than simply a way of equalizing the opportunities for economic advancement." As radicals, they were estranged from the middle-class culture of their origins and, as a result, "identified [themselves] with other outcasts and tried to look at the world from their point of view." This was not generally the case with the subjects of this study. Although very much aware of one another as reformers with similar goals, they neither identified with the outcasts of American society (two tried, briefly) nor were susceptible to the "confusion of politics and culture" that Lasch finds "so essential to the new radicalism." They engaged, instead, in paternal top-down reform, were generally comfortable with their middle-class origins and continued status (if not always comfortable with themselves for feeling that way), and clearly saw the issues of the day in economic and religious rather than cultural terms. They posed religious means of achieving economic democracy by urging, in short, the application of the golden rule to industrial life. They were therefore more akin to Daniel Aaron's "men of good hope" than to Lasch's new radicals.[4]

They were not even radicals, although sometimes accused of being so. It is important for our understanding of these figures to define the difference between reformers and radicals. The traditional distinction suggests that reformers favor nonviolent, gradual, educational, evolutionary means to their goals, while radicals urge violent, sudden, conspiratorial, revolutionary means. In *Radicalism and Reform*, Ross Paulson challenges this distinction, insisting instead that "it is a man's ultimate goal, not his immediate means, that determines whether he is a radical or a reformer." The reformer accepts the basic assumptions and values of his society, Paulson writes, and finding them unfulfilled, seeks "change in order to fulfill the promise of the assumptions," thus bringing the performance of his society up to the standards professed in its accepted values. The radical, on the other hand, not only criticizes the practices of his society but also totally rejects its basic assumptions. "In a sense, the reformer ultimately loves that which he tries to change; the radical hates it and rejects it totally."[5] By this definition—and the traditional one as well—the subjects of this study, except perhaps George Herron, are reformers. Their methods were nonviolent and educational and their ultimate goals were historically consistent with those of American society; they accepted most of its basic assumptions and promises, seeking only to see them fulfilled. Indeed, their goals were quite conventional, even conservative. They sought to apply original Christian principles, as set forth in the Sermon on the Mount, to the fulfillment of original American principles, as enunciated in the Declaration of Independence and countless Fourth of July speeches. Such simplicity in goals may in itself be a radical idea, especially when confronting ecclesiastical and political institutions that had long been violating their own principles (or so it seemed to these reformers). They frequently found their way back to fundamental principles through those of Jesus and various European social thinkers. And yet, despite their frequent appeals to Europeans such as Tolstoy and Mazzini, they sought to change American society precisely because they loved it, especially its professed ideals.

Or did they? Paulson's simple and useful definition, even in the context of his brilliant story of the reformist and radical members of the Vrooman family, has its weaknesses. Any intellectual's view of the basic assumptions of his society is bound to be an ambivalent one, subject to his definition of those assumptions and his probable mixed affirmation and denial of them. Staughton Lynd illustrated this ambivalence in the preface to his *Intellectual Origins of American Radicalism*. "Any critic of the American present," he wrote, "must have profoundly mixed feelings about our country's past.

On the one hand, he will feel shame and distrust toward Founding Fathers who tolerated slavery, exterminated Indians, and blandly assumed that a good society must be based on private property. On the other hand, he is likely to find himself articulating his own demands in the Revolutionary language of inalienable rights, a natural higher law, and the right to revolution."[6] Lynd reflects the ambivalent view of a critic from the 1960s. Late nineteenth-century critics, however, who generally ignored the violations of rights of Afro-Americans, Native Americans, and women and who were not so inclined to speak in revolutionary language, were nevertheless ambivalent about different parts of the basic assumptions of American society.

What does one do, for example, with an individual who accepts the political-legal assumptions of American society, namely, democratic participation through the ballot, constitutional safeguards for the individual through due process of law, and orderly changes of government, but who rejects the economic assumptions, namely, capitalistic free enterprise, limited governmental interference in the market, and a reverence for private property? As Lloyd put it in *Wealth against Commonwealth* in 1894, "politically we are civilized; industrially, not yet."[7] Many other intellectuals in the late nineteenth century, including Walt Whitman, Bellamy, Rauschenbusch, and even the Vrooman brothers, concluded that America had achieved an acceptable degree of political democracy but had failed to achieve economic democracy, a failure they attributed to the misguidedness of the original economic assumptions. Thus, they repudiated part of the assumptions of their society but accepted another part. Does this make them reformers or radicals according to Paulson's definitions?[8] Why is Eugene Debs generally considered a reformer before he was imprisoned for breaking the injunction in the Pullman strike and a radical after he left Woodstock Prison? Is it because he changed from a trade unionist to a socialist, thus rejecting the economic assumptions of American society? Or did the experience of violating a legal maneuver to protect corporate institutions, and being imprisoned for it, create in him an awareness of the integral relationships among political, legal, and economic institutions, causing him to reject the political-legal assumptions of American society as well? If anything, in terms of behavior and methods, Debs was more radical before his imprisonment than after. In 1894 he was an angry activist labor leader, disrupting the transportation network and therefore endangering the economy of the nation, and breaking the law (or so ruled the Supreme Court) to do it. After 1894 he was a political campaigner, in no way threatening the vitals of American society by his futile quadrennial presidential campaigns. Was he not a radical in large part because the Pullman strike episode thrust him into the public eye as a dangerous and threatening figure?

Both the traditional and Paulson's distinctions between radicals and reformers place the burden of the definition on the individual's own self-perceptions and actions, either of goals or of means. Both leave out his public image, that is, the response of the official institutions of his society, as represented by courts, police, newspapers, employers, ministerial societies and boards of inquiry, or political officers, to his profession of goals and overt behavior. If an individual is publicly perceived and treated as a radical for long enough, there is a strong possibility that he will become a radical, both in means and in goals. This is similar to the principle of the self-fulfilling prophecy: a person becomes what he thinks he is, or is called. If a generally good child is called a brat and treated like one, he will probably become a brat, altering his behavior to fulfill the image held by others. This is not to say that just because a state governor calls a college professor a radical he will become one, or because Robert Welch calls a president a communist dupe he will become one. But if a court will imprison a person for alleged radical behavior, or even detain him through a lengthy trial which results in an acquittal, or if an employer will fire someone for alleged radical behavior, then these are rather solid guarantees that that person will thenceforth act in ways fulfilling the image held by the court or employer, whether or not the image was originally accurate. Many radical strategists have long known that the best way to radicalize a young person is to induce him into a violent demonstration in which he is maced or beaten by a policeman, and possibly jailed.

The result of the imprisonment or firing of a reformer who had previously espoused the assumptions of his society is to cause him to question seriously those assumptions. Combining the traditional, Paulson's, and the public definitions of a radical, then, one arrives at the conclusion that a radical is a person whose goals are so antithetical to those of the society in which he lives and whose actions are so threatening to the productive efficiency of that society that he becomes, in public terms, an outcast. He either begins as a member of an oppressed group or is forced by his political behavior and public image to renounce his membership in a privileged class and to identify himself with the oppressed. There must be costs. He must accept the consequences of his ideological and tactical beliefs, whether they are genuinely held or alleged. The path to radicalism is irreversible: he cannot return to a secure, publicly accepted status in his society. In short, he must either win, that is, carry out his revolution, or die a public outcast—or, at least, be personally unfulfilled. By this definition also the ten intellectuals studied here were not radicals, although Herron, Jones, and even Howells and Scudder at times suffered vigorous public denunciation or ridicule. In Herron's case, the more widespread and vicious the denunciation the more radical in espoused goals he became. And yet, for the most part, these intellectuals, despite their repudiation of some of the assumptions of American society, were not considered dangerous enough to be publicly censored and branded to the point that they were compelled to act like radicals. If anything, their beliefs and active commitments mellowed and diminished with age and frustration. None ever went to jail and only Herron was dismissed from a position, a ministry (but for the reasons of a scandalous divorce and remarriage, not for his ideological convictions). These intellectuals were simply too genial, respectable, and tactically restrained to be regarded as very dangerous to the well-being of the society. Except for Herron and Scudder, both teachers, they were not even accused of corrupting the minds of youth. After an irate letter to the editor or indicting article or speech, the intellectual reformer could always escape a hostile response—if indeed there was any response at all—by a trip to Europe, or by secluding himself at a summer home in Maine, or by attending a conference on the banks of the Hudson. He could escape everything, that is, but himself.

But if they were not radicals, neither were they moderates, always working within the conventional limits of major party politics and believing in the possibilities of a reformed capitalist economic system. Some of these figures joined and worked for the Socialist party, others hovered on the periphery of the radicalism of their day, and all of them, except Flower, defined themselves in some way as either socialists or anarchists. They were, it can be concluded, reformers—idealistic, ethical reformers—afflicted with, in Emerson's words, "too much intellect." Partly for this reason (and for arbitrary limitations of size and scope), I have chosen not to include more moderate figures such as Washington Gladden, Lyman Abbott, Richard T. Ely, Jane Addams, Robert A. Woods, Edward Everett Hale, Clarence Darrow, or Brand Whitlock. A brief look at these reformers, whom I shall call realists (or lesser knights), provides a useful contrast with the idealistic crusaders.

The realists were kindred souls with the idealists in many ways, but held fewer doubts about the assumptions of American society or about themselves. They were more inclined to work with existing political-economic institutions than to seek to build new ones. They preferred piecemeal reform to total social and spiritual regeneration. Hence, they focused their reform activity narrowly on a settlement house, industrial controversy, legal case, economic association, or pending labor law. Although not without vision, they were more comfortable initiating tangible reforms, which were immediate and satisfying, rather than prophesying the idealistic ends of reform, which were impractical and frustrating. They looked more often at the present and very near future than to some vaguely distant golden day when the kingdom of God would be ushered in on earth. The most crucial factor, however, that distinguishes the realistic reformers from the idealists is that the ideological and ethical views of the idealists were profoundly influenced not only by the usual American sources—Jefferson, Emerson, George, and Bellamy—but also by European social prophets, most notably Leo Tolstoy, John Ruskin, and Giuseppe Mazzini.

On the surface, no three European luminaries of the nineteenth century seemed to be as different as Mazzini, Ruskin, and Tolstoy. Mazzini, the self-proclaimed exile and propagandist of Italian unification and republicanism, was a Christian collectivist. His self-chosen role was that of a conspirator, although he was at various times literary critic, poet, journalist, educator, and non-Marxian champion of the laboring classes of Europe. For a few weeks in the spring of 1849 he was a Triumvir of the abortive Roman Republic. Mazzini's social and political thought, which stressed the unity of the human race, was inextricably bound up with his religious vision of a unified and autonomous Italy, the "Messiah-people," leading the way to the creation of a republican "United States of Europe." The two major institutional obstacles to the fruition of his vision were the Austrian Empire and the Roman papacy; he spent his entire adult life, mostly in exile, conspiring to overthrow them both. The two major philosophical currents of his century, from which he dissented, were the French revolutionary slogans of liberty, equality, and fraternity and the political economy of the English utilitarians. According to Mazzini, both taught false doctrines of the rights of man and individual self-interest. What was needed instead were the "duties of man," collectivism, which he called "association," and self-sacrifice. Only through association with the whole of humanity could individual liberty be realized. The utilitarians pursued the ideal of individual rights as an end in itself, he charged, which resulted in egoism and self-interest. They promised the happiness of men, yet "the condition of the people has not improved." Finding these doctrines wanting, Mazzini urged self-sacrificing love of others and the duties of man to his family, his country, and humanity. In 1852 he wrote that man "must not be taught to enjoy, but rather to suffer for others; to combat for the salvation of the world." And in his diary after a spiritual crisis in 1837, he wrote, "Life is a mission: duty, therefore, its highest law. In the comprehension of that mission, and fulfillment of that duty, lie our means of future progress." His comprehension of the mission was to work for the unification of Italy, and then all Europe, as initial steps in preparing the way for the coming of God's kingdom on earth.[9]

Mazzini sought to impose Christian ethics on the institutions of mankind; Ruskin sought to transform the minds and hearts of men. His life has been conventionally seen as split between his early career as an art critic and his later one as a critic of the blighting effects of industrialism and its selfish Manchesterian rationales on late nineteenth-century England. But Ruskin's life is not so easily compartmentalized; his art and social criticism were one. "Every nation's vice, or virtue, was written in its art," he wrote, concluding that England was a sick nation. "Brittania of the Market" worshiped the "Goddess of Getting-On." The architectural monuments to this goddess were not stately cathedrals and Gothic spires, but railroad stations, black chimneys, harbor piers, warehouses, and exchanges. Worse yet, the mass of English laborers were leading joyless, starving lives, economically and aesthetically. In 1859 he wrote to Charles Eliot Norton, "As I grow older, the evil about us takes more definite and overwhelming form in my eyes, and I do not care to write any more or do anything more that does not bear directly on poor people's bellies—to fill starved people's bellies is the only thing a man can do in this generation." Ruskin's response to this growing awareness of evil was twofold. On the one hand, he sought to improve the artistic and architectural styles of England, modeling his standards of taste on the craftsmanship of preindustrial medieval life, where the art of society reflected the moral health of its people. Emotionally he was, as Norton said after his death in 1900, "meant for the thirteenth century." But on the other hand, he found it necessary to study and criticize the prevailing rationales of economic life in his contemporary England. In a speech to businessmen at Bradford, he chided the impiety of those economists who urged that "to do the best for yourself, is finally to do the best for others." He urged instead the rule of Jesus, who said that "to do the best for others, is finally to do the best for ourselves." The best statement of his own political economy is contained in *Unto This Last*. In this work Ruskin stressed the duties of employers to employees, which he conceived as a paternal relationship in which the employer instituted profit-sharing and factory-beautifying programs in order to produce not wealth but happy people. The essence of wealth was the recognition that "the persons themselves *are* the wealth." Ruskin also advocated welfare statist, paternal programs such as government training schools and workshops for youth, unemployment insurance, state responsibility for the aged and destitute, and other means by which the upper classes would "keep order among their inferiors," raising them "to the nearest level with themselves of which these inferiors are capable."[10]

As Mazzini was a Christian collectivist and Ruskin a Christian medievalist and paternalist, Tolstoy was a Christian anarchist. The great Russian novelist suffered a spiritual crisis of self-doubt in 1878, as he neared his fiftieth birthday. In *My Confession*, written in 1879, reviewing the last thirty years of his sated but unsatisfying life, he realized that he had helped neither the life of others nor his own. The characters in his novels had revealed Tolstoy's own difficulty in reconciling his comfortable life with the poverty and misery he observed in the Russian cities and countryside. Levin, in *Anna Karenina*, "had always felt the injustice of his own abundance in comparison with the poverty of his peasants" and therefore resolved to "work harder and allow himself still less luxury," a resolve that Tolstoy himself later made. Pierre Bezukhov, in *War and Peace*, learned from the peasant philosopher Platon Karataev that to love life in spite of suffering was to love God. Tolstoy reached the same conclusion in his often morbid but illuminating confession. With *My Confession* he turned from fiction to the writing of didactic religious tracts and criticisms of the institutions of church and state in Russia. In *My Religion* (1880) he set forth his faith in the literal application of Jesus' Sermon on the Mount, especially the exhortation to "resist not evil." The Russian count henceforth became a philosophical and practicing nonresister, preaching against all forms of violence and advocating the abolition of the institutions of society: capital punishment, prisons, courts, churches, property, and government itself. He refused to pay taxes, use the courts, accept royalties for his books, hold property in his own name, support wars, or participate in the sacraments of the church. He dedicated his life to improving the standard of living of the peasants at his Yasnaya Polyana estate and set up an experimental school for them there. He dramatized his rejection of conventional society (as well as his own dissipated youth) by wearing a simple smock and eating peasant food, by renouncing tobacco, wine, meat, and sex, and by toiling in the fields alongside the peasants. The rich man, he believed, could not enter the kingdom of heaven until he had renounced his wealth and emulated a simple peasant life. "If all men practised Christ's teaching, the kingdom of God would have come upon earth; if I alone practise it, I shall do what is best for all men and for myself."[11] His message was highly individualistic as well as anarchistic, yet he hoped nevertheless that others would follow his example.

Each of these three thinkers, then, was unique. Yet they were also strikingly alike, especially to the American intellectual reformers who were influenced by them. Their social message was profoundly ethical, humanitarian, idealistic, and essentially Christian in sources and direction. They all criticized the competitive avarice, mammonism, and rampant selfishness of the industrial era and were concerned with the laboring and farming poor who were victimized by that age. They all looked to the ultimate triumph of the brotherhood and unity of man to be realized in the kingdom of heaven on earth. For Mazzini the kingdom was seen as a new world order of association, the desired end of the progress of humanity toward unity; for Tolstoy and Ruskin the kingdom would come not from without but from within. The path to either kingdom required the same human responsibilities: self-sacrifice, the duties of man to his fellowman, altruism, and love. All three suffered self-doubts over their own egotistic passions and failures, realizing that genuine contentment came from selfless service to others and living by one's principles. All three were actively involved in the social and political problems of their respective countries, and all three typified the intellectual in practical affairs who is not always very practical. The form of their impact in America was equally impractical, and no less visionary.

The distinction between the realists and idealists can be clarified by a brief examination of the contrasting ways in which they responded to the influence of these Europeans. The realists read widely in European thought and were influenced by it, but tempered their enthusiasm, as the idealists did not, with appeals to practicality and common sense. Lyman Abbott, for example, who often quoted Ruskin, Mazzini, and Tolstoy, owed the origins of his moderate reform tendencies and liberal theology to Horace Bushnell and Henry Ward Beecher. He recognized the prophetic qualities of Ruskin and Thomas Carlyle in their indictments of the wage system, but criticized them for calling "us to turn about and march with our faces to the past and our backs to the future."[12] Washington Gladden, the "prophet of the social gospel," as he has been called in Joseph Dorn's biography, was similarly restrained. His liberal theology was also derived from Bushnell and his social Christianity from George, Ruskin, and English Christian socialism. But he rejected Ruskin's paternalism and anticapitalism and was extremely hostile to the Christian socialist doctrines held by Herron. Tolstoy's form of nonresistance, Gladden wrote, deserved "a respectful toleration," yet he nevertheless felt that Tolstoy's program was unrealistic. He called Tolstoy's view one of "philanthropic nihilism," one that does not "commend itself to our common sense."[13] Richard T. Ely went further than either Abbott or Gladden in advocating a more socialized Christianity in America. He, too, often quoted Ruskin and Tolstoy in his many works, but he went to the German scholarship of Karl Knies and others with whom he studied in the 1870s for his economic thought, and to his reading of Jesus and the apostle Paul for his religion. Ely's "new economics" stressed the golden mean between the cooperative, Fabian, nonclass conflict aspects of socialism and the regulatory possibilities of the reformed capitalist state. And when his concern for security and status within the academic community was threatened in the early 1890s, he moderated his already moderate economic theories and retreated from labor reform into the less threatening domain of economic scholarship and political progressivism.[14]

Robert Woods and Edward Everett Hale were both leaders of the settlement house movement; both traveled to England to observe Toynbee Hall, a settlement house founded in part by Ruskin, and the Working Man's College established by the Christian socialists Frederick Denison Maurice and Charles Kingsley. Yet neither was swept off his feet by these experiences. Woods returned from England to establish Andover House in Boston and wrote several books on English and other settlement movements. His visit to England, according to his wife, gave him "a quickening realization of spiritual kinship with the antecedents of social reform culminating in the teaching of Ruskin of whom he was unswervingly a disciple." Woods himself, however, a rather unimpassioned and restrained man, recognized that "although getting its specific clue from England, the American settlement was compounded of qualities and sentiments distinctively of the soil." The American social movement could learn from English movements, Woods wrote, but "we do not . . . need to go over the sea to learn about evil social conditions."[15] Hale was influenced not only by Maurice and Ruskin but also by Tolstoy, whom he discovered in 1889. He founded a Tolstoi Club of some seventy-five college students in Cambridge, Massachusetts. Yet, as he wrote to Ely, the choice of the name of the club was "not from any profession of adherence to Tolstoi's creeds, but because the club is made to find out 'how other people live.' " In a review in *Cosmopolitan*, Hale compared Tolstoy's life to that of "an intelligent New England farmer who chooses to show his workmen that he can work as well as they can" and suggested that reading the Russian's religious tracts would do neither good nor harm.[16] In 1895 the Tolstoi Club established a social settlement in Boston called Hale House.

Among a coterie of reformers clustered around Governor John Altgeld of Illinois in the mid-1890s were Clarence Darrow, Brand Whitlock, and Jane Addams. Darrow and Whitlock often met in the governor's office in Springfield where they discussed Tolstoy and the other great Russian writers. Darrow rarely missed an opportunity to talk about Tolstoy, especially about his exhortations against capital punishment and the Russian penal system. In the preface to his little book *Resist Not Evil*, published in 1903, Darrow wrote that his ideas were inspired by Tolstoy's writings because he was the only author to justify the doctrine of nonresistance intelligently. But Darrow's enthusiasm for Tolstoy was short-lived. In his autobiography he admitted that the anarchism of Tolstoy and Prince Kropotkin had impressed him, but "only as the vision of heaven held by the elect, a far-off dream that had no relation to life." The tenuous hold that Tolstoyan pacifism had on him was shown when Darrow, like so many others, supported the Allied cause in World War I. As early as 1914 he renounced his adherence to pacifism, saying that although "for many years I had been an ardent reader of Tolstoy, and regarded myself as one of his disciples, . . . when Germany invaded Belgium I recovered from my pacifism in the twinkling of an eye." Cynically, he concluded that "pacifism is probably a good doctrine in time of peace, but of no value in war time."[17]

Whitlock's devotion to Tolstoy was even shakier than Darrow's. When first exposed to the Russian's writings, he told all his friends to read them. And in a speech in 1904 in memory of Samuel Jones, his predecessor as mayor of Toledo, Whitlock called Tolstoy "beyond a shadow of a doubt, the greatest man of our day and the greatest novelist of all time." He compared him to the Hebrew prophets, Buddha, Jesus, Socrates, Lincoln, and Samuel Jones. But Whitlock was given to many enthusiasms and at various times in his life called himself a disciple of George, Whitman, Altgeld, Howells, Jones, and Thomas Hardy. The most enduring influences on him were American ones. As much as he admired Tolstoy, he never called him "master," as he called Howells. He wrote to Darrow in 1900 that for years Howells had been his literary divinity. He gave his greatest political adoration to Jones, whose unrestrained idealism and unorthodox political styles Whitlock could never equal. Indeed, one of the themes of Jack Tager's biography of Whitlock is the contrast between the freewheeling mystical idealism of Jones and the temperamental and tactical restraint of his realistic disciple. Whitlock never quite resolved his conflict whether to be a political reformer or a successful novelist, and the resultant tension had its cost in consistency of purpose and social vision.[18]

Jane Addams often recalled her father's heartbroken reaction to the death of Mazzini in 1872, though as a little girl she did not understand why he should have cared so much about the death of a total stranger to the point of weeping unashamedly. She therefore read Mazzini herself, finding out that he "made a most significant step between the eighteenth-century morality and our own by appealing beyond 'the rights of man' to the 'duties of humanity.' " But for Addams, who was always skeptical of excessive idealism, Mazzini was a poor model for emulation, for "he shared the eighteenth-century tendency to idealization." Like Woods, she visited Toynbee Hall in England and studied the English social movements of the Ruskin tradition. But she was too practical a person, rooted in the work of Hull House, to adopt Ruskin's philosophy fully. Addams was filled with social idealism, but tempered it by placing greater emphasis on the processes rather than the ends of democracy. In *Democracy and Social Ethics*, reflecting the influence of the pragmatism of her Chicago friend John Dewey, she wrote that "life consists of processes as well as results," which led her to the conclusion that democracy was more than "a sentiment which desires the well-being of all men," but rather "a rule of living." She placed a high value on action as "the sole medium of expression for ethics" and wrote that "a situation does not really become moral until we are confronted with the question of what shall be done in a concrete case."[19] It is this pragmatic preoccupation with processes, action, and concrete cases, illustrated by her total involvement in Hull House, that distinguished Addams from the idealistic reformers.

Her response to Tolstoy reflected this same practical cast of thought. She read *My Religion* when she was twenty-one and often thereafter, but never could agree with Tolstoy's whole message, which she considered impractical and illogical. Yet she was sufficiently inspired by him to travel to Russia in 1896 to visit him at Yasnaya Polyana. As she described the visit in *Twenty Years at Hull House*, she went to Tolstoy "with the hope of finding a clew to the tangled affairs of city poverty. I was but one of thousands of our contemporaries who were turning towards this Russian, not as to a seer—his message is much too confused and contradictory for that—but as to a man who has had the ability to lift his life to the level of his conscience, to translate his theories into action." She found Tolstoy clad in a peasant cloak. He made fun of her puffy dress which had, he said, "enough stuff on one arm to make a frock for a little girl." He plied her with questions about Hull House and chided her for buying the food for the settlement rather than making it there herself. She felt guilty about her dress and the management of Hull House and also for her choice of meat for dinner while the count dined on a simple peasant porridge. She left Yasnaya Polyana resolved to read everything by Tolstoy that she could find and to work two hours a day in the little bakery recently added to Hull House. But when she arrived back in Chicago, she abandoned the idea in the face of "the demand of actual and pressing human wants." In 1898 she visited the Tolstoyan communal colony, the Christian Commonwealth in Georgia, which was dedicated to the practical application of the principles of nonresistance and equality of labor and ownership. She observed its inconsistencies and failures in keeping with Tolstoyan ideals and concluded that the colony "portrayed for us most vividly both the weakness and the strange august dignity of the Tolstoy position."[20] Jane Addams herself, though, in her own failures to live by the Tolstoyan ideals she admired, demonstrated the inspiring but limited effects of Tolstoy's influence in America, particularly on those of a moderate, realistic disposition.

Contrast the restrained enthusiasms and tempered judgments of the realists with the experiences of the idealists, who often underwent sudden and dramatic, almost religious, conversions of thought and life-style when exposed to these European thinkers. Scudder, for example, wrote in her autobiography that hearing Ruskin lecture at Oxford in 1884 "marked a turning point in my mental, and later in my outward, life." Howells said of Tolstoy, "I can never again see life in the way I saw it before I knew him." Crosby was a well-to-do international judge on duty in Egypt when he picked up a copy of Tolstoy's *My Life* in 1894. He read it to the end one Sunday and reported that "since that day the world has never looked to me quite as it used to." He immediately renounced his judgeship and went on a pilgrimage to Yasnaya Polyana, feeling that he had "risen to a loftier plane, and that there was something immortal within me." Herron, whose commitment to some form of social change was present throughout his life, reported that as a small boy in Indiana he had absorbed "the spirit of Mazzini as the bread and wine of my life!"[21] These germinating experiences were in no way temporary, but bore fruit—sometimes bitter fruit—for years after.

The ten idealistic intellectual reformers responded in a recognizably consistent manner in their continued acceptance and attempted application of the ethically inspiring message of these and other European reformers, a manner that distinguished them from their realistic contemporaries. And it was precisely the quality of the influence of their European models that helped to cause their idealistic impracticality. The major European inspirers of their social thought, besides Tolstoy, Ruskin, and Mazzini, were Victor Hugo, William Morris, and Thomas Carlyle; Christian radicals such as Francis of Assisi, Savonarola, and Robert de Lamennais, the French priest excommunicated for his support of the revolutions of 1830 and 1848; and Maurice and Kingsley, the English Christian socialists. Among American social prophets, they were influenced, like the realists, by Emerson, Whitman, George, and Bellamy. The most profound ethical inspiration on them all, however, was the life and words of Jesus.

There are many forces that impel a seemingly contented individual to become a reformer or radical. Among them, as many historians and social scientists have shown, are parental influence, the ethical climate of one's childhood and youth, status anxiety, economic dislocation, cultural alienation, religious conversion, identity crises at various stages of one's life, causing guilt and psychic discomfort, the intrusion of contemporary events, and purely ideological influences.[22] Any attempt to assign a single cause to a whole generation of reformers, much less one person, is a risky venture at best. Any individual's commitment to reform is of course a result of multiple influences and should be treated as a separate case. For these reformers, the mixture of impelling forces varied in each case, but in all of them included the ethical inspiration and ideological influence of the many social prophets mentioned above; in most of them it included early childhood influence and the impact of contemporary events. The moral climate of a person's formative years and the events of his life serve to make him susceptible to an ethically inspiring experience. He may think he has been suddenly converted, when in fact he was psychically ready for the experience, a concept understood by the Puritans as "preparation for grace." In *The Varieties of Religious Experience*, William James explained that a spiritual conversion, which is similar to an ethically inspiring experience, involved two stages, or types. The first was the volitional type, in which "the regenerative change is usually gradual, and consists in the building up, piece by piece, of a new set of moral and spiritual habits." The second was the type of self-surrender, in which subconscious factors were at work, and which thrust the volitional type forward more rapidly.[23] Thus, Howells, for example, who absorbed enlightened humanitarian ideals in his youth, and which built up slowly throughout his early life (volitional), was propelled forward to new heights of ethical consciousness by particular political and intellectual events in his life in the mid-1880s, some of which he understood and some he did not (self-surrender). The decision to commit oneself to reformism or radicalism, then, is not unlike a religious conversion. But what, more specifically, is ethical inspiration?

Erik Erikson has offered a distinction between morality and ethics which is helpful in defining what is meant here by ethical inspiration. For Erikson, morality refers to "moral rules of conduct to be based on a fear of threats to be forestalled," threats that derive first, externally, and second, from within. The acquisition of a moral sense, then, occurs in childhood. By adolescence an ideological sense develops, defined by Erikson as the ability "to anticipate the future in a coherent way, to perceive ideas and to assent to ideals." Not until one reaches young adulthood, however, is one ready for an ethical sense, defined as "ethical rules to be based on a love of ideals to be striven for—ideals that hold up to us some highest good, some definition of perfection, and some promise of self-realization." The young adult, unlike the adolescent, is less susceptible to the delusions, illusions, and excesses of ideology and is more capable of moral restraint and ideal vision. He is not, however, less susceptible to the pain of self-doubt and guilt in failing to fulfill his commitment to ethical ideals.[24] Thus, when one is ethically inspired he is filled first with a love of ideals and second, with discomfort over the hiatus between things as they are and as one conceives they ought to be. The first implies a need for action; the second demands it. In order to achieve the promise of self-realization, one must commit himself actively to the narrowing of the gap. It was the requirement for action, especially for the effective practical kind, that most often caused guilt and self-doubts in these intellectual reformers, for failure of deeds revealed serious deficiencies in one's self-concept. A gap between the is and the ought to be existed at two levels: within the society the reformer was trying to change, and within the reformer himself.[25]

One could, of course, seek salvation by conventional religious experiences or take refuge in the traditional theological meaning of inspiration, which involved "the breathing in or communication of divine wisdom to men or literature." George Herron, however, reinterpreted this theological idea of inspiration to make it pertinent to late nineteenth-century social questions and reformers: "*The real problem of inspiration*," he wrote with emphasis, "*is not as to the manner in which holy men of old were inspired, but whether there are now holy men willing to be inspired and consumed in the service of truth and justice.* Inspiration is always the passion for righteousness in human relations, and the passion for righteousness is always inspiration." Mazzini, Ruskin, and Tolstoy were the new holy men, pointing out current iniquities in human relations and pointing the way toward what ought to be. They were, in the minds of their American followers, social prophets. As Rauschenbusch wrote in 1907: "The men of our own age who have had something of the prophet's vision and power of language and inspiration have nearly all had the social enthusiasm and faith in the reconstructive power of Christianity. Maurice and Kingsley, Ruskin and Carlyle, Lamennais and Mazzini and Tolstoi, were true seers of God, and they made others see."[26] They made others see their vision of a new Christian social order by the brilliance, passion, and power of the language they employed in their writing and by the inspiring, dramatic ways in which they lived. Although not without their own self-doubts, they appeared to be the living embodiments of their message, which made its inspirational effect all the more compelling.

The ten knights of the golden rule, then, shared common ethical inspirations and visions, deriving in large part from the influence of Tolstoy, Ruskin, and Mazzini. Moreover, most of them had middle-class origins and were reared by ardently religious parents. Five of the ten—Lloyd, Flower, Herron, Rauschenbusch, and Crosby—were sons of Protestant ministers, and Bliss and Scudder came from missionary families. Howells's father was a printer-journalist with strong Quaker and Swedenborgian beliefs. Only Markham and Jones, of this group, grew up in some poverty and had limited religious training in their youth. Although half of them were born and reared in small towns, all ten eventually settled (or at least developed their social philosophy) in cities, where the ills of industrial society were most manifest. They were all engaged in some sort of reform endeavors during part or all of the period from 1886, the year in which Lloyd and Howells were incensed by the "civic murder," as Howells called it,[27] of the Haymarket anarchists, until 1904, when Samuel Jones died. Jones was the one to whom all looked as best embodying and applying the golden rule in action. For this reason, even though all but Lloyd outlived him, I have focused my study of each person on the period between 1886 and 1904, thus emphasizing the origins and earliest manifestations of an individual's commitment to reform. In order, however, to portray each person completely, I have sketched out the major developments of his or her life after 1904. In 1886 their median age was thirty-two, with Howells the oldest at forty-nine and Herron the youngest at twenty-four. In 1904 their median age was fifty. The years in which their social conscience was awakened and most active, therefore, were the most productive years, at least potentially, of a person's life.

They frequently joined the same or similar reform organizations during the era and carried on vibrant correspondences with one another. For example, Bliss and Howells were both members of the Nationalist Club of Boston, and Scudder joined these two in the Society of Christian Socialists, founded by Bliss in 1889. Bliss, Howells, and Lloyd were members of the American Fabian League, also founded by Bliss, and he and Scudder belonged to the Christian Social Union in the mid-1890s. Herron, Jones, Lloyd, Flower, and Markham all attended Bliss's conference at Buffalo in the summer of 1899, in which he sought to unify reformers into one Social Reform Union, and Howells sent a letter of regret. Jones and

Flower were executive vice presidents of the American Peace Society, and Crosby was a member of the same society as well as president of the New York Anti-Imperialist League. Crosby and Howells were members of the New York Social Reform Club, served on the executive committee of the Tolstoy Fund to rescue the persecuted Doukhobors from Russia, and jointly issued various appeals for peace in 1898. Crosby, Lloyd, Bliss, and Markham attended some of Rauschenbusch's summer conferences of the Brotherhood of the Kingdom at Marlborough, and Jones was invited but could not attend. Lloyd, Markham, and Herron all went to Toledo to campaign for Jones's reelection as mayor in 1899, and Crosby wrote a biography of the Tolstoyan mayor. Markham, Crosby, Bliss, and Herron launched a social crusade in New York in 1901, another effort at reform unity. Flower, Crosby, and Markham attended a dinner in 1905 commemorating the twenty-fifth anniversary of the publication of *Progress and Poverty*. Markham and Jones were influenced by the Christian socialism of Herron; Herron and Lloyd influenced each other as did Crosby and Jones; Scudder was decisively affected by Rauschenbusch; and all the younger members of the group constantly sought the moral (and often, financial) support of the two older and better-known reformers, Lloyd and Howells.

But these are rather superficial indications of similarity. A more significant element in the pattern was the similarity of their social and religious ideals, caused by their largely common backgrounds, their role as professional intellectuals, and the common sources of their ethical inspiration. Despite the fact that the Christian anarchism of Tolstoy led Crosby to espouse the individualism of the single-tax movement and a form of philosophical anarchism rather than socialism, they all preferred, in its broadest sense, cooperation to competition. They believed in self-sacrifice rather than self-interest and often contrasted the golden rule to the "rule of gold." They all believed that the golden rule ought to be applied to industrial life and were all, even Crosby, closely associated with socialism. They preferred the gradualistic, ethical, and cooperative aspects of socialism to the dialectical, class conflict, and revolutionary elements, which they did not always understand. They tried often to reconcile the two sides of socialism, but their preference was clearly for the soft Fabian brand of American socialism (via Bellamy and Laurence Gronlund), rather than the hard doctrinaire European kind (via Daniel De Leon). They all believed in the dignity of the individual, like Ruskin and Tolstoy; yet, paradoxically, they sought to preserve this dignity within a vague, collective idea of the unity and brotherhood of man, like Mazzini. They were all zealously democratic and expressed enormous faith in and love for the humble and poor, like Tolstoy; yet, they often distrusted the ability of the common man to govern himself except under the paternal guidance of an intellectual elite, like Ruskin. Only Jones and Lloyd, for example, were comfortable with working-class audiences or meetings. The most persistent problem that afflicted them was the painful contrast between the idealism of their words and the practicality of their deeds. They shared common blind spots as well as common convictions and inconsistencies. Their reforming orientation was toward the white, male, urban poor; they generally ignored farmers, did not take woman's rights seriously (except Scudder and Flower), and almost totally ignored the plight of blacks reenslaved to southern peonage or northern urban destitution.[28]

Like Mazzini, the ten reformers believed that all political questions were social questions and all social questions were religious questions. Their common religious creed, like Tolstoy's, stressed the ethical teachings of the Sermon on the Mount, most notably those of peacemaking, nonviolence, antimammonism, the virtues and rewards of poverty, service to others, and the injunction that "whatever you wish that men would do to you, do so to them" (Matt. 7:12). Their reading of the golden rule was not the negative Judaic version, "what is hateful to you, do not do to your neighbor," which was limiting, self-restraining, and required self-negation, but rather the Christian version, which was expansive, self-asserting, and required a keen conscience and active expressions of empathetic love. As Erikson has pointed out, Jesus' version was not a warning for "egotistic prudence" but an exhortation to "altruistic sympathy," suggesting a genuine love of oneself as a prerequisite to love of others.[29] This alone was an enormous challenge for the ten knights of the golden rule.

The Sermon on the Mount as a whole presented even greater challenges. They all believed, as Markham put it in a lesson learned from Herron, that it was "the greatest sermon in the world. . . . It is the Constitution of the Kingdom of Heaven, the Kingdom of Comrades. Christ's New Social and Industrial Order is to be governed by these lofty principles." The Sermon on the Mount has long been regarded by biblical scholars as "the perfect portrait of the Christian life." According to Amos N. Wilder, the sermon arouses a strong and serious sense of responsibility which, because of the intensity of its implied obligations, "plants a seed of permanent dissatisfaction in the soul." Once exposed to the message of the sermon, one is compelled "to confront and do homage, not to what the natural man but to what the Spirit demands. And this makes for pain, for inner division, and for fateful consequences." No one knew this better than these ten Christian reformers. As if fulfilling the ethical injunctions of Tolstoy or Mazzini was not challenging enough, they also felt an obligation to live by the teachings of Jesus' sermon. Failing to fulfill those teachings added to their self-dissatisfaction. Moreover, their political interpretation and application of the sermon was an erroneous one. The context of the sermon, according to Wilder, was not political but religious salvation: Jesus was preparing his disciples for the imminent coming of his kingdom.[30]

The central concept in their religious thought, besides the golden rule and the Sermon on the Mount, was their idealistic vision of the kingdom of heaven on earth. But this, too, was conceived in ethical, political, and economic terms, not redemptive ones. They all bemoaned the failures of the institutional church to respond to the social needs of American life by adopting and advocating their form of social Christianity. Led by Herron and Rauschenbusch, however, they went a long way in bringing a portion of American Protestantism around to their position; Rauschenbusch's conception of the kingdom, however, had a much sounder theological and ecclesiastical basis than Herron's. Although they did not think in these terms, they were all postmillennialists, believing that the Second Coming would follow the thousand-year reign of peace, love, and harmony. The duty of the Christian reformer, then, was to work toward the creation of the millennium, or kingdom, that alone would guarantee the return of Jesus Christ. Their emphasis, however, was on the socioeconomic forms of the millennial era rather than its conclusion. They frequently differed in their definition of the right path to the kingdom, as well as their conception of its precise form. Scudder often looked back to monastic medieval models, and Howells back to agrarian, preindustrial ones. But all ten also looked forward to the collectivist Christian socialist ideal whereby modern industry and urban life could be changed so as to realize the kingdom of heaven on earth. At one time or another, all of them seriously asked themselves the question posed by Maurice: "Must we not either socialize Christianity or Christianize socialism?" Rauschenbusch paraphrased Maurice's question in 1896 when he wrote that social Christianity would be "immeasurably more valuable to the world than either an unsocial Christianity or an unchristian socialism." In a conversation with Flower, Markham expressed in a more moderate way the same problem: "Reformers fail because they reject Christianity; and churchmen fail because they reject reform."[31]

The guiding ideals and sources of ethical inspiration of the ten intellectual reformers were so strikingly similar that they, and some of the realists as well, constituted what Robert T. Handy has called "a new religious movement." Handy dates the movement from 1897 to 1899 and calls it "the religious aspect of the social movement of the period; it gave its very life blood in furthering American socialism."[32] Handy's dates, I believe, are too restrictive. The effort to infuse American socialism with religious idealism was the motivating purpose of Bliss's founding of the Society of Christian Socialists in 1889 and was the primary intellectual effort of Vida Scudder throughout the second decade of the twentieth century. The period between 1897 and 1899, however, contained the movement's highest intensity and clearest examples of purpose and failure. The respected elder advisers of the new religious movement were Howells and Lloyd. While Howells revealed the limits of practical application of the idealistic goals of the movement, Lloyd provided the clearest statement of a workable political economy of the golden rule. Bliss, Flower, and Scudder struggled for organizational and doctrinal unity among Christian intellectual reformers; Vida Scudder had a more serious struggle, harmony within herself. Herron was the charismatic leader of the movement, and he and Rauschenbusch best expressed its essential vision—the kingdom concept—in sociological and religious terms. Crosby and Markham were the poet laureates of the movement, and Golden Rule Jones embodied and practiced its ideals.

As middle-class intellectuals, the efforts of the ten knights were primarily educational, far removed from the bloody battleground of steel mills, coal mines, labor union halls, and picket lines. Their absence from the arena of conflict caused them discomfort, which no armor could protect against, but these irrepressible knights of the golden rule persisted in tilting at the windmills of competitive injustice, inequality, selfishness, and war. As Henry George had said in 1883: "Social reform is not to be secured by noise and shouting; by complaints and denunciation; by the formation of parties, or the making of revolutions; but by the awakening of thought and the progress of ideas. Until there be correct thought, there cannot be right action; and when there is correct thought, right action *will* follow."[33] George's priorities, which they endorsed, brought some solace to their troubled consciences. They could justify postponing action until more "correct thought" had permeated their society, a not easily detectable or even reasonable possibility. This much they knew: their own correct thought was not enough, but had to be spread to others by both words and deeds. It was to this difficult purpose that they committed themselves.

2

CHRISTIAN INSPIRATION RESTRAINED: WILLIAM DEAN HOWELLS AND HENRY DEMAREST LLOYD

We are theoretical socialists, and practical aristocrats. But it is a comfort to be right theoretically, and to be ashamed of one's self practically.

HOWELLS *

No man can love mankind who does not love his country. To love his country, a man must love his city, to love his city he must love his family and to learn to love his family as it deserves, a man must love himself.

LLOYD †

ONE AFTERNOON in 1896 the self-styled American itinerant Josiah Flynt was tramping across the fields of Yasnaya Polyana with Count Tolstoy, and the Russian told Flynt that there were four men in the world whom he was anxious to bring together in a conference. In a letter to Henry Demarest Lloyd six years later, Flynt recalled that three of the four were Lloyd, George, and Howells: "The Count seemed to think that if all of you got together, and had a long soulful conversation, an advance would have been made toward the regeneration of degenerate humanity."[1] Such a conversation unfortunately never took place. If it had, it is likely that, while agreeing generally on the need for the regeneration of humanity in order to transform the institutions of society, the four would have had difficulty agreeing on the precise form a reconstructed social order would take. Tolstoy and George were committed to the idea of the negative state (Tolstoy more than George) and stressed individualism and personal freedom in their social thought; Lloyd and Howells endorsed a form of Fabian socialism and argued that individual freedom could only be achieved through collectivized social institutions. Furthermore, it is highly doubtful that a conference of the four intellectual reformers, despite the probable elevation of their discussions, would have accomplished much concrete human regeneration, except perhaps in themselves.

All four premised their social analysis on Christian principles, but in Howells and Lloyd the practical application of their analysis was often restrained. Partly for this reason, Tolstoy most admired Henry George, who was not without his own restraints. "The reading of every one of your books," Tolstoy wrote to George, "makes clear to me things which were not so before, and confirms me more and more in the truth and practicability of your system." Tolstoy read *Progress and Poverty* aloud to his peasants in 1894 and tried for years to persuade both the czar and the duma to enact the single tax in Russia. He sought, also in vain, to meet with the American single-taxer. He told Jane Addams that if George would attend a land reform convention in Berlin in 1896, he would break a long-held personal vow and travel outside Russia to meet him there. Although flattered by Tolstoy's admiration, George did not reciprocate the enthusiasm. They exchanged several letters, but never met. Tolstoy's admiration for Howells and Lloyd was not nearly as zealous. Although he respected Howells's fine spirit and had high praise for Lloyd's *Wealth against Commonwealth*, his enthusiasm was clearly and understandably for George, the land reformer.[2]

Of the three Americans, Howells held the most reverence for Tolstoy, and he and Lloyd were most similar in their interests, aims, and roles as reformers. Both shared George's concerns about injustices in American society, but neither was particularly excited about the single tax or George's two mayoralty campaigns in New York. They enjoyed a personal acquaintance and mutual respect. On two occasions Howells's editorial influence enabled Lloyd to secure publication of his assaults on Standard Oil. As an editor of the *Atlantic Monthly*, Howells printed "The Story of a Great Monopoly" as the lead article in March 1881. Thirteen years later, after *Wealth against Commonwealth* had been refused by four publishers, Lloyd turned again to Howells who succeeded in persuading Harpers to publish the work. "I am reading your great book as I get the nervous strength for it," Howells wrote Lloyd, "and I find that it takes a good deal of nervous strength. To think that the monstrous iniquity whose story you tell so powerfully, accomplished itself in our time, is so astounding, so infuriating, that I have to stop from chapter to chapter, and take breath." Doubtful about the effect the book would have on the present generation, Howells nevertheless correctly anticipated that later it would "form the source from which all must draw who try to paint the evillest phase of the century." Lloyd, who turned to Howells on more than one occasion for solace and support, wrote to a friend that Howells "is a very noble-hearted man, and takes the whole world into his sympathy." When Lloyd died in 1903, Howells wrote to his widow that "the public sorrow will grow, great as it already is, when it is fully realized how generous and how wise and how helpful a champion of humanity the public has to mourn in him."[3]

Howells and Lloyd had more in common, however, than lack of interest in Henry George and admiration for each other. With George and Edward Bellamy, they were the earliest and most prominent supporters—and hence the patrons—of the new religious crusade in America. Both were influenced in their youth by Lincoln, Emerson, and other American heroes, but owed their mature reform thought to Europeans. Lloyd was inspired by Ruskin and Mazzini in the 1880s, and Howells by Tolstoy in 1886. Both sought to convey the ideas of these European thinkers to other Americans. As a result of the combination of intellectual influences and a journalist's keen observation of developing social conditions, both were disturbed by the increasing gap between the promises and the achievements of America, particularly in the industrial life of the common laborer. Both were dismayed by the irrelevancy of the platforms of both major political parties to social and economic questions. Both despaired of the neglect of these questions by organized religion. Both preferred cooperation to competition and self-sacrifice to self-interest; both advocated various collectivist means of alleviating economic injustice in America. Both espoused the gradualistic and humanitarian brand of English Fabian socialism, rejecting the revolutionary class-conflict socialism of the European continent. Both sought, above all, to apply the message of the golden rule and the Sermon on the Mount to public affairs, as well as to practice that message in their own lives.

The efforts of Lloyd and Howells to awaken other Americans to the Christian social implications of European thought were frequently diluted and ineffective, however, partly because of their commitment to indigenous American ideas and institutions and partly because of the restraints caused by their wealth and elevated social status. Lloyd was known as the "millionaire socialist" and Howells was widely regarded—unfairly, perhaps—as the symbol of the late nineteenth-century genteel New England literary establishment. Both used their positions of wealth and respect to contribute moral prestige, intellectual ideas, and financial support to reform causes. Their effective impact, however, was at once heightened by their prestige and diminished by their personal inability to practice completely what they preached. This was a cause of distress for Howells more than for Lloyd, mainly because Lloyd was a more active participant in the daily struggles of the farmer-labor movement. Together they represent the plight of the well-intentioned intellectual reformer who, when confronted with the highly idealized and visionary ideas of Mazzini, Ruskin, and Tolstoy, had difficulty reconciling this idealism with the practical realities of achieving change in American life. In his notebook in 1888, Lloyd wrote: "Inspiration must come first, experience must follow. How to reconcile the schools of inspiration and experience?"[4] This was a problem neither he nor Howells ever successfully resolved. That Lloyd had less difficulty reflected, in part, his stronger claim for self-respect.

The first critical test of their idealistic commitment in the stark arena of practical politics came in the Haymarket affair. On May 4, 1886, a protest rally was held at Chicago's Haymarket Square. The meeting was called and led by the anarcho-syndicalist Black International to protest the police violence and strike-breaking that had occurred the day before at the McCormick Harvester Works. As the peaceful rally was concluding (most of the crowd already having left along with the mayor of Chicago), a squad of police marched to the square to order the meeting to disperse. Suddenly, a bomb exploded in the front lines of the police, setting off a battle. When the smoke cleared, seven policemen and several demonstrators were dead and more than a hundred were wounded. Hysteria over the incident in particular and the strike for an eight-hour day in general swept Chicago's citizenry. Within two months, in a highly suspect trial, seven leading Chicago anarchists were found guilty of murder and were given the death sentence. Four of them had not even been present at the Haymarket rally. A few Americans, who regarded the trial as a farce and believed the convicted men guilty only of anarchist opinions, argued for executive clemency and a commutation of their sentence to life imprisonment. Lloyd and Howells were among the most eminent Americans to defend the anarchists. Their impassioned attempt to save the lives of the condemned men marked a turning point in their own lives and was a revealing example of the frustration of the intellectual as reformer.

Lloyd, who was living near Chicago at the time, attended the trial, visited the anarchists in jail, and worked tirelessly for a commuted sentence. He printed a number of appeals and circulated them among prominent Chicago business leaders and jurists. On November 9, 1887, two days before the date set for execution, he personally visited Governor Richard Oglesby and pointed out that "the words and acts for which these men are sentenced to be hanged grew out of the great labour struggle of our day." Therefore, he argued, their punishment should be less than death. As a result of Lloyd's and other appeals, the sentence of two of the anarchists was commuted to life imprisonment. Lloyd personally carried the commutations to them on November 10. That night one of the five still condemned to hang the next day committed suicide in jail. Lloyd was despondent. He wrote his father that "if it were possible to do everything I would attempt to rescue the victims of all injustice.... I am on the side of the under dog. The agitators on that side make mistakes, commit crimes, no doubt, but for all that theirs is the right side. I will try to avoid the mistakes and the crimes, but I will stay by the cause." On the next day the four remaining anarchists were hanged. Lloyd wrote a two-stanza verse in which he incorporated Albert Parsons's last words, "Let the People's Voice Be Heard," as a refrain. On the evening of Parsons's funeral two days later, the Lloyd family sang the song, after which Lloyd wept bitterly.[5]

On the same day that the Lloyds were mourning Parsons's death in Winnetka, Illinois, William Dean Howells, deep in Tolstoy at the time, was writing to his father from Dansville, New York: "All is over now, except the judgment that begins at once for every unjust and evil deed, and goes on forever. The historical perspective is that this free Republic has killed five men for their opinions." In September he had written Roger Pryor, one of the several counsels for the anarchists, saying, "I have never believed them guilty of murder, or of anything but their opinions, and I do not think they were justly convicted." Howells had in mind a public appeal in the form of an open letter, which Pryor encouraged. After discarding a hastily written and emotional first draft, Howells's letter finally appeared in the *New York Tribune* on November 6. He reported that he had both petitioned and written personally to Governor Oglesby for a commuted sentence. Then he appealed to those who believed that the execution of the anarchists "would be either injustice or impolicy" to petition Oglesby to mitigate their punishment.[6] His effort may have helped save two lives, but not the other five. After the hangings, Howells drafted another letter to the *Tribune* in which he excoriated the press and public, first, for executing four men "*for their opinion's sake*" in "one of those spasms of paroxysmal righteousness to which our Anglo-Saxon race is peculiarly subject," and second, for celebrating their death in a "hymn of thanksgiving for blood" on the morning after. Howells sarcastically apologized for interrupting the "Te Deum" and went on to say that "by such perversion of law as brought the Anarchists to their doom," Garrison, Emerson, Parker, Phillips, Thoreau, and other abolitionists would have all been executed. Whatever the cause of the anarchists' "craze against society," Howells continued, "it was not through hate of the rich so much as love of the poor."[7] This powerfully impassioned letter, however, was never sent.

Howells's angry stand against the anarchists' death sentence was totally unexpected. For some twenty years, as an editor of the *Atlantic Monthly* and *Harper's New Monthly Magazine*, Howells had been a genteel formulator of literary taste and conventional manners and morals. Despite an abolitionist background, there was little in his recent past to indicate a bold stand on this or any other controversial social issue. He had been generally unenthusiastic about political and economic movements of any sort prior to 1886. His defense of the anarchists could easily jeopardize his growing reputation as the "Dean of American Letters," and, indeed, his stand evoked countless letters and editorials of abuse and ridicule. Reawakened humanitarian convictions and principles led him to send the first letter; personal restraints prevented him from sending the second. Lloyd's position in defense of the anarchists, however, was predictable. He had always pursued causes, beginning with his work soon after graduating from Columbia Law School for the Free Trade League and the Liberal Republican movement in 1872. By 1886 he had become one of America's most outspoken critics of monopoly and for years, as chief financial editor of the crusading *Chicago Tribune*, had been exposing the corrupt practices of trusts. When *Tribune* policy changed in 1885, he traveled to England where he acquainted himself with William Morris, Thorold Rogers, and other leaders of the English Fabian and Christian social movements. He returned to Chicago to devote himself full-time to scholarship and writing on behalf of labor and antimonopoly causes. He was an editor for the *Knights of Labor* when the Haymarket affair occurred.

Lloyd and Howells were both profoundly upset by their inability to prevent the hanging of the four anarchists. In their despair they resolved to devote their lives to the cause of justice for the laboring poor. Lloyd's life reflected a renewed commitment to the problems of workers. He wrote in his notebook a solemn resolution based on the last words of Albert Parsons: " 'Let the voice of the people be heard,' *The voice of the people shall be heard.*"[8] After 1887 the emphasis of his discontent with America shifted from negative criticisms of monopoly to a positive commitment to the labor movement and the development of a new social philosophy. He wrote less about financial, judicial, and industrial evils and more about social and ethical solutions.

The events of November 1887 were particularly shattering for Howells. On the day of what he called the civic murder, he wrote to a friend and recalled how they had once argued about Blaine and Cleveland. "How trivial the difference between them seems in this lurid light." A week later he wrote to his sister that he and his wife "no longer care for the world's life, and would like to be settled somewhere very humbly and simply, where we could be socially identified with the principles of progress and sympathy for the struggling mass. . . . Someday I hope to do justice to these irreparably wronged men."[9] To be identified with the struggling mass, however, is not the same as to share its oppression, a question of great concern to the guilt-ridden man. Nevertheless, as a writer Howells did what he could, and his new resolves were reflected in both his literary criticism and his own fiction. As a critic, he was concerned less with the aesthetic requirements of fiction and more with the humanitarian obligations of the novelist. As an author, he wrote less about the manners and morals of the drawing room and more about socioeconomic conditions of life and the relationships between rich and poor. For both Lloyd and Howells the execution of the anarchists in 1887 brought the social question in America into focus and added an emotional impetus to their growing intellectual commitment to seek justice for the "struggling mass." How well they succeeded and what happened to them in the process are the themes of this chapter.[10]

William Dean Howells

Early in his life Howells determined as his career goal "the conquest of the whole field of polite learning."[11] For some twenty years before his seemingly sudden conversion by Tolstoy in 1886, he had been living the comfortable genteel life of a Boston editor, writing novels of manners and discussing literature with James Russell Lowell, Thomas Bailey Aldrich, Charles Eliot Norton, Oliver Wendell Holmes, and other Boston Brahmins clustered around Harvard and the *Atlantic Monthly*. His literary tastes prior to the 1880s had included, among others, Lowell, Irving, Scott, Cervantes, Wordsworth, and Tennyson. None of these, except perhaps for Lowell, had taken strong public positions on socioeconomic issues. Except for brief periods of depression, Howells had led a wholly satisfying literary life. He had come out of the West, gained respect from the cultural establishment of New England, and had indeed conquered the field of polite learning. He had not as yet, however, conquered himself. The roots of both his success and his discontent were in the years of his youth.

Born in 1837 in Martin's Ferry, Ohio, Howells was reared in a Quaker atmosphere of abolitionism, Owenite utopianism, and Whiggery. His earliest recollections were of abolitionist lectures, his father's printing office, steamboat rides on the Ohio River, and, after a move to southwestern Ohio, of a thoroughly joyful life swimming in and playing by the Great Miami River. William C. Howells's printing ventures were often unsuccessful, especially with the proslavery inhabitants of southern Ohio. Young William Dean, therefore, lived in a succession of mostly small Ohio towns, each one further to the northeast from the last: Hamilton, Xenia, Columbus (where he proudly wore a Louis Kossuth hat), Ashtabula, and finally Jefferson, where the only school he attended was his father's Free Soil printing office. Although he was received into the communion of his father's Swedenborgian faith, he also attended Baptist, Methodist, and Roman Catholic churches. As he grew older, young Howells increasingly distrusted any religious faith in its organized form. He also grew to dislike the printing business and politics.

The exciting realities of nominating conventions and elections, he wrote, "did not concern me so much as the least unrealities of fiction." He worked throughout the 1850s as a reporter-editor for antislavery journals, but his interests were primarily in the literary aspects of the political events he covered. "I felt the ethical quality of the slavery question, and I had genuine convictions about it; but for practical politics I did not care." Indeed, as he confessed in

1916, despite being in the midst of political rallies and conventions throughout his almost eighty years, he had never listened to a political speech to the end. This was, he added, a pity for a realistic novelist.[12] Howells's aspirations were plainly literary, and in the years prior to the Civil War he acquired not only cultural ambitions and facility of writing but also, to his shame, an attitude of social snobbery toward the West. His campaign biography of Lincoln earned an appointment to the consulate in Venice during the Civil War, and when he returned to the United States in 1866 he firmly committed himself to a literary career in New England.

After settling himself in Cambridge, however, there were indications that Howells was not entirely satisfied with himself and his life and that he was susceptible to guilt and self-doubts. As he launched his career with the *Atlantic Monthly* in 1866, he wrote Norton, "I am constitutionally depressed, and innately ashamed of all I do." Two years later he suffered greatly over his neglect of the family back in Ohio. He was too busy and absorbed in Boston to visit his mother during her serious illness. And when a turn for the worse compelled a hurried train ride west, he arrived at her bedside three hours after she had died. His mother's death brought him closer to his father. They corresponded often and, despite their many differences, Howells revealed his innermost thoughts in these letters. One of their recurring arguments was whether or not belief in the divinity of Jesus was necessary for the good life. Dismayed by theological hairsplitting, Howells told his father in 1872 that "at times I'm half-minded never to read another word of theology; but to cling blindly to the moral teachings of the gospels."[13] This was a prophetic statement, for by the late 1880s he had indeed resolved, like Tolstoy, to do just that.

Throughout the 1870s Howells solidified his position as a member of the inner circle of leading New England intellectuals and wrote several novels that treated "commonplace America." His subjects and themes included not only the wedding journeys and lives of the wealthy but also the lives and perceptions of black domestics, Irish and Italian immigrants, shop owners, and hotel clerks. His rise to prominence, however, was not without its setbacks. The financial panic of 1873, the depression that followed, and the scandals of the Grant administration caused him to doubt the healthiness of American society. Declining circulation of the *Atlantic* and a frank assessment of his literary accomplishments to date, as compared to the example of Ivan Turgenev, caused him to doubt his abilities as an editor and author. Finally, his wife's ill health was a constant source of anxiety. In the early 1880s Howells suffered one of his most serious psychic and physical breakdowns, caused in part by the discovery of a nervous disorder in his oldest daughter, Winny, and in part by the pressures of writing *A Modern Instance* (1882). The novel was virulently criticized for its explorations of divorce as a literary theme and for its underlying sexual intimations of the passion between a father and daughter. Writing the novel—at a feverish pace to escape the anxiousness of Winny's illness—sapped his strength far more than reading the many critical reviews.[14]

Howells came out of the crisis a dedicated advocate of literary realism. Although he and his friend Henry James disagreed on the extent to which American life provided appropriate literary themes, together they championed realism and were ardent proponents of Emile Zola and Turgenev. In politics Howells still clung to Republican orthodoxy, but with less and less conviction. He wrote to Mark Twain in 1884 that he intended to "vote for Blaine. I do not believe he is guilty of the things they accuse him of." Yet to James he confessed that it made him blush to think of voting for Blaine. As an editor he introduced more articles on social and economic issues, but his views on labor and the poor were naive, as indeed they always would be. He was appalled at the living and working conditions of American cities, yet fearful of the potential of organized labor for violence and social disruption. He liked John Hay's *Breadwinners*, particularly because it showed that workingmen "are no better or wiser than the rich *as* the rich, and are quite as likely to be false and foolish." Describing the contrasts between uninhabited wealthy homes and the crowded houses of the poor in Boston in a letter to his father in 1884, Howells wondered why "men are so patient with society as they are."[15] And yet, as Tolstoy made painfully obvious to him, he would never successfully bridge the hiatus between his comfortable life (including maintaining three or four empty houses while living somewhere else) and that of the masses of workers in cities. Despite his apparent conquest of the society of polite learning, Howells's rise to literary prominence was not without its moments of self-doubt and fumbling, insensitive attempts at socioeconomic analysis. By 1885 the troubled man was more than ready for a new purpose for his life and writing.

The trial and execution of the anarchists was not the only crisis in Howells's life in the mid-1880s. His favorite sister died in 1886 and, after an illusory period of good health, Winny's illness suddenly worsened. Her worried parents lived out of suitcases for several months in search of medical specialists, sanitariums, and restful resorts. Winny deteriorated until her death in 1889. In the midst of these painful and emotional events, he discovered Tolstoy, which he later described as something like a "religious experience." In the spring of 1887 Howells and Edward Everett Hale met at the train depot in Albany. During an hour's wait between trains they talked about Tolstoy and, as Hale later explained to his wife, they "came round to the most serious subjects man can talk to man about. You know how deep he is in Tolstoi. Tolstoi had really troubled him, because he does not know but he ought to be ploughing and reaping. But he is as sweet and good and eager to do right as he can be. I dare not begin to write down what he said and I, I went nearer the depths than perhaps I have ever done to any one but you." Six months later, a week following the Haymarket hangings, Howells asked his sister if she had read Tolstoy's "heart-searching" books. "They're worth all the other novels ever written"; he told her that he could "never again see life in the way I saw it before I knew him."[16]

Howells had hardly even known Tolstoy's name when he read the *Cossacks* in 1885. But it was *Anna Karenina*, which he began in the fall of 1885, that first awakened his appreciation of Tolstoy. "How good you feel the author's heart to be," he wrote to T. S. Perry while only partway through the novel. Within the next two years Howells read all Tolstoy's fiction and nonfiction translated into French or English and was urging his friends to do likewise. In the summer of 1887 he was at Lake George, mainly for Winny's sake, writing his first Social Gospel novel, *Annie Kilburn*, in a study in which pictures of Lincoln, Hawthorne, and Tolstoy hung above his desk, and preaching Tolstoy's doctrines to a visiting reporter. To the many writers and critics who gravitated to Howells in the mid-1880s, as they did throughout most of his career, he talked mainly about Tolstoy. His enthusiasm was infectious. Four months after the encounter and discussion in the Albany train depot, Hale wrote Howells to explain that he had not been corresponding because he had been busy reading Tolstoy all summer. On May 28, 1887, former President Hayes jotted in his diary the simple notation: "Yesterday W. D. Howells and his sister called. A happy greeting and meeting. He warmly commended Tolstoy's writings." The next day Hayes noted that he was reading *Anna Karenina*. Even the aging Walt Whitman, who was generally insensitive to Tolstoy, as well as to Howells, remarked in surprise to Horace Traubel after reading Howells's introduction to *Sebastopol:* "I never knew Howells could enthuse so much—could take such an interest in any one. . . . Certainly if this continues I shall have to warm towards Tolstoy!" There were many intellectual influences on Howells in the mid-1880s—Gronlund's *Cooperative Commonwealth*, the tracts of William Morris, the Fabian essays—but as he said in 1898, "the greatest influence . . . came to me through reading Tolstoi. Both as an artist and as a moralist I must acknowledge my deep indebtedness to him."[17]

Howells's enthusiasm at first was for Tolstoy's fiction. As one of America's foremost proponents of literary realism who had for several years been exploring new fictional modes and themes, Howells was enthralled by Tolstoy's realism. What he admired most about *Anna Karenina* was Tolstoy's faithfulness to life in showing the self-destructive effects of Anna's guilty love affair. "As you read on you say, not, 'This is like life,' but, 'This is life.' " Howells found that in all Tolstoy's novels and short stories, one seemed "to come face to face with human nature for the first time in fiction. All other fiction at times *seems* fiction; these alone seem the very truth always." The second requirement for fiction, according to Howells, was that it must be morally instructive, and this, too, he found in Tolstoy's novels. After a summary of the Russian's fiction in an article for *Harper's Weekly* in 1887, Howells confessed that he was not very objective about Tolstoy's works and could not criticize them aesthetically because, as he said, "I have found myself thinking of them on their ethical side." He concluded that the understanding, love, and ultimate renunciation of Karenin, the betrayed husband in *Anna Karenina*, was "incomparably good aesthetically," but "still greater ethically."[18] Howells was particularly impressed with the eagerness to emulate the simple peasant life of toil in such characters as Olenin, Levin, and Pierre Bezukhov, which partly explains why he told Hale that he thought he should be ploughing and reaping. His own experience confirmed those of Tolstoy and his characters that the poor were more capable of following the moral precepts of Jesus than the rich. Tolstoy's fiction, then, struck two responsive chords in Howells's literary sense of what the novel should do: it should be aesthetically realistic and ethically instructive.

As much as Howells celebrated Tolstoy's fiction, he reserved his warmest enthusiasm for the Russian's personal confessions and religious tracts. The novels showed what fiction could do to improve literature, but the essays revealed what a person could do to improve humanity. In his Christmas editorial in 1888, Howells cited Tolstoy's essays as an example of what he called the new Christmas literature. He decried the charitable practice of giving turkeys and other palliative gifts to the poor as mere provisional measures and suggested that what was needed was not charity but a new social and political system. Tolstoy reminds us, Howells wrote, "that there is and can be no happiness but in the sacrifice of self for others." Although he found exemplary lives in Tolstoy's novels, Howells found the Russian's life itself "by far the most impressive spectacle of the century." He admitted that he was "helpless before the spirit" of Tolstoy's confessions and religious essays. Tolstoy "compels no man's conscience, he shapes no man's conduct"; if one cannot but be compelled and shaped by his teachings, which are the same as those of Jesus, Howells added, then it is "because this reader's soul cannot deny it."[19]

Howells's soul was troubled by the contrast between his comfortable life and the poverty he saw all about him, especially after his move to New York in 1886. As early as April of that year, in a review of *My Religion*, in which Tolstoy enjoined the rich man to renounce material pleasures and possessions, Howells admitted that Tolstoy's example caused in him "some pangs of disagreeable self-question." Tolstoy "tells us that in this century thirty millions of men have perished in war; and he asks us how many have given up their lives for Christ's sake. These things give one pause." Reviewing *What to Do?* a year later, in which Tolstoy said that the rich man ought not to give alms but rather should demonstrate that he could and would work with his hands, Howells was again forced to pause and question his own life. When Tolstoy asked others to emulate the life of Jesus, Howells confessed that he did not like that prospect. Moreover, Tolstoy's successful example "makes it impossible for one to regard it without grave question of the life that the rest of us are living." In perhaps the most illuminating statement of Tolstoy's influence on him, Howells said in 1887 that "this far-fetched Russian nobleman is precisely the human being with whom at this moment I find myself in the greatest intimacy; not because I know him, but because I know myself through him."[20] And because he could not emulate Tolstoy's personal example of self-denial, he did not particularly like what he knew about himself. This confirmed a long-held but well-hidden inner conviction.

In *My Literary Passions*, Howells summarized his debt to Tolstoy ten years after his initial exposure. The Russian taught that the life of Jesus provided the only ideal of a perfect life. "There is no other example, no other ideal, and the chief use of Tolstoy is to enforce this fact in our age." Because he aspired to live an ideal life himself, Howells reiterated that "I can never look at life in the mean and sordid way that I did before I read Tolstoy." Failing to achieve this ideal life caused Howells shame and guilt, while at the same time offering hope: "I learned from Tolstoy to try character and motive by no other test, and though I am perpetually false to that sublime ideal myself, still the ideal remains with me to make me ashamed that I am not true to it." Despite his adoration and shame—or perhaps because of it—Howells was capable of finding fault with his master. Although Tolstoy posed Christian anarchist solutions for remaking the world, Howells's remedy was a collective one. He objected to the Russian's withdrawal from society and insisted that "it is as comrades and brothers that men must save the world from itself, rather than themselves from the world."[21] This, however, was a minor quarrel in an otherwise highly eulogistic account of his foremost literary passion.

Tolstoy's ideas did not convert Howells, as he and others often claimed, so much as they reawakened and confirmed inner beliefs that had long been dormant. His upbringing in a Quaker, abolitionist home had inculcated him with strong Christian beliefs in justice, equality, and service to others. Howells's adherence to these principles had been impeded by the glitter of his popularity in literary circles in New England. And in the midst of his enthusiasm over Tolstoy, he continued to recognize Emerson as "the foremost of our seers." Howells's move to New York, the execution of the anarchists, his daughter's illness, and the discovery of Tolstoy all contributed to the reawakening of his earlier commitment to the ethical teachings of men such as Emerson, Jesus, and his father. These events and discoveries shocked Howells into an awareness not only that America had lost sight of Christian ideals but also that those ideals had become obscured in his own life.[22]

For more than a decade after 1887, Howells espoused, if somewhat reluctantly and inactively, various programs of reform. The themes to which he repeatedly returned in the late 1880s and in the 1890s were those of the renunciation of wealth and riches, the gap between rich and poor, the nobility of menial work, nonresistance to evil, and the equality, dignity, and brotherhood of man. Calling himself a socialist (with something less than definitional precision), Howells preached replacing economic competition and private charity with industrial cooperation and self-sacrificing social justice. Involved in all his manifestations of concern was the shame he felt in the inadequacy of his own attempts in living up to these ideals and in practicing himself, as Tolstoy did, the ethic of Jesus. His inability to express his concern in deeds, as he did in words, caused Howells eventually to soften, or perhaps to rationalize, the importance of Tolstoy. The nature of this rationalization, the restraints on his activism, and his own proposed solutions are revealed in his writing, especially his novels, during the years after 1887.

At the time of the execution of the anarchists, Howells was completing a new novel, *Annie Kilburn*, which, as he told his sister, dealt with humanity rather than with love. The hero, a Tolstoyan minister named Peck, preached the life of Jesus rather than the doctrine of Christ.[23] The novel reveals the ambivalence of Howells's response to his Russian master and demonstrates both the possibilities and the impracticabilities of Tolstoy's, that is, Howells's, social theories. Peck was a Unitarian minister in Hatboro, a small city in Massachusetts. In Old Hatboro were the summer homes of wealthy old Boston families, while in South Hatboro, a growing industrial section, lived the poor workers. Thus, the town was a mixture of Howells's old life in Boston, where his interest in socioeconomic questions had been minimal, and his new life in New York City, where these questions were inescapable. The rich in

Old Hatboro were dabbling with the creation of a Social Union, an experiment in charity by which the wealthy and worker families would be brought together for the moral benefit and uplifting of the poor. The Social Union would sponsor paternalistic programs such as reading rooms, joint theatrical productions, and sending poor children to the beach for the summer. The experiment was a monstrous failure in communication and intent. The wealthy, who were hosts at a joint dinner-theatrical affair to raise money for the union and, presumably, to mix with the poor, separated themselves from their guests by a rope.

Peck, of course, objected vehemently to the experiment as an insidious form of patronizing charity. He told Annie Kilburn, a wealthy young woman in Old Hatboro, that "money is a palliative, but it can't cure. It can sometimes create a bond of gratitude perhaps, but it can't create sympathy between rich and poor." After the fiasco of the theatrical, in his last sermon before renouncing his ministerial position to go work with the poor in the mills, Peck preached that authentic brotherhood and justice were holier than charity. The only way to understand the poor and help them was to work and to live with them. Earlier he had told Annie that "those who rise above the necessity of work for daily bread are in great danger of losing their right relation to other men." But before Peck could begin his new life, he was killed (like Anna Karenina) by a train in the local depot. The novel was, as Howells told Hamlin Garland, "from first to last a cry for *justice*, not *alms*," precisely the message of Tolstoy in *What to Do?*[24]

The only person in town who partially understood what Peck had been trying to say was Annie. His influence on her was not unlike the influence of Tolstoy on Howells. Peck gave her an unfamiliar but inescapable challenge and despite some initial reluctance, "she began to see that one ought to have a conscience about doing good." After Peck's death she donated her money not to Old Hatboro's Social Union but to a cooperative boardinghouse for workers, called the Peck Social Union. This was but a partial application of Peck's theories, as Howells himself could only partially apply Tolstoy's. Annie's restraints (and Howells's) were exposed by a friend who chided her at the end of the novel, saying, "she was the fiercest apostle of labour that never did a stroke of work."[25]

Letters written during and after the writing of *Annie Kilburn* revealed the depth of Howells's guilt. In reply to a letter from Garland, who was trying to convert him to the single tax, Howells expressed doubts about outright confiscation of property which landlords did not wish themselves to give up. Howells made it clear that he had not yet rejected single-taxism, but only that he was "reading and thinking about questions that carry me beyond myself and my miserable literary idolatries of the past. . . . I am still the slave of selfishness, but I no longer am content to be so." Hale's letter of congratulations on the novel elicited a reply from Howells in which he insisted that he had solved nothing "except what was solved eighteen centuries ago. The most that I can do is perhaps to set a few people thinking; for as yet I haven't got to doing anything, myself." Two months later Howells was utterly depressed, partly because of Winny's worsening illness and partly because of his inability to do anything about social conditions he increasingly believed to be unjust. He wrote Henry James that he was "not in a very good humor with 'America' . . . . I should hardly like to trust pen and ink with all the audacity of my social ideas; but after fifty years of optimistic content with 'civilization' and its ability to come out all right in the end, I now abhor it, and feel that it is coming out all wrong in the end, unless it bases itself anew on a real equality." It was not just America that he was out of sorts with, but himself: "Meantime, I wear a fur-lined overcoat, and live in all the luxury my money can buy." In another letter to Hale his shame for not doing anything was even more manifest. He admitted that he used to believe that America provided all men a fair chance but now had become convinced that this was not so. "I am neither an example nor an incentive, meanwhile, in my own way of living." He confessed that he was capable only of "words, words, words! How to make them things, deeds,—you have the secret of that; with me they only breed more words."[26]

One reason Howells was incapable of deeds was that he was unable to accept, much less adopt, Tolstoy's example in its extremes. He found it difficult to give up his material possessions, particularly as his own financial success as a writer and critic skyrocketed in the early 1890s.[27] How best to rationalize one's failings, as judged by a Tolstoyan standard, than to find Tolstoy himself inapplicable? Although Howells admired the Russian's sincerity and motivations, he quarreled with the extent to which Tolstoy carried his ideas of renunciation. Tolstoy not only renounced the life of ease but also withdrew from society and denounced its institutions: marriage, courts, prisons, the church, and ultimately, government itself. This was going too far. Tolstoy's extremism could only be explained by his Russian environment. *What to Do?* was "another of those Russian books which have given some people the impression that Russia cannot be an agreeable country to live in." In Russia, Howells thought, Tolstoy's extreme pessimism and denunciations were warranted because the country was backward and despotic; therefore, it needed a total upheaval of its social, economic, and political systems. Russia was different from America, where "the smiling aspects of life" were more obvious and abundant, a fact that all who read Tolstoy should keep in mind. "We are still far from justice in our social conditions, but we are infinitely nearer it than Russia." For this reason, "we can endure much that is wrong and hideous," but only because these things are "merely temporary and disciplinary."[28] Howells's guarded optimism here contradicts the despair expressed in his letters to James and Hale, but his explanation served to relieve some personal guilt for not following Tolstoy's example to the letter. As good as Tolstoy was, therefore, it was not always necessary to follow him, for his impractical actions were warranted only by his Russian environment.

The citizens of Old Hatboro arrived at a similar conclusion in explaining Mr. Peck. They called him a sentimentalist and a dreamer. After his death they "revered his goodness and his wisdom, but they regarded his conduct of life as impractical, . . . impossible to follow." Peck would have been a more useful man, "if he could only have let impracticable theories alone." This opinion was precisely the usual response of most Americans who read Tolstoy and increasingly became Howells's own view. He was no more capable of following Tolstoy's practical example than Annie was of following Peck's. Annie's plight—and Howells's—was best expressed by the doctor in *Annie Kilburn*, who concluded, "We can't hurry any change, but we can make ourselves uncomfortable."[29] In the years between 1888 and 1898 Howells's position on social questions was characterized by a desire for change without hurrying it. His inner life revealed a tension between assailing impractical programs for change on the one hand, and making himself uncomfortable by self-condemnation for his own impracticality on the other.

As he always did, Howells revealed his social beliefs and inner turmoils in his fiction. In *A Hazard of New Fortunes*, written in 1889, he painted his economic theories and personal dilemmas onto a vast canvas of life in New York. Again, as in *Annie Kilburn*, he employed Tolstoyan characters, Lindau, the proud old self-renouncing socialist, and Conrad Dryfoos, the young and gentle Christian socialist son of an unscrupulous entrepreneur, to criticize American social and economic evils. These same characters also revealed the impracticality of their own positions. Again, the most significant character in the novel is not a radical but Basil March, the comfortable middle-class editor who has recently moved from Boston to New York. Initially, March is generally uninterested in socioeconomic questions, but gradually he is sensitized to the corruptions of American capitalism by Lindau. His first stand is in support of the principle of Lindau's freedom of opinion, but eventually Lindau's opinions and principles become in part his own. March finds himself, like Howells, wandering on Sundays into churches where Christianity is treated "as a system of economics as well as a religion," but is incapable of fully adopting or acting on any of the new creeds. Conrad's Christlike martyrdom in trying to serve as peacemaker of a streetcar strike challenges March to sort out his confusion. His anticapitalist conversion, it appears, is less than complete, for he fears for his own security and right conduct in a society he knows will not change: "And so we go on, pushing and pulling, climbing and crawling, thrusting aside and trampling underfoot; lying, cheating, stealing; and when we get to the end, covered with blood and dirt and sin and shame, and look back over the way we've come to a palace of our own, or the poorhouse, which is about the only possession we can claim in common with our brothermen, I don't think the retrospect can be pleasing." In the end, despite March's sympathy for Lindau, Conrad, and the laboring, striking poor, he concludes that personal acts of renunciation and activist socialism are impracticable. He tells his son that other than suffering for the sins of others, like the exceptional Conrad, only through the vote can American life be improved. "Men like Lindau, who renounce the American means as hopeless, and let their love of justice hurry them into sympathy with violence—yes, they are wrong; and poor Lindau did die in a bad cause."[30] Like Howells himself, in spite of his personal discomfort, March was in no hurry.

Throughout the novel Howells, as author, and March, as protagonist, are far removed from the action. Most of the scenes take place in aristocratic drawing rooms where petty romances are unfolded and in the editorial offices of March's journal. And when, against his wife's advice, March's curiosity sends him into the streets looking for scenes of activity or violence in the streetcar strike, the author never lets him see them, except for one brief, yet central, passage. Howells's own experience was too limited. Henry James compared the novel to Zola, but unlike Zola, Howells could not portray the stark urban life of tenements, poverty, and industrial warfare because he did not understand it. All he could do, as he told Mark Twain, was to let his book "preach its great sermon without seeming to take sides or preach at all."[31] The sermon itself was as ambivalent as Howells's commitment to it. And yet, he was still determined to do something, by deeds, for the causes in which he believed.

While in New York in the winter of 1888–1889, Howells attended and was impressed by the sermons of Heber Newton, head of the New York branch of the Society of Christian Socialists. When he moved back to Boston after finishing *A Hazard of New Fortunes* late in 1889, he identified himself with W. D. P. Bliss's Christian Socialist Brotherhood of the Carpenter, Bellamy's Nationalist Club of Boston, and Hale's Tolstoi Club. Howells shared the beliefs of both the Christian socialists and the Nationalists but, as he told his father, he decided not to "openly act with either for the present." He preferred, instead, a Senate bill then pending "to lend farmers money from the Treasury surplus on their mortgages,"[32] hardly a measure to initiate a new socialized society. Howells placed more faith in the ballot and legislation than on the utopian panaceas of Bliss and Bellamy. These simply were too impractical in America.

Howells's dilemma was still with him in the early 1890s, but without the intensity of the late 1880s. He wrote to his father in 1890 that a discussion at dinner with the Twains had revealed Twain, Howells, and their wives to be in agreement. "We are theoretical socialists, and practical aristocrats. But it is a comfort to be right theoretically, and to be ashamed of one's self practically."[33] When Howells left *Harper's* in the spring of 1892 to write for the newly reformist *Cosmopolitan*, he carried with him a bust of Tolstoy and a map of Altruria, indicative of the persistence of his desire to be right theoretically. He was, however, as incapable of writing a sociological study, as he later called his Altrurian novels, as he was in realistically depicting the violence of a streetcar strike.

A Traveller from Altruria and *Letters of an Altrurian Traveller*, serialized in *Cosmopolitan* between 1892 and 1894, were presented not as sociology but as utopian romance. The imaginary Altruria, described to a group of American aristocrats at a fashionable seaside hotel by Mr. Homos, is an idyllic, peaceful, mostly rural Christian republic. All its citizens, true followers of Jesus, work with their hands as artisans or as cultivators of the earth. Such work, the now Jeffersonian Howells wrote, "brings man into the closest relations to the deity." Altruria had evolved from an anarchic and violent era of rapid technological development and selfish monopolistic accumulation, an era identical to the conditions of the United States in the late nineteenth century. The old order had been peacefully overthrown by its own evolution into monolithic economic units, as in Bellamy's *Looking Backward*, and by the ballot. The new society preserved the family, rural virtues of neighborliness, and beautiful, useful factories and mills. The citizens of Altruria pursued not rights and self-interest but fulfilled Christian ideals of duty, fellowship, and altruism. Indeed, said Mr. Homos, "we have the kingdom of heaven upon earth already."[34]

Howells's utopian conception owes some of its character to Tolstoy, but much more to American sources: Bellamy, Jefferson, Emerson, and his own boyhood Quaker-Owenite heritage. Indeed, when Howells's description of Altruria is not confused with the White City of Chicago's Columbian Exposition, which he visited, it seems very much like the small Ohio towns of his youth. Tolstoy appears in the work as a crank, the only man in "the whole civilized world—outside of Altruria, of course—who is proud of working at a trade." The point of the romance, as Howells reiterates frequently, is that the ideals actualized in Altruria are precisely those espoused in America. "I imagine," the Altrurian said one day, "that the difference between your civilization and ours is only one of degree, after all, and that America and Altruria are really one at heart." Both aspired to be Christian republics, but the difference in the degree to which national principles were fulfilled was much wider than any of the naive American aristocrats was willing to admit. Through the narrator, Mr. Twelvemough, a famous writer, Howells achieves a more credible portrayal of American hypocrisies than he does of Altrurian fulfillments. The solution he poses is to Altrurianize America, which is to say, to Americanize it. The most positive signs that America might be Altrurianized, according to Howells, were the Columbian Exposition, Central Park ("a bit of Altruria"), and the twenty-two electoral votes cast for the Populist party in 1892.[35] These examples indicate how theoretical, and possibly naive, Howells's Altrurian serials were.

The implications of the Populist reference were explored more thoroughly in another novel written at the same time. The *World of Chance*, published in 1893, was a more convincing expression than his Altrurian serial of Howells's beliefs in the possibilities for political reform in America. The novel also revealed how far he was moving away from Tolstoy. David Hughes, the protagonist of the *World of Chance*, was an old disillusioned communitarian who was extremely bitter in his denunciations of American capitalism. He explored, like Howells, the solutions offered by Tolstoyan anarchism and nonresistance, Bellamy Nationalism, Christian socialism, and the American way of the ballot. He found all wanting except the last. Most characters in the novel called Hughes "Tolstoyan," but he was in fact more vehement in repudiating Tolstoy's renunciation of social institutions than he was in criticizing American monopolies. By "quitting the scene of the moral struggle, and in symplifying himself into a mere peasant," Hughes said of Tolstoy, "he begs the question as completely as if he had gone into a monastery." Although Tolstoy "struck out some tremendous truths" about the conditions of civilization, "his conclusions are as wrong as his premises are right." Tolstoy was not even consistent, one character charged. He wore the dress and ate the food of his peasants, but "he has not been able to give up his money. . . . He's a monumental warning of the futility of any individual attempt to escape from conditions." Hughes insisted many times in the novel that he was not Tolstoyan, that his views were actually opposed to Tolstoy's. In a particularly illuminating statement, Howells has him say that "practically, I don't follow him. We shall never redeem the world by eschewing it. Society is not to be saved by self-outlawry. The body politic is to be healed politically. The way to have the golden age is to elect it by the Australian ballot. . . . What

I object to in Tolstoi is his utter unpracticality."[36] As he moved away from Tolstoy himself, Howells used Hughes, as he had used March, to repudiate his former master's extremism and to express his own restrained solution to social problems.

Hughes's solution, like Howells's, was by the ballot and an exercise of rationality. And yet, as Howells knew, the likelihood of getting a reformed America through the vote was doubtful. Both major parties were decaying and he looked to "the growth of a new one that will mean true equality and real freedom." If the two major parties did not alter themselves to embrace the needs of the workers and farmers, he wrote his father, he hoped that "a party 'of the people, for the people' will rise up in their place, and make this a country where no man who will work need want." He told Perry in 1888 that "if there were a labor party, embodying any practical ideas I would vote with it; but there's none." And yet, when the Populist party emerged in the 1890s, Howells found himself wishing that "the populists had kept the middle of the road" and voted in 1896 for McKinley. Although in sympathy with the labor cause, he was critical of strikes and any form of labor violence. In a letter to his father he deplored the Homestead strikers for their lawlessness, arguing that their cause would have been better served had they "suffered the Pinkertons to shoot them down unarmed. Then they would have had the power of martyrs in the world."[37] Howells's honesty here (and perhaps even his tactics) are commendable, but only a detached and cynical intellectual observer could make such a suggestion.

Although Howells never was comfortable with either labor leaders or Populists, he supported many of the planks of the Omaha platform, as well as the specific demands of many socialists. In 1897 he wrote Frank Parsons, a leader of the municipal reform movement, that he supported the initiative and referendum and was "heartily in favor of municipal ownership of street railways." He was frequently in demand as a speaker before various socialist and Christian socialist meetings, and many reform groups sought to add Howells's prestigious name to their honorary membership rolls. "Even if you cannot attend our meetings, your name will help us," Ernest Crosby wrote in asking Howells to join the Social Reform Club of New York. Howells was chosen to preside over the Bellamy Memorial meeting of the Reform Club on June 7, 1898;

as a theme for his speech he chose, significantly, Bellamy's literature and "the charm and nobility of his personality" rather than Bellamy's utopianism. He was invited to a gathering of most leading Christian intellectual reformers in Buffalo in the summer of 1899, but could not attend. His letter to the conference said that if he were there he would speak for the initiative and referendum, public ownership of railroads and streetcars, state-supported insurance and pensions for labor, public ownership of monopolies, and a national plebiscite on war, peace, and the ratification of treaties.[38]

His endorsement of a plebiscite on war and peace reflected Howells's bitter disgust with American imperialism in the Caribbean and Asia at the close of the century. His opposition to the Spanish-American War was derived in part from Tolstoyan nonresistance, but had its roots in his Quaker youth and his father's stand against the Mexican War. He was, however, no doctrinaire pacifist, like Tolstoy, but opposed imperialism on practical grounds of domestic priorities. Early in April 1898 Howells wrote his sister that he thought American interference in Cuba would be "wickedly wrong" and would cause "a thousand times more suffering than Spain has inflicted or could inflict on Cuba." Howells's predictions were remarkably accurate: "After war will come the piling up of big fortunes again; the craze for wealth will fill all brains, and every good cause will be set back. We shall have an era of blood-brought prosperity, and the chains of capitalism will be welded on the nation more firmly than ever." Two weeks later, after McKinley's war message to Congress, he wrote Henry James that "the most stupid and causeless war that was ever imagined by a kindly and sensible nation" would "set every good cause back." By July, Howells was sure that the stated reasons for the war were a sham: "Our war for humanity has unmasked itself as a war for coaling stations."[39] Although he continued to denounce American imperialism as manifested in the annexation of the Philippines, the old fire was clearly gone from the restrained reformer.

In 1895 Howells told a young man, Jonathan Sturges, whom he encountered in Paris, to take advantage of his youth, to avoid Howells's mistakes, and to "Live!" In a mood of profound despair, as Sturges reported, the aging writer told the young man: "Now I'm old . . . too old for what I see. Oh, I do see, at least—I see a lot.

It's too late. It has gone past me. I've lost it."[40] He reached his sixtieth year in 1897, and he and his invalid wife, Elinor, spent less time in New York, which they detested, and more time at their summer home at Kittery Point, Maine. Howells enjoyed the role of patron of reform, lending his name and support to various causes and encouraging young realistic writers like Garland, Stephen Crane, and Frank Norris. He was generally pleased with the progressive mood Theodore Roosevelt brought to American politics. He revisited Altruria in 1907 in a sequel, *Through the Eye of the Needle.* But like most utopias revisited, it was disappointing: his criticisms of the present and visions of the future were much less sharply defined. Howells was more optimistic about America; consequently, Altruria was less attractive and full of imperfections. His sadness was still present, for as he wrote to Norton, "All other dreamers of such dreams have had nothing but pleasure in them; I have had touches of nightmare." In 1907 Howells was still a man of words, not deeds, and his own dreams brought little pleasure. At age seventy-five he marched down Fifth Avenue in a suffragists parade, but he was no longer committed to reform as much as he was playing at reform. When he had an opportunity in 1909 to deliver a sermon in Kittery Point, he got, as he wrote to his wife, "the Trav. from Altruria, and gave 'em a good dose of socialism." Howells was pleased that the people, who were mostly vacationing wealthy Bostonians, "liked it so well that they all shook hands and thankt me. Marthy reported later that it was the greatest hit ever known in K.P."[41]

When Tolstoy died in 1910, Howells faithfully called him "the greatest novelist and one of the best men, the truest philosophers who ever lived," but turned down an invitation to speak at a memorial meeting. He was understandably more upset by the death of Mark Twain, his close friend for almost forty years, in the same year. Four years earlier, Howells had written Twain that he cared more for praise from him than from any other person in the world with the one exception of "perhaps Tolstoy; but I do not love him as I love you."[42] This was not an idle preference. It was symptomatic of Howells's preference for all things American, including not only personal admirations but also the way in which he believed reform should be achieved. Tolstoy made a profound impression on Howells, perhaps as profound as any person can make on another, but he was simply too Russian for the American. Turning it around, perhaps Howells was too American for Tolstoy. The restraints of Howells's temperament and status rendered him incapable of significant reformist deeds. Discovering Tolstoy back in the 1880s had jolted Howells from the complacency of years of literary success and had revived his latent impulses to do good, serve humanity, and emulate Jesus. These impulses, learned in his youth, were as American as Martin's Ferry or Jefferson, Ohio. They brought Howells added prominence and distinctiveness, new literary themes, and not a little guilt and personal anguish. His was, on balance, thoroughly a life of the mind.

Henry Demarest Lloyd

By the late 1890s Henry Demarest Lloyd was moving in an opposite direction from Howells. Both alternately despaired of and were optimistic about America, but as Howells's reform efforts diminished, Lloyd's increased. Like Howells, Lloyd had difficulty resolving the dilemma between idealistic ends and practical means, but unlike his contemporary he did not let the problem paralyze his reform participation. He put his mind to work. Lloyd also was proud of his Americanness, which tempered the influence of European thought and acted as a restraint on his reformist ideology. And like Howells, Lloyd, too, looked forward to a utopian day when "we are to be commoners, travellers to Altruria," a vision of utopia that was often more comfortable than were the practical ways of getting there.[43] The activist ways he pursued, however, were closer to the suffering objects of his concern, and he was therefore less susceptible than Howells to the agonies of conscience.

Born in New York City in 1847 into a morally strict and sober Dutch Reformed ministerial family, young Lloyd received an excellent formal education. At Columbia he studied with the leading free trader, Francis Lieber, and distinguished himself with his facility as an orator and writer. He passed the New York bar examination in 1869 and immediately embarked upon a reformist career, first joining the battle against Boss Tweed and then as an ardent crusading Liberal Republican against the tariff. He wrote to a friend in 1872 that he yearned for public distinction and power without obligation to any interests. The most independent avenue to power, he concluded, was neither law nor the ministry, but journalism. He joined the staff of the *Chicago Tribune* in 1872, married Jessie Bross, the wealthy daughter of one of the paper's owners, and soon achieved prominence as financial editor and general editorial writer from 1875 to 1885. While in England in 1885 he met William Morris and other European reformers who, as he wrote his wife, made him long to be his own man. He therefore decided to resign from the *Tribune* to devote himself to a larger constituency.[44] He returned to the United States to do just that. Despite his resignation from the *Tribune* and the loss of his father-in-law's financial favor over his Haymarket stand, Lloyd was assured a continuing wealthy income through his wife's independent resources and his own wise money management. By the mid-1880s he had achieved the independence, distinction, and power which he had sought as a young man. There was no question that he would use his favorable status and skillful pen on behalf of those suffering citizens and socioeconomic issues which the Haymarket affair had brought into focus. How far he would or could go as a reformer was another question.

Lloyd's reformist philosophy was worked out in the 1880s. The application of his beliefs took place in the 1890s when he was an active participant in a wide variety of reform causes and organizations. His diverse commitments were derived from two fundamental positions developed in the 1880s, founded upon a mixture of personal observations of American life and the influence of both European and American intellectuals. His first belief was that nineteenth-century doctrines of laissez-faire, classical economics, free market competitiveness, and self-interested pursuit of wealth as a means of social benefit were fallacious and bankrupt. Capitalism was both immoral, corrupting its beneficiaries and victims alike, and impractical, operating neither cheaply nor efficiently; it did not even operate competitively. Free competition inevitably led to monopolistic combinations and tyranny. Simply stated, he believed that "liberty produces wealth, and wealth destroys liberty." The old self-interest, as Lloyd called prevailing economic theories and practices in *Wealth against Commonwealth*, should be replaced by the "new self-interest." This was his second fundamental belief, which he variously called the new conscience, the social self-interest, and the gospel of social sympathy. Whatever he called it, the new self-interest was distinctly cooperative and collective and was directed toward the application of Christian ethics, particularly the law of doing unto others as you would have them do unto you, to political and industrial life. "The golden rule is the original of every political constitution, written and unwritten, and all our reforms are but the pains with which we strive to improve the copy."[45] His primary inspirations for this new self-interest, besides Jesus, were the Fabians, Mazzini, Ruskin, and Emerson.

It is not easy to define Lloyd's social philosophy precisely, for he was an eclectic and enigmatic person. He was known as the "millionaire socialist." His brother called him "temperamentally a practical idealist." Chester Destler defined his social philosophy as non-Marxian socialist welfare democracy.[46] Lloyd himself believed that the phrase cooperative commonwealth best defined his political, economic, and religious beliefs. He wrote in his notebook in 1894:

> What Party do you belong to?
> The Cooperative Commonwealth.
> What school of Political Economy?
> The C.C.
> What God do you worship?
> C.C.

In one of Lloyd's most paradoxical and illuminating statements, he said that when asked to define himself, "I say that I am a socialist–anarchist–communist–individualist–collectivist–co-operative–aristocratic–democrat, for, as I survey the world, the very complicated thing we call society is rolling forward along all these lines simultaneously."[47] Lloyd was not being purposefully evasive; he was genuinely all of these, according to his own definitions. The inherent contradictions in his list reflect Lloyd's quest for a social philosophy which was both collectivist and individualist and an approach to reform which was both idealistic and practical. In his attempt to balance these polarities he espoused a plethora of reform causes and movements, many of which floundered on either ideological inconsistencies or tactical ineffectiveness. An examination of his own definitions will partially clarify his ideological contradictions, as well as show the intellectual influences on his social thought.

Lloyd's socialism was distinctly non-Marxian. Although he defined the struggle in America as one between the "Money Power" and the "Labour movement," he rejected outright the doctrine of historical class conflict. If he were in England, he said, he would be a Fabian socialist, and generally he preferred to be called a Fabian or a democrat than a socialist of any kind. His socialism was grounded not on dialectical materialism and the conflict of classes but on Christian principles of moral concern for the welfare of others. In a talk on Mazzini in 1889, Lloyd said that Mazzini, with whom he agreed, had deep sympathy with all plans for advancing the worker, but that he rejected the materialism of the socialist schools. Lloyd stressed the religious, cooperative, and anti-monopolistic side of socialism. "I care nothing for any system of economics that does not include co-operation and anti-monopoly. Call it socialism, if you like, I do not care. . . . The people of a community are as able to co-operate as the people of a corporation."[48] He moved in a circle of secular and Christian socialists, supported socialist programs with money and his organizational ability, but never fully committed himself to an organized socialist party. He sympathized with the anarchists, not for their terrorist methods and pronouncements against government but for their love and trust for ordinary people. He never forgot Albert Parsons's dying words that the voice of the people should be heard, and he incorporated that principle into his social philosophy. When Governor Altgeld pardoned Fielden and Schwab in 1893, the two anarchists for whom Lloyd had secured a commuted sentence six years earlier, he and Howells were again among the few prominent Americans who defended Altgeld's unpopular decision.

Lloyd's communism was founded upon a misplaced hope in the communitarian experiments in America and England in the 1890s. He visited the Shaker community at Mount Lebanon, New York, in 1894 and admired the Shakers' spirit and economic arrangements. In 1896 he was elected president of Eugene Debs's Social Democratic organization, the Brotherhood of the Cooperative Commonwealth, but declined to accept the position, partly because he could not devote all his energies to the experiment. He delivered the major address at the laying of the cornerstone of the Ruskin College of the New Economy in 1897. He followed the efforts of the Christian Commonwealth colony in Georgia with sympathy and admiration, but believed that the colonists' rigid adherence to Tolstoyan doctrines of nonresistance to evil were too narrow and limiting. The failure of all these communal experiments convinced Lloyd that the new order had to be founded on a broader basis; not by isolated successes or failures, he said, but "in the bosom of society by all for all."[49]

The most difficult paradox for Lloyd to resolve was that of reconciling collectivism with individualism. He was unquestionably a collectivist in his political economy, but was determined to salvage the kind of individual independence which he believed had made America a great nation. Rather than destroying the individual, collectivism ennobles him. "We are individuals, persons, only so far as we have achieved union with others." In the concluding chapter of *Wealth against Commonwealth*, Lloyd said that the new self-interest would enhance, not destroy, individualism. "We can become individual only by submitting to be bound to others. We extend our freedom only by finding new laws to obey." Again, quoting Mazzini, as well as showing the influence of his other master, Emerson, Lloyd wrote that American industrial life needed "a retempering of the individual life through communion with the universal life." Lloyd's conception of the universal life was cooperative, democratic, and ultimately, redemptive. "The next Messiah will be a collective Messiah," he wrote, promising political and economic democratizing for the redemption of the world. The purpose of democratizing the people, he said, was not to create mediocrity and monotony, but to regenerate the individual with equal rights and opportunities.[50]

The other paradox in Lloyd's thought, as he had written in his self-definition, was his allegiance to both democratic and aristocratic ideals. His concept of democracy, which had its origins in Jacksonian antimonopolism, was expanded in the 1890s to include the Populist, Swiss, and New Zealand examples of direct democracy. Lloyd believed, like Mazzini, that the people should rule, saying that "when the People complain, they are always right." He wanted to expand rule by the people beyond political life, where in America it operated with some effectiveness, to economic life, where it did not: "We are a Postoffice People, a Police People, a War People, a Courts of Justice People, a Ballot People, . . . [yet] we are not yet a Telegraph People, a Railroad People, a Postal Savings

Bank People, a National Insurance People, a Right-of-all-to-Employment People."[51]

Lloyd's faith in democracy, however, was complicated and restrained by his aristocratic notions, attributable partly to his own elevated status, but mainly to an Emersonian intellectual elitism. Curiously, although many of his speeches were before audiences of workers, Lloyd hoped to influence not the lower or middle classes but the intellectual elite—editors, ministers, and scholars. The nearly 500 pages of *Wealth against Commonwealth* prior to the magnificent eloquence of the final two chapters present a weighty, thoroughly researched and documented case against the corruptions of Standard Oil. Only a few readers could possibly have had the dedication and patience to wade through the whole sordid story. Yet he believed strongly in the impact of ideas on events: "before every revolution marches a book—the *Contrat Social*, *Uncle Tom's Cabin*. 'Every man nowadays,' says Emerson, 'carries a revolution in his vest-pocket.' " Or so he hoped. He was, as Daniel Aaron pointed out, "the first of the great reformers to be equally at home among musty business records and court files and in the rarefied atmosphere of transcendental ethics." Portraits of Emerson, Ruskin, and Morris hung in his Winnetka study, and Lloyd's elegance of style and effective epigrammatic sentences as well as his ethics were clearly patterned after Emerson. But the influence of the Sage of Concord, whom Lloyd called "the greatest mind of our times," went far beyond literary style.[52]

One of Lloyd's most significant public addresses, "The Scholar in Contemporary Practical Questions," was aimed at converting American intellectuals to practical participation in social reform. In tone and content the speech was modeled after Emerson's "American Scholar" address in 1837 and Wendell Phillips's Phi Beta Kappa speech in 1881, both delivered at Harvard. Lloyd's oration was given as a commencement address in 1895 at Iowa College in Grinnell, upon the invitation of President Gates, who called it "the finest Commencement address I ever heard," and George Herron, whose students had been reading *Wealth against Commonwealth*. The influence of Emerson, Phillips, Ruskin, and Mazzini, all of whom were both advocates and exemplars of the intellectual's responsibility in reform, was clear throughout Lloyd's speech. Both Emerson and Phillips, he said, spoke out against slavery and criticized other intellectuals who did not. Mazzini, in the face of Austrian despotism, "spread the principles of political freedom by essays and arguments for literary freedom, its twin brother." Ruskin wrote about art, but he had "for his real subject the contemporary practical questions, the ethics of the common life." It was Ruskin, Lloyd said, who initiated the agitation about the London slums. Although laughed at by political economists, he was the man to whom all political economists must look for practical suggestions for reform. It was difficult to decide, Lloyd said, whether to call Ruskin "England's first literary artist, or its first political economist, or its first practical reformer." Contemporary scholars, Lloyd continued, should profit by the examples of these four, for "never was this courage of scholars and literary men to deal with the social wrongs and social remedies so clear as in our times." There was a crisis at hand, and the scholars should respond, as they always had, first in thought and then in action.[53]

Lloyd was as disturbed by the problem of concrete deeds as was Howells. Throughout his speeches and writings he insisted that the scholar was as responsible for practical action as he was for idealistic thought. In the Grinnell speech he predicted that an ethical rebirth was about to be "put into action, here, now, and practically in farm and mine, stockmarket, factory, and bank!" The scholar must be both herald and executor of the renaissance. He must "put scholarship to its highest use," as Lloyd himself had done in *Wealth against Commonwealth*, in order to find the social solution which would free twentieth-century humans from their nineteenth-century chains. The social solution that was foretold and practiced by nineteenth-century prophets was the gospel of social sympathy. Although he believed that the labor movement was in the vanguard of the new conscience, he called not upon labor leaders but upon the intellectual elite—men such as Ruskin, Mazzini, Carlyle, and Emerson—to lead the movement.[54]

Lloyd's insistence that such men as Emerson and Ruskin were practical reformers reveals the intellectual constraint from which he could not completely escape. The lens through which he perceived the world were those of a scholar. Why else would he have spent so much time and thought trying to resolve contradictory polarities between individualism and collectivism, elitism and democracy, and idealism and practicality? His difficulty with these contradictions, which few working men and women engaged in the daily struggles for survival could afford to worry about, was in large part the result of his intellectuality and the elevated level of those who influenced him. Still, since inspiration (thought) preceded experience (action), the nature of his intellectual inspirations is critical to an understanding of Lloyd.

Ruskin's influence was not startling and sudden, as was Tolstoy's influence on Howells. Rather, Lloyd underwent a continuing process of new discoveries and reawakenings to Ruskin's faith in cooperation, brotherhood, and social love. Lloyd began reading the English critic in the late 1870s; it was then that the protests of Ruskin, Carlyle, and Emerson against the rampant materialism of the nineteenth century first persuaded him to attack the economic theory that justified the exploitation of men in the name of free enterprise. Throughout his career, Lloyd sprinkled his speeches and writing with epigrammatic quotations from Ruskin. The Englishman's influence on him, however, was by no means continuous and complete. Lloyd was too much a product of American thought and life. Like most American reformers at the turn of the century, including Bellamy and many Populists and progressives, Lloyd was proud of America's material accomplishments. He sought only to "bring the size of our morality up to the size of our cities, corporations, and combinations." He did not, like Ruskin and Morris, want to return to a medieval society of small craftsmen. Lloyd preferred to believe that the excursions of Morris into medievalism and utopianism "were precisely the measure of his devotion to the present." The American did, however, share Morris's and Ruskin's discontent with the theory and practice of nineteenth-century industrialism, particularly the American manifestations. Under the influence of Ruskin, he therefore set about to criticize this theory and expose these practices. According to Chester Destler, "Ruskin's aesthetic protest against a sordid, grasping industrialism conditioned Lloyd for affirmative reaction to his denunciation of orthodox economics and his plea for application of the Golden Rule to business."[55]

Lloyd's first well-known assault on American business, "The Story of a Great Monopoly," in which he exposed the practices of Standard Oil as early as 1881, was based more on Lloyd's meticulous research skill in uncovering corrupt behavior than on any intellectual source. But the influence of Ruskin was pronounced in "The Political Economy of Seventy-three Million Dollars," Lloyd's first attack on the system of classical economics which often was used to justify these business practices. "Our high thinkers, like Ruskin, Carlyle, and Emerson," he wrote, "have refused from the first to acknowledge its [orthodox political economy] authority. According to Ruskin, nothing has ever been so disgraceful to human intellect as the acceptance among us of the common doctrines of political economy as a science." The most valid political economy, he said quoting Emerson, "is the care and culture of men." Political economists who ignored this human concern and taught instead that individual pursuits of profits and wealth were validated by science were neither scientific nor moral. Such doctrines, in practice, lead to national destruction by allowing a few like Jay Gould to amass a fortune of $73 million while the many languish in poverty. Lloyd continued by quoting Ruskin, who said that the orthodox political economists were "aiding and abetting the cruelest form of murder on many thousands of persons yearly for the sake simply of putting money into the pockets of the landlords." Drawing on Emerson again, and on Ruskin who wrote that "there is no wealth but life," Lloyd concluded that the "world of wealth is the world of soul, over-soul, and under-soul." In the "Lords of Industry" in 1884 Lloyd concluded with a theme, adopted from Ruskin and Emerson, that he would repeat many times. An era of material inventions in the industrial revolution had created monopoly. What was needed now, he said, was an era of moral inventions in a moral revolution to make social control of monopolies possible. The first revolution was capitalistic and industrial and had produced wealth and monopoly. The second, he predicted, would be social and moral and would promote citizenship and antimonopoly. The first had created competitive trade; the second would stimulate competitive morals.[56]

Lloyd's trip to England in 1885 confirmed his conviction that the old self-interest was immoral and that a new moral revival was imperative. Meeting Morris and other leaders of the English Christian socialist and trades union movement convinced him that Morris was the intellectual son of Ruskin, practicing the preachings of the father. But before practicing himself what he had learned in England, and before devoting himself to a larger constituency than the readers of the *Chicago Tribune*, Lloyd had to refine his social philosophy. He had not yet concluded what form the new morality should take, or what role other than intellectual prophet he would play in the revival.

When he returned to the United States in the fall he had still not recovered from his nervous disorder and insomnia. He therefore devoted a full year and a half to study, interrupting his study to make his bold effort to save the Haymarket anarchists from the gallows. He read Ruskin and Emerson again, the English socialists, Kant, Hegel, Comte, William James, and many others. He also read George and Bellamy. Rejecting their single tax and nationalist panaceas as too narrow, he sought a social philosophy that would reconcile the best in both doctrines. After discovering Mazzini in 1888, his philosophy underwent further refinements. Mazzini and Gronlund's *Cooperative Commonwealth* led him to diminish a persisting emphasis on individualism and to expand the collectivist side of his new thought. Mazzini provided him with the understanding that collectivism ennobles the individual and that all social, political, and economic questions were at heart religious, moral questions: " 'The first one who makes a religion of Democracy will save the world,' Mazzini wrote in substance. He reiterated that the religious idea is the very breath of humanity. His constantly repeated declarations that Humanity was not an accident but an aim, life its mission, and duty its highest word have never been surpassed for inspiration." According to Destler, Lloyd clearly admitted "that Mazzini was the reformer most akin to his own spirit and intellectual approach to the social problem."[57] Most significantly, Mazzini provided him with the example of the prophet-idealist as activist.

Throughout most of 1888 Lloyd read Mazzini's essays, filling six notebooks with quotations from and comments about the Italian idealist. In these notebooks Lloyd thought through the Mazzinian concepts of duty, equality, and love as the basis for a religion of humanity and labor. From Mazzini, Lloyd learned to place more value on equality than on liberty, which was only a means to an end. The liberty of the individual is nothing by itself, he said, quoting Mazzini, for "the free conscience of the individual is powerless to found a social faith." Only a new dogma could save them: that new dogma was association. "There is one finer thing on earth than a perfected individual," Lloyd wrote, and "that is an association, a group of such." The way to actualize association in practical affairs is for the idealist, the intellectual, to act. "Action is the word of God," Mazzini said; "thought alone is but his shadow." The brotherhood of man, Lloyd wrote, could not be achieved by talking about it. "Mere words have never led, will never lead men, not intellect, but faith, not mere faith, but faith in action. The faith of Christ, Dante, Mazzini." Lloyd took great delight in observing, however erroneous the fact, that "the practical Cavour declared the unification of Italy 'a Utopian idea'—the idealist Mazzini achieved it."[58] Practical action alone was shallow without the idealistic spirit of the intellectual behind it.

After studying Mazzini throughout 1888, Lloyd was ready to talk about him. In his basic speech, "Mazzini: Prophet of Action," Lloyd said that the Italian was one of those "few rare faces lifted above the rest, and always turned toward the light." Like William Clarke, whose collection of Mazzini's essays had first attracted Lloyd to the Italian, Lloyd realized that he was a prophet not only of Italy but of the whole world. His greatest contribution, according to Lloyd, was that "he saw that there was but one principle at the foundation of all growth and reform, from religious to economic—the principle of 'one God, one humanity, one law, one love from all for all.' " Only Emerson was as capable of such ethereal and high-minded thinking. The principle of oneness led Mazzini to his motto, "God and the People," and to association as a way of organizing all the people under a political economy of the golden rule. Mazzini "carried into government the principles which Christianity proclaimed in religion," which Lloyd believed must be expanded further into industrial life. The question of activism and practicality inevitably brought Lloyd back to earth. The most compelling part of Mazzini's message, he said, was that he was both the voice and the arm of reform. Although called a dreamer by the despots and aristocrats of Europe, Mazzini was practical enough to defeat their plans and re-create Italy.[59]

In this and other speeches, Lloyd stressed Mazzini's sacrifices of his inheritance and of a promising literary career in order to serve the revolution. He had himself lost an inheritance from his father-in-law and given up a potentially successful career in law or politics. In an unpublished notebook entry, Lloyd wrote that if a reformer were tempted to relax in his commitment to the poor, his temptation could "be stilled by the vision of Mazzini standing at the counter of the London pawnshop." The example, of course, surely did not apply to Lloyd. Although blessed with enough wealth to maintain the house in Winnetka and two summer homes, Lloyd used his resources for others. His Winnetka home was so open and full of visiting reformers that Jane Addams called it "an annex to Hull House." Unlike Howells, Lloyd did not often personalize the impact of the intellectual influences on him; hence, he was spared many of Howells's personal agonies. Where Howells was soft, introspective, and concerned with the individual conscience, Lloyd was tough, externalizing, and concerned with the collective conscience. His version of Christian ethics was applicable not to individual lives but to the whole social and economic fabric of the nation. "We have not been able to see the people for the persons in it," he wrote in *Wealth against Commonwealth*, going on to quote a favorite passage from Mazzini referring to the "man called million."[60] Lloyd preferred to deal not with persons but with people; he painted with a broad brush. His own Christian ethic was expressed in terms of social love and the political economy of the golden rule.

Lloyd's theory of social love owed a great deal to the influence of Mazzini. Man is a creator, he wrote, who discovers and proclaims love as "the original of all social forces." It was manifested not only in the self-interest of the individual but more importantly in the self-interest of the community. Like Mazzini, Lloyd believed in the inevitability of progress, to be achieved on earth, not in heaven. In order to promote progress, men, as creators, must associate, thus creating social love, which in turn begets more social love and more association. Like Mazzini in the *Duties of Man*, Lloyd believed that although social love began with love of the individual, it spread to love of family, state, country, and ultimately, to all of humanity. The best contemporary example of social love was the labor movement, which was not, as the Marxians claimed, an economic movement, but rather a democratic and religious one. Labor was, in fact, "the most religious movement of the day, for it carries the Golden Rule into the market."[61]

The second (and related) expression of Lloyd's Christian social ethic was the political economy of the golden rule. "Our special task," he wrote, "is to iterate and reiterate to the people that Society is organized love, and the Golden Rule its law." Among the many titles he considered for his major work, before settling on *Wealth against Commonwealth*, was *The Rule of Gold and the Golden Rule*. To pursue one's own interest, thus eliminating the poor and the weak on the way to wealth, Lloyd wrote, "is the golden rule of business." In one of his most gruesome and hard-hitting passages, he depicted the fruits of this perverted rule of gold: "These intolerabilities—sweat-shops where model merchants buy and sell the cast-off scarlet-fever skins of the poor, factory and mine where childhood is forbidden to become manhood and manhood is forbidden to die a natural death, mausoleums in which we bury the dead rich, slums in which we bury the living poor, coal pools with their manufacture of artificial winter—all these are the rule of private self-interest arrived at its destination." The challenge of the new self-interest was to restore the golden rule to its original purpose. It was, for Lloyd, no impractical solution to "put the principles of Christ into practice," for many citizens through their family devotion, neighborliness, and self-sacrificing commitments to others were doing just that. These efforts needed to be extended beyond individuals to institutions. To change the minds and hearts of men and women was insufficient: "change of heart is no more redemption than hunger is dinner." Institutions, following the laws of association, of which "the golden rule is the first and last of these," would translate the spirit of love and justice into laws, customs, and habits. Only with the institutionalization of new forms, thus eliminating the old apparatus, could the political economy of the golden rule be made operative.[62]

Once Lloyd's social theory was developed, he had to act on it. As both Mazzini and Emerson had said, the reformer had to be both voice and arm; thought without action for the scholar was only half a person. Beginning in the late 1880s, especially after his year of reading Mazzini, Lloyd supported, encouraged, and worked with the labor movement more ardently than ever. His first concrete act after the Haymarket affair was to go to Spring Valley, Illinois, in 1889 to bring food, clothing, and legal help to suffering miners locked out by their owners. Writing a book about it, *A Strike of Millionaires against Miners* (1890), however impassioned, was the least of his contributions to their cause.

After his Spring Valley participation, he was frequently in demand as a speaker at meetings of worker and liberal reform groups; he argued consistently against sweatshops and child labor, and for the eight-hour day, the right of unions to organize and bargain collectively, and the compulsory arbitration of industrial disputes. In 1893 he delivered a strong plea at the annual convention of the American Federation of Labor (AF of L) for organized labor. A year later he supported the controversial Article 10 on public ownership of the means of production, by which the socialists tried to gain control of the AF of L. He deplored the use of the injunction against Debs's American Railway Union in ending the Pullman strike, calling the injunction legal, but immoral, and quoting Emerson that "the highest virtue is always against the law." And when Debs was released from prison, Lloyd welcomed him back at a mass meeting in Chicago as "the martyr of government by injunction."[63]

One of Lloyd's best known efforts in the mid-1890s was his attempt to effect a Populist-labor alliance in Illinois, uniting farmers, trades unionists, socialists, single-taxers, Nationalists, and reformist intellectuals. He even ran in 1894 for Congress himself, but lost. With great political skill he managed for two years to hold the shaky alliance together. Inevitably, however, it broke apart, completing its demise with what he called the betrayal of the People's party by the free silverite's fusion with Bryan at the Saint Louis convention in 1896. A failure of "principle which alone keeps parties together," he wrote to Ely, allowed the Populists to be "seduced into fusion" and into the parasitical silver plank. The convention, he told Ely, was "the most discouraging experience of my life." In the election he voted for the Socialist Labor party, which he hated, less out of doctrinal allegiance than as an expression of his bitter disillusionment with Populism and Bryanism.[64] He had engaged himself actively in the reform movement as spokesman, organizer, and candidate. He had won the respect of other reformers and many workers. Yet he lost. His optimism however, if shaken a little, was soon restored.

Immediately after the election Lloyd wrote again to Ely and rejoiced that "the free-silver fake has received its death blow," for this meant that the field was now cleared away for the reform forces to unite in a new direction. He was certain that socialistic measures could not unify reformers and the labor movement. But what could? Typically, his first approach in an effort to find the new direction was a scholarly one, by traveling, reading, observing, and reflecting. In the late 1890s he concluded more and more that communitarianism and the labor cooperative movement offered the best solutions to the labor question. He went to Europe to represent the Ruskin colony at the Third International Cooperative Congress in Holland, and while at the conference was impressed by reports of English labor cooperative and copartnership experiments. He traveled to England to observe them firsthand and, noting the influence of Ruskin, Carlyle, and the English Christian socialists on the apparently successful movement, regretted that he had not discovered labor copartnership sooner. He wrote wistfully in his notebook of "reading our Ruskin & Carlyle & sighing for the abolition of the cash nexus, & dreaming blissful dreams of the C.C." After returning home he wrote to an English friend that he had been "very much encouraged by what I saw in England of the Co-operative movement; and I am going to make our people familiar, as far as my powers permit, with its remarkable developments there."[65] As usual, this determination resulted in a book, *Labor Copartnership*, describing his observations and pointing out to American readers that the experiment with cooperative factories and farms in Great Britain was "applied brotherhood, . . . the Golden Rule realized." He had found a "political economy of the kind that seeks wealth for itself by creating wealth for others." His travels to New Zealand and Australia in 1899 and to Switzerland in 1901–1902 convinced him that the new direction of unity for American reformers was in the areas of cooperatives, social insurance, compulsory arbitration, direct democracy, and the nationalization of railroads, telephone, and telegraph.[66]

Lloyd's search for an effective way in which to organize the reform forces of America continued. The foreign experiments he endorsed hardly seemed possible in the United States, particularly with the new mood of activity without substance reflected in the White House by Theodore Roosevelt. Lloyd voted for the Socialist Labor party again in 1900; in 1903, shortly before his death, he almost joined the newly formed Socialist Party of America. He even drafted a manuscript, "Why I Join the Socialists," in which he centered his justification around a conviction that "Christianity is the religion that was, socialism is the religion that is to be." He had difficulty, however, satisfying himself with this justification. Death intervened and he never completed either the manuscript or a membership application card.[67]

Despite his indecision about joining the Socialist party in 1903, Lloyd kept his faith and trust with the American labor movement. With Clarence Darrow he argued the case for compulsory arbitration of the anthracite coal miners' strike in 1902 and 1903. When the battle was won, the miners offered him a small reward, which he refused. He was a selfless and tireless campaigner. He made his winning argument for collective bargaining before the Anthracite Strike Commission in February 1903. A week later he, Darrow, and the leader of the coal miners, John Mitchell, spoke before a victory celebration in Chicago. On March 12 and 13 he appeared at hearings before the Committee on Federal Regulations in Maine and Massachusetts, arguing in support of petitions before those state legislatures calling for national ownership of anthracite coal mines. Two months later he spoke before the Massachusetts Reform Club on the failure of Roosevelt's feeble attempts at railroad regulation with the Elkins Act, advocating public ownership instead.[68] Throughout the summer of 1903 he campaigned for Golden Rule Jones's reelection as mayor of Toledo and was engaged in a bitter conflict with the traction companies in Chicago. On September 28, 1903, he died, an active reformer to the end.

Lloyd kept his faith with American workers and they kept theirs with him. Two months after his death a memorial service was held for him at the Chicago Auditorium. Besides the Village Council of Winnetka and Hull House, the principal organizers of the memorial were the United Mine Workers, the AF of L, the Chicago Federation of Labor, and the Carpenter's and Typographer's unions. Labor unions contributed $650 for the service and a delegation of Pennsylvania anthracite coal miners attended because, as John Mitchell put it, "the miners loved Henry D. Lloyd." Except for Mitchell, however, the speeches were given by such moderate and respectable intellectual reformers as Jane Addams, Edwin D. Mead, Clarence Darrow, Tom Johnson, and Samuel Jones. The speeches reiterated Lloyd's many contributions to the humane improvement of the lives of the laboring poor, as he had pledged on the night of the execution of the anarchists back in 1887. A pervasive theme stressed by all the eulogizers was his democratic commitments. He overcame his wealthy status and background in order to work with the poor and the weak. He was rich, Darrow said, "but uncorrupted by wealth. He was an aristocrat, but unspoiled by aristocracy." Mead pointed out that when a woman asserted that "Lloyd always seemed to me a prince condescending to be a democrat," Lloyd would have "told her that the way from prince to democrat is upward." The two mayors, Johnson and Jones, both said that Lloyd could have lived a life of luxury and used his wealth to become a governor or senator. He could have enjoyed "the comforts of life" (Johnson) or gathered titles and drifted into "the ranks of the dilettantes" (Jones). Instead, he took his place with the outcasts of society, as Jones put it, "that he might be true to the highest and holiest impulses of his soul."[69]

Another theme of the memorial speeches was Lloyd's profound patriotism and fundamental commitment to and enthusiasm for the principles of Washington, Jefferson, Franklin, Sam Adams, and Emerson. He believed, as Mead pointed out, that the remedy for current American evils and corruptions was to be found not in a radical "general reorganization of society," but by being "faithful to the cardinal principles" of the founders of the republic. Lloyd often worried that his advocacy of reforms enacted in New Zealand, Switzerland, and other countries would be misunderstood and his patriotism impugned. He wrote to E. E. Hale in 1899 that people "seem to think I want the United States to imitate New Zealand; on the contrary, I want our country to give New Zealand something to imitate."[70]

Lloyd was deeply proud of America's past, and though he turned to many Europeans for inspiration, his speeches were full of historical pride and innumerable references to Washington, Jefferson, and other Founding Fathers. His great-grandfather had fought in the American Revolution. One of his most persistent themes was that America had awakened politically in 1776 and morally in 1861; in the 1890s it needed only to be awakened industrially. New Washingtons, Lincolns, and Garrisons were needed to "abolish the money-bag monopolist" as the "throne monopolist" had already been eliminated. In a not untypical burst of patriotic rhetoric, Lloyd said in a speech on Washington's birthday in 1890 that the man who had achieved political liberty for America from King George would, if alive, seek to achieve industrial liberty from the King Georges of coal, sugar, whiskey, and steel.[71] Although fearful of the kind of chauvinistic patriotism that was misdirected to foreign wars, he was nevertheless no pacifist on concrete issues of foreign policy. He defended the Cleveland-Olney stand on enforced arbitration of the Venezuelan boundary dispute, at the risk of war with England, and as late as May 1898, he supported American intervention in Cuba. His enthusiasm paled, however, as events in Cuba and the Philippines made clear to him that American imperialism was benefiting the trusts and diverting attentions from domestic reforms.

One of Lloyd's quarrels with Tolstoy, in addition to Tolstoyan anarchism and renunciation, was the Russian's condemnation of patriotism as a sin. As Samuel Jones pointed out in his memorial speech, patriotism for Lloyd was synonymous with religion, and religion was identical to labor and love. In his posthumously published *Man, the Social Creator*, Lloyd equated these concepts with a "Church of the Deed." In his new church the religion would be love; the worship, work; the congregation, humanity; and the creed, the golden rule. Tolstoy's denunciation of patriotism, Lloyd said in 1902, was wrong for the significant reason that he misunderstood the relationship between love of country and love of self: "No man can love mankind who does not love his country. To love his country, a man must love his city, to love his city he must love his family and to learn to love his family as it deserves, a man must love himself."[72]

Unlike William Dean Howells, Henry Lloyd was able to love himself. He had a healthy acceptance of his wealth and elevated status and believed that he had used his advantages consistently for the cause of reform, as indeed he had. Because he was so actively involved in the daily struggles of the reform movement, his troubles and self-doubts were not, like Howells, over an inconsistency of words and deeds, but over which tactic, or which direction, the movement should follow next. He was, in short, so heavily engaged in reform that his involvement and his optimism in America assured his psychic well-being.

And yet, although his self-respect was warranted, his optimism was not. Neither Lloyd nor Howells, despite their frequent disappointments with America, ever reached the despair of Tolstoy with Russia or Ruskin with England. Like Howells, Lloyd was an incurable optimist. He believed that the new conscience was already being manifested in the labor movement and political life, in religion and the family, and even in industry. As early as 1894 he said that "it is our happiness to live so near the end of this era that we can see over the crest of the mountain to the smiling valley beyond of a cooperative commerce, and a humanity where men will have learned that they become more 'individual' as they become more brotherly."[73] The last chapter of *Wealth against Commonwealth* is a paean of praise to the awakening conscience, the spirit of reform, the free institutions of press, speech, and political process, and the new tools of science and technology in America, all of which were available to the cause of change. There was little doubt in his mind that they would be used for that purpose, and indeed, one mark of his relative success as a reformer has been the great number of twentieth-century fulfillments of his turn-of-the-century proposals.

But Lloyd's analysis was flawed. Because of his and Howells's optimism—and their devotion to American heroes and the American past—both were restrained in the extent of their ideological and tactical commitments to reform. Both had an abiding faith in the ballot. Both romanticized the labor movement. Both shied away from advocating anything like violence or revolutionary upheaval and condemned those who did. Lloyd, however, understood well the dynamic of change: "The question is not whether monopoly is to continue. The sun sets every night on a greater majority against it. We are face to face with the practical issue: Is it to go through ruin or reform? Can we forestall ruin by reform? If we wait to be forced by events we shall be astounded to find how much more radical they are than our utopias."[74] No liberal establishment leader could have said it better, and in the years after Lloyd's death a succession of liberal reformers averted revolutionary ruin by enacting minimal evolutionary reforms. Abolition of monopoly has not been one of them. Lloyd and Howells were inspired by European ideas, many of which had radical implications, but both sought to effect American solutions to American problems and thereby were restrained in pursuing the implications of their European masters.

Their restraint, ultimately, was twofold. The first, in what I call the limits of practicality, was that neither Lloyd nor Howells ever completely resolved the problem of appropriate activism. Neither could actually live by the code of Mazzini or Tolstoy, and in Howells's case, the frustration and guilt in not fully emulating Tolstoy acted often to paralyze rather than to activate practical participation in reformist endeavors. Howells was not nearly as active as Lloyd, and his literary stature and personal temperament were more restraining than Lloyd's wealth. As a literary critic, Howells encouraged younger novelists to write with a kind of realism he could not do himself; as a reformer he pointed the way to Altruria for others to follow, but could not provide effective leadership himself. His humanitarianism was large and sincere, but as an active reformer he was, as Walt Whitman said, tame and almost colorless. Because he was "unable to follow up radically the lead of his rather remarkable intellect," Whitman said, Howells was no revolutionary. "He goes a certain distance—then hauls himself in with a shock: that's enough—quite enough, he is saying to himself."[75] Howells knew this, of course, and suffered over his inconsistencies and restraints. His agonies of conscience over the gap between words and deeds were acted out by the characters in his novels. Lloyd was spared Howells's suffering primarily because his words and beliefs were translated not into fictional deeds but into his own.

But even Lloyd had his restraints, caused partly by his station in life and partly by his flawed analysis and ideological eclecticism. He argued that the protest movement should be unified, but when he failed to effect an alliance in 1894, he committed himself to a variety of often contradictory and warring reform positions and groups. He reasoned that the scholar should be a practical reformer, but his activism was limited to books, speeches, and organizing. Other than to his health, perhaps, there were no costs to his reformism. He lost neither wealth, nor comfortable life-style; neither friends among the intellectual elite, nor respect. He could renounce Winnetka no more than Howells could renounce Kittery Point. Nor could Lloyd shake his Emersonian belief that the true leaders of reform were the intellectual elite. He could not realize that the workers, despite their token appearance at his memorial service, looked for leadership not to him but to Gompers, Debs, and

Mitchell. The image of Lloyd standing in the pawnshop like Mazzini was one with which no worker could identify. Only a fellow intellectual like Darrow (who had his own restraints) could say that although "Henry D. Lloyd was a scholar, . . . he was the most radical man I ever knew."[76]

The second restraint was what I call the comforts of utopianism. Howells and Lloyd both found comfort in their zealous enthusiasm for Altruria: whether Howells's Tolstoyan Christian anarchist kind or Lloyd's Mazzinian Christian cooperative kind. Howells's utopianism went beyond his Altrurian romances and his anguished efforts to live according to the example of Tolstoy. His father had been a devoted disciple of Robert Owen around the time of William Dean's birth, and his wife was the niece of John Humphrey Noyes, the founder of the Oneida colony. He spent two summers in the 1870s at a Shaker village in western Massachusetts and wrote a novel, *The Undiscovered Country*, about the idyllic Shaker community. Utopianism, then, was part of his heritage and never left him. Lloyd, too, was full of utopian yearnings. He took an interest in the Ruskin and other communal experiments, and as he was battered by one defeat after another, dreamed wistfully of the elusive "C.C." Even Lloyd wrote a utopian piece, "No Mean City," in which he envisioned the transformation of Chicago's Columbian Exposition into a cooperative commonwealth. But like the utopias of Howells and Bellamy, the new age was defined more by spiritual, moral, and aesthetic qualities than by economic ones. Churches, universities, and cultural centers loomed as large as the means of making a livelihood.[77]

The dreams of Howells and Lloyd of what ought to be were so intense and gratifying that they were often unable to see or cope with what was. Their desire to lead America to Altruria compelled them to support and patronize innumerable causes, which diluted their efforts. They knew what their goals were but were uncertain of their means, except that they be nonviolent and rigorously Christian. The road to Altruria for these two brave knights was full of pitfalls and misleading turns. Their efforts, therefore, were diffused, restrained, and full of frustrations, disappointments, and, for Howells, guilt. It was easier, then, to proclaim a vision of the distant millennium than to inch one's way toward an imperfect and partial realization. It was more comforting to focus one's eyes on the utopian vision, proclaiming one's ideals and hoping for their fulfillment. Or was it? Is it not another case of perceptive self-condemnation that Howells has one of his most self-reflective characters say, "I abhor dreamers; they have no place in a world of thinking and acting"?[78] The thinking was easy enough; it was the acting that caused problems.

3

THE STRUGGLE FOR CHRISTIAN REFORMIST UNITY: W. D. P. BLISS AND B. O. FLOWER

I believe in the One Life;
I believe in all the people;
I believe in all the people in the one life.

BLISS *

Yesterday men dreamed; to-day they are thinking; to-morrow they will act.

FLOWER †

THE DIFFICULTY of Howells in reconciling words and deeds showed clearly that the kingdom of heaven in America would not be realized by visionary proclamations of Altruria and impassioned declarations of the dignity of labor alone. Lloyd's eclectic experience in moving from one reform group and position to another illustrated the frustration of American reformers in the 1890s. As they looked about them, they saw a seemingly infinite array of organizations, each convinced that the gap between the promises and achievements of America had to be closed, and each pursuing a different path to that end. Socialist laborites, social democrats, Nationalists, Christian socialists, single-taxers, Populists, anarchists, cooperationists, and trade unionists all vied with one another for leadership. Moderate intellectual reformers joined the others in clamoring for the ear of the worker. Often the worker was not even listening, yet the rivalry went on anyway. Each group claimed that it had found the only path to the kingdom of heaven on earth. It was unimportant whether the kingdom was a secular or a religious one, because in either case, brotherhood, justice, and the reign of love were guaranteed. In quest of the kingdom, the different groups fought more with one another than with the plutocracy they universally despised. Their factional fights frustrated and often paralyzed effective action.

For two Boston intellectual reformers, William Dwight Porter Bliss and Benjamin Orange Flower, the wasted effort of this factionalism was tragic. What American reformers needed, they said, was unity. As Flower wrote to Lloyd in 1895, "unless those who understand and fully believe in fundamental reforms get together at once they will most certainly soon find themselves a powerless minority." There were two ways of effecting a unity of reformers that would render them something more than a powerless minority. One was organizational; the other was doctrinal. Each was dependent upon a large-scale educational effort to awaken others to the imperative need, first, for a reform thrust spiritualized by the moderating influence of Christian intellectuals; second, for minimizing doctrinal differences; and third, for concerted effort. "Only through the education of the units and the quickening and development of the individual conscience," Flower wrote, "can a nation be raised to a nobler and juster estate." Bliss, likewise, saw a need for developing within the nation "a conscience, not only that something is wrong, but that every one of us is to an extent responsible for that wrong. . . . *Hence, the practical thing to do to-day is to educate.*" The formula was simple: education would create an aroused class of reformers who, with more education, would see the need for reform unity. With unity accomplished they would sweep away the forces of selfish materialistic greed and usher in an age of selfless love and brotherly cooperation.[1]

Flower and Bliss both sought to educate and unify American reformers according to this formula. Both tried to find unity in a single organization, and both minimized doctrinal differences, often at the cost of accuracy and discriminating sophistication. Each was a minister-turned-journalist, which accounts for the elevated religious thrust each brought to his journalistic campaigns. Flower's efforts were primarily educational; Bliss was a unifier. Their common quest, however, was essentially an inspirational one. They believed that through the diffusion of socioeconomic facts and the ethical ideals of European and American social prophets, they could awaken the American social conscience and direct it on a single path toward the kingdom of heaven on earth. Curiously enough, although engaged in the same effort and in the same city, their own paths rarely crossed.

Both found their way to Boston from diverse places. Bliss was born in Turkey in 1856, the son of Congregational missionaries.[2] He was educated at Phillips Academy, Amherst, and Hartford Theological Seminary, where he was ordained in 1882. After briefly serving in Congregational pastorates in Denver and in South Natick, Massachusetts, he joined the Episcopal Church in 1886, largely as a result of his admiration for the Social Gospel activities of Anglicans in England, particularly the Christian socialists Frederick Denison Maurice and Charles Kingsley. In the mid-1880s he was at Saint George's Episcopal Church in the factory town of Lee. Influenced by his friend George McNeill, an eight-hour-day advocate and universal reformer, Bliss joined the Knights of Labor and soon became a Master Workman and ardent crusader for the cause of organized labor. He was an unsuccessful Labor party candidate for lieutenant governor of Massachusetts in 1887. Discouraged by the struggle between socialist laborites and single-taxers for control of the United Labor party, he abandoned politics and went to South Boston as minister at Grace Church. While in Boston he read widely in the history of Christianity, finding pro-labor, socialist antecedents in nearly everything he read. He met together with Laurence Gronlund, Walter Vrooman, O. P. Gifford, and others at the church of Francis Bellamy, Edward Bellamy's cousin, in an effort to find a way for middle-class moderate socialist clergymen to influence the labor movement and heal the widening breaches caused by factional conflicts. On January 26, 1889, Bliss printed a notice in the *Workmen's Advocate* in New Haven, an organ of the Socialist Labor party still under the influence of moderates, and called for the formation of a society of Christian socialists. Those making the call, he wrote, did not wish to antagonize socialists or Nationalists, with whom they agreed in economic goals, but they saw a need for a distinctly Christian society basing their socialism on the fatherhood of God and the brotherhood of man.[3] A few ministers and middle-class intellectual reformers answered the call, but on the whole, the response was far from overwhelming. Bliss was to have many similar experiences in the years ahead.

Flower came to Boston from the Midwest. He was born near Albion, Illinois, in 1858, the son of a farmer and zealous Disciples of Christ preacher.[4] His grandfather had come from England in 1816 with letters of introduction to Thomas Jefferson, with whom he spent part of one winter before moving westward. Flower was educated in a schoolhouse built on his father's farm, in public schools in southern Indiana, and at the University of Kentucky, which he left after one year. He also attended Transylvania University Bible School in Lexington, and was a liberal minister in Owensboro, Kentucky, for a short while. His interests, however, were in journalism, not the ministry. In 1880 he and a friend founded and edited the weekly *American Sentinel* in Albion to compete with the one newspaper in town. Flower's first editorial showed a crusading educational style which, except for adding new causes, would change very little in the next thirty years. The *Sentinel*, he wrote, "will be a bold fearlessly and out-spoken advocate of Temperance. . . . We believe that agitation is the great means of education, and therefore invite communications and questions relating to this great growing evil [liquor]." Flower sold out eight months later and went to Boston to help an older brother with a medical business venture. In Boston he became increasingly interested in reform, psychic research, and a socially purposeful literature and theater. The source of Flower's commitment to reform is difficult to assess, for records on his early life have been destroyed, but it was probably rooted in a midwestern heritage of piety and dissent and in his exposure to slum conditions in Boston in the 1880s. Whatever the source, his admiration embraced Europeans such as Hugo, Mazzini, Ruskin, and Morris, and practically every American active in reform in the 1890s. Like Bliss, he saw the need for exposure of social evils and for responsible, middle-class leadership of the splintering reform movement. Toward these ends he founded the *Arena*, America's "first successful muckraking magazine."[5] In that same year, also in Boston, Bliss began editing the *Dawn*, a journal of Christian socialism.

W. D. P. Bliss

As editor of the *Dawn* and founder of the Society of Christian Socialists, Bliss's major efforts were directed at effecting organizational and doctrinal unity among intellectual reformers, especially those of Fabian or moderate socialist persuasion. He had an irrepressible faith that a reconstructed social order would be realized once a socially educated and spiritually awakened middle class was receptive to the programs offered by a unified reform movement, which was itself educated to its common ideological commitments. He was neither a shrewd strategist nor a practical activist, but rather was best at making superficial syntheses of radical and reformist ideologies and at declaring vague and idealistic visions of a more humane—or, in his word, Christianized—American society. Repeated organizational failures and an inability to hasten the coming of the new order, however, never dampened his enthusiasm or diminished his efforts.

It was in the late 1880s that Bliss began in earnest his indefatigable efforts in achieving his twin goals of an awakened American middle class and the unity of American reformers. A partial list of his activities in the period between 1887 and 1901, his most active years, will illustrate his indomitable will. He was one of the primary organizers of two Episcopal Social Gospel societies, the Church Association for the Advancement of the Interests of

Labor in 1887 and the Christian Social Union in 1891. He was a charter member of the Nationalist Club of Boston in 1888 and the American Fabian League in 1895, both dedicated to the implementation of the principles espoused in Bellamy's *Looking Backward*. He organized the Society of Christian Socialists (1889), the Mission and Church of the Brotherhood of the Carpenter (1890), which he founded after being forced to resign from Grace Church because of his socialist views, and the Wendell Phillips Union (1891), an intellectual settlement house for Christian socialist and labor union gatherings. In 1895 he formed the ineffective National Educational and Economic League, an attempt to educate trade unionists to the virtues of Fabian socialism. Bliss was not discouraged by the demise of these early efforts at reform unity but went ahead and organized the Union Reform League in 1897, the Social Reform Union in 1899, and the Civic Council of New York City in 1901.

As president, secretary, or organizing secretary of these many organizations, Bliss traveled back and forth across the United States several times forming chapters of his various leagues and unions and enlisting reformers in his selfless crusade. With pathetic regularity, he could be counted on to appear at almost every large gathering of religiously oriented socialists or socialist-oriented clergymen held during the 1890s. In addition to these organizational activities, Bliss founded and edited almost single-handedly the *Dawn* (1889–1896), the *American Fabian* (1895–1896), the *Social Forum* and *Publications of the Social Reform Union* (1899–1901), and the *Social Unity* (1901). He edited the Social Science Library, a series of books containing selected works and passages of John Ruskin, Thomas Carlyle, William Morris, John Stuart Mill, and Thorold Rogers and wrote a number of socioeconomic tracts for the Christian Social Union. In 1895 he published the *Handbook of Socialism*, a catalog history of communal and urban socialist utopian experiments, and two years later produced the first edition of the massive *Encyclopedia of Social Reform*.

Although Bliss was a prolific writer, he was neither a profound nor an original thinker. He borrowed freely from the ideas of the many social prophets for whom he had enormous enthusiasm. Most of Bliss's organizations were English in origin. The Society of Christian Socialists, the Christian Social Union, and the Fabian

League were little more than American branches of English societies. Modeling himself after the English Christian socialists, Bliss believed that "the aim of Socialism is embraced in the aim of Christianity" and that "the teachings of Jesus Christ lead directly to some specific form or forms of Socialism." In the inaugural issue of the *Dawn* he announced that "our aim is to arouse all Christians, to arouse the Church, to arouse the unchurched, to arouse all men, to apply, in a definite, lawful, democratic way, our Christianity to practical social order." For over thirty years he never strayed from this fundamental purpose. Bliss agreed with the injunction of Maurice that "Socialism should be christianized, and Christianity socialized." Like Maurice, he believed that competition, self-interest, and "the rule of Gold" should be supplanted by cooperation, self-sacrifice, and the golden rule. Insisting, correctly, that his view of Christianity was no narrow theological one, he pointed out that Christian socialists simply sought to apply the Sermon on the Mount to the structure of society.[6] Bliss rarely defined or elaborated on these large ideas, which he reiterated tediously, other than to expound such equally vague principles as love, association, and brotherhood.

Nor was his definition of socialism any clearer. He assured the readers of the *Dawn* that his kind of socialism was not communism, nor a specific economic scheme, nor undemocratic statism, nor a class-conflict doctrine setting poor against rich. With characteristic oversimplification, he defined socialism as "democracy in business." When showing what Christian socialists proposed to do, he was more specific, if no less imitative. He advocated profit-sharing, the eight-hour day, trade unionism, arbitration of industrial disputes, municipalization of urban services such as light, heat, and local transit, the nationalization of telegraph and railroads, the establishment of postal savings banks, the taxation of all real estate, and government hiring of the unemployed. After enumerating these specific reforms and indicating that they could be achieved by gradual, nonviolent means, Bliss returned, as he always did, to his central point: that Christian socialists must place their main reliance upon character, conscience, and religion.[7]

In addition to generalized thinking, Bliss demonstrated a fondness for simplistic paradoxes. In an article on the sources of his Christian socialism he wrote, "I was made a Christian by Karl

Marx, and a Socialist by Jesus Christ." It was while studying Marx and other socialists, he said, that "it flashed on me what Christ was, and what Christianity was." At the center of Christian thought, he realized, was the concept of individual self-sacrifice for the good of the collective body, as symbolized by the cross. With this understanding, "one must come out a Socialist. Jesus made me a Socialist." The lesson of the cross saved Christian socialism not only from the excesses of the Marxian position but also from the extreme individualist position of Tolstoy and other Christian anarchists. Tolstoy, Bliss said, followed "the letter, but not the spirit of Christ. Jesus Christ taught Brotherhood. Tolstoy is a grand sentimental Individualist who feels but does not think." Unlike Jesus, who "was a socialist, seeing all truth," Tolstoy was "an individualist seeing and living magnificent half-truths." Although Bliss made exceptions of Marx and Tolstoy, mainly to show what Christian socialism was not, he freely labeled as Christian socialist most other humanitarian social prophets in history. These included, among others, Maurice and Kingsley, Dante, Lamennais, Savonarola, de Laveleye and Mazzini, as well as the leaders of the American Social Gospel movement: Lyman Abbott, Washington Gladden, Heber Newton, and Richard T. Ely. Above all these, however, Bliss turned to Jesus, whom he called "the first Christian Socialist."[8]

Obviously, Bliss's definition of Christian socialism had to be broad and vague enough to include many diverse minds. Abbott and Gladden, for example, were Christian socialists only by Bliss's definition. But it was not his habit to make fine distinctions to clarify ambiguities. His primary purpose was to awaken, educate, and unify all who were discontented with the existing social order. Hence, he was constantly assuring other reformers that their aims and ideologies were the same as his. In a discussion of the similarities between his principles and those of Nationalism, as described in *Looking Backward*, Bliss emphasized that "Christian Socialism is much larger, better, truer than any book" or any single reform panacea. In 1889 he examined the platforms of the Nationalists, socialists, Knights of Labor, AF of L, Greenbackers, Prohibitionists, and Grangers and found a startling consensus on the economic issues of the day. He interpreted this discovery not as an indication that a new union party ought to be started, for with the exception of a brief flirtation with the People's party he opposed the formation of a third party, but rather as evidence of how much union already existed. He urged them toward even greater union. Although the single-taxers, he found, differed slightly from the others, his concept of socialism could include them. Bliss's insistence on doctrinal unity was irrepressible. And as he suffered one disappointment after another throughout the 1890s, his definition broadened. By 1901 he claimed that even Jews, Hindus, and Theosophists qualified as Christian socialists.[9]

Like most American socialists in the late nineteenth century, Bliss found it necessary to argue that socialism and individualism were compatible. In a debate in 1890 with Benjamin Tucker, a philosophical anarchist, Bliss urged blending the two doctrines. "The Socialist who sees no good in individualism is as narrow as the individualist who sees no good in Socialism." His preference, however, was clearly for socialism, "the mother of individuality." The progress of the nineteenth century indicated, he said, that the twentieth century would bring an end to the plutocracy of Jay Gould (his example of a typical individualist) and the beginning of a truer individuality that flowed from socialism. Bliss often cited John Stuart Mill in showing the compatibility between individualism and socialism. Despite evidence to the contrary, Bliss was convinced that most of Mill's writings were on socialism. He edited a book of carefully selected passages from Mill's writing in order to demonstrate his conviction. He argued, somewhat speciously, in an introduction to the volume that Mill's distaste for the paternalism of socialism would have been dispelled had the Englishman seen the changes in socialist theory which occurred after his death in 1873. In fact, Bliss said, few have advanced socialism more than Mill.[10]

Once it was clear that anyone was a Christian socialist who wished, however remotely, to see vague Christian principles applied to the social order, the next step was to expand the educational process so that unified action might be taken. The role of the church was therefore of singular importance. "Churches are discussing how 'to reach the masses,' " he wrote. "The truer problem is how to rouse the Church." In 1891 he suggested to Ely, secretary of the newly founded Christian Social Union, that the union should provide ministers with tracts on relevant social and economic issues. Ely's reply expressed reluctance to embroil the church in economic debates. Bliss responded that he was certain that Episcopal clergymen were convinced that the church should speak out on social questions, but that they were afraid to say anything because they did not know what to say. Therefore, he went on, it was imperative that they be educated with factual and inspirational evidence with which to justify their convictions.[11] Bliss was successful in persuading the Christian Social Union to publish a series of economic tracts, many of which he wrote himself.

Bliss frequently put together reading lists for those interested in social problems. His reply to the question "what to do?" was inevitably: read, reform yourself, then educate others. Although he felt that the Bible was the basic textbook of Christian socialists, he usually recommended beginning a study of socialism with *Looking Backward*, Gronlund's *Cooperative Commonwealth*, and the *Dawn*. Most issues of the *Dawn* included a list of suggested titles, available from the "Dawn Library" for thirty-five cents each. For a general introduction to socialism, Bliss suggested the titles listed above as well as *Das Kapital* and a number of English monographs. The *Fabian Essays*, Bliss believed, contained the "best all around statement of modern practical scientific Socialism." On Christian socialism, he recommended the biographies and works of Maurice and Kingsley, Heber Newton's *Social Studies*, Ruskin's *Unto This Last*, Mazzini's *Duties of Man*, and, strangely, Tolstoy's *My Religion*. For other categories—the history of socialism, American socialism, the land question, and political economy—Bliss urged reading, among others, George, McNeill, Ely, Mill, Morris, Carlyle, and Ruskin.[12]

Bliss was particularly fond of Ruskin because he was primarily a teacher. He argued that Ruskin, like Jesus, did not originate a social theory but served to fulfill one and teach it to others. As Jesus led men to love their neighbors, Ruskin led men to love beauty and to live according to "the Gospel of Noble Things." Ruskin was a constructive social thinker who saw things "as they are *and as they ought to be*"; therefore, Bliss said, there were many thoughtful socialists who will say that they were led to socialism by Ruskin. The impressionable Bliss admired Mazzini for essentially the same reasons. Mazzini was a teacher and a social prophet, as well as a man of action. "His writings are full of the best Christian Socialism. He puts more emphasis upon duties than upon rights, and pleads for unity, through sacrifice."[13] These were among Bliss's dearest personal convictions.

In his desire to stir the conscience of America, Bliss relied not only on lofty examples of inspiration like Ruskin and Mazzini but also on the facts of economic life. Bliss had a penchant for encyclopedic cataloging—of books, wage statistics, reform organizations, church affiliations of reformers, and almost anything that would educate toward greater unity among reformers. In 1890 he edited a book of selections from Thorold Rogers's *Six Centuries of Work and Wages*, a statistical history of English labor. Bliss included a preface, some wage charts, and an appendix, in which he summarized Rogers's conclusions and added a few of his own. It was necessary to issue Rogers's work in an accessible form, he wrote, because facts were needed to achieve the goals of labor. Facts can even convert: Rogers himself had been an orthodox, anti-trade-union economist when he began his study, but finished it, Bliss emphasized, "converted by his facts into an ardent believer in Trade Unions and defending many a formerly denounced Right of Labor." It was Bliss's hope that others might be similarly converted. Enthusiastically, he concluded: "What a record! People ask for facts; here they are in all conscience—multitudinous, grim, denunciatory, unimpeachable."[14]

In 1895 Bliss was criticized by a Prohibitionist who disagreed with his contention that poverty led to drink rather than the reverse. He answered with a barrage of statistics. In the waning issues of the *Dawn*, while Bliss was preaching socialism on the lecture circuit and neglecting his editorial duties, a series appeared entitled "Facts for American Socialists," an alphabetical compendium of social statistics and short sketches of reform organizations and Bliss's heroes. In 1897, with a team of editors and contributors which itself reads like a roster of American reformers in the 1890s, Bliss collected these facts and hundreds of others into the monumental *Encyclopedia of Social Reform*. Ten years later he brought out a larger edition. He boldly announced that the new volume included "all social-reform movements and activities, and the economic, industrial, and sociological facts and statistics of all countries and all social subjects."[15] He was as good as his word, too, for the *New Encyclopedia* contained over 1,300 pages of small print on topics ranging from abandoned farms and the reward of abstinence to working women's clubs and the Zoar community, and on individuals ranging from Lyman Abbott and Jane Addams to John Wyclif and Charles Zueblin.

Bliss could never be criticized for lack of thoroughness or effort. The only respite for the tireless crusader came in 1894 when, following countless disappointments, a spell of family illness, and the death of his daughter, he traveled to Europe for a rest. Close observation of European (especially English Fabian) social action and progress revived his sagging spirits. He returned to the United States late in the year with renewed dedication and optimism. He announced in the *Dawn* that although his fundamental ideological position was unchanged, he planned to concentrate more on concrete action than on discussion of principles.[16] The time for words was over, and the time for deeds, as Bliss conceived them, had come. It was difficult for him, an inveterate editorialist, to refrain entirely from the propagation of principles; nevertheless, his varied activities were intensified in the mid-1890s and it is surprising that he found the time to accomplish all that he did.

In 1895 and 1896, for example, he wrote the *Handbook of Socialism*, contacted contributors and began work on the *Encyclopedia*, simultaneously edited the *Dawn* and the *American Fabian*, and wrote several pamphlets for the Church Social Union, a revitalized Christian Social Union. Like all Bliss's endeavors, the aim of the *American Fabian*, which he launched in February 1895, was "to unite social reforms and lead the way to a conception of Socialism, broad enough, free enough, practical enough to include all that is of value, no matter whence it comes, and replace jealousy between reformers by co-operation for the general good." The method, as usual, was primarily educational. As he did in the *Dawn*, Bliss provided a lending library for all subscribers. He also announced that he would go anywhere to preach, lecture, or organize Fabian clubs. Apparently, his new commitment to concrete action meant that he would use more of the old words. In the summer of 1895 he conducted a course of ten lectures on "The Economics of the Labor Movement" in Philadelphia, New York, and Boston. He presented a lecture each on individualism, philanthropy, the single tax, municipal reform, the agrarian movement, trade unionism, the eight-hour-day movement, and Utopian, German, and Fabian socialism. The stated purpose of the lecture series was to present various economic theories and let the facts dictate how the listener would respond. Sensible listeners, of course, responded by embracing Bliss's brand of Christian socialism, which he faithfully worked into every topic. In the fall and winter of 1895 he traveled throughout the Northeast and Midwest attempting to organize Fabian clubs. The response of reformers was so limited that he was unable to unite the various local clubs into a national American Fabian League. His schedule for January 1896, as announced in the *American Fabian*, showed that he would conduct meetings on twenty-two days of that month and added that six days were free if anyone should want him to speak. During this same period, he was also organizing secretary of the Church Social Union. In December 1896 he reviewed his work for that fall and proudly reported that he had preached, lectured, and organized branches in a list of cities from Syracuse to Seattle to San Diego.[17]

This was the basic pattern of Bliss's efforts in the 1890s: start an organization, publish a journal, establish a lending library and lecture bureau, and go on a tour to organize branches. Despite the magnitude of his effort, the measurable accomplishments were limited, both in the duration and number of readers of his journals and in the size and effectiveness of his clubs. The Society of Christian Socialists in Boston, for example, never had more than twenty-five members. In the face of his failures, however, he was undaunted. He campaigned vigorously for William Jennings Bryan in the midst of his other activities, supported the Democrat strongly in the *American Fabian*, and was not discouraged by Bryan's defeat. He wrote to Lloyd before the size of the loss was known and expressed his optimism: "I do not think a *narrow* defeat will discourage reform, so much as a narrow victory might cause reaction."[18] Thus encouraged by the election of 1896, Bliss looked forward to 1900. He was also becoming increasingly political.

While on the West Coast in 1897 on another of his lecture-organizing tours for the Church Social Union, Bliss and some San Francisco Bay area reformers conceived a plan to unite all reformers, even nonsocialists, into a national federation. They formed the Union Reform League, with Bliss as its president. Despite a promotional scheme in which any person who enrolled twelve other persons in the league was given a free copy of the *Encyclo-*

pedia of Social Reform, support was largely confined to the West Coast. In quest of national participation, Bliss and some eastern religious reformers issued a call to all reformers to attend a conference to be held in Buffalo in late June 1899. The ensuing National Social and Political Conference, called for the purpose of planning for reform unity in 1900, was the gallant organizer's most ambitious project and his most disappointing failure.

Bliss's open letter, "Unite or Perish," sent to all who had been invited, set the tone for the conference. His letter began with an old theme: "Reformers, unite!" He urged the adoption of a platform including the programs with which most reformers could agree: direct legislation, public ownership of monopolies, taxation of land values and incomes, and anti-imperialism. He advised that the conference should "form itself into a great Reform League" in order to pressure one of the major parties, presumably the Democrats, into adopting these programs in its platform. If unsuccessful, Bliss advocated converting the league into an independent third party.[19] This last suggestion alienated the social democrats, who expected that their recently formed party was the appropriate political home for leftist dissenters.

The conference was attended by a potpourri of radical and moderate reformers, including Christian socialists, Fabians, social democrats, Prohibitionists, Populists, Democrats, Republicans, and advocates of woman's rights, direct legislation, academic freedom, and free silver. The meeting was dominated by Bliss and the fiery George Herron, who had recently been dismissed from his chair of Applied Christianity at Iowa College. Significantly, on the Sunday in the middle of the conference, Bliss, Herron, Golden Rule Jones, and many other delegates scattered throughout Buffalo delivering sermons in sympathetic churches. In a burst of enthusiasm later, Jones compared the conference to the gathering of early Christians in the upper room. Despite the religious emphasis, the topics discussed in Buffalo reflected a wide variety of reform thought: monopolies, municipal reform, public ownership, direct legislation, the single tax, and arbitration of domestic and international disputes. Extremely vigorous debates were held on socialism and imperialism. But the most hotly contested issue was whether or not to form a new party. The question was resolved by adopting Bliss's suggestion and converting the Union Reform

League into a nonpartisan Social Reform Union. Bliss was its president and a whole host of prominent figures, including Lloyd, Herron, Jones, Howells, and Markham (who had thrilled the participants with a reading of his poem "Brotherhood"), agreed to serve as vice presidents. The union's motto was "Plutocracy is combining, let the People unite." In addition to uniting reform groups into a single federation, the primary purpose of the union was, as usual, to educate the nation on socioeconomic issues. For this purpose, departments were established for Publications, Lecturing, Summer School, Circulating Libraries, a College of Social Science, and Bliss's personal favorite—Bible Lessons in Social Reform. The College of Social Science, a correspondence school of sorts headed by such distinguished activist social scientists as E. W. Bemis, Frank Parsons, and John Commons, was well financed but collapsed within a year, largely from internal dissensions between impartial researchers and political propagandists. The other departments were put in Bliss's hands and suffered the same fate, less from conflict within than from lack of interest without.[20]

After the Buffalo meeting the delegates returned to their respective special interests and squabbling, leaving Bliss to run the Social Reform Union essentially by himself. He did so with the customary zeal and in the familiar pattern. He carried the major burden for editing the monthly *Social Forum*, a fortnightly *Bulletin*, and a weekly *Publications* of the Social Reform Union. The stated objectives of the union had Bliss's trademark on them, but he was forced to phrase his aims in a way that reflected the splintering of interests at Buffalo:

> objects (a) to unite the reform forces of the United States in a federated body, in which individuals and organizations, while retaining separate existence and freedom in pursuing separate lines of work, *may yet unite* for those practical immediate measures upon which they agree
>
> (b) to educate the people at large upon the measures upon which the reform forces are agreed. [my italics]

This was hardly a statement to strike fear into the hearts of the established order! The death knell of the union was implicit in the word yet. Undeterred by having to wait still longer for reform unity, Bliss set up the circulating library, went on a tour to organize branches of the union in every state, and recited economic facts in the pages of the *Social Forum*. The *Publications* consisted mostly of "Bible Lessons in Social Reform," in which Bliss selected a topic (e.g., "Christianity and Wealth" or "Christianity and Social Evils"), stated what Jesus said about it, cited contemporary statistics to show how awful things were, and asked: "is that Christian?" An editorial note in the *Bulletin* on November 1, 1899, can serve as an obituary for Bliss's Social Reform Union. He announced, almost proudly, that "North Dakota is at present being better reached by our thought than any other State," and reported that total membership in the country was 594![21] Moving his headquarters from California to Chicago did little to increase membership or to bring unity to the reform movement.

By October 1900 all three publications were defunct and, for all intents and purposes, so was the union. The election of 1900 shattered even Fabian unity, as many radical ministers followed Herron in his support for Eugene Debs, while Bliss, Jones, and others voted for Bryan. A second National Social and Political Conference was held in Detroit in 1901, but only 230 persons attended. In a letter to Lloyd during the conference, Bemis wrote that the sessions "rapidly degenerated into ridiculous effervescence by extreme radicals and cranks."[22] Fortunately, the ever-present Bliss was this time absent, for he was already on a new project. In January of 1901 Bliss had initiated the new year with a new journal, called optimistically the *Social Unity*, which repeated the identical pattern of his earlier magazines; within eight months it, too, folded. He did, however, resort to one new tactic, which sadly illustrated his growing desperation.

In the first issue of *Social Unity*, Bliss printed an open letter, "The Political Situation with a Definite Proposal," in which he rejected the growing movement for socialist unity in the form of a new party and urged instead the unity of all the people. "These are not vapid words," he wrote, but "are practical as well as theoretical, economic as well as spiritual." With unbelievable persistence in view of his past experiences, the intrepid reformer announced a proposal: another national union of reformers! This one, he indicated, would be open to all and would have "no opinions, no principles, no platform." If principles were to be developed, he said, they would be decided upon democratically by national referendums. He conducted the first referendum in the *Social Unity* on the question of whether his subscribers favored the doctrine of class consciousness for American socialists. He received sixty-five replies, fifty-two against and thirteen for. Encouraged by the outcome, if not by the numbers, he took another poll of his readers asking whether American reformers should form a new party. In July, on the eve of the socialist unity convention in Indianapolis, Bliss added a little creed to his masthead declaring that "the *Social Unity* aims at Socialism, but not through party nor a class struggle." He favored, instead, a referendum. In a long article, "The Faith of a Socialist," Bliss tried several different ways of expressing his socialist faith in order to distinguish it from the heretical beliefs he thought would be stated in Indianapolis. The article represented, in a way, Bliss's farewell address to his ever-diminishing little band of followers.[23]

The *Social Unity* was Bliss's last magazine. He took a pastorate on Long Island and worked for a while for the American Institute of Social Science in New York. With Josiah Strong as editor-in-chief, Bliss helped put together *Social Progress* in 1904 and 1906, "An International Year Book of Economic, Industrial, Social and Religious Statistics." Bliss compiled a bibliography which included his old favorites: Mazzini's *Duties of Man* ("full of inspiring social utterances"), and Ruskin's *Unto This Last* and *Fors Clavigera* ("full of incisive and suggestive social thought"). He continued to cling to his original assumption that in the broadest sense socialism and Christianity were synonymous. Under the auspices of the Institute of Social Science he sent out questionaires to over a thousand reformers and found, to his delight, no doubt, that 74 percent were church communicants. After working as an investigator for the United States Bureau of Labor between 1907 and 1909, Bliss joined the Religious Citizenship League and became its secretary; he was a member of the Christian Socialist Fellowship in New York. In 1912 and 1913, armed with new statistics, he wrote a series of articles on "Industrial Problems and What to Do about Them" for Strong's *Studies in the Gospel of the Kingdom*. The facts were new but the solution was not: "In the spirit of Christ we must learn what we can and then bravely, patiently, and continuously labor so to bring in the kingdom of God on earth."[24] The consistency of the zealous founder of the *Dawn* a quarter of a century earlier was altered only by his increased patience.

Bliss's optimism persisted in these later years, bolstered no doubt by his religious faith. In 1910 he expressed the hope that there would be "a resurrection of spirituality as applied to social problems." His spirit, too, remained indomitable. In 1924, at the age of sixty-eight, he wrote to George Herron and admitted that fundamentalism and the Ku Klux Klan made him more pessimistic than ever before in his life. Certainly, some pessimism was warranted at long last. But in spite of a chronic asthma condition, and some forty years of tireless efforts and countless disappointments in the service of an elusive reconstructed social order, he told Herron, "I feel good for 25 years more."[25] He died a little over two years later.

Bliss suffered throughout his career not only from frustrated efforts but also from severe criticism from the fellow reformers he so desperately wanted to unite. In 1894 he quarreled with Lloyd, whose support he needed for one of his leagues, over the controversial plank on government ownership in the 1894 AF of L platform. Lloyd refused to give Bliss the help he needed and wrote to a union official that Bliss "is a good fellow; one of the best. But he must be, agitationally, a mere child." In an open letter to the *American Fabian* in 1896, English Fabians chastised Bliss for his support of free silver. And when he announced in 1897 that the emblem of the Union Reform League would be a red flag, he alienated moderate members of the league and horrified conservative nonmembers. Bliss accommodated, as he usually did in any controversy, by adding "a white cross, symbol of peace, of love, of Christ, of sacrifice" to the red background. He explained, moreover, that the red was the symbol "not of anarchy and destruction, but of society, of fraternity, of that common humanity which makes of one blood all nations upon the earth." But the severest criticism of Bliss came not from moderates but from radicals to his left. After hearing one of his lectures on "Socialism and Trades Unionism," the communitarian Alexander Longley observed that "it was amusing to see him dressed in a long white gown and to hear his denunciation of plutocrats and his pitiful appeals for the poor, while his slim audience of well-dressed people in their costly church made it seem like he was accusing a lot of masters in the absence of their servants." The criticism was both cruel and revealing. Socialist laborites picked up Longley's report and reprinted it in the *People*. Perhaps Bliss's most serious failing was his inability to identify with and appeal to workers; there was simply too much of the Christian intellectual in him.[26]

Partly as a result of this weakness, Bliss's dream of a unified league of reformers eluded him, with perhaps the exception of a few ebullient moments at Buffalo in 1899. Sadly, he seems never to have recognized his failures. His Fabian gradualism and optimistic faith in the regenerative influence of study groups and the written and spoken word buoyed up his spirits, yet limited his effectiveness. He was in this sense, as Lloyd observed, a mere child. Moreover, his overwhelming desire for doctrinal unity led him into intellectual shallowness and vague pronouncements. It was indeed difficult to pull Marx, Maurice, and Mazzini under the same doctrinal umbrella, just as it was no simple task to unite single-taxers, social democrats, and Christian socialists. At the very least, Bliss's contribution to American reform consisted of shaming and awakening a few ministers and of introducing one kind of middle-class reformer to the ideas and activities of another. The same can be said for Benjamin Flower. But where Bliss was limited by his single-minded devotion to Christian socialism, however vaguely defined, his fellow Boston journalist crusader, Benjamin Orange Flower, knew no limits to the many and diverse causes he could embrace.

B. O. Flower

Flower was one of the many reformers who left Bliss's Buffalo conference pleased that a new third party had not been started. Like Bliss, he was convinced that reformers should pursue two goals. First, as he said in 1899, they should cease their intergroup fighting and unite in support of common programs; second, "they should further in every way possible systematic educational agitation."[27] These were not new goals for Flower. For ten years, as editor of the *Arena*, the *New Time*, and the *Coming Age*, he had crusaded for an awakening of the public conscience and for unity of purpose among reformers. Where Bliss stressed organizational unity, however, Flower emphasized educational agitation. Where Bliss was inclined to catalog facts, Flower gushed forth inspirational rhetoric. Where Bliss sought a more Christianized socialist society, Flower preferred a more Christianized democratic society. Where Bliss ended up proclaiming his readiness to continue the struggle for a spiritually infused social movement, Flower ended up proclaiming the menace of the papacy to American institutions.

At the heart of Benjamin Flower's social thought in the 1890s was a paradoxical belief both in an imminent apocalyptic crisis for American society and in the inevitability of spiritual and material progress. The first derived from his staunch religious origins in the lower Midwest; the second was a result of his studies of nineteenth-century history and his insatiable interest in newness: new ideas, new religions, new technological inventions, new social or economic panaceas, new centuries. Both beliefs, however paradoxical, were essential to his purposes. On the one hand, a receptive audience to his ideas was guaranteed by his apocalyptic threats. If enough persons were jolted into an awareness of imminent catastrophe, they might rouse from their complacency and do something to avert it. On the other hand, those already aroused or activated by his message had to be assured that they were working in the service of a coming golden age. He thus sought to keep his readers walking a tightrope toward the "golden dawn" of brotherhood and justice while ever alert to their suspension over "the storm and wrath of violence and animal savagery."[28] Personally optimistic himself, he much preferred to depict the ethical qualities of the New Man in the New Day than to dwell on the horrors of an imminent apocalypse. What he was not very good at was in providing practical advice for maneuvering the tightrope. The only guides he offered for balance were the ethically inspiring ideals of his many intellectual heroes. As he described these ideals and heroes, they were certainly elevated and airy enough for the walk.

Flower was intrigued by the tactical significance that could be made of the transition from one century to the next. In the mid-1890s he wrote, "The closing years of this century will be a grand climacteric period in the history of the world. *It is in a very special sense a day of judgment.*" To survive the crisis, which could very well be bloody and brutal, he warned, it was necessary to renounce one's selfishness and adopt the new spirit of altruism and justice. The choice was one between the brutality of Caesar and the gentleness of Jesus. At present Flower saw the reign of Caesar infesting business, politics, the schools, and national morality. The time was therefore ripe for a reformation in the name of Jesus in which a vanguard of citizens in every town and village would educate others to an awareness that "*the conscience of the individual must be awakened*. He must be brought to the point *where he is willing to be just regardless of personal profit or loss*; to do right, heedless of consequences." Once an awakened populace were mobilized, Caesarism would be routed from the land. The nineteenth century had been an age of notable material progress, Flower pointed out, but had brought with it countless industrial, social, and moral evils. Caesarism, in the form of plutocracy, still prevailed in American life, but the twentieth century promised to bring in an age of moral progress more than matching the achievements of the nineteenth. Signs everywhere pointed to the new awakening. Books like *Looking Backward* and *Progress and Poverty* and the rapid growth of single tax, Nationalist, and socialist societies were "signs which reveal most eloquently the fact that the moral nature of man is being awakened; that the higher impulses are being quickened." By November 1899 he was even more certain that "egotism is receding and altruism advancing." Certainly, full social and spiritual redemption must be right around the corner of the new century.[29]

As an illustrative example of how the United States could be saved from plutocracy at the turn of the century, Flower looked to what he thought was a comparable episode in England in the 1840s: the anti-Corn Law movement. In the 1840s great English humanitarians such as Maurice, Kingsley, Gerald Massey, Charles MacKay, and Mazzini had produced, Flower noted, a literature that "awakened the sleeping conscience of old England and rendered the repeal of the unjust Corn Laws inevitable." Maurice gathered workers around him and taught them to believe in the oneness of humanity, the brotherhood of man, and the literal truth of the Sermon on the Mount. Maurice's outspoken disciple Charles Kingsley prodded the conscience of England with his Christian socialist novels. Massey, "the radical prophet-poet of progress," and MacKay, "the poet of the Anti-Corn-Law League," contributed a "*conscience* literature" to the moral ferment of the era. Mazzini, especially, contributed to the crusade while in England. In Flower's opinion, these young idealistic agitators had been successful in "educating the conscience of the nation to such a degree that practical advance became comparatively easy." Their method had been entirely educational and nonviolent, thus averting a revolution by force. They had held mass meetings, delivered lectures and sermons, and distributed tracts, poems, songs, and novels. These were, he said, the right methods of effecting change. The lesson for American reformers in their struggle against plutocracy was obvious:

follow the same example of moral awakening, unity of purpose, and peaceful educational agitation.[30]

As editor of the *Arena*, Flower had a perfect forum and medium for this approach. He thoroughly believed that by stirring consciences and awakening minds he could foster a spirit of moral idealism which would "drive out the base with the pure; destroy hate with love, brutality with gentleness, and elevate man by touching all the well-springs of spirituality, by playing upon the notes of his higher being."[31] This was typical of Flower's effusive style and faith in the regenerative power of moral idealism. His favorite quotations, repeated frequently, were Hugo's "life is conscience" and Mazzini's "life is a mission." Flower was himself a man with a mission, believing that as an editor he could arouse the consciences of his readers by the moral force of his exuberant missionary idealism.

The *Arena*, like its editor, had a mission. In the second issue Flower stated the purposes of his magazine: "What then is our duty? to agitate, to compel men to think; to point out wrongs inflicted on the weak and helpless; to impress higher ideals on the plastic mind of childhood; to labor at all times and in all places for the triumph of that which is pure and noble, unselfish and humane; to stimulate a love for truth, for liberty and justice." In 1897 he retired from the *Arena* for a short period to join Frederick U. Adams of Chicago in a journalistic venture, the *New Time*. The lesson of Bryan's defeat in 1896, according to Adams in his announcement of the new magazine, was the need for more effective voter education. He quoted Flower's determination "to establish a great review, which shall be, above all, reconstructive in influence and tendency, a veritable torch bearer, . . . a thought stimulator, a quickener of the higher ethical sensibilities." The *New Time* lasted until December 1898, when Flower merged it with the *Arena*. A month later he began a new magazine, the *Coming Age*, devoted to "the quickening and development of the individual conscience," a familiar theme. He quoted Mazzini's "life is a mission," as he did in his usual introductory editorial, but within two years the mission of the *Coming Age* ended as Flower returned to the *Arena*, which had been faltering under a number of editors in his absence. An introductory editorial in November 1900 rehashed the old themes of imminent crisis and the need for an awakened conscience at the dawn of a new century. Nine years later, when the *Arena* finally collapsed, an undaunted Flower founded the *Twentieth Century Magazine*, again a "magazine with a mission," dedicated to arousing man's "moral and civic idealism," so that "the conscience side of life" could match "industrial advance."[32] The repetitiveness of these quotations and themes illustrates Flower's consistency; he changed very little between 1890 and 1909 both in the language he employed and in the fundamental purposes of his life.

Hamlin Garland, whose Populist protest literature was encouraged by Flower, wrote, "I have never known a man who strove more single-handedly for social progress, than B. O. Flower. He was the embodiment of unselfish public service, and his ready sympathy for every genuine reform made his editorial office a center of civic zeal." Flower was even more undiscriminating than Bliss in his espousal of a wide variety of reforms and causes. His own political creed was ambiguous, yet was predominately democratic and Populist; he supported, however, almost any new idea that he believed would usher in the New Day. He endorsed most of the financial and political platforms of the Populist party: free silver, postal savings banks, the initiative and referendum, presidential primaries, direct election of senators, and full and equal woman's rights. He called direct democracy "the most important immediate political reform to meet existing conditions [because] it places the tools of democracy in the hands of the people." He supported many labor and moderate socialist programs as well: municipal socialism, corporate profit-sharing, worker and farmer cooperative experiments, immigration restriction, and the compulsory arbitration of industrial (and international) disputes. Flower's primary commitment was to personal freedom and social justice. He therefore had "no faith in any theory of government that distrusts human freedom." This meant socialism. In an editorial, "Is Socialism Desirable?" he cited the arguments of Herbert Spencer to declare that the socialists were wrong both in their diagnosis of the causes of current social problems and in their proposed remedies. According to Flower, not individualism but faulty education was at fault for socioeconomic ills. The remedy, therefore, was not governmental paternalism but more individualism and more liberty.[33] Despite his distrust of socialism, he was by no means averse to the kinds of socialism advocated by Bellamy. Yet even Bliss's brand of socialism was too strong for him.

Flower's clearest political allegiance was to Bryan, whose campaign in 1896 he worked for ardently. Bryan's election, he predicted, would mean "the rejuvenation of democracy and the salvation of republican government from a lawless plutocracy." Each of three earlier tyrannies in American history had been overcome by the ideals and actions of a great man: Jefferson thwarted the power of England, Jackson's veto destroyed the tyranny of the bank, and Lincoln defeated the slave power. Bryan appeared, Flower said, to turn back the tyranny of privilege and plutocracy. He was particularly proud of pointing out that the *Arena* "was the only leading review or magazine in the East which supported Bryan."[34]

Despite his partisan support of Bryanism and particular Populist or labor reforms, Flower's fundamental trust in freedom of thought led him to open the pages of the *Arena* to views and proposals with which he disagreed—without, of course, giving up his right to have the last word. His favorite technique was the symposium. In this way, between 1890 and 1896, the *Arena* dealt with the election of 1892 (but not 1896), tenement houses, child labor, municipal reform, government control of telegraph, the race question (even including an article by Wade Hampton suggesting deportation), women on social problems, and practical Christianity. He also included symposia on topics not necessarily of national concern but of particular interest to him. In this category were those on women's clubs, dress reform, age-of-consent laws, prostitution, gambling, women on the single tax, George Herron's Christian socialism, and the Bacon-Shakespeare controversy. Flower himself wrote most often on nineteenth-century social prophets, early childhood education, the political and sexual rights of women, and various aspects of psychic research. His articles and editorials in the 1890s, however, ranged far and wide, covering slums, saloons, and prostitution, kindergartens, child rearing, and divorce, the death penalty and lynching, religious intolerance and censorship, and mesmerism, hypnotism, and dreams. It was not unusual for him to write one month about the menace of plutocracy and the next about winter days in Florida. The personalities he wrote about included not only social prophets such as Jesus, Hugo, and Ruskin but also scientists and musicians such as Darwin, Alfred Wallace, Handel, and Christoph Gluck.

Although Flower had eclectic interests, the underlying purpose of the *Arena* and of his own contributions was, as he had said in

1890, to point out wrongs and to impress higher ideals on his readers in order to arouse, educate, and elevate the ethical sensibilities of the American people. He pursued two means of accomplishing this high purpose. The first was by muckraking. The second was by sermonizing.[35] Flower's usual technique was to lead his readers into the depths of the "social cellar" by exposing ugly social conditions and then to lift them out by gushing over the lofty ideals of his favorite prophets.

In *Civilization's Inferno*, or "Studies in the Social Cellar," serialized in the *Arena* during 1891–1893, Flower laid bare the life of society's exiles in the slums of Boston. His study, based on but three afternoon walks, earned him a reputation as "the Jacob Riis of Boston." The city he described was truly an inferno of tenement cellars and attics, diseased babies, evictions, suicides, and hard-luck stories. The "real inferno," however, was underneath even the social cellar, in the "pseudo-pleasures" found in saloons, poolrooms, gambling halls, and brothels, all of which Flower saw one afternoon while accompanied by a policeman. Typically, he was as horrified that "ethical exaltation or spiritual growth is impossible with such environment" as he was with the physical conditions of the environment itself. He blamed slums and vice on monopoly, tax laws, the saloon, unrestricted immigration, and the general decline in morality caused by material greed. His solution was a familiar one, reminiscent of Bliss: study the slums, gather statistics, and let the churches unite in a program of educational agitation to eradicate the evils. Flower was not too interested in the practical details of how this was to be done; he was certain only that palliative measures would not satisfy the people. He concluded his book with the assurance that the inspiration of Victor Hugo would lead men to a better life and with William Morris's visionary poem "The Day Is Coming." He warned his readers that they could expect disappointments in the near future, but assured them that he believed "*the dawn to be breaking*."[36]

Flower much preferred to spend two hours with a poem by Morris than he did two hours in the slums and assumed that his readers did likewise. Therefore, he wrote more often about Tolstoy, for example, than about tenements; he spent more time dreaming of what ought to be than exposing what was. Like Bliss, Flower found it easier to synthesize and express others' ideas than to propound his own. His magazines, therefore, were filled with the prophetic utterances and ideals of such nineteenth-century Europeans as Hugo, Mazzini, Tolstoy, Morris, and Ruskin, and of such contemporary American reformers as Bryan, Lloyd, Markham, and George. Flower's lists of prophets usually began with Jesus. What these men shared in common were those traits that Flower deemed most virtuous: vision, love, duty, sacrifice, and moral idealism. Above all, each had an ability to inspire others.

As a critic of art, literature, and the theater, Flower believed that the office of any artist was to serve humanity, not art, and "to make the people think, act, and grow morally great." For this reason, he proclaimed the writing of Hugo and Mazzini, the poetry of Massey, Whittier, Morris, and Markham, and even the acting of Joseph Jefferson. Hugo was one of Flower's earliest enthusiasms. *Les Miserables*, he wrote, was "a prayer for a higher ideal of justice, a heart-cry for a more humane public spirit, a noble picture of the divine in man." Flower described Hugo as a man of pity, love, and vision of a better life for the sick and hungry of Europe. His ethics were "amplifications of the Sermon on the Mount, and the Golden Rule. . . . He had an abiding faith in the ultimate redemption of humanity." Flower learned from Hugo that the criminal and prostitute were victims of an unjust society and male lust and were therefore not responsible for their sins. This did not, however, justify licentiousness. Ultimate responsibility was always on the individual, Flower pointed out, so long as human freedom was preserved. Hugo, he said, saw that human progress could not be achieved by sacrificing liberty on the altar of socialism. Above all, the French poet awakened others to dedicate themselves to the service of humanity.[37]

Flower's favorite poets were always lovers of humanity and mystical seers of the New Day. His books on Massey and Whittier, serialized in the *Arena* during the mid-1890s, were long panegyrics to their humanitarian and mystical visions. In his introduction to a volume on Massey, Flower said that he wanted to bring the verses of this underrated poet to the attention of all good persons, "believing that his noble ideals, his passionate appeals for justice, his prophetic glimpse of the coming day, would serve to awaken some sleeping souls." Because Massey was a humble man who scorned convention in his hatred for ignorance and cant, Flower admired and honored him; and because he was a prophet of "freedom, fraternity, and justice, ever loyal to the interest of the oppressed, I love him." He loved Whittier for the same reasons. The American abolitionist poet was "a prophet of freedom" and "poet of the *inner light*" who, like Massey, was primarily a dreamer and apostle of higher ideals.[38]

Morris's death in 1896 evoked an obituary from Flower, who seemingly liked nothing better than an excuse to eulogize. Morris's special distinction, he said, was in being a poet-mystic who, despite his business success, became a more effective practical reformer in his later years while at the same time retaining his mysticism. By practicality he meant inspiring others: "The seeds he has sown will never die; the inspiration he has shed abroad will touch, light, and fire other brains," and many others will have the courage to carry on Morris's divine causes because of his influence. Elbert Hubbard, an American craftsman of book printing, was an example of one who had heard Morris's message and was "determined to test the practicability of the poet's dream." Flower's unrestrained enthusiasm for Morris and Massey paled when compared to his admiration for Edwin Markham. Flower had heard Markham recite his poem "Brotherhood" in Buffalo and recalled the moment as the most thrilling of the conference. Markham's more famous poem, "The Man with the Hoe," like Millet's painting which inspired it, was for Flower the epitome of art for humanity's sake. Markham's response to Millet illustrated "the fact that the artist, no less than the poet and philosopher, wields a godlike power which in the service of progress exerts an undreamed of influence for the advance of an enduring civilization." Markham was a far greater champion of the masses than Massey or Morris, Flower wrote, because he had known poverty and been touched by the new conscience, rising to become a spokesman for the oppressed.[39]

Besides admiring the vision and inspirational qualities of these poets, Flower also emphasized their willingness to sacrifice. Massey gave up his wealth and suffered with the poor in his old age because he believed that the spiritual life was greater than the material life. Whittier and Markham embraced the humble life, and Morris, Flower pointed out, could have been poet laureate had he not been an agitator for justice and brotherhood. The greatest prophets of the nineteenth century, in fact, "have been primarily the apostles of an austere morality. In each the conscience dominated the intellect, and the spirit of the Puritan or the ascetic has been very much in evidence."[40] This was dramatically the case with Tolstoy.

Flower was introduced to Tolstoy's writings in 1890 when the *Kreutzer Sonata*, Tolstoy's graphic portrayal of male dominance in marriage, was censored in America. Although finding the Russian's book extremely repulsive, Flower argued that its motive was moral elevation and not sexual stimulation. He defended Tolstoy from the "pseudo-moralists" of the Post Office Department, calling him "a moral pillar in the far East [*sic*] . . . denying self everything that he may by life, example, and influence better and gladden the lives of his fellowmen." In his many articles on Tolstoy, Flower emphasized his renunciation of social eminence and the wealthy life in order to live by his literal interpretation of the Sermon on the Mount. He was, Flower said, "the greatest living exemplar . . . of the Christian ideal." Tolstoy was not, however, to be held up as infallible. Like many Americans, Flower thought the Russian too pessimistic. In comparing Tolstoy unfavorably to Ruskin and Elbert Hubbard, he said of the Russian that rather than uplifting the poor, he descends to their level; rather than preaching beauty, he practices ascetic austerity.[41] It is curious that Flower criticizes Tolstoy for doing the very things he admires in others. Perhaps he objected to the fact that Tolstoy actually did descend to the level of the poor, whereas Markham and Whittier simply talked poetically about doing so. Flower himself talked a great deal about renunciation but never made any costly sacrifices personally. Still, he admired Tolstoy as a real inspiration, particularly on young men. One of those young men was Ernest Crosby, who was so influenced by Tolstoy's writings that he abandoned a promising political career in order to emulate his master by serving humanity. In Crosby's books and life, Flower wrote, was found "the rugged democracy of Whitman and something of the austerity of Tolstoy . . . and the luminous love that glorifies the Sermon on the Mount." Tolstoy's influence on Crosby, Flower pointed out, was immediate, profound, and lasting.[42]

In contrast to Tolstoy, Flower wrote, John Ruskin had not imprisoned beauty in his own breast. Rather, his "passionate love for the beautiful and an enthusiasm for art, born of an appreciation of its potential usefulness in enriching, brightening, and ennobling life," had elevated him to a higher plane than Tolstoy. Ruskin's art and social criticism had done more than any other English writings of the century to awaken the conscience of England. The moral exaltation of his writing compelled readers to a new appreciation for nature and art; more important, Ruskin created in men "an intense desire to uplift and dignify humanity." Flower commended Ruskin's political economy, but concluded that his writing was not nearly as remarkable as the example of his life. He was a model of the self-sacrificing philanthropist, Flower said, for he used his fortune for the benefit of the workingmen, disposed of most of his inheritance and book royalties for public good, and even gave up his young wife to an artist friend.[43]

Flower's impassioned admiration for Tolstoy and Ruskin was often qualified. Tolstoy was too austere and pessimistic; Ruskin was too narrow-minded and pedantic. Flower's love for Mazzini, however, was rarely, if ever, qualified. More than any other man, Mazzini possessed those traits that Flower revered. The Italian was inspired by more "moral enthusiasm," more "passionate love," a "broader intellectual vision . . . and a sweeter, saner, and truer ideal of man's duties, obligations, and proper relationship to all other men" than any other nineteenth-century figure. Flower's essay on Mazzini dwelled on his sacrifices and the perils of a life of exile. But as usual, Flower's fondness for purple prose and the superlative impelled him to his conclusions: Mazzini was one of the "most single-hearted apostles of unity and freedom who ever left an impress on the brain of the world." His ideals of duty, mission, freedom, brotherhood, and justice were those which must be pursued if civilization was to continue to advance. Most importantly, Mazzini knew that "moral ideas never die" and that the way to human progress was by the martyr's inspiration to "thousands of other men to carry forward the great cause . . . of Freedom, Fraternity, and Justice." Mazzini was himself, Flower wrote in another essay, the most effective awakener of the social conscience of the century. His influence preceded, and was greater even than, that of Ruskin, Tolstoy, Hugo, and George. The eulogist's enthusiasm, rarely restrained, was never as impassioned as it was for Mazzini.[44]

Flower's obsession with the influence of Millet on Markham, Morris on Hubbard, Tolstoy on Crosby, and Mazzini on multitudes suggests what is common to these seemingly endless panegyrics. He was, as Howard Cline has written, a "middleman dealing in ideas of others." He conveyed these ideas to his readers, stressing the process by which one person was influenced by another. His hope was that the moral idealism of these prophets would catch fire in others in order to carry America to the golden age. His concept of inspiration and influence, however, was not confined only to great prophets. Flower was too democratic for that. His own creed, itself inspired by Mazzini, was that every person has some influence and some work to do.[45] This conviction was the basis for Flower's closest attempt at a concrete reformist act: the Union for Practical Progress.

In 1893, after four years with the *Arena*, Flower reported that letters from readers indicated the need for a unified reform organization. He therefore proposed the creation of a Union for Practical Progress, a loosely federated union of local Arena clubs. Actually, Flower's proposal had already been attempted by Frank and Walter Vrooman in their Union for Concerted Moral Effort in Worcester and New York. This organization, begun in 1892, was intended to mobilize the concerned citizens of a community in a concerted effort to abolish urban evils. They floundered in tactical, financial, and public-relations difficulties, so when Flower made his announcement, the Vrooman brothers were eager to join. The purpose of Flower's union was "to unite all moral forces, agencies and persons for concerted, methodical and persistent endeavor in behalf of the public good, and especially for the abolition of unjust social conditions." The method was by raising and discussing "a definite moral issue every month." Each club was essentially autonomous, for Flower recognized the special needs of different localities. He nevertheless strongly suggested adopting "Leagues of Love" or "Federations of Justice" as suitable names for the clubs (he was afraid the word Arena might alienate potential sympathizers), and he was insistent that the same moral issue be discussed in each club in the same month. The topics for 1894 included sweatshops, tenement house reform, saloons, child labor, parks and playgrounds, penal and municipal reform, unemployment, and political corruption. The clubs did more than discuss; they were also active lobbying with public officials against the evils they condemned, working to establish reading rooms, meeting halls, and public parks and baths, and spreading their message by distributing protest literature and encouraging subscriptions to the *Arena.* There was even a mail order People's University. Flower's role in the union was as an organizer and inspirer, suggesting ideas for discussion topics, for better ways of spreading the word, and for dividing cities into workable units. Most of all, he provided the material and moral support of his *Arena* editorial office to the unions and their members. He assured them that their work of propaganda, like that of the Fabian Society and anti-Corn Law League in England, was awakening millions of people and, more importantly, was averting the bloodshed and violence which might potentially convulse society. By the end of 1894 he announced that there were fifty clubs in operation. The experiment soon ended, however, with the absorption of the clubs into other civic betterment organizations and with Flower's increasing interest in other things, namely his year-long series in the *Arena* on the century, the life, and the utopia of Sir Thomas More.[46]

Flower's shift of interest from the Union for Practical Progress to the life of Sir Thomas More was typical and illustrates his most serious weakness as an effective reformer. He was not an activist, but a word-monger. This was not by any means an unnecessary role, and it was certainly the one he conceived for himself. Perhaps his panegyric tributes to Mazzini, Markham, and others, or his exposures of life in the slums of Boston did, in fact, inspire a few readers to pick up the cause of social justice. But one wonders if there were perhaps too many wasted words, however well-intentioned, on his readers. Flower's subscribers, like Bliss's, were other middle-class intellectuals like himself who already agreed, no doubt, with his positions on social evils and the appropriate methods of reform. He intended the *Arena* to be read by affluent families (it cost $5.00 per year, expensive by late nineteenth-century standards) and by intelligent people.[47] His eulogistic biographies of great moral prophets and his obsessions with dress styles, age-of-consent laws, and psychic research were generally irrelevant to all but an educated middle class. And his increasing absorption with Christian Science, medical freedom, and the menace of the papacy in later years were even more remote from working-class needs, although certainly many workers shared these concerns. Like Bliss, Flower was tactically a child and temperamentally a middle-class intellectual. And therein was the source of his failures as a reformer.

Both Bliss and Flower had too much faith in the regenerative influence of study groups, in the Bible-lesson-a-week or moral-issue-a-month method of awakening minds and therefore eradicating evil. What did these methods have to do with the needs of the American worker and tenement dweller? Despite his democratic principles, Flower assumed, even more than Bliss, that reform came from above, from dutiful employers, charitable organizations (the *Arena* had a fund for the poor), and a socially awakened and spiritually aroused middle class. Flower had little contact with the poor. He understood their lives and needs hardly at all. He avoided the doctrinal and tactical struggles of trade unionists and socialists (being always on a "higher" level) and stayed away from union halls, worker meetings, and strike conflicts. On his three, two-hour afternoon walks through the slums of Boston, accompanied by a policeman, he placed oranges in the hands of little children, and saw all he needed to write a 237-page book on "civilization's inferno." Near the end of his book he described a dream he had after his walk in which he was visited by an angel. In his dream he saw first a plague cast over Boston and then a Bellamyite utopian city of the future. The city had no slums or factories, but instead was filled with flowers, music, grassy parks, playgrounds, pools, gymnasiums, eating halls, reading rooms, theaters, lecture halls, and night schools.[48] Karl Marx, quarreling with Hegel, described the successive stages of human need as beginning with food and shelter, and moving upward to organization of the means of subsistence through division of labor and ownership of the means of production and distribution, and finally to the highest stage, the production of ideas and mental life through education, religion, and culture. Flower, turning Marx upside down without knowing it, started at the top with theater, lecture halls, and flowers. Only the oranges offered a hint of reality.

There is little evidence that Flower doubted the effectiveness or righteousness of his cause. Practical activism, self-sacrifice, and incisive intellectual analysis were not within his capacity. He was not one to suffer self-doubts, and never apologized, as far as I know, for not emulating the sacrifices of his many heroes. He went on until his death an ardent professional crusader and believer in himself. The causes changed, but not the style or methods. By 1911 the *Twentieth Century Magazine* under Flower's editorship was promoting Christian Science, although he was not himself a Christian Scientist, and was lobbying against the creation of a national health bureau for fear that it would suppress faith healing, mesmerism, and similar practices which he supported. In the second decade of the twentieth century he edited an anti-Catholic journal, the *Menace*, and wrote *The Patriot's Manual*, a scurrilous, pocket-sized handbook of facts "Showing Why Every Friend of Fundamental Democracy Must Oppose Politico-Ecclesiastical Romanism in Its Un-American Campaign to Make America 'Dominantly Catholic!' " In 1917 Flower brought *How England Averted a Revolution by Force* up to date by substituting "Romanism" for "plutocracy" and showing how the lesson of the anti-Corn Law agitation in England should be followed in order to repel the Catholic menace.[49] He died a year later, believing that the pope had caused World War I.

4

THE STRUGGLE FOR PERSONAL HARMONY: VIDA SCUDDER

Our idealists are too often ideologists. . . . The great mass of misery, corruption, and injustice remains practically unaffected by our efforts. The appeal to purely moral incentives, while it brings blessing to many individuals, is helpless to attain, unaided, the decent society which, to our shame, two thousand years of Christianity have failed to reach.

SCUDDER *

THE EFFORTS of Bliss and Flower to achieve organizational and doctrinal unity failed. Part of their failure was in shallow analysis and tactical naiveté; part was a result of their inability to make contact with anyone but those in middle-class intellectual circles. Neither, however, suffered many self-doubts about their tactical approach or personal limitations. Vida Scudder had the same goals and was to a large extent able to overcome both sources of failure that plagued Bliss and Flower. She was a much more sophisticated and critical thinker than either of her two Boston contemporaries, and through strike involvement, Socialist party membership, and settlement house work she was able to contact those who were the objects of her social concerns. Unlike Bliss and Flower, she understood the chief limitation of the intellectual as reformer to be the ineffectiveness of "the appeal to purely moral incentives." But because she was a more sensitive and introspective person and because she was more practically involved than either Bliss or Flower, she was more vulnerable to self-doubts and self-accusation. She did not doubt the righteousness of her cause, but she certainly questioned the quality of her involvement and her own internal consistency. To the quests for educational agitation and reform unity, she added a personal quest, that of self-knowledge and inner harmony. The compelling question for Vida Scudder was how a reform-minded, highly principled person, as teacher, could make an impact on creating a better world. Her story reveals the often painful process of the professor who seeks to balance a professional obligation to the pursuit of learning with a personal commitment to social and political activism.

It was axiomatic for Benjamin Flower that he attempt to influence his readers; not to do so would have been a denial of his journalistic responsibilities. But to seek to influence others is itself a serious responsibility, as Scudder knew well. In her youth she had been profoundly influenced by Ruskin, as well as by a host of other European social and religious prophets. Consequently, she maintained a sensitivity to the dangers, as well as the opportunities, inherent in exposing one mind to the ideas of another. As a young teacher in 1890, she expressed her concern that many people closed their minds in fear of being influenced. It was wrong, she said, especially where the exercising of influence was free and open, "to refuse to be helped by it." But it was equally wrong, she added, to refrain from exerting one's influence.[1]

In her autobiography, *On Journey*, written a half-century later, she reiterated her commitment to the potentially redeeming influence of the written and spoken word. There were pedagogical difficulties, she wrote, in exposing young minds to model lives from history, for this often fostered an imitative life. Moreover, as an innovative teacher, who normally used twice as many discussions as lectures, she struggled with the difficult challenge of both insuring her students' freedom to explore and "steering them toward a right conclusion." Would her own sympathies intrude? "Suppress them, and you are dull; give them play, and you imperil the direct impact of the book on the student." Like most teachers, she straddled the delicate line, recognizing that however much she sought to be impartial it was inevitable that she would teach best that which she cared most about. Although acutely sensitive to the dangers of hypocrisy, subjectivity, and imitation, she nevertheless concluded that her responsibility was to give her sympathies the play they demanded and to expose her students to "the whole human heritage."[2]

Vida Scudder had herself assimilated that heritage and been thoroughly influenced by it. Born in India in 1861, the only child of a Congregational missionary, she was brought to the family home in New England as an infant after the death of her father. She attended a private girls' school and the new Girls' Latin School in Boston. Because of the influence of Phillips Brooks and Frederick Denison Maurice, she and her mother converted to the Episcopal church in 1875. In her rather lonely youth, much of it spent in European art galleries and cathedrals, Vida acquired a devotion to beauty and a rich appreciation of the human past. Although exposed to the usual classical writings, she developed a particular fondness for the social passion of Christian activists such as Lamennais, Maurice, and Kingsley. Going to college was a significant family event. In her fantasies Vida disguised herself as a boy and "crept into Harvard"; actually, she entered Smith College in 1880, where she thrived on English literature and remembered herself as "a little intellectual snob." After graduating from Smith she became one of the first women to attend Oxford. It was at Oxford that her intellectual emptiness and social complacency were transformed into "a social radicalism nebulous enough, yet thundery and intense." The teaching of John Ruskin, she said, was largely responsible for this transformation.[3]

Years before going off to Oxford in 1884 Scudder had spent long hours of summer reading in New Hampshire devouring Ruskin's art criticism. He had introduced her to an appreciation for painting and architecture. Like many other genteel Americans, however, she felt that Ruskin's career had gone wrong when he began "meddling with political economy." It was a tragedy, she wrote, that he had turned to social criticisms, and "would write no more lovely descriptions of sunsets or Venetian palaces." As she enrolled for Ruskin's lectures, therefore, she was predisposed to view him critically, almost antagonistically, as well as with keen interest. To her surprise she saw not "an unstrung fanatic," as she had expected, but a prophet.[4]

In later years Scudder could not remember much of the substance of Ruskin's lectures, but she recalled being struck by his "life-communicating" presence, his gentle "childlike simplicity," and his "unswerving rectitude, intellectual and moral." When he departed from his manuscript and spoke directly to his audience, she was nearly carried away with rapture. Ruskin suggested questions and relationships which represented, for her, a quite new point of view. She learned that political economy and art were related and that the contemplation of art was not the exclusive privilege of the wealthy. She learned that a nation which did not provide beauty and leisure for its workers was an unhealthy nation. He taught her to ask the question whether social idealism should lead one to choose the study of the past or the world of modern fact. She came away from his lectures motivated to read Ruskin's social criticism. The first book she turned to, *Unto This Last*, Ruskin's assault on Manchesterian economics, marked a turning point in her life. She resolved to devote herself to awakening others to the plight of the poor, as well as to work with the oppressed herself.[5]

The impact of Ruskin prompted Vida Scudder to ask new questions and make new resolves; it also caused guilt and stimulated her to action. She was particularly impressed with Ruskin's influence on the English university settlement house movement, most notably Toynbee Hall. While still at Oxford she joined the Salvation Army, somewhat impetuously and masochistically, she recalled.

> The point of my desire was an intolerable stabbing pain, as Ruskin, and the rich delights of the place, forced me to realize for the first time the plethora of privilege in which my lot had been cast. That pain has continued at intervals to stab my spirit broad awake ever since; though for the most part it has become merely a dull chronic ache. But when I first felt it, I yearned to banish it by extreme measures. A desperate wish to do violence to myself drove me to the dirty garrets, to the strange street meetings, where the Army was in evidence.

This passage reveals a recurring compulsion and largely unresolved dilemma of Scudder's long life. The stabbing pain that affected her in her youth, and continued throughout her life, was caused not only by Ruskin but also by Tolstoy, whom she began reading in the late 1880s. "The more intimate I grew with Tolstoy, and the more I became afflicted by my sense of severance from the wholesome world of manual labor, the more respect I developed for the idea of 'domestic work.' "[6] By the late 1880s, everyone that she read, including Ruskin, Tolstoy, Carlyle, Arnold, Shelley, and More, she interpreted in terms of this social passion. From them she caught a glimpse of a more humane society and received an inspiration for social service and personal sacrifice. Her inability fully to renounce the worldly comforts of her modestly wealthy inheritance, however, assured the continued persistence of her pain.

In the early 1890s she turned to Marx's works and other economic writings and became a socialist. Ruskin and Tolstoy had been influential in her decision, she recalled, as well as More's *Utopia* and Shelley's *Prometheus Unbound*. "But the book which clinched my socialism and furnished me with a definite set of concrete economic convictions, was the 'Fabian Essays.' " In them she found economic facts and analyses to bolster the tenuous and emotive influence of Ruskin and Tolstoy. "Poets and dreamers had fed my imagination," but had left her in a "fog." In the Fabians "my mind found the practical, constructive ideas for which it had been avid." But she still was left with a doctrinal dilemma. The original source of her passion for humane service was Christianity, and she was determined to reconcile materialistic socialism with spiritual Christianity. In 1890 she joined Bliss's Society of Christian Socialists in Boston, where, as she recalled much later, "we feasted on ham and pickles and found intense relief in talking without reserve of the Christian Revolution." She met once a week with other Christian socialists in Bliss's Church of the Carpenter. She argued in the *Dawn* that humans had both physical and spiritual natures, and that the material improvement of the body was a necessary prerequisite for the progress of the soul. Therefore, the Christian, she said, was obligated to work in the world. Five years later, in "Socialism and Spiritual Progress," she speculated on what kind of people they would be in a socialist society. She concluded that under socialism persons not only would be economically better than under capitalism but also would be ethically better. Socialism itself, she wrote, would not make men more ethical, but would create the social context within which men could more easily exert their instinct to do good. Ultimately, it would free man's soul.[7] Scudder was not, however, yet entirely convinced by these still vaguely defined arguments. Much of her writing in the 1890s and for the rest of her life was devoted to finding a suitable doctrinal unity between the idealistic and spiritual inspiration of social prophets and Christianity, and the tough-minded economic analyses of socialists. This quest for unity was accompanied by another, more personal one.

The influence of Ruskin and others led Scudder not only to socialism but also into a personal quandary. On the one hand, she looked eagerly toward a Christian socialist society, to be brought about by persistent social activism and agitation. On the other hand, she yearned wistfully for the contemplative, self-sacrificing, ascetic life of the medieval monk. A visit to the shrines of Saint Francis of Assisi in 1901 intensified her dilemma. "Friends are justified," she wrote, "who tell me laughing that my real home is either in the Middle Ages or in the Utopian future." She did not know whether to ally herself with the labor movement and agitate for radical reform or to retire to a comfortable academic post and teach English literature—or even to hide away at her summer cottage in New Hampshire and contemplate art and nature. Of one thing she was sure: Ruskin and common sense had taught her that the social order was seriously diseased. Whether to cure the disease or to flee from its infection was the question that haunted her life. One possible solution was to synthesize her conflicting compulsions. "But where was unity for me?" she wrote about her life in 1901. Under the influence of Tolstoy and Saint Francis, the life of poverty was compelling. But her missionary inheritance was calling her also to work in the world, arousing social passion in others. But where was unity? In 1910 Scudder wrote that "the moments when two ideas, thought to be irreconcilable, are perceived to be supplementary, are the most radiant in history."[8] The quest for those radiant moments, intellectually and personally, constituted the primary objective of her life. In this quest for unity, she followed three paths: teaching, settlement house work, and socialism.

The first path was an academic one. Vida Scudder returned to the United States from Oxford as a young woman "kindled with the flame of social passion." She accepted a job teaching English literature at Wellesley in the fall of 1887, not without serious reservations or trepidations, and remained there until she retired in 1927. One of her first academic tasks, which she tackled eagerly, was to edit a collection of Ruskin's writings for use by students. "No man," she wrote in the introduction, "is a wider exponent of the life and thought of the nineteenth century than John Ruskin." Because of his scathing criticisms of industrialism and his illuminations of both art and humanity, she wrote, "we are eager to study him." His accomplishments, she noted, were both practical and inspirational. In her volume she included selections from Ruskin as naturalist, art critic, sociologist, and ethical teacher. The common denominator of Ruskin's many interests was his singular unity in serving both God and man. Although he defied easy classification, she concluded that he was a socialist, not of the "crude" type but of the "higher and of the Christian type."[9] Her book on Ruskin was a labor of love; so also was her teaching, despite occasional periods of self-reproach.

At Wellesley she found ego gratification, security, and a measure of fame. Florence Converse, in her history of Wellesley, noted that Scudder was to the Wellesley of her day what Norton, Longfellow, and Lowell had been to the Harvard of theirs. After her initial concerns about the frightening responsibility of interpreting the experience of others, she found that she delighted in teaching. Her almost obsessive shyness disappeared (as did the preclass nausea) when she entered a classroom, and she often left "walking on air." In her courses she ranged widely from Arthurian romance to nineteenth-century literature and modern poets. She had time to write and thrived on the "sustaining routine of professional life."[10] Her somewhat cloistered position, however, did not satisfy her passion for social service. In a letter to a colleague shortly after her career began, Scudder confessed that teaching did not enable her "to do any of God's work." The injunctions of Tolstoy and Saint Francis to embrace poverty and live with the poor prompted the disquieting thought that perhaps she had made the wrong decision when she chose to teach. The comfort and security of her life in Wellesley occasionally filled her with self-hate. She was ashamed to draw her pay, but told herself that earning money was more respectable than inheriting it. In 1896 she was distressed by an endowment Wellesley received from Standard Oil. She had recently read Lloyd's *Wealth against Commonwealth*, and her conscience urged a dramatic resignation. She traveled to Chicago to seek advice from Lloyd, who chided her about her emotional denunciation of the corporation and probably urged restraint. Her dilemma was resolved by signing a vehement protest against accepting the money and by staying at Wellesley.[11] What better way to arouse social passion in others?

In 1896, against the indifference of her department and the opposition of the Wellesley administration, Scudder began offering a course in "Social Ideals of English Letters," which she later made into a book. The course provided a link between her social concern and her love of letters. The underlying theme was that English literature, which originally had been concerned with the individual, had become in the nineteenth century "a series of social documents," which she interpreted as socialist documents. The purpose of her course, she said, was to awaken a sense of responsibility on the part of her generation toward a practical solution of urban and industrial injustices. She began, not very practically, with the fourteenth-century Christian socialist vision of William Langland and went on to discuss More's *Utopia* and Swift's satires. The awakening of the English social conscience, she said, was prompted by Carlyle's *Sartor Resartus* and intensified by Ruskin's social criticism. After describing the indictment of English economic and moral life by Carlyle, Ruskin, Arnold, and the Christian socialists, she turned to their various proposals. The emphasis in her chapters on "What to Do?" was on Ruskin's charge to employers to extend moral consciousness to areas of production and consumption, as discussed in *Unto This Last*. According to Ruskin, employers had a paternal duty to simplify their own lives by renouncing their wealth and sharing it with their workers. Her interpretation of Ruskin, Carlyle, and Arnold held that the thought of each was moving toward a more democratic society, while at the same time searching for some kind of paternal or governmental authority to restrain the excesses of democracy. Admittedly, this was a paradoxical quest, and Scudder had difficulty making Arnold, especially, into a democrat. Nevertheless, she predicted "a synthesis of forces in which all the inconsistencies of Victorian thought are solved." Straightforwardly, she asked: "Will that synthesis be the social democracy of the future? Will it be the socialist state?"[12] Stuffed full of Shelley, More, Ruskin, and Carlyle by the end of the course, her students were then encouraged to do some utopian speculation of their own. Presumably, they envisaged the same socialist synthesis that she did.

With these partisan objectives and enthusiasms, she had to be careful not to proselytize in her course. Well aware that she was "skating on the thinnest ice on which my pedagogic feet ever ventured," she insisted that "the ice never broke." She disapproved of two colleagues, one of whom dragged the *Communist Manifesto* into an astronomy course, and the other who introduced a questionnaire on sex in a medieval history course. Scudder avoided these academic transgressions, she wrote, by balancing her own sympathies with texts expressing other viewpoints. But what is one to make of her comments that she taught the "conservatives with special gusto" or that Edmund Burke was "valuable pedagogic 'material' "? Despite her disclaimers, her course on English social ideals was little more than a partisan socialist interpretation of English literature. And the students loved it, enrolling in large numbers despite the department's refusal to accept the course for the major. In retrospect, that didn't bother Scudder: "more alumnae thank me for it than for any other course I ever taught; they tell me that its worth to them grows with the years."[13]

More than once she embroiled herself and her course in controversy. Trustees wrote irate letters, indignant parents threatened to withdraw their daughters from the college, and many alumnae pointed at Scudder's activities as justification for refusing to bestow gifts on Wellesley. She was troubled but not deterred by these criticisms. In the spring of 1912, for example, she took part in the

Lawrence textile strike, attending strike meetings, visiting workers' homes, and delivering an impassioned address to a meeting of women in sympathy with the strike. She charged the police with rough treatment of female strikers and the courts with denying bail to strike leaders. She assailed the woolen industry of Massachusetts and advocated a minimum-wage law. The major thrust of her speech, however, was a plea for nonresistance and obedience to law. To the strikers, whom she honored as martyrs "*for justice's sake*," she urged both more patience and more solidarity. In time, she said, they would achieve their sacred goals.[14]

An editorial in the *Boston Transcript* demanded that Scudder resign from the Wellesley faculty. College officials, deluged with similar letters, called her to account. In a letter of explanation, she expressed regret that the public held the college responsible for her views, but defended her decision and right to speak at the meeting. Any Christian, she said, would have done what she had done. She admitted that "conscience and logic" had impelled her to join the Socialist party. Although she carefully avoided propaganda in the classroom, she guessed that she inevitably interpreted literature from her socialist point of view. The letter was concluded with an offer to resign. Her resignation was refused, but the course was dropped for a year. Scudder's disappointment was expressed in a letter to Walter Rauschenbusch, in which she told him that it was impossible for her to proselytize her students, partly because her own judgment prevented it, and partly because she taught literature, not economics. But the main reason she could not speak out, she wrote, was because "my course . . . has been suppressed." Indomitably, she added, "I shall make a fight to have it restored next year. It's a good course!"[15] Long before the Lawrence affair, however, Scudder had realized that teaching alone could not satisfy her desire to pursue both the contemplative life and the activist life. The second path she followed in her quest for unity was in the college settlement house movement which, like her social teaching, was inspired by Ruskin.

In the fall of 1887 Vida Scudder and a group of Smith alumnae pledged themselves to start a settlement house. In addition to proving that college women could assume a responsibility for social service without turning hearth and home on its head, they were motivated by a desire to share, a need to learn, a sense of gratitude toward the community, and a genuine desire to promote social justice. An initial attempt failed, Scudder recalled with embarrassment, because of family ties and professional obligations. But by the fall of 1889, antedating the opening of Hull House by two weeks, the group succeeded in opening a settlement house in New York, followed in the next three years by others in Philadelphia and Boston. The College Settlements Association, which Scudder and her friends founded, was the integrating organization. Settlement work was an opportunity for combining social activism with self-sacrifice. "Those who live in a settlement house," she wrote, have "achieved the end of righteous living by the simple process of refusing to receive more than a just share of the world's goods." She knew well that the main value of the settlement was less to help the community participants than to educate and enlighten the college women residents. But even this value was incidental rather than essential to the ultimate purpose of the settlements. Unlike the settlements started by Robert Woods and other social scientists in the 1890s, which sought primarily to study the community and amass statistics on the life of the poor, Scudder's purpose was not academic but redemptive. A settlement, she wrote, represented a spiritual ideal in which the life of the settlement participants approached the example of Jesus. Although each settlement was a small experiment, limited in its influence, it stood firmly on the assumption that "large ideals grow from small endeavors."[16]

Vida Scudder's activity in and study of the settlements convinced her that the most dangerous weakness in America was the intellectual and moral disunion caused by the vast gap between the privileged few and the deprived many. In 1902 she wrote a series of articles for the *Atlantic Monthly* in which she showed how the lack of a common physical, intellectual, and ethical life in America could be diminished. A nation, to be truly democratic, must possess spiritual unity, a common life. A few weeks' living in a tenement, she said, would demonstrate the gravity of divisiveness and disunion. There were two options. Americans could admit that democracy was a sham and retreat to an aristocratic theory. Or they could dedicate themselves to the development of a common life which would make of democracy a substance, rather than a shadow. The three articles that followed showed how this unity could be effected in education, society, and the church. She began with the settlements as an experiment in education toward unity. "In order to promote the common life, it is necessary to live the life in common." She was fully aware, however, that the settlements and organized charities could not provide fully the unifying force that was needed, but they could point the way. The whole framework of society had to be reconstructed. The process would be a gradual one but it must begin along the lines of Ruskin's concept of the duties of employers to sacrifice for the good of their workers. But Scudder went beyond Ruskin's paternalism: not only employers but all persons, she said, should suppress their selfish desires in order to practice the simple life and social fellowship required to bring about a common life. Her final appeal was to the Christian church, which had become allied with the rich, and to Christians in ordinary walks of life to follow Jesus toward the realization of "that spiritual democracy of which our fathers dreamed."[17]

The settlement, which Scudder described as "the most engrossing interest of my life, after my profession," was a fitting way of fulfilling her need for simplicity, limited activism, and what she called "fellowship." She spent her vacations, weekends, and late afternoon hours at one of the houses, well aware, of course, that she could always return to the comforts of her home near Boston. Her home was both refuge and prison: "Ever since my Oxford days," she wrote, "I had been beating my wings against the bars,—the customs, the assumptions, of my own class. I moved in a garden enclosed, if not a hothouse, an enclosure of gracious manners, regular meals, comfort, security, good taste." She liked the comfortable life, she admitted, although at times it suffocated her, pressing upon her the need to escape. Although she had theorized on the purposes and functions of the settlement house movement, her own motivations for settlement work were a need to escape the stultification of Wellesley life and genteel living, "a biting curiosity about the way the Other Half lived, and a strange hunger for fellowship with them." She therefore used every moment she had toward acquiring a "vivid feeling of life in the social depths."[18]

At Denison House in Boston, headed by Scudder's close friend Helena Dudley, and by Mary Kenny, who married Jack O'Sullivan, an active local AF of L organizer, she found fellowship and feelings enough. There she partied, sang songs and chanted poems (a favorite was William Morris's "Chants for Socialists"), redecorated the old tenement that served as the settlement, and taught literature to working girls. There she was able, temporarily, to escape from her "class prison," as she called it. She admitted, however, that she found it easier to love the adults, for she was not very good with boys and small children: "they scared me and I bored them." She established a Social Science Club in which businessmen, students, and workers discussed such topics as trade unionism and socialism. Attendance reached forty to fifty in the beginning but soon dwindled, and the club collapsed within three years. A few years later she shifted her efforts to newly arrived Italian immigrants. Unlike many settlement workers who insisted on teaching English to immigrants and who refused to communicate in native languages, Scudder learned Italian in order to maintain fellowship with the Italian peasants who increasingly frequented Denison House after the turn of the century. But her class prison extended even to Denison House, for she had difficulty relating to lower-class immigrants. Her Italian, she was told, often sounded more like Latin. She therefore set up a Circolo Italo-Americano, a carefully selected club intended to appeal to intellectuals and professional classes. Meetings were held in Italian and usually featured lectures or debates and music. One debate, between socialists and anarchists, turned into a near-riot and was broken up only by tear gas.[19]

Her activities at Denison House were not confined to clubs and debates; they also included direct contact with the struggles of the labor movement. In the mid-1890s, during the difficult depression years, the settlement became at times a strike center for union meetings, picket-organizing, and placard-making. Vida Scudder and Helena Dudley were appointed delegates to the Central Labor Union in Boston, where they attended meetings and were "suffocated by smoke" and subjected to "interminable speeches." At the meetings, she thoroughly absorbed the immediate needs and realities of the class struggle. "Here was escape from cool academic atmosphere!" She even invited Jack O'Sullivan to Wellesley to speak to younger faculty members. He tried to organize them into a teachers' union, however, and Scudder's colleagues were outraged. The work of the women at Denison House, she recalled, "incurred horrified criticism from our patrons uptown."[20]

Scudder's involvement at the settlement house prevented her

from completing work on her doctorate. In 1893 she had taken a two-year leave of absence from Wellesley in order to finish her work, but spent the time instead at Denison House. Scudder's failure to finish her degree condemned her, she wrote, to a subordinate place in the academic world, a fitting sacrifice: "I deliberately renounced personal ambition. . . . What I cared for was to keep my students as well as myself in the presence of significant racial experience." Through the settlement house and her courses she was able to provide her students (and herself) both with the ideas of liberal culture and with direct experiential learning—and, with both, the impetus to remake the world. "To permeate the middle class with conviction that the social order in which its members moved tranquil and prosperous, should be intolerable to any decent person—such was the end to which I was devoted. Residence among the workers seemed to me the best means to that end."[21] Moreover, her absorption with the settlement houses and strike activities partly resolved one of her personal quests. By working with the poor, she was able to fulfill, to some degree, her Tolstoyan compulsion to renounce comfort and her Ruskinian desire to share beauty with the underprivileged. Her quest for self-fulfillment through the college settlement house was portrayed in a thinly disguised and somewhat sentimental autobiographical novel, *A Listener in Babel*, published in 1903. The protagonist was a young girl, Hilda Lathrop, who, like Ruskin and Vida Scudder herself, changed from a student of art to a student of society.

As a sensitive, lonely young woman, Hilda longed for both artistic beauty and social justice. Her youth was spent in Europe and at a women's college in the United States where she learned that "individuals can be [as] exciting as cathedrals." Her self-sacrificing compulsions were demonstrated by giving up an eligible socialist suitor she had met in England to a friend. In deciding whether to teach art in a college (the "Voice of Learning") or to work in a settlement (the "Voice of Justice"), she chose the settlement, but only after a visit to the shrines of Assisi. Her explanation of this decision to a disapproving mother noted that "of course I shall miss beauty, but I shall find significance." At the settlement Hilda was a listener, searching for the key to the social problem. Through her life paraded philanthropists, clergymen, educators, anarchists, labor leaders, and socialists; none, however, provided her with an answer. She was soon disillusioned, finding little in the reform movement "but opiates that deaden sensation and quicken disease." Each potential instrument for reform—the church, the university, democracy itself—was found sorely wanting. Her faith in democracy was revived, however, by the friendship of two Irish working girls. "Have you found God?" a friend asked. " 'I dare not say that,' responded Hilda, 'any more than I dare deny it. But I have found Katie Donovan.' " Ultimately, the solution chosen by Hilda was a blend of Tolstoyan and Ruskinian principles. She left the relative comfort of the settlement to work at a trade with Katie Donovan, while at the same time continuing her art studies in order to spread the beauty of art and handicrafts to other working girls. She was, she admitted, "in part a disciple of Tolstoy." She believed that "the intellectual classes, so-called, will never be healthy again until they return to a more natural life, including some productive labor with their hands." And like Ruskin, she believed that although "life without industry is guilt; industry without art is brutality."[22]

Hilda Lathrop made all the decisions which Vida Scudder did not make. She chose the settlement, not the college. She disobeyed her mother's wishes. She resigned from a temporary job in a People's University because of a "tainted money" gift from a Rockefeller-like millionaire. She chose working girls for fellowship instead of settlement house colleagues. And finally, she renounced material comforts in order to work with her hands in industry. In her own life Scudder was unable to make such sacrifices, and her guilt over the inability to live permanently at Denison House was bitter to her. A self-conscious shyness, she explained, "inhibiting personal contacts, except when I faced my college classes," as well as a responsibility to care for her widowed mother, prevented her from leaving the college for the settlement.[23] Thus she compromised, working in the settlements during vacations and teaching social ideals in her courses.

Scudder attempted to rationalize her compromises through a paradoxical blend of common sense and utopian thinking. In 1898 in "Christian Simplicity," she wrote that beyond the duty of helping the poor lies the attractive ideal of complete surrender, of total rejection of the world for the world's sake. Only a few individuals, she said, were capable of such a martyrdom. For most persons, however, there was no need for such dramatic renunciations. Rather, if all ordinary people in their daily lives were to strive toward greater simplicity and a modest renunciation of worldly things, "Christianity would at once gain a new force of actuality in the minds of men." At the same time, she approved the experiment in Christian simplicity, love, and brotherhood going on at the utopian Christian Commonwealth colony in Georgia. In a letter to the editors of *Social Gospel*, the colony's official organ, she wrote that "many of us are watching you wistfully and lovingly. . . . I see more and more clearly that the difficulty is not to state the truth, but to make it operative." A few months later she wrote again to explain that she could not join them, for she belonged "to that inferior and outer circle . . . of persons who . . . still seem entangled in the present state of things by many threads of private duty."[24] Vida Scudder was unable to renounce her comfortable life to live in either a settlement or a utopian community. Like Bliss and Flower, this was not her role in the social movement; she was primarily an intellectual, an advocate, a synthesizer, not an active participant. Her personal quest for harmony she could never resolve: her intellectual quests, she might.

The third path in her search led to organizations and to the resolving of their doctrinal conflicts. She joined groups which would provide her with needed fellowship while at the same time affording her an opportunity to work toward remaking the social order according to both Christian and socialist principles. The solution offered by most of these organizations was socialism, and the tactics she preferred were at first educational, and later political. Among others, she joined the Society of Companions of the Holy Cross (a group of Episcopal women who prayed for reform), the Church Association for the Advancement of the Interests of Labor, the Society of Christian Socialists, the Christian Social Union, the Intercollegiate Socialist Society, the Women's International League of Peace and Freedom, the Church Socialist League, and the Church League for Industrial Democracy, of which she was president. With Mary Kenny O'Sullivan, Jane Addams, Lillian Wald, and others, she helped to organize the National Women's Trade Union League in 1903. In her autobiography she recalled, in fact, belonging to "fifty-nine dues-paying societies bent on reform."[25]

In a sense, Scudder's lifelong quest for unity was a gradual movement toward joining the Socialist party, which she finally did in 1911. Her self-appointed role within the party was, as in the settlement, not that of an activist but rather that of a doctrinal synthesizer. If she were to embrace socialism, it would have to be the sort by which she could reconcile the economic determinism of socialism with the spiritual, Christian aspects of her life. She wrote to Rauschenbusch in 1912, imploring him to join the party and indicating the kind of socialism she preferred. "I never regret having joined the Socialist party. I am sure that it is immensely important for people of our type to be *within* the political movement, both in order to preserve it so far as possible from that hard dogmatism of which you speak (& it *can* be preserved if sufficient numbers of persons with religious tradition get into it) *and* to vindicate the honor of Christianity." A year later she argued in *The Intercollegiate Socialist* that "a gap yawns wide" between "the theorists and the fighters." It was the responsibility of socialist theorists like herself, she argued, to bridge the gap and join the party to save it from the hard dogmatism she referred to in her letter to Rauschenbusch.[26]

In an English journal in 1909 she argued that a moral preparation for socialism was imperative. If the socialist state were achieved without having been preceded by a spiritual transformation of individuals, many persons, she said, would resent the loss of their individuality, turn to violence, and destroy the state at its inception. By moral preparation, she meant the individual's willingness to sacrifice himself for the whole society. She argued that individuality would in fact be enlarged under socialism, but only if the denial of self were imposed from within, not externally coerced. "Social welfare is a wider term than personal liberty; but it includes that liberty. . . . The fruit of inner liberty is ever obedience to law. Only he possesses who refrains, and the way of renunciation is always the way of freedom." Moreover, she said, spirituality as well as liberty would be enhanced under socialism. The new religious spirit would not be a contemplative one, as in the East, but would be an active one of each working for all. Religious life, in fact, would be liberated because "if there be a God, the socialist state will offer Him a better opportunity than we of the Western world have ever given Him before to draw the hearts of men upward to

Himself." These were difficult ideas to accept, especially for a hardened socialist, and in 1912 she expanded them into a book, *Socialism and Character*. Its purpose, as she wrote to Rauschenbusch, was "to break down the barriers between the socialist world and the religious world, and show each its need of the other, by presenting the affiliations between them."[27]

Vida Scudder was able to reconcile socialism and spirituality, to herself if not to others. She still had, however, to effect a unity between her old Tolstoyan and Ruskinian idealism and her increasing acceptance of the factual realities of economic socialism. In an article in 1910 she contrasted the ideas of Mazzini and Bakunin, as they expressed them in a conversation on socialism in 1871. Mazzini preached an idealistic, religious, anticlass warfare, moral, evolutionary socialism, she said, while Bakunin urged a socialism that was realistic, economic, deterministic, distinctly class-conscious, amoral, and revolutionary. One might expect Scudder's sympathies to lie with Mazzini, as would Flower's; this, however, was not the case. She noted that although Mazzini had many disciples "by virtue of his exalted ideas and magnetic personality," he "lived and died alone" and founded no tradition. With Mazzini, she wrote, "we are dealing with a glorious nature in unstable equilibrium: treading too often, not the *terra firma* of the actual, but a tight-rope gossamer spun spiderlike from within. Here is a great man; here is no founder of a great or living school." Where he had failed, his opponents, Bakunin and Marx, had succeeded. Marx's ideas, shorn of Mazzini's lofty idealism, were the ideas which Scudder observed among the working classes, a point that Flower never saw. She found that even her youthful inspiration, Ruskin, was guilty of this hopeless idealism. He wavered "between fact and dream" and many of his "obstinate theories" had to be laid aside. "Our idealists are too often ideologists," she wrote, and their approach was futile and ineffective. "Listen to the pleadings of Hugo, Carlyle, Tolstoi, Ruskin,—tragic voices uttering a summons that few indeed follow and that when obeyed leads too often to no country of social salvation, but to solitary and erratic paths, where personal satisfaction may perhaps be won, but where social utility, in the broader sense, is wholly dubious." Therefore, it was time, she said, to turn away from the idealists and study the scientific, economic determinists, who realistically understood social conditions. "Tolstoi, Ruskin, and the others are on the wrong tack. . . . Close these gentlemen! Open your Engels, your Jaurès, your Bebel; and realize with refreshment and repose that here at last we are in the presence of minds free from sentimentality, and at grip with the actual facts of social progress." Admittedly, she said, economic determinism, labor theory of value, and class warfare were not very pleasant things to consider; but they had the future on their side.[28]

When it seemed that the economic determinists had won her mind, Scudder asserted that the idealists still held a place in her heart. "We may not say that the exponents of idealism are routed. The accents of Carlyle, of Victor Hugo, of Ruskin, of Tolstoi, still echo down the decades." Rather than excluding one or the other of these two sides, she advised blending mysticism with economic determinism. The idealists, she wrote, needed the determinists' practicality, economic clarifications, and understanding of the workers; the determinists needed the idealists' lofty expressions and exemplifications of purpose and will. The spiritual consciousness of the idealists was "the final blossoming of material and economic life." If this spirit were cut, the "growth shall perish from the earth. But let the Mazzinis, the Ruskins of the future," she said, "look to it that their blossoming be rooted in the soil of economic reality, and the day of rich harvestings shall be sped."[29] Thus, she sought to effect a doctrinal unity which would give the Socialist party she had joined a spiritual, idealistic thrust to complement its economic realism.

Theory was confirmed by experience which, after all, "is better than theory." As Vida Scudder looked back in her autobiography to the idealism of her activist days, and to the countless organizations and "groups of earnest well-to-do theorists" she had associated with, she could not recall "a genuine working-man" ever joining them. Her old "comrades . . . lacked actuality. Utopists all." But in the early labor movement, in which she had also played a limited part, she recalled "grimly practical" leaders grappling not with theory but with daily struggles for survival. "No lack of actuality there." But also, alas, no vision. What was needed was fusion of the two groups. But under whose leadership? She was not quite sure. Her instincts told her that "direct proletarian leadership is bound to increase, and I welcome it." But she wanted her revolutionary leaders "from the educated strata," such as Lenin and Norman Thomas. She therefore approved of "all the young intellectuals who are pressing into the communist ranks," and especially admired labor leaders like a British workingman she had met who had the works of Ruskin on his shelves and a young Italian immigrant working in a rubber factory in Boston who could recite from memory portions of Mazzini's *Duties of Man.* To leaders like this, who combined proletarian roots and experiences with intellectual idealism, sympathetic middle-class intellectuals "should be wholesomely ready for a subordinate role."[30]

Scudder's analysis achieved a balanced synthesis and degree of realism far beyond that ever achieved by either Flower or Bliss. The reason for this, apart from her greater intellectual sophistication, was precisely in her closer relationships and wider contacts —limited as they were—with the working class, which gave her a more concrete understanding of their needs. She spent her time and energies not only in lecture halls, editors' offices, and churches, but also in union halls, strike meetings, and settlement houses. She understood that "middle-class radicalism needed to be purged of its Utopian ideology . . . [and] the taint of condescension."[31] She did not, therefore, have an undiluted faith in the effectiveness of study groups and in the regenerative influence of unrestrained and indiscriminate propagation of the ideals of European social prophets. She even outgrew Ruskin to some extent, but still remained as limited by her middle-class origins and intellectual temperament as were Bliss and Flower. Her most significant difference from them, however, was the degree to which she was aware of these limitations. But this, of course, is what caused her self-doubts. If she cloistered herself at Wellesley she felt guilty because she was not doing enough of God's work. When she left Wellesley for Denison House, she felt personally bitter because she was unable to live there permanently. Given these persistent "stabbing pains," she turned more and more, in later years, to her attempt to promote unity between ethical idealists (the church) and economic realities (the Socialist party).

It was one thing to promote doctrinal marriages, however, but quite another to see them consummated. The outbreak of World War I was a staggering blow to those in the radical movement. Theoretical arguments over the economic and spiritual qualities of socialism gave way to questions of patriotism, pacifism, and sedition. Tolstoy and the New Testament had led Scudder to pacifism in matters of personal nonresistance to evil, but she nevertheless believed that Christian nations had a "duty to defend the weak, and to fight in a righteous cause." She distrusted Wilson's idealistic proclamations as a mirage, but did not regret the American decision to enter the war in 1917. The pacifists erred, she said, in not connecting their opposition to war to the social and economic forces which bred wars. "The days of war will never be ended till war is seen not as an isolated phenomenon, but as part of the whole system of human relations gone wrong." She tried during the war to rally the disintegrating unity and sagging hopes of socialists, but her arguments against pacifism and for a "less materialized . . . less formula-ridden" postwar socialism compromised her influence with other radical theoreticians.[32]

She was also becoming increasingly more interested in the church than in socialism, which hardly helped her influence in socialist circles. In 1917 she put together a collection of essays and speeches from the period between 1913 and 1917, titled *The Church and the Hour* and subtitled "Reflections of a Socialist Churchwoman." The introduction to the volume indicated that she hoped "to promote better understanding between the religious world which fears social revolution, and the unchurched world of radical passion which desires it." But the essays and speeches that followed clearly revealed that she was speaking as a churchwoman to the religious world and not as a socialist to the world of radicals. The titles alone indicated her emphasis: "Why Does Not the Church Turn Socialist?" (because it was false to its master and its own socialist origins), "The Alleged Failure of the Church to Meet the Social Emergency" (the word alleged, she said, was ironic; she argued, as she did in all these essays, that the church had more to do to promote industrial democracy than it was doing), and "The Church's Opportunity" (for material renunciation and active support of the dispossessed). In one selection, "Two Letters to 'The Masses,'" written in the winter of 1915–1916, she objected vehemently but tactfully to *The Masses*' cynical, iconoclastic contempt for Christian dogma. But on the whole her efforts were clearly aimed at awakening the churches to an awareness that "social action becomes the swift correlative of spiritual vision." And she gave them a heavy dose, too, endorsing not only the Social Creed adopted by the Federal Council of Churches in 1912, which advocated many social-justice and rights-of-workers measures, but also social revolution and the abolition of private profit. She ended the book, however, with "a plea for social intercession," that is, prayer as a cure-all for reconciling classes, for uniting the church and the unchurched, and for achieving social justice. The purpose of prayer, she added, was not to elicit a response from God, but to purify oneself.[33]

Vida Scudder's conclusion to her reflections was a highly personalized and private one. None of her efforts was succeeding. In her attempt to reconcile and unify the churches and the socialist movement, she ended up only isolating herself from both. More and more, she said, she had "a desperate and tragic sense of playing a lone hand." In 1917 she predicted with remarkable accuracy the loss of liberties and political reaction of postwar America, but she did little to protest the antiradical hysteria that followed the war. She was uncharacteristically quiet during the crises of 1919 and, with the death of her mother in 1920, she went off to Europe for a year's vacation.[34]

Although her home in Wellesley continued to be a meeting place for Boston radicals during the 1920s, Scudder increasingly withdrew to her own intellectual preoccupation with what she called the "Christian Apocalyptic . . . element in Marxist philosophy." She worshiped privately at an altar in her home consisting of the red flag "placed beside the Crucifix" and, as she said, was "doing my best to align a catastrophic and dialectical conception of history with my Christian thinking." In the communist revolution she saw a divine judgment as a sign of an approaching redemption. She decided, however, that it was impossible for her to join the communists in America, not because she disapproved of their atheism, but because they would object to her religion. In a mystical book written in 1921, the *Social Teachings of the Christian Year*, she interpreted the social implications of the various seasons on the Christian calendar, complete with meditative social readings from the *Book of Common Prayer* for each season. She had, by this time, totally shifted her emphasis from making Christians out of socialists to making socialists out of Christians. But this attempt at unity served her quest no better than earlier efforts. In 1937 she wrote with sadness that "the separation between the Church of

Christ and the forces making for a new social order is to me the supreme tragedy in the modern world." This failure of unity constituted "the central sorrow of my life."[35]

Scudder could not effect the fruition of the intellectual synthesis of which she dreamed, nor could she resolve her personal dilemma between ascetic medievalism and social utopianism. Much of her work after she left Wellesley in 1927 was devoted to the Episcopal church and to studies of medieval Franciscans. Her interests in these later years leaned toward the past rather than to the present or future and looked within rather than without. "I am keen as ever on the struggle," she wrote in 1937, "though my part in it must be largely inward now." Her role was not entirely inward. Ten years later, at the age of eighty-six, Scudder contributed a chapter on "Anglican Thought in Property" to a volume dedicated to her by seven other contributors. The dedication pointed out that the seven had "conspired" against her, for "Vida Dutton Scudder's humility would never let her consent to this dedication: to her." It went on to acknowledge her enormous influence on them all, as well as on "hosts of her former students," who "brighten when her name is mentioned." She refused to rest on her well-deserved praise. At the age of ninety-one, two years before her death in 1954, she wrote another autobiography, *My Quest for Reality*, arguing in it that religious concern was not an evasion of but a commitment to social responsibility.[36]

Although Scudder was not primarily a feminist ideologically, her experiences as a woman gave her a perspective and insight that helped synthesize the varied strands of her life. Curiously, not once in *On Journey* did she refer to the struggle for the suffrage in the years from 1890 to 1920, a period that directly paralleled her own activist years. Although she was sensitive and committed to feminist issues, her goal for a restructured social order in America demanded much more than the vote for women. Socially, she and her settlement house friends zealously organized women workers, helping to found the Women's Trade Union League and supporting women strikers at Lawrence and elsewhere. It may have been teachers like Vida Scudder who prompted a fellow New Englander, Calvin Coolidge, to comment that women's colleges were "hotbeds of radicalism." Professionally, Scudder's main energies for over half a century were dedicated to the higher education of women.

She attended Smith and taught at Wellesley in an era when such colleges were new and widely challenged. She knew, however, that the opportunities, both social and psychological, afforded women by these colleges was stimulating a "transformation of status, actual and prospective, which is no less than epoch-making."[37] Her own status, indeed, had been transformed by them.

Vida Scudder never married; in fact, according to her autobiography, she never loved or had sexual relations with a man. Contrary to the popular thought inspired by Freud, she wrote, "Sex is not the only clue to human behavior; I am not even sure it is the chief." She believed that her independence and chastity were more opportunity than deprivation. Rather than bemoaning her single status, she was thankful that she had not married, for "how much it would have excluded!" Marriage, she observed, "looks to me often . . . terribly impoverished, for women." Although she confessed to a desire to fall in love (as opposed to being loved) before she was thirty, she was convinced "that a woman's life which sex interests have never visited, is a life neither dull nor empty nor devoid of romance . . . and significant personal relations." Her many female friendships were intense and close, tied together by the bonds of mutual struggles, "shoulder to shoulder, in a world always misunderstanding and often hostile." It was difficult enough to preserve one's solitude and identity in friendship with women. But in marriage, she noted, the "insidious lust for power" and possessiveness that was often confused with love all too frequently poisoned the relationship and destroyed individual identity. Unlike friendship, marriage sought complete union, which was both impossible and undesirable. "Too great straining after identity mistaken for unity destroys that air of liberty in which alone love can breathe." Her liberty and her love were more precious in the search for other kinds of unity. Francis and Catherine of Siena, whom she called "the prototype of all modern women idealists," had taught her that much![38]

Except for her own confessions of an inferiority complex and fear of rejection ("nobody I do not love can hurt me much"), there is no reason to believe that Vida Scudder was either rationalizing or deluding herself. Her attitudes toward sex and marriage were thoroughly consistent with her larger philosophy and lifelong quests. She had read Marx and Engels and had observed many marriages; she therefore understood that the acquisitive and proprietary instinct inherent in marital life was the equivalent of the drive for private property and material accumulations in economic life. Possessiveness in personal relations, in fact, was far more dangerous. Therefore, in both the conjugal and commercial worlds, she said, it "must be exiled, must be slain." Furthermore, consistent with her socialist aspirations, she believed that when society had progressed to an age of the cooperative commonwealth ("one big family"), the generations of training women as household managers, however misguided, would make them more valued and necessary in the management of civic life.[39] Scudder's quest for harmony between socialism and Christianity, and between social activism and contemplative solitude, was challenge enough for one lifetime. She did not need the false and demeaning unity or probable frustrated fulfillments of marriage. Her life had too much meaning for that.

If she was satisfied with choices made about her personal life, how did Vida Scudder see her life as an intellectual reformer? At the end of *On Journey* she recalled her career as a mixture of occasional accomplishments and frequent frustrations—but in sum, a life of "defeat." As she thought back to her youthful aspirations and dreams, "waves of sadness" swept over her. The Wellesley years were especially disheartening. The old stabbing pain of guilt arose again as she recalled "sending young people out into difficulties and tests which I seldom shared, remaining, as I did, in shelter while they met the storm." Teaching and writing had provided some gratification, to be sure, but she confessed that interpreting other lives was not as fulfilling as living a fuller life herself. "Was it not my fate, always to live at second hand?" She was far more bitter, however, when she took stock of the defeat of the causes she had tried to serve, a fate she shared with all idealists. From the vantage point of 1937, she saw Western civilization in crisis, brought near to catastrophe by greed, hate, industrial warfare, and rampant international militarism. Although she bemoaned the frustrations, she acknowledged, with pained irony, that she would "find it harder to realize inner unity with the forces that redeem the world" than with those that led to fulfillment. Indeed, "denial" and renunciation, she concluded, provided the "leitmotif" of her life. And in failure she found, at last, the reality of her existence that had long eluded her.[40]

Scudder's honest and illuminating self-appraisal was excessively self-disparaging. She was entirely conscious of her limitations as an intellectual reformer and freely admitted them. She was not an activist like her friend Mary Kenny O'Sullivan, nor was she capable of acts of renunciation like her fictional alter ego, Hilda Lathrop. Recognizing this (not without guilt) she worked for social change in the milieu she knew and did best: teaching Wellesley students, speaking to the church, and working out a spiritual-material synthesis of socialism—which is precisely what she should have done.

Back in 1890, in the introduction to her book on Ruskin, she had said of him that "the best results of his life are written in the souls he has awakened to the love of beauty and the vision of the right." Such were the fruits of her life as well. She estimated in 1937 that she had taught between two and three thousand young women, many of whom, according to Jessie Bernard, "took her idealism home with them and filled countless voluntary and civic organizations with it." It is doubtful that these efforts radically transformed the social order. But Scudder's influence in changing consciousness was undeniable. "When you touch her," one student said, "sparks fly," igniting students who, in turn, "inflame hundreds of communities with sparks from that torch." Henry Adams once said that one can never tell where a teacher's influence will stop. Scudder understood this with characteristic humility and sadness. "When disciples have gathered around me, as they have done, when my words have been quoted as expressions of faith which all crave and few possess, when I have been most dogmatic and most seemingly assured—then all Thy waves and Thy billows have gone over me, and I have struggled vainly toward the shore." The context of this metaphor was a recurring dream, prompted, she thought, by her father's death by drowning. In the dream she struggles against the waves, groping for the shore, only finally to "Accept, surrender! I sink into those green deep waters" to find peace and contentment. "That dream," she wrote, "has come to me at intervals all my life. I don't know what it means. But reality is in it."[41] Indeed.

Vida Scudder's dream reveals a profound understanding of the subtle tension between a reformer's momentary successes within the context of ultimate failure. What is important for Scudder, as for Camus's Sisyphus, is the struggle against the waves, or the rock, knowing that, in the end, one will fail. Unlike Bliss and Flower, and many other intellectual would-be reformers as well,

Scudder did not delude herself into believing that words alone would bring about the changes she sought. Moreover, unlike Howells, she matched her words with deeds: not just changing the consciousness of her students, but also building settlement houses, organizing trade unions, and participating in strikes. Given where she had started from, her life was a humane and noble one, as true to the dictates of her conscience as was humanly possible. She apparently forgot the aphorism prefacing the chapter in her autobiography on "Adventures in Pedagogy," in which she quoted Matthew Arnold: "We experience, as we go on learning and knowing, the need of relating what we have learnt and known to the sense which we have in us for conduct, to the sense which we have in us for beauty."[42] If at times she was too harsh on herself for violating her own high standards of conduct, she never violated Arnold's precept. Self-deprecation and denial was her fate, but the quest for right conduct and for beauty was her triumph over fate. No matter the inevitable failures. What finer challenge is there than for a teacher to realize in one's conduct the injunctions of one's study, especially if that study has been of moral prophets such as Ruskin and Tolstoy—or of Vida Scudder herself?

5

THE KINGDOM OF HEAVEN ON EARTH: WALTER RAUSCHENBUSCH AND GEORGE HERRON

O Christ, thou hast bidden us pray for the coming of thy Father's kingdom, in which his righteous will shall be done on earth. We have treasured thy words, but we have forgotten their meaning.

RAUSCHENBUSCH *

I will arise and be the brother that I am—
The brother that I was before Moses or Jesus spake;
The brother that I was before St. Francis or Mazzini came;
The brother that I was before the Socialist went unknowingly
preparing the way of the Lord.

HERRON †

WHILE W. D. P. Bliss and Vida Scudder were feasting on ham, pickles, and dreams of the Christian revolution in 1890, two young men saw signs that the revolution had already begun. Walter Rauschenbusch, speaking before a Baptist conference in Toronto in 1889, cited Mazzini's assertion that the French Revolution emphasis on rights rather than duties marked the end, not the beginning of an age, and proclaimed the beginning of a new era. The age of selfish individualism, Rauschenbusch argued, was over. "We have come now to the era of cooperation and association, and all these attempts at combining and associating which we see about us in every sphere of life are only humanity's blind gropings and its feeling through the dark towards the goal which Christ Himself has pointed out to us," a goal which Rauschenbusch understood to be the kingdom of heaven on earth. A year later George Herron proclaimed that the kingdom was "at hand," as manifested by the unrest evident throughout the land. Similarly indebted to Mazzini, Herron urged that the achievement of industrial freedom by cooperation and association depended upon taking a stand on "the platform of duties, and not that of rights."[1] Both men applied Mazzini's vision of the brotherhood of men to the Christian prophecy of a kingdom of heaven on earth; both sought to awaken a sinful nation to that imminent hope and to lead it into the new era. Rauschenbusch later came to believe that he had largely achieved his goal; Herron was never able to hold such a belief.

Bliss and Flower were journalists and organizers; Herron and Rauschenbusch were, by profession, ministers and educators, and their impact, such as it was, flowed from these roles. Beginning with his well-known and widely read "Message of Jesus to Men of Wealth," delivered first in 1890 before the Minnesota Congregational Club, Herron stirred up innumerable controversies as he stumped the nation for the coming Christian socialist revolution. Rauschenbusch, a more temperate man, was unquestionably the most successful Social Gospel clergyman in influencing other progressive middle-class religious leaders. Among scores of others, Harry Emerson Fosdick, Norman Thomas, Reinhold Niebuhr, and Martin Luther King, Jr., all acknowledged their intellectual debt to Rauschenbusch. In 1909 Ray Stannard Baker toured the country asking clergymen what recent book had best illuminated social questions for them. "By all odds," he reported, "the book most frequently mentioned" was Rauschenbusch's *Christianity and the Social Crisis*.[2] The title is significant: Rauschenbusch and Herron, like B. O. Flower, assumed that the socioeconomic and spiritual crises at the *fin de siècle* indicated the imminence of a new social order, which they equated with the kingdom of heaven. Yet as their careers progressed, they differed in the degree to which they believed the kingdom was attainable in the United States. After an initial account of the similarities of their religious and social thought, this chapter tells how two Social Gospel clergymen responded to similar intellectual influences and espoused almost identical creeds, yet moved in opposite ideological directions. The reasons for their divergence are many, but of primary significance is the effect of an intellectual's personal and professional life on the quality of his beliefs and behavior as a reformer.

Rauschenbusch and Herron were born within four months of each other, Rauschenbusch in October 1861 in Rochester, New York, and Herron in January 1862 in Montezuma, Indiana. Rauschenbusch's father, a German-born immigrant to the United States in 1846, taught church history at the Rochester Theological Seminary for over thirty years. A converted Baptist, he was a sixth-generation minister in the family (the first five had been Lutherans). Herron's father came from a long line of devout dissenters dating back to the Scottish Reformation; he was an evangelical Presbyterian minister and stern disciplinarian. Rauschenbusch's formal education was spent alternately in Germany and the United States, culminating with an A.B. at the University of Rochester in 1884 and a divinity degree from his father's seminary in 1886. At Rochester he acquired sound disciplined training in orthodox Christian theology.

Herron grew up in poverty, and his schooling was irregular. From the ages of ten to seventeen he worked as a printer and followed a course of reading prescribed by his father. In 1879 he attended Ripon Preparatory Academy in Wisconsin, but dropped out in 1881 due to lack of finances and ill health. He edited newspapers in Wisconsin for two years, married the daughter of the mayor of Ripon, and in 1883, while working again as a printer in Saint Paul, Minnesota, resolved to enter the ministry. Entirely self-trained in theology, he was given a doctor of divinity degree by an Iowa Congregational school, Tabor College, after speaking there in 1892.

Rauschenbusch's first church position was as a summer replacement in a small German Baptist church in Louisville, Kentucky, in 1884 and 1885. On June 1, 1886, he was called to the Second German Baptist Church on the edge of the infamous Hell's Kitchen area of New York's West Side. He remained there until 1897, when he returned to Rochester to inherit his father's chair and become a professor of church history. Herron held small Congregational pastorates in various villages in the Dakota Territory, Ohio, Wisconsin, and Minnesota in the late 1880s. His first major church position was as associate pastor to the retiring Reverend William Salter at the First Congregational Church in Burlington, Iowa in 1891. In September 1893 he was appointed to the richly endowed E. D. Rand Chair of Applied Christianity at Iowa College in Grinnell, where he remained until his sensational resignation in 1899.[3]

Both Rauschenbusch and Herron began as evangelical ministers with conservative theologies, seeking to convert individual souls to Jesus Christ. But by a combination of experience and reflective study in the late 1880s, both soon developed a position best defined as Christian socialism. Rauschenbusch joined Bliss's New York branch of the Society of Christian Socialists in 1889; a year later Herron became the first Minnesota member of the society. Herron had known poverty personally throughout his early life; Rauschenbusch witnessed poverty and urban suffering in New York City during the depression years of the 1890s. The primary ideological source of their Christian social beliefs was the New Testament. Each was inspired in his study of the gospel by Tolstoy's literal interpretation, especially by his injunction of self-renunciation to men of wealth. They also were influenced by their study of Francis of Assisi, F. D. Maurice, Henry George, and Edward Bellamy, all of whom they were both reading in the late 1880s. The deepest and most sustained inspiration on them both, however, was Mazzini.

As a consequence of these experiential and ideological influences, both Herron and Rauschenbusch believed that the United States was in the midst of a social crisis in which the business and commercial classes, allied with a misdirected and errant Protestant church, were arrayed against all other classes. A small minority of church leaders alone understood the true meaning of the social teachings of Jesus. This minority had a special responsibility to reform the church so that it could fulfill its appointed mission and lead the struggle against mammonism. "If the Church cannot conquer business," Rauschenbusch wrote, "business will conquer the Church." The church and the money power, he said in 1893, should be as irreconcilably opposed to each other as God and the world. The most important chapter in *Christianity and the Social Crisis*, he thought, was one in which he showed historically how the loss of the original social teachings of Jesus since his crucifixion had prevented the church from undertaking the work of social reconstruction. He was certain, however, that by 1907 the church was "fitter for its social mission than ever before." Herron also believed, as he said in 1895, that the church had forgotten the message of the cross and the Sermon on the Mount and had become part of the world in its worship of mammonism. "The existing order has already served over-time," he wrote, and predicted that a "revolution of some sort is not far off." He was, as he said, a pessimist about the church but an optimist in his expectations for the coming of the kingdom. He believed that a single generation of Christians could revitalize civilization.[4] Unlike Rauschenbusch, Herron's confidence that social regeneration would emanate from the churches diminished with the years.

Most of Herron's and Rauschenbusch's writings and preaching were concerned first with a social interpretation of the teachings of Jesus; second, with the responsibility of the church to preach the Social Gospel; and third, with the application of the gospel to the institutions of an unregenerate yet redeemable society. "*To reform society*," Herron wrote, "*is to Christ-form it*." For both men, the message of Jesus dictated that human institutions, presently individualistic, would become collectivized. The church's duty, Herron wrote, was to achieve "the Christianizing of industry, the gospelizing of commerce, [and] the moral enforcement of the Sermon on the Mount." The basic principles of Jesus' life and gospel were self-sacrifice and cooperation. First, men must be converted to the message of the cross, thereby solving social problems by being disciples, usually requiring acts of self-renunciation. Second, "*human institutions must be gospelized. . . .* The principle of Christ's life must be the principle of the market, the social room, the gas company, the college, the kitchen, the locomotive, the bed room." Many thought, as we shall see, that he applied the doctrine of collectivism to the bedroom too literally. He believed, nevertheless, that the need for "gospelizing" institutions (which, as his career progressed, increasingly meant by socializing them) was both imperative and immediate.[5]

Rauschenbusch's analysis was similar. The American social order, he said, was full of unregenerate sections, particularly the business segment, which was the source of current troubles. It was clear that business (i.e., capitalism) was not a passive force, but one that actively threatened to subdue those portions of the social order already "christianized." Capitalism split mankind, resisted the worker's struggle for freedom and dignity, created inequalities, and stifled love. Christianity, on the other hand, created unity and solidarity, promoted freedom for labor, and bred equality, dignity, and love. Rauschenbusch was convinced that "the Father of Jesus Christ does not stand for the permanence of the capitalistic system." He therefore recommended christianizing the social order, which meant bringing those unregenerate portions "into harmony with the ethical convictions which we identify with Christ."[6] To christianize, for Rauschenbusch, was to humanize, to democratize, and to socialize. For both men, the burden of responsibility for social change was on a few Christian intellectuals who, by words, would show others the compelling need for a new social order.

This message of Herron and Rauschenbusch was reiterated in many books and articles throughout the period from 1890 to World War I. Herron's most influential and productive period of speaking and writing occurred in the 1890s, while still a young man. He published nine volumes of collected sermons and lectures between 1891 and 1899. Rauschenbusch was more patient and let his ideas germinate for several years before publishing them as *Christianity and the Social Crisis* in 1907. Six other volumes followed in the next ten years. Their ideological divergence came in the last three years of the century, when Rauschenbusch left the ministry for seminary teaching and Herron left teaching for politicking. Significant personal and professional events caused their ideological paths, which up to then had been remarkably similar, to diverge. Curiously, at no time—not even during the mid-1890s—did they ever meet each other.

Walter Rauschenbusch

When Rauschenbusch arrived in New York in 1886, he had little concern for socioeconomic questions. His formal theological training had taught him that the minister's primary responsibility was to save individual souls. Then he began to work in New York, where his social education began. Admitting that he "had had no social outlook before," he understood for the first time the connection between religious and social questions. Social work and Christian work became synonymous for the young minister.[7] While serving the poor near Hell's Kitchen, he saw men toiling long hours for starvation wages and women suffering under the burdens of poverty. He was frequently called upon to hold funeral services for children who had died of malnutrition or disease in the tenements. During the great blizzard of 1888, while recovering from epidemic influenza, he left his sickbed to minister to his suffering parishioners, the result of which was damage to his hearing which worsened throughout his life.

Rauschenbusch's reading confirmed his experiences. During this period he read *Progress and Poverty* and witnessed Henry George's mayoralty campaign in 1886. His first paper on a topic other than religion was written on George in 1887, in which he concluded: "there is a social question. No one can doubt it, in whose ears are ringing the wails of the mangled and the crushed, who are borne along on the pent-up torrent of human life." Years later he wrote that he owed his "first awakening to the world of social problems to the agitation of Henry George in 1886, and wish here to record my lifelong debt to this single-minded apostle of a great truth." Rauschenbusch's social concern was intensified by reading Edward Bellamy's *Looking Backward* in 1888. He especially admired Bellamy's Christian spirit and vision and became increasingly critical of both capitalism, which he believed caused the suffering he observed in New York, and the church, which ignored it. In his desire to substantiate his new understanding that social and religious questions were related, he turned anew to the Old and New Testaments. He began as early as 1891 the research and reflection that would culminate sixteen years later in *Christianity and the Social Crisis*.[8]

Rauschenbusch's new study of the Bible was influenced by Tolstoy's interpretation of the teachings of Jesus. He told Ray Stannard Baker that he had never understood the Sermon on the Mount until he read Tolstoy's *My Religion.* He later recalled that when the teachings of Tolstoy first became known in the 1880s, they surprised many people by asserting that the words of the sermon were obligatory laws of Christian conduct. He got over his initial shock, however, and eventually adopted much of Tolstoy's creed. The Russian never led him to question his own Christian conduct, mainly because it was beyond reproach. Tolstoy did, however, give him a clearer understanding of Jesus' message to men of wealth. Citing lessons learned from both Tolstoy and George, Rauschenbusch wrote that "the greatest and most searching moral teachers of humanity have agreed with Jesus in his moral diagnosis of the classes that live on unearned wealth." Tolstoy's demand for voluntary poverty might seem excessive and unnecessary to the average man, he wrote, but nevertheless represented "the heroic corollary of the moral condemnation of unearned riches." He was particularly disturbed with clergymen like Russell Conwell and other advocates of the "gospel of wealth," who rationalized Jesus' message in order to justify rich men's ease in entering heaven. Rauschenbusch believed that if the rich man would not give up his riches voluntarily by an act of personal renunciation, such as Jesus and Tolstoy enjoined, then a reorganized society would be compelled (and would have the right) to take his wealth away forcibly and share it with others.[9]

He was also profoundly influenced in the late 1880s by Mazzini. The Italian prophet, he wrote, was "not the kind of prophet that tells you on what day of the year 1889 this poor world will turn to cinder," but rather a prophet with a "passion for justice and liberty" which he envisaged as the hallmarks of the new era. Rauschenbusch's enthusiasm for Mazzini was unrestrained, advising his readers to "listen to him and learn." Mazzini's *Essays*, he concluded, make up a book of religion, even to some, a book of devotion.[10] The young minister's growing conviction that social and religious questions were identical was confirmed by Mazzini, whose vision of the reconstructive power of Christianity provided him with a spiritual rather than material basis for his incipient socialism.

Rauschenbusch's biographers uniformly attribute his social

awakening to this combination of his Hell's Kitchen experience and the influence of Mazzini, Tolstoy, Bellamy, and George in the years between 1886 and 1891. His reading in the early 1890s also included Jacob Riis, with whom he worked in the New York tenements, Richard T. Ely, Marx, Lamennais, and Ruskin. Rauschenbusch's preparation for a career in seeking to bring about the kingdom of God on earth was furthered by a visit to Europe in 1891–1892. He wrote to Ely that he was going to England and Germany "to get in contact with the various currents of sociological thought, & to see what has been actually accomplished in municipal life, in the care & education of the working people, in cooperation, etc."[11] In England he stayed with Beatrice and Sidney Webb, from whom he absorbed the spirit of Fabian socialism and the English Christian social movement.

Once he had studied and reflected upon these many ideological influences and day-to-day experiences, Rauschenbusch was prepared to promulgate his version of Christian socialism. In 1889 he joined the New York branch of Bliss's Society of Christian Socialists and together with other Baptist ministers founded a monthly paper, *For the Right*, which was full of folksy parables and Sunday school lessons for workers. The paper's objective, as stated by the editors in the first issue, was "to discuss, from the standpoint of Christian-socialism," those questions which reflected "the needs, aspirations, and longings of the tens of thousands of wage-earners who are sighing for better things." The sole aim of the editors was to promote "the advancement of that kingdom in which wrong shall have no place, but Right shall reign forever more."[12] The paper, however, was righteous and paternalistic in tone and revealed little understanding of the workers it claimed to support; it perished for lack of funds early in 1891.

It was during these early years in New York that Rauschenbusch's concept of the kingdom of heaven on earth was developed. In describing his spiritual growth some twenty years later, he said that his attempts to secure justice for workers had led him to the conviction that the kingdom concept was so large that none of his interests were excluded from it. Although the kingdom idea was born in individuals, it had to be spread throughout the world. "Does not the Kingdom of God consist simply of this—that God's will shall be done on earth, even as it is now in heaven? And so, wherever I touched, there was the Kingdom of God. That was the brilliancy, the splendor of that conception—it touches everything with religion."[13] As Rauschenbusch and other Baptist ministers in New York became more convinced of the seminal importance of the kingdom concept, they formed a little group, "The Brotherhood of the Kingdom," to study the social implications of the idea more thoroughly.

The Brotherhood of the Kingdom originated in the friendship among Rauschenbusch and two fellow ministers, Leighton Williams and Nathaniel Schmidt, meeting in Rauschenbusch's home late in 1892. They were disturbed that the kingdom of God had been abandoned or perverted by the Christian church; they formed the brotherhood to reestablish the idea of the kingdom of God on earth in the church. The spirit and aims of the brotherhood were adopted on August 11, 1893, at Williams's pleasant summer home at Marlborough on the banks of the Hudson River, north of New York City, where they held conferences almost every summer for twenty years. The spirit of the brotherhood was to promote the practical realization of the kingdom in the world. The aims, which were enumerated, were to exemplify the ethics of Jesus in their own lives, to propagate the social aims of Christianity, to keep in contact with the common man, to hold frequent meetings with one another to discuss how these aims might best be fulfilled, and to issue regular reports and papers on these questions. Membership was carefully screened so as to exclude all but those with intellectual or professional interests and backgrounds.[14] Each summer, therefore, usually in August when the heat in the city was most unbearable, the members of the brotherhood retired to Marlborough-on-the-Hudson to read papers to one another.

The best single statement of the brotherhood's concept of the kingdom was by Rauschenbusch, who issued a leaflet in keeping with the publicity aims of the brotherhood. He wrote that the members "believe that the idea of a kingdom of God on earth was the central thought of Jesus, and ought ever to be the great aim of the church." This goal had been consistently misunderstood, which was the cause of the present "social ineffectiveness of church life." Laymen thought the kingdom referred to an afterlife in heaven, mystics saw it as the inner life of the reconciled sinner, ecclesiastics equated the kingdom with the church, and most Christians looked to the reign of Christ after the Second Coming. None of them were right, Rauschenbusch said, for "the kingdom of God is larger than anything contained in any one of these ideas." Although the kingdom began within individual hearts, he wrote, it was applicable to all the institutions of society: in government, in the administration of justice, and in education. The kingdom would not come with a cataclysmic day of judgment, but was already structurally evident in the social order.[15]

In his later works Rauschenbusch departed very little from this definition, consistently emphasizing the developmental nature of the kingdom. In *Christianity and the Social Crisis* he wrote that while early Christians "were waiting for the Messianic cataclysm that would bring the kingdom of God ready-made from heaven, [Jesus] saw it growing up among them." The kingdom appeared gradually, growing organically from one person and group to another. In this sense, Rauschenbusch could say that the kingdom was "already here." His focus was clearly on earth and on man's social institutions. "It is not a matter of getting individuals to heaven, but of transforming the life on earth into the harmony of heaven." In *Christianizing the Social Order* in 1912 Rauschenbusch reiterated what Jesus had meant by the kingdom. It was to be achieved by gradualist, peaceful means and was equated with a new social order. It was intrinsically democratic and demanded not charity and philanthropy, but the mercy and social sympathy which accompanied social solidarity. It meant the brotherhood of all men regardless of particular national identity. It meant that spiritual values were higher than economic ones (a reply to the socialists), yet translated Christian spiritual principles to the economic affairs of men. And finally, the kingdom was not in heaven but on earth: Jesus "never transferred the Kingdom hope from earth to heaven. The Kingdom was so much of this earth that Jesus expected to return to earth from heaven in order to set it up."[16]

The kingdom concept, however central, was only one of the many topics discussed at the annual summer conferences at Marlborough. Others included the nature of Christian thought generally, the relationship of the kingdom to social questions specifically, and the role of the intellectual as a reformer. Many of the sessions were devoted to studying the thought of Christian social prophets. Mazzini, a favorite of Williams and Rauschenbusch, was often discussed, as was Tolstoy, especially because of the frequent presence of his ardent follower Ernest Crosby. At the close of the conference in 1897, Rauschenbusch suggested that, among others, Augustine, Wycliffe, and Mazzini be discussed the following summer. A year later there were papers on Wycliffe, Mazzini (by Lloyd), Tolstoy (by Crosby), Lamennais (by Williams), the apostle Paul (by Rauschenbusch), and the Hebrew prophets. In 1900 there were again lectures on various Hebrew prophets, as well as on George Fox, Wesley, Maurice, and Ruskin. In 1906 a series on the "socialized views of the great reformers" was held, including talks on Wycliffe and Savonarola, Luther and Calvin, Wesley and Whitefield, and Mazzini and Tolstoy. From 1907 to 1909 the brotherhood published a journal, *The Kingdom*, with Rauschenbusch, Williams, and the ubiquitous Bliss on the editorial board. The journal was largely a vehicle in which to publish the papers delivered at Marlborough, garnished with devotional readings by such luminaries as Ruskin, Carlyle, Mazzini, Lammenais, and Tolstoy. Thus, there was a constant flow of European inspirational ideas into the discussions at Marlborough. The topics discussed by the Brotherhood of the Kingdom usually reflected the interests of Rauschenbusch and Leighton Williams, the guiding leaders. One participant described them as the "constructive prophet" and the "constructive interpreter," respectively. Although Marlborough was Williams's home, it was known as "Rauschenbusch's Assisi."[17] He spoke more often than any other member and after 1907 was a nationally known figure. Rauschenbusch's several topics for his talks at Marlborough revealed an evolution of interests from the social teachings of Jesus to the kingdom of God, and from the kingdom to its relationship with socialism.[18]

It was inevitable that the relation between the Brotherhood of the Kingdom and socialism would be raised. When speaking of socialism, Rauschenbusch consistently avoided defining it but rather relied on ambiguity of definition in order to serve his purpose of extracting those socialist principles that were compatible with Christianity and rejecting those that were not. In 1894 he told a reporter in an interview for the *New York Press* that most members of the brotherhood did not endorse socialism, but rather were Christian socialists. He was certain, however, that no one could read the Sermon on the Mount and remain an individualist and indicated to the reporter that a religious element was essential to all social movements. In the "Ideals of Social Reformers" in 1895 he said that one of the tasks of the brotherhood was "to wed Christianity and the social movement, infusing the power of religion into social efforts, and helping religion to find its ethical outcome in the transformation of social conditions." It was important, he said, to avoid the error of many well-intentioned reformers who embraced scientific socialism. The two ideals of the social movement were individual human dignity and the Mazzinian principle of association. In adopting this latter ideal, he said, reformers were sympathetic with socialism. He cautioned them, however, to avoid those principles of socialism which denied individual liberty, threatened the stability of the family and the nation, advocated force and violence, and preached materialism to the neglect of spiritual forces. "We must be social reformers *and* Christian disciples," he wrote, "and stronger and saner in each capacity because we unite the other with it."[19]

Although on friendly terms with many American socialists, Rauschenbusch, like Lloyd, never joined the Socialist party, nor did he ever accept the crucial doctrine of public ownership of production. "How largely we press in the same direction!," Vida Scudder wrote to Rauschenbusch in 1912 while trying to persuade him to join the party as she had done. Although she failed to sign him up, her judgment on their similarities was largely correct. In 1907 he had written that "socialism is the ultimate and logical outcome of the labor movement," but added that the workers needed the help of idealistic religious leaders to guide their progress, a belief held consistently throughout his career. In a passage strikingly similar to Scudder's attempted reconciliations at the same time, he wrote that religious idealists and practical workingmen needed each other: "The new Christian principle of brotherly association must ally itself with the working class if both are to conquer. Each depends on the other. The idealistic movement alone would be a soul without a body; the economic class movement alone would be a body without a soul. It needs the high elation and faith that come through religion."[20] His position was fleshed out by advocacy of such specific measures as social justice legislation (better wages, hours, and working conditions for labor), workmen's compensation, labor cooperatives, profit-sharing schemes, the public ownership of natural monopolies, and the legitimacy of trade unions, strikes, and collective bargaining. He did not recognize, however, that these were palliative measures, designed to christianize the present economic order but hardly to subvert or change it fundamentally. Far from undermining or weakening American capitalism, as both the Progressive and New Deal reforms revealed, these measures only strengthened it.

Rauschenbusch's endorsement of semi-socialistic programs was primarily theoretical, aimed at other intellectuals for educative purposes. In 1912 he expanded his belief that Christians and socialists needed each other in order to uplift workers and bring an end to the unchristian aspects of capitalism. He noted that many idealistic intellectuals, literary men, and artists were socialists, and asked: "If in any great historic movement the men of property are on one side and the young and idealistic intellects are on the other, on which side is God?" It was a loaded question. He recognized, however, that socialism was repellent to many Christians. "Socialism inevitably involves a menace," he admitted, but added that "it is our business to make its menace small and its blessing great." Socialism, he was confident, would become more moral and less objectionable as it matured. Eventually it would pass away while Christianity continued to prevail. In the meantime, he wrote, God worked through socialism in order to eliminate capitalism. "The great danger is that our eyes will be blinded by ecclesiastical prejudices so that we do not know God when he comes close to us."[21] Thus, Rauschenbusch came about as close as one possibly could to embracing socialism without joining the party. His detachment, however, was revealing, derived from his intellectual conviction that the kingdom of God, however similar in broad outlines to socialism, was larger than any single doctrine and in fact encompassed all social movements which were "for the right."

A second, and perhaps more significant, reason why Rauschenbusch was not as willing as Vida Scudder to embrace socialism in 1912 was that he was more optimistic than she about the social progress and institutional changes that had been achieved in the preceding twenty years. As early as 1907, while in Germany, he wrote to his fellow members of the Brotherhood of the Kingdom to tell them that he was "impressed with the amazing changes in public thought since the Brotherhood was founded." He noted that

Christian unity was more secure, politics was purer, the antitrust movement was progressing, and the kingdom concept had become foremost in Christian thought. "It would be folly for us to claim that we created these changes," he warned, but added that the vision of the brotherhood "did *help* to create the change." In 1908 the Federal Council of Churches of Christ in America was organized in Philadelphia; four years later the council adopted a "Social Creed" which included most of the specific socioeconomic measures which Rauschenbusch and others had been advocating for twenty years. For Rauschenbusch, the 1890s had been a "time of lonesomeness," when it was possible for Terence Powderly to charge that he could count on his fingers the number of clergymen interested in the labor problem. By 1912, however, in *Christianizing the Social Order*, Rauschenbusch could celebrate the great progress that had occurred in the church's response to social problems. The crisis was over; the family, the church, education, and even politics had already been "christianized." He confidently pointed out the "direction of progress" and the "methods of advance" in order to complete the task of christianizing the social order. The Marlborough conference a year later, recognizing the achievements of the Brotherhood of the Kingdom, had a sense of finality to it. And by 1917 Rauschenbusch observed that the Social Gospel was no longer a vision, but had "become orthodox."[22]

Rauschenbusch could afford to be self-satisfied by 1912. Since the publication of *Christianity and the Social Crisis* in 1907, he had become a well-known and respected leader of the Social Gospel in America. The book was translated into several languages and sold over 50,000 copies, making its impact on two generations of Social Gospel clergymen. When he left his New York ministry for a teaching position at Rochester in 1897 (partly because increasing deafness was less of a handicap as a professor than as a minister), he left behind him more than the personal pain of presiding over tenement funerals. He also escaped the insecurity of a poverty-stricken urban pastorate, where his maximum annual income was $1,200, and was relieved of constant exposure to socialist, anarchist, and militant unionist pressures. Rochester had its own urban problems, to be sure, but it was not New York. Nor did the seminary classroom provide the burdens and intense personal experiences of his Hell's Kitchen church. He was able to teach his church history and Christian socialism without interference, and only his deafness prevented him from becoming president of the Rochester Theological Seminary in 1911. His family life was especially comforting and joyous. His wife of twenty-five years bore him three sons and two daughters, and their life together was a model of Christian affection and decent living.

This is not to say that Rauschenbusch lost his crusading fervor and vision of the kingdom, but rather that the move to Rochester provided him with an opportunity to reflect and write in a tranquil environment. He received many offers to lecture at other schools, among them Ohio Wesleyan University, the Pacific Theological Seminary in Berkeley, and the Yale School of Religion. Rauschenbusch was no longer an activist minister and organizer, but had become an eminently respectable and honored professor-prophet, experiencing none of the pains of self-doubt and guilt suffered by Vida Scudder in a similar role. He had served his activist role in New York; it was time to reflect upon that experience and educate others to their sense of responsibility for finishing the job of christianizing the social order.

In his new role as educator, Rauschenbusch faced a dilemma which revealed his central weakness as a reformer. Like many progressive social gospelers and reform social darwinists (Josiah Strong, for example), he espoused racialist theories of Teutonic and Anglo-Saxon superiority. In a "Commencement Day Address" in Rochester in 1902 he expressed his pride in the German origins of American educational theory and practice from kindergartens to universities. The Teutonic races, he said, were "a princely stock" who rightly ruled and dominated the world as a result of providential purpose. He saw the innate virtue and stability of the German middle classes in Rochester threatened by the influx of new immigrants at the turn of the century. He feared that "alien strains of blood," specifically mentioning the French, Spanish, Slavs, Bohemians, Poles, and Russian Jews, would dilute the Teuton virtues by amalgamation.[23]

He also believed in an intellectually elitist position that social change came from middle- or upper-class professionals who had proved their moral fitness for leadership. These paternal and elitist qualities, evident in *For the Right* and the Brotherhood of the Kingdom, were clearly demonstrated in a crisis in the Rochester school system in 1908. The Board of Education had responded to the new lower-class immigrants in Rochester by introducing progressive reforms, stressing a child-centered, vocational, practical education for democracy. Rauschenbusch, like his father in his work in the 1850s with the American Home Missionary and American Tract Societies, believed in authority-centered German discipline and liberal arts education not only for moral reformation by the fittest toward social change but also for social control of the unregenerate lower classes. At a series of public meetings in 1908, Rauschenbusch led the attack on the progressive methods of the Rochester school board. As chairman of a committee investigating abuses in the school system, he wrote a long report which revealed his elitist, conservative educational theories. His report deplored the lack of discipline, homework, respect for authority, rigorous drill and examination, and classical liberal learning in the schools. Nowhere in his report did he show an interest in the specific needs of the lower classes he theoretically supported. Ironically, his educational elitism led him to solidify existing class relationships, thus inadvertently strengthening the capitalist oppression of workers which he condemned in his writing. This dilemma was at the heart of his ineffectiveness in achieving his long-range goals.[24]

Rauschenbusch's basic conservatism was displayed not only in his approach to public schools but also in his other means of education: writing books. In addition to his *Prayers of the Social Awakening*, a collection of devotions applicable to various Social Gospel concerns, Rauschenbusch wrote three books from 1910 to 1919. Each work included the familiar themes of the social teachings of Jesus, the responsibilities of the church, and the evolving manifestations of a christianized kingdom of heaven on earth. As contrasted to his earlier works, however, the tone in each of these books was gentler, milder, less crisis-oriented, and more conciliatory. The sting had gone out of his work, and with it much of the economics. Thus, *Dare We Be Christians?* in 1914 was a call for love in human and social relationships based on an analysis of the apostle Paul's famous first letter to the Corinthians. The *Social Principles of Jesus* in 1916 was written as a voluntary college study guide for the Young Men's Christian Association and a subcommittee of the College Courses Sunday School Council of Evangelical Denominations. Although continuing to emphasize the ethical significance of the Sermon on the Mount and the importance of the kingdom concept, *The Social Principles of Jesus* was a relatively conventional guide to Christian living, complete with daily readings and biblical texts, anecdotes relevant to college students, and suggestions for thought and discussion.[25]

His most significant book in this period was *A Theology for the Social Gospel*, Rauschenbusch's attempt to provide a sound theological basis for his ethical ideas of the Social Gospel, particularly the kingdom of God. The work is disappointing in its conciliatory tone and lack of theological sophistication. Although he often assailed orthodox Christian doctrines, he took much care to accommodate with conservatives by showing how the doctrines of the Social Gospel were neither alien nor novel but in harmony with the original ethical teachings of Old Testament prophets and Jesus. He assured his readers in the foreword to the book that his approach was "wholly positive and constructive" and was "just as orthodox as the Gospel would allow." *A Theology* rehashed the historical abandonment of the central ideas of the kingdom of God and the law of love which he had developed so thoroughly in *Christianity and the Social Crisis* ten years earlier. He argued throughout the book how the Social Gospel reacted on the orthodox theological doctrines of sin, redemption, God, inspiration, eschatology and atonement. His usual treatment of each doctrine was to review briefly its original meaning, its loss and abandonment, and how the Social Gospel could restore the doctrine to the purposes intended by Jesus. The doctrine of baptism, for example, was not meant originally to guarantee the salvation of an individual soul but rather to commit the individual to work for the coming kingdom of God; baptism was "the symbol of a revolutionary hope, an ethical act which determined the will and life of the person receiving it."[26] His most extensive treatment, however, was of the doctrines of sin and redemption.

Theologians had defined sin, according to Rauschenbusch, as individual human selfishness, transmitted biologically through the generations in accordance with the doctrines of original sin through Adam's fall. Rauschenbusch, however, defined sin as social wrongdoing, transmitted socially and racially (by which he meant the human race) from generation to generation. The "true standard of holiness," he wrote, was not Adam in the Garden of Eden before the fall but Jesus' effort to establish the kingdom of God and the law of love. "It is Christ who convicts the world of sin and not Adam." The worst sins of human history, he wrote, were those "permanent evils of mankind" which killed Jesus and which had persisted to the present day: religious bigotry, graft and political power, corruption of justice, mob spirit and action (by both rich and poor, conservatives and radicals), militarism, and class contempt. Mankind's redemption from these social or group sins, according to the theology of the Social Gospel, could not be achieved only by individual salvation but required "solidaristic consciousness," by which he meant the understanding that submission to God implied submission to the common good.[27] No matter which theological doctrine was under examination, the theology of the Social Gospel consistently rejected individualism, autocracy, personal salvation, mysticism, asceticism, and pessimism. It argued instead for social salvation, solidarity (the brotherhood of man), democracy, the law of love, and devotion to the developing kingdom of God.

Perhaps the most revealing, and confounding, chapter in the book is the one on eschatology, for in it Rauschenbusch wavered between optimism and pessimism in his attitude toward the possibilities for the kingdom's presence in America. He clearly rejected the premillennialist hope for an apocalyptic, catastrophic day of judgment which would usher in the thousand-year reign of Christ. Rather, he was a postmillennialist, believing that the thousand-year reign of social peace and harmony must precede the Second Coming. He made it clear that the "social life in which the law of Christ shall prevail" would involve both spiritual and economic life (i.e., both love and the common good), and that the new order would come not by catastrophe but by development. Yet, unlike his earlier optimism, Rauschenbusch seemed to be uncertain whether the kingdom was imminent or already present. He concluded that it was both. On the one hand, the kingdom has no final consummation, but was always coming; it was never fully here. On the other hand, he cited Jesus' belief that the kingdom was both present and future. In order to achieve the full realization of the kingdom in heaven, one needed the preparation of "partial realizations" on earth. These were already evident in American life, as he had long recognized. Indeed, he had rejoiced in one of his "prayers of the social awakening" that the belief in the kingdom had become "the clear faith of millions."[28] By 1917 Rauschenbusch was therefore generally pleased with social and spiritual progress in America; his optimism and tranquillity was disturbed only by the world war.

George Herron

Rauschenbusch's optimism and moderation after the turn of the century increased with his growing stature and respectability, as well as with the widespread acceptance of his ideas. His midwestern counterpart, however, moved in opposite directions. "We steered clear of the ultra-radicalism of George Herron," a participant at Marlborough wrote, for his protest books contained an impatience and implied advocacy of force and hatred missing in the members of the Brotherhood of the Kingdom. Bliss noted as early as 1894 that "Dr. Herron has a noble scorn of schemes and plans and arrangements. He scores the instituted church with eloquent yet with vehement words. He by no means would destroy, though he would radically revolutionize the church. For institutions of any kind, he seems to have small respect." Even the eulogistic Flower, although finding in Herron "a prophet's message to the sleeping church which reminds one of the clarion voice of Savonarola," admitted that Herron was, perhaps, overly dogmatic.[29] Herron's vehement dogmatism was the result of the inextricable mixture of personal, professional, and ideological forces in his life. Each of his personal and professional crises in the late 1890s intensified his radical analysis of the contradictions in American society and what he thought to be appropriate solutions. The roots of his radicalism, however, were deep in his childhood and youth.

Early in his life George Herron was convinced that he was destined to be a messenger of God to his fellowmen. His family instilled such religious fervor in him as a child that he could not remember, as he said, "when I began to live with God. I have never been without the inner consciousness of God's compelling and restraining presence." His mother filled him with devotional piety to the point that he was not sure but that "I may have been converted before I was born." By the time he was ten, through reading George Bancroft, he had absorbed God's plan for history, especially the divine mission of the United States. He grew up, he reported, "in the company of God, with a daily deepening sense of a divine call which sooner or later I must obey." His solitary childhood was spent with Old Testament prophets, medieval Catholic saints, and Cromwell, Wesley, and Charles Sumner as his "imaginary playmates." From his maternal grandfather he received an emphasis "upon inspirations from Italy. Virgil and St. Francis and Dante and Mazzini were almost my personal companions."[30]

Herron was obsessed with a sense of his own sinfulness, suffering, and duty. In a sermon in Lake City, Minnesota, in 1890, he said that "God permits our thorns in the flesh as reminders that self-enjoyment is not the business of life. . . . Our business in the world is not happiness but duty." At the same time he wrote that "it would be a joy to be pilloried and disgraced before the world."[31] In his "Confession of Faith" in 1891, upon taking the pastorate in Burlington, Herron admitted, in language borrowed from Jonathan Edwards, that he was a redeemed sinner. The Lord had heard his cries of anguish, he said, and had taught him that his sole purpose on earth was to do the will of God. Despite the traditionalism of his evangelical orientation, the Social Gospel was already part of his faith. In his "Confession" he stated that "the grace of Christ is as sufficient for the affairs of state, the construction of society, the reformation of politics, the management of traffic in labor or wares, as it is for the saving of my soul." He was as certain as Rauschenbusch that Christ's kingdom was on earth: "I have here all that I can do; I see enough for all the sons of God to do." Six months earlier he had written to Richard T. Ely, introducing himself as a "young man in the ministry" who had thought long on the relation of Jesus Christ to the problems of his day.[32]

Herron's letters and illuminating confession reveal that at an early point in his career he was in both the evangelical and Social Gospel traditions. His faith was two-pronged: the duty of the clergyman was to save souls and to change society. His wide reading as a young man gave him ample support for both tasks. From the Bible, Calvin, Wesley, and Charles Finney he acquired a fervent belief that his soul and others' had to be redeemed that they might serve the will of God. From Sumner, George, Garrison and Tolstoy he learned what the will of God required: namely, that the purpose of Christianity was to gospelize society's sinful institutions which were, like men, in need of redemption. By the late 1890s, Herron's concern for the second task so outweighed his interest in the first that he abandoned the ministry for the Socialist party. His language, immediacy, and messianic self-conception, however, were unaltered in his new role. He sought to transform institutions to socialism as fervently as he had formerly sought to convert individuals to Jesus Christ. Early evangelical influences like Edwards and Finney inevitably gave way to a devotion to socialists like Eugene Debs. The most sustained inspiration in his life, however, with the most profound impact on his religious and social philosophy, was Mazzini, "my best beloved master, next to Jesus."[33]

In 1905 Herron wrote that Mazzini "was one of the two or three formative influences in my life, and I felt as though I knew him personally." He thought it a suitable testimony to the Italian's widespread influence that in an obscure little town in Indiana he had absorbed "the spirit of Mazzini as the bread and wine of my life!" His allegiance to that spirit remained undiminished throughout his life. At the heart of Herron's thought was the concept of the cross, which he said meant that men must be taught, as Mazzini said, not to enjoy but to suffer for others. In the sermon that established his reputation, "The Message of Jesus to Men of Wealth," delivered first in 1890, Herron said that the cross "was not our release from, but our obligation to, sacrifice." Taking a stand directly opposed to the gospel of wealth, Herron enjoined rich men not to acquire riches but to renounce them. All men, rich and poor, must sacrifice their self-interest and rights, Herron said, in order to fulfill their duties. Citing Mazzini's declaration that life was a mission, he called men to emulate the mission of Jesus in order to remake the world.[34]

As individuals had a mission, so also did the state. Herron's analysis of the social crisis of the 1890s, like Rauschenbusch's, concluded that there was not enough Christianity in the social order. The cross would teach the duties of love and self-sacrifice requisite to the creation of a Christian state. "As Mazzini once said," Herron wrote, "the nation is perpetuated by men who die for humanity." He was convinced that "a Christian political philosophy will teach us how to translate Christ's law of sacrifice into economic association and political organization." The conflict of Jesus with Caesar, Herron said, was as economic as the contemporary Christian conflict with Caesarism. The current crisis in America was not between capital and labor, but between Jesus and the existing social order. Herron's diagnosis of the social order found it suffering from an excess of individualism, capitalism, and mammonism, which had created anarchy. The cure, he said, quoting Mazzini, was "a social faith which may save us from anarchy, [and] the moral inspiration which may express that faith in action." Resolution of the conflict between Jesus and the existing order would require the synthesis of religious and political forces. Only then could "the Christ order" be established in America.[35]

Translating these vague ideas into a still vaguer vision of the Christian state, Herron again borrowed heavily from Mazzini's similar vision, and suggested that "the Christ order" would be one of association, cooperation, and the oneness of humanity. The God of Abraham and Isaac, Jesus and Paul, and Mazzini and Lincoln was not an individualistic but a collectivist God. What had been lacking in America, Herron charged, was enough government and unity of purpose to counteract the anarchic consequences of individualism: "The want of a common centre of unity to associate the energies and institutions of men in a collective and harmonious progress toward a common fulfilment of life, has been the fundamental ailment of the world." The mission of the state was to discover this missing center of unity, which Herron suggested was Jesus. Since social, economic, political, and religious questions were one, the state would be theocratic. "If I am my brother's keeper as a religious man, I am equally my brother's keeper as an economic or political man." Although theocratic, the state would not be undemocratic. In "The Gospel of Jesus to the Poor," Herron asserted that Christ's gospel was undeniably "*the democracy of the people*. Pure democracy and pure theocracy are one." The Christian state, then, was for Herron, as it was for Mazzini, a theocratic, democratic association, guided by the lessons of sacrifice exemplified by the cross.[36]

Herron also believed in the special mission of the United States, as had Mazzini in that of Italy, to begin the spiritual and political rebirth of the world. With America as an example, he wrote in 1895, "the dream of the federation of the nations in the holy universal church will yet be realized."[37] Some twenty-three years later Herron still held the same dream while serving during World War

I in a semiofficial position in Switzerland for the Department of State. Throughout his life, Herron alternated between Italy and the United States as embodying the spiritual leadership of the world. After his disillusionment with America at the end of the century, he turned to Italy, his spiritual home. For a short period at the end of the war he believed that the redemptive torch had been passed to Woodrow Wilson. He soon doubted, however, that America could assume the missionary role that Mazzini had envisaged for Italy and turned again to Italy for leadership.

Herron's thought was so similar to Mazzini's that he was often compared to the Italian prophet. A close friend said that Herron's philosophy marked him "as the Mazzini of our day—the political prophet and supreme apostle of labor in America. Thus has he made a synthesis of the spiritual and social; the political and the religious truth, which is the demand of the hour." In 1896–1897, under advice from his doctor, Herron went to Europe for health care and a needed vacation from increasing personal and professional difficulties. Although he spent some time in England explaining Populism to skeptical audiences, he passed most of his vacation in Italy. He had the "strange sense of being at home in Florence" and wrote that until he visited Florence, he had never felt that he belonged on earth. The cause of his love for Florence, he explained, was that the chief influences of his life had all been Italians. He visited the shrines of Francis at Assisi and the places where Savonarola had preached and been imprisoned. The happiest part of his tour, however, was his visit to Mazzini's Genoa during the week of the twenty-fifth anniversary of the prophet's death.[38]

"Genoa was all Mazzini to me," Herron wrote, and although he did some sight-seeing, every day he worshiped at "one of the Mazzini shrines, praying for such small portion of his spirit as I might be able to attain." He ended each day at the Mazzini monument, a stone column capped with a statue of Mazzini set at the top of a little hill. Here he found his greatest joy. The solemn and simple monument seemed to Herron to be "truly suggestive of the man, forever enshrined in the love and thought of many as the incarnation and ideal of all that is noble and truly great, beautiful and truly good, gentle and truly strong, knightly and truly pure, self-denying and truly brave." Mazzini was, he said, the only man in all Europe feared by Metternich and the monarchs of Europe, as well as "the one sole man to whom the spirit of Bismarck bowed in reverence." Such enthusiasm inevitably required a comparison with Jesus. Like Jesus, Herron wrote, Mazzini was unsuccessful during his lifetime. The heritage he left to the world was his ideal.[39] By visiting the shrines of Mazzini in Genoa, Herron accomplished a symbolic laying on of hands. He achieved vicarious physical contact with his spiritual master and was even better prepared for the task of crusading for the establishment of the true Christian state. Messianic apostleship was transferred from Mazzini to Herron; the burden of national spiritual leadership passed from Italy to America.

Herron genuinely believed that the Christian state could be realized in the United States in his lifetime, and he agitated to that end. The Sermon on the Mount would be the Christian Constitution of the new state, for the sermon was the "most perfect expression in letters of the divine government of the world, of the unseen yet appearing just social order." One could discern the outlines of the new order, Herron maintained, not only by studying the teachings of Jesus but also by exploring the history of western social thought through the study of what he called Christian sociology. This discipline was a science of sacrifice, redemption, and atonement. The study of sociology would compel men and women to commit themselves to eradicating every social sin in economic and political life. Individuals would sacrifice their selfish acquisitive instincts so that institutions could be changed from their protective, paternal, individualistic purposes to redemptive, fraternal, collectivist ones.[40]

Herron's faith in the redemptive power of sociology was the guiding assumption of the course in "Christian Sociology" which he taught at Iowa College in his new chair of Applied Christianity, richly endowed by Mrs. E. D. Rand, who followed Herron from Burlington to Grinnell. When he first taught the course in 1893–1894, it consisted of 100 lectures and twenty-six required books. Among them were Hegel's *Philosophy of History*, Maurice's *Social Morality*, Ruskin's *Unto This Last*, Mazzini's *Duties of Man*, John Seeley's Christian socialist vision *Ecce Homo*, Gronlund's *Cooperative Commonwealth*, and several titles by Gladden, Ely, and Herron himself. The purpose of his course was "not to do a technical work in sociology, but rather to interpret the teachings of Jesus in relation to the problems of the day." The course began with definitions and the historical background of Christian sociology and Christian society. With more misplaced optimism than accuracy, Herron then traced recent historical developments away from individualism, paternalism and competition toward altruism, cooperation, and unity. In the middle of the course he described the Christian constitution of society and presented his evidence to show that the kingdom of God was imminent. The final part of the course, "The Realization of the Kingdom," analyzed the contemporary crisis in American society and indicated the ways in which American life could be redeemed. They were hardly specific. "We need no programs of action," he had written in 1892, "save the words of our Lord," a visionary, nonprogrammatic position he never abandoned.[41]

Herron's forte was neither organization nor concrete proposals, but charisma. His presence at Grinnell, then under the presidency of George Gates, himself a liberal reformer influenced by Mazzini, transformed Iowa College into a midwestern center of Christian radicalism. Herron's courses were so large, swollen by student auditors and visitors from Grinnell and throughout the nation, that they were moved to the college chapel. Evening meetings led by Herron, intended as noncredit discussion groups, were attended by over a hundred students. The small college of some 500 students even added a graduate program in Applied Christianity for Herron. One of Herron's colleagues, John Nollen, who later became president of Grinnell, described Herron as "a forensic wizard" with an intense, hypnotic platform appeal. The impact of his personality and teaching on the college and community, Nollen wrote, was electric and soon became nationwide. Herron's fame (and Mrs. Rand's money) attracted figures of the stature of Lloyd, W. T. Stead, Robert A. Woods, Ellen Starr, Hamlin Garland, and Graham Taylor to the campus to give lectures.[42]

But Herron was not content simply to bring Christian reformers to Grinnell; he needed to preach his controversial gospel of Christian socialism throughout the land. From his base at Grinnell, he traveled widely, lecturing on the Christian society to enormous audiences. In the spring of 1894, for example, he delivered lectures at the University of Michigan (an estimated 3,000 attending), Princeton, Indiana University, Union Theological Seminary, and at Montreal, where one observer compared his impact to the explosion of a "dynamite bomb . . . in a public square of the city." An appearance by Herron was inevitably the cause for a heated dispute. His commencement address at the University of Nebraska, for example, precipitated an embittered exchange with the governor of the state, who followed Herron to the rostrum and castigated him as an anarchist. While on a lecture tour in California in the spring of 1895, he embroiled himself in a nasty dispute with a Congregational minister, the Reverend C. O. Brown, who denounced Herron as "a lunatic and an anarchist." Herron's assertion that "*revolution is the Christian's business*," his dogmatic interpretation of Christian sociology, and his repudiation of most social, economic, and even religious institutions endeared him to few with any stake in the existing social order. Only his students, who saw less and less of him, regretted his absence.[43]

Partly because Herron desired a broader pulpit than Grinnell, the American Institute of Christian Sociology was founded at Chautauqua in 1893. Herron was one of the principal organizers and was the third president of the institute after Ely and Josiah Strong. One of its functions was to sponsor "schools for the Kingdom" at Grinnell during the summer. The idea for the schools, modeled on the Chautauqua example, originated at a summer retreat held in 1892 by President Gates. Inviting Ely to attend the retreat, Herron wrote that "our purpose is to make a brief, earnest, and prayerful study of the gospels in their relation to the social crises that are pressing upon us." By the summer of 1894, now under the auspices of the institute, the schools addressed themselves to the study of the kingdom of God and to "the ways and forces for realizing that kingdom in a Christian social order." The topics for discussion included the whole range of economic and social problems in the mid-1890s. Although Herron provided the integrating theme of the schools by essentially repeating a shorter version of his course in Christian sociology, there were also lectures by Ely, Gates, Strong, John Commons, and others. Many of the same persons appeared at both Herron's Grinnell and Rauschenbusch's Marlborough in the 1890s, and the discussions in both places focused on the kingdom of God. There was, however, more impatience at the midwestern school. Herron was never invited to Marlborough and Rauschenbusch stayed judiciously away from Grinnell. Lloyd was a close friend of both kingdom movements, speaking on Mazzini and the responsibility of scholars in the social movement at both places. He corresponded often with Herron, calling him "a consecrated soul of the new order that is coming." Herron returned the compliment by assigning *Wealth against Commonwealth* in his classes.[44]

Lloyd was particularly in sympathy with a venture by Herron and Gates to publish a family newspaper of "applied Christianity," the weekly *Kingdom.* Lloyd lent money to the paper, wrote for it, and secured Clarence Darrow as a defense counsel when the *Kingdom* was sued by the American Book Company for an exposé by Gates in 1897 of that company's monopoly of the schoolbook business.[45] The *Kingdom* lasted from 1894 to 1899, when the loss of the suit caused the paper's demise, despite the funds poured into its defense by Lloyd, Jane Addams, and other sympathizers. The *Kingdom* was largely dominated by Herron's ideas; it serialized and advertised his books, offered free copies of *The Christian State* with each subscription, and defended him in his many controversies.

In the first issue Gates explained that the *Kingdom* was inspired by Herron, whose "unswerving loyalty to Jesus" and "consuming passion for righteousness" had influenced the entire kingdom movement. Gates included a letter by Herron to a critic as the best statement of the aims of the paper. In his letter Herron reiterated his conviction that his vision of the kingdom did not depict a distantly future society but one which was "at hand." "I have not supposed the kingdom to be coming because of my words," Herron wrote with false modesty, "but have believed my words to be spoken because of the kingdom's coming." He castigated the church for dragging its feet on social questions and asserted that the proper work of the Christian was "to lay the axe at the root of the trees of social wrong" and to prepare the nation for the sacrifices necessary to create the new Christian social order. No kingdom, he said, had ever been achieved "without a Calvary."[46] During the *Kingdom*'s five-year existence, Herron's impassioned editorials and articles became more and more strident, exhorting readers in violent language to adopt his increasingly revolutionary principles.

Another of Herron's endeavors in the mid-1890s, in addition to his teaching, lecture tours, the summer schools, and the *Kingdom*, was his support of the Christian Commonwealth Colony in Georgia.

His influence on Ralph Albertson and George Gibson was one of the factors leading to their founding of the colony. As in the past, Herron again sought Lloyd's financial and moral support in getting the colony started. In 1896 he requested money from Lloyd, stating that he would "make almost any sacrifice . . . to start this movement rightly. It seems to me very important." Although Herron did not live at the colony, he was an associate editor of its mouthpiece, the *Social Gospel*, which took as its motto, "The Kingdom of Heaven is at hand." The *Social Gospel*, reflecting Herron's and Tolstoy's inspiration, announced in its introductory issue that its purpose was "to inspire faith in the economic teachings of Jesus. . . . [The Social Gospel] is the proclamation of the kingdom of heaven, a divinely ordered society, to be realized on earth. It is the application of Christ's Golden Rule and Law of Love to all the business and affairs of life." The early issues contained many of Herron's lectures and sermons, which revealed a growing socialist and revolutionary radicalism. Even his interpretations of Jesus were more extreme. In "Christ's Economic of Distribution," for example, Herron asserted that none of Jesus' teachings was "practicable in any other than a communistic order of society." In the summer of 1898 he said that Jesus was "the most radical revolutionist that ever came to the earth." Compared to Jesus, he wrote, Tolstoy, Marx, and George were "dogged conservatives." Only Jesus risked and lost his life in the cause of revolution.[47]

By the end of the decade Herron had purged himself of the individualistic influences of Tolstoy and George, both of whom sought to promote change by personal example, limited government, and other nonrevolutionary means. His attitude toward Tolstoy was at best ambivalent, and at worst, intensely critical. He revered the Russian as a "lofty prophet" and "consummate artist" and continued to quote him and recommend his religious books. But as Herron became increasingly socialistic, he lashed out at Tolstoy's individualism. Before a group of single-taxers in 1899, he said that he could not agree with the Christian anarchist "of the noble Tolstoi sort" who persisted in being "his own kingdom of heaven," adding that he also disagreed with single-taxers. A year later, in an address in Chicago, in which he enumerated alternative roads out of bondage to the kingdom, he said that a single-taxer would stay in Egypt and a Tolstoyan would deny his responsibility to others and start to the promised land by himself. A Moses, however, would lead his people out, and a Jesus would give his life for others in that effort. Herron's repudiation of Tolstoy was particularly vehement, especially because his name was often linked with the Russian's. He rejected Tolstoy's program because it seemed to him very reactionary. In his lectures at Grinnell he was even more vituperative, calling Tolstoy's philosophy "the most mischievous philosophy that has perverted and deluded the minds of men for many centuries." Herron charged correctly that as a young man Tolstoy had lived a satiated life of luxury and sensuality; after he had "drained the cup of the world to the dregs," he then demanded that young people deny themselves the pleasures he had enjoyed. "Now men," Herron said, "that is not love, that is Hell." Tolstoy was a "spiritual inebriate" and his religion was one of "shame and cowardice." His philosophy was not one of unselfishness and self-denial, as he claimed, but was "treason to the human life of which he is a member." Although Herron's disenchantment seemed complete, curiously, he told Edwin Markham that he hoped to spend some time with Tolstoy while on a trip to the Holy Land early in 1900. His trip was cut short, however, because of his eagerness to return to the United States for the Debs presidential campaign. Also, his domestic life was coming apart.[48]

Herron's stormy public and private life reached its climax in the years between 1898 and 1901. Increasingly under attack from the organized church and from former admirers at Grinnell, he had shifted steadily to the left. On the basis of a survey of church periodicals, R. T. Handy concluded that Herron had "passed the peak of his influence in church circles by 1896" and had been condemned for his false Christology, his criticisms of churches and capitalism, his anarchism, and his impractical, nonconstructive utopianism. Herron's predictable response to this rejection was to intensify his fervent missionary activism and to escalate his radical analysis of and assaults on American institutions. His bombastic rhetoric became increasingly denunciatory and no institutions were spared his verbal broadsides. In April 1899 he charged that America's intervention in Cuba had been overtly commercial, not humanitarian. He castigated the exploitation, "commercial debauchery," and "slaughtering" of innocents in the Philippines. In his speech at Bliss's Buffalo conference in July 1899, modestly titled "An Address to the American People," he denounced militarism and plutocracy as the two evils which most menaced American economic and moral well-being. In *Between Caesar and Jesus*, published in 1899, he described his sense of alienation as an American citizen and concluded that "wickedness . . . prostitutes every sacred national and religious function."[49]

As early as February 1897, the Board of Trustees of Iowa College had complained in a letter to Herron that the results of his "intemperate and unsafe" teachings were being manifested in declining student interest, hostile reactions from the Christian community of Grinnell, and fewer donations to the college. In his reply—a thirty-seven page handwritten letter from Geneva—Herron spent seven pages graciously acknowledging the just bases of the trustees' concern and twenty-six pages pointing out where he thought their criticisms of him were in error. He concluded by insisting that, although he would use his free speech "more wisely and patiently," he would continue to do his "duty to the founder, to Christ, to the cause I represent, [and] to the college" by carrying the message of social salvation to the unregenerate. "You will never find me posing as a martyr, whatever you do," he wrote, and then asked that his letter be read in its entirety at the June meeting of the trustees.[50]

Despite his disclaimers, as John Nollen pointed out, Herron responded to increasing vilification by retaliating in kind: "His self-confidence easily took the form of overweening pride, his intense conviction made him impatient and censurious, his eloquence ran into exaggeration and wild invective. . . . There came into his manner an acerbity and a martyr-complex neither of which could gain him sympathy. His scathing condemnation of existing institutions aroused bitter antagonism and even alienated many who had once been his ardent partisans." His enemies launched a determined effort early in 1899 to force his resignation from Iowa College. Their case was based on neglect of his duties despite being the highest paid member of the faculty, smaller enrollments in his classes, false and harmful teachings, and the loss of gifts to the college as a result of his nationwide notoriety. Herron refused at first to resign; his own actions, however, added to the charges against him. Increasingly estranged from his wife of fifteen years, he spent more and more time in the home of his benefactress, Mrs. Rand, and her daughter, Carrie. He even had a room there to rest in between classes. Observers commented that he had an insatiable need for feminine adulation, which Carrie willingly provided. Soon he separated from his wife entirely, and rumors were spread that Herron had confused the doctrine of Christian love with that of socialist free love.[51]

At the June meeting of the Iowa College trustees, an attempt was made to oust him. It failed, however, probably because of the intervention of Gates and Mrs. Rand, who had given the college not only a troublesome professor of Applied Christianity but also a new gymnasium and library. But in October, after months of bitter controversy, Herron unexpectedly resigned from Iowa College without taking Mrs. Rand's $35,000 endowment with him. His letter of resignation, which was full of uncharacteristic goodwill, as well as the familiar protestations against martyrdom while at the same time emphasizing his sacrifices, was widely reprinted in radical and reformist journals. Although generally lauded for his courageous and magnanimous stand, Herron's resignation evoked criticism from as sympathetic a friend as Lloyd, who told Herron in a letter that he was "too angry to keep quiet." Lloyd charged Herron with abdicating the endowed chair and leaving the cause of applied Christianity to the hands of trustees. Lloyd's unexpected criticism hurt, and in his reply Herron pleaded: "I could do no differently from which [*sic*] I did, and be consistent. In no other way, could I practice what I preach. . . . I am now free to give myself wholly to the social movement."[52]

The first deed of the reborn Herron was the trip to Europe with the Rands for a rest. He soon returned, however, to deliver one of the speeches nominating Debs for the presidency in 1900 and to campaign vigorously for Debs and other social democrats. After the election he wrote to Lloyd to thank him for his help in the campaign and said that he needed to be in the midst of the socialist movement. Debs's loss convinced Herron that it was imperative for American socialists to cooperate with one another and to heal the divisions that marked socialism at the turn of the century. "If we stand for brotherhood," he said in December 1900, "we must act like brothers, and not like the so-called Christians who call one another brother and then proceed to devour one another." That same month he wrote Bliss that his primary responsibility was "to help spiritualize the international Socialist movement."[53]

By 1899 Herron had begun to stress that socialism itself was a new religion and that God worked through it. His concluding words in the last issue of the *Kingdom* stated that "never was there a time when the world seemed to be so without religion as it is now, and yet the world was never so religious. The world is deserting the churches but it is discovering God," by which he meant socialism. In a speech before the Social Reform Club of New York prior to his European trip in January 1900, he asserted that "socialism is the only living religion." A year later he joined J. Stitt Wilson's "Social Crusade," a movement to arouse American citizens to the evils of capitalism and to infuse socialism with a Christian spirit. Herron stressed more and more that social redemption would be achieved not by Christianity but by a spiritualized socialism. He denied charges that his participation in the Social Crusade was an attempt to start an entirely new religion. "The people," he said, "are ready for a great socialistic movement that shall be political in its aspects and yet wholly religious in its spirit." The first step was to overthrow the capitalist class system: "civilization must be born again before society can see the kingdom of God."[54] To serve as midwife to that rebirth consumed all his energies; his efforts were interrupted again, however, with the intrusion of his personal life.

In the spring of 1901 Herron's wife sued for divorce and support of their four children. Despite the help of Clarence Darrow in his defense, he lost the settlement. The ensuing financial burden was gladly assumed by Mrs. Rand and Carrie, whose own personal fortune of $60,000 was given for support of Herron's ex-wife and children. Two months after the settlement, on May 25, 1901, Carrie Rand and Herron were married; moral outrage was expressed by the press throughout the nation. The scandal was magnified by their unusual marriage ceremony which sought neither religious nor civil sanction, symbolic of their opposition to "all coercive institutions." Before a group of friends, George and Carrie simply declared their love for each other, and that was that. After the brief ceremony, friends read poems and Carrie played Beethoven sonatas on the piano. As she played, Leonard Abbott recalled: "the memory of a ghoulish press, of human vultures, of slave-marriage, of cruel capitalism, was blotted out. We saw only the vision of the New Life of Socialism." Herron's remarriage completed the severing of his connections with conventionally respectable institutions. Within two weeks he was expelled from the Grinnell Association of Congregational Churches and "deposed from the Christian ministry," not for heresy or socialism, but for "immoral and unChristian conduct."[55]

Herron had contributed to the decision by a long letter to the Grinnell Church Committee, written the day before his marriage to Carrie, in which he had repudiated the sanctity of marriage vows. He bemoaned the loss of his former friends in the ministry of Iowa and said he would abide by the committee's decision. His children belonged to their mother, he said, for "the life of a man given to the socialist revolution cannot fail to be more or less the life of an outcast." And an outcast he was. The citizens of Grinnell vilified him as "a cruel and faithless husband," and old friends like Josiah Strong called his conduct "despicable and a crime against society." One New York minister based his repudiation of Herron's economic statements on the evidence of "the sobs of his deserted babies." The *Outlook* called his letter of defense "self-indulgent sensuality" and declared that Herron was "self-exiled from the society of honorable men, and we hope that his name may be omitted from the columns of honorable papers." Except to condemn him, honorable papers followed the *Outlook*'s advice.[56]

Although expulsion from the ministry and the calumny of the press hurt him personally, Herron's martyr complex, which had been revealed again in his letter to the church committee, was fulfilled. He now had even more reason to give his life to the socialist cause. Personal abuse fed economic conviction and furthered his alienation from organized Christianity and American society. In an article in 1901 he called the church "a huge and ghastly parasite," squeezing hard-earned money out of laborers, thereby keeping "the people in economic and spiritual subjection to capitalism."[57] Herron's disenchantment with the church was complete. He was now more than ready to abandon the pulpit for the political platform; he was also tired of his own talk and inaction.

An anecdote on an experience in Mazzini's Genoa in 1897 illustrated his concern. One day a boatman rowed Herron out into Genoa Bay and delivered a tirade to the captive listener about the wasted funds the city had expended in celebrating the anniversary of a man who "had never done anything for Genoa except talk about social equality." Herron's arguments that Mazzini was a doer were in vain, and he noted that "I took the lesson he taught me to heart." One wonders, however, what Herron meant by doing something. Other than severing his relationship with the institutions of marriage, college, and church (which were deeds of a sort), he simply translated one set of words for another. From his emphasis on what was socialist about the Christian kingdom of heaven, he shifted to an emphasis on what was Christian about the socialist commonwealth. He continued to associate only with other intellectual reformers like himself, rarely spoke at a union meeting, and participated in no strikes or other forms of direct action. His milieu was words, and it was words he continued to use. He still refused to support or endorse specific programs, believing, as he always had, that words alone were sufficient to convert nonbelievers. He keynoted the socialist unity convention in Indianapolis in July 1901 and was chosen temporary chairman by acclamation. In the platform debates he opposed enumerating specific immediate demands, but lost. At his insistence, a statement was added declaring that the immediate demands were but a step toward "the overthrow of capitalism and the establishment of the Co-operative Commonwealth." When a unified Socialist Party of America was created at long last, Herron declared that "Socialist unity has passed from desire and struggle into accomplished fact; and it is important that all forces related to the socialist movement should now be centered upon the one work of building up a great revolutionary party, that shall conquer all the seats of power in the nation."[58] His own efforts to work actively for the new so-called revolutionary party, however, were short-lived. Words for old themes resolved themselves into a final seemingly inexplicable deed: self-exile.

On September 17, 1901, Herron departed with the Rands to live in a luxurious sixteenth-century villa near Florence, Italy. Ironically, he became a Tolstoyan after all, setting up his own kingdom and leaving the active battle to others. He maintained his contacts with the international socialist movement, wrote poetry and letters of encouragement to his friends back in America, and sent $25–$200 annual contributions to various American socialist and radical party organizations. He returned to the United States briefly in 1902 and to renominate Debs for president in 1904. These, however, were token acts and, despite his continuing rhetoric, he was no more a threat to the stability of American institutions than Rauschenbusch. He never really had been.

Why did Herron exile himself in 1901? In part, the controversies of the previous four years had worn him down physically and his doctor advised rest. Also, as Nollen observed, Herron had always been "at heart a sybarite," enjoying not only the adulation of women but also the luxuries and comforts of the wealthy life. Moreover, he and Carrie were the victims of constant abuse wherever they went; rumors were spread that Mrs. Rand had bought him as a husband for her daughter and that the newlyweds had started a free love colony in New Jersey. Morris Hillquit, who was close to Herron at the time, reported that "the newspapers, eager for a ground of attack on the apostate minister and radical revolutionist, launched a relentless campaign of persecution against him.... The newly married couple were followed at every step by hordes of newspaper reporters and photographers. Their union was publicly denounced from the pulpits. They were socially ostracized." There is no question that these scurrilous attacks pained him deeply. Herron had had a martyr complex all his life and at least could take comfort in his martyrdom. He had written in 1890 that "it would be a joy to be pilloried and disgraced before the world," a prophecy he fulfilled. But he also saw how the calumny heaped on him was a way of discrediting socialism. On June 15, 1901, he wrote to Joseph Labadie that the abuse by church and press was an attempt to destroy "his influence as a socialist and thereby reach the cause itself," which he said caused him the "deepest suffering." Therefore, it was only proper that he martyr himself for socialism by an act of expatriation. Herron wrote to Labadie that he and Carrie, "who have gone through this storm together, and through many years of suffering and work before the storm came, have more than ever placed our lives on the altar of human need."[59] One suspects that his martyr complex, however sincere his devotion to causes, was bound up with his need for female adulation. He was incapable of living without a woman and could endure any abuse if accompanied by an adoring wife. Carrie Rand Herron died in 1914 and within a few months he was married again, this time to a wealthy German woman. She died soon thereafter, and by 1919 Herron was living with his fourth wife. He lived in comfort in the land of Mazzini for the rest of his life, dying of a heart attack while on a trip to Munich in 1925.

It may help to follow again the ideological lines of Herron's and Rauschenbusch's lives. In Herron's youth he was inculcated with midwestern evangelical piety and a personal sense of mission. Rauschenbusch's education was provided by his German-born father and formal theological training. Both began as orthodox ministers seeking the salvation of individual souls, but early in their careers moved to a position of promulgating the doctrines of social Christianity. Both were inspired by common intellectual influences and developed strikingly similar religious and socioeconomic beliefs. Their ideas converged in the mid-1890s in the Christian socialist schools and Brotherhood of the Kingdom. But by the turn of the century, as Herron left Iowa for socialist rallies in Chicago, and Rauschenbusch left Hell's Kitchen for the Rochester seminary, their ideological lines diverged. Herron abandoned the ministry for political activism and eventually exiled himself from the United States. Rauschenbusch moved deeper into Christian history and theology and translated patriotic American documents for use by German-American youth. Herron stressed the socialist dimensions of revolutionary Christianity; Rauschenbusch, the Christian qualities in evolutionary socialism. After 1900 Herron boldly proclaimed: "Why I am a socialist." Rauschenbusch gently asked: "dare we be Christians?"

Most significantly, they differed widely in their attitudes toward the possibilities for reform, that is, the kingdom of heaven on earth, in American life. Ironically, Herron made several ideological shifts, yet remained constant in his expectation that the kingdom, however defined, was at hand. It never was closer. Rauschenbusch, on the other hand, remained ideologically consistent, yet evolved from a sense of the imminently coming kingdom to a belief that partial realizations of the kingdom had already been achieved.

How is this divergence to be explained? They ended up in different ideological places in large part because of events in their private and professional lives. To put the thesis simply: Herron embroiled himself in so much controversy, involving a scandalous divorce and remarriage and loss of professional position, that he had little to lose by taking increasingly radical positions. He ended up profoundly disillusioned with his country and its failures in fulfilling its promises. His continued vitality seemed to depend on failure, on never achieving his goals. Therefore, he exiled himself from the socialist movement in America at the very moment of its highest promise. Rauschenbusch, by contrast, enjoyed a happy family life and achieved enormous professional success and respectability; he had a great deal to lose by taking radical positions like Herron. He had served his society both as activist urban minister and as scholarly prophet, and it was comforting to be relatively confident in his country and its accomplishments. Besides, the thrust of his work was theoretically reformist but practically conservative, a dilemma he never resolved.

These outcomes are not just the result of family life and differing degrees of professional respectability; they are also the product of the widely separated environmental origins and childhood experiences of the two men. Their ultimate divergent attitudes toward the pace of reform in America represents the differing expectations of a midwestern native American who expected the United States, given its ideals, to become what it ought to be, and those of a second-generation immigrant who was proud of what was. Origins provide clues to later attitudes. Herron, for example, was imbued with frontier democratic values through his love for Lincoln and his reading of George Bancroft. He grew up expecting American performance to match its promise. When it did not, his radicalism and eventual disillusionment were assured. Rauschenbusch grew up in a family proud of its adopted country and, as his native Germany became increasingly despotic, he was fully aware of the difficulties of fulfilling national promises. To the extent that the performance of the United States moved closer to its promise in the early years of the twentieth century, he was proud of his own role in that progress and increasingly feared only the abandonment of elitist leadership.

One final look at these two men in their differing responses to World War I illustrates both the mixed quality of their feelings toward America and the agonies of the intellectual as reformer. Ironically, the anti-American socialist, George Herron, enthusiastically embraced the Allied cause in the war, while the pro-American nonsocialist, Walter Rauschenbusch, opposed the war and maintained a strict neutrality in word and deed. Both were avowed pacifists. Rauschenbusch's pacifism, however, was more genuine and trustworthy than Herron's, partly because of his more peaceful, gentler temperament. Herron supported America's entrance into the war because he saw it serving the holy cause of world peace and brotherhood, and because he had often rhetorically endorsed violence as a solution to social conflicts.

In March 1918, shortly before he died, Rauschenbusch wrote that "since 1914 the world is full of hate, and I cannot expect to be happy again in my lifetime." With a German origin, German name, and continued German contacts, he was accused of unpatriotic, pro-German motivations for his pacifism. Although undeniably proud of his German heritage, his belief in nonviolence was deeply rooted in his studies of the gospel and Tolstoy. His treatment of the unregenerate portions of American society had been done with such charity and sympathy that the success of his books has been attributed to his gentle and forgiving spirit and style. Under pressure, however, to defend his antiwar position, he wrote an open letter, his *apologia pro vita sua*, to a friend. "I was born an American citizen," he wrote, "and have never dreamed of being anything else." He declined from reciting incidents of patriotic feelings and pride as "too intimate for a public statement," but cited his work in translating patriotic hymns and documents for German-American young people, as well as writing a textbook for them on American civics, as evidence of his loyalty and love. American democratic ideals, he wrote, dominated his intellectual life. He pleaded that his Christian social convictions directly negated the autocratic and militaristic philosophy then dominating Germany. One of his fears, in fact, was that the United States might "travel the same old way toward an aristocratic distribution of property and consequently an oligarchal Junkerism in politics; I am, therefore, not merely an American in sentiment, but have taken our democratic principles very seriously and used my life to inculcate and spread them here and abroad."[60] His pacifism during World War I, like his confidence in the progress of domestic reform, was an affirmation of his Americanism. He died in July 1918, thus being spared the task of coming to terms with the decline of progressivism and the social gospel. Herron was not so fortunate.

For all his domestic radicalism, Herron wavered briefly at first with other socialists (and Italians as well) when the war broke out, yet emerged militantly on the side of the Allies. At first, his motivations were less the result of a positive commitment to the Allies as negative hatred of Germany. Eventually, however, his analysis of the war had the Herron stamp on it: he polarized the conflict into one between Prussianism, autocracy, and the will to power on the one side, and Jesus Christ, democracy, and the will to love on the other. Critical of those who derogated his pro-Ally idealism, he wrote, "*Only Utopia is practicable. We shall see that no peace is procurable, either by a world or by nations or by individuals, save in the realization of the ideal. . . . It is Utopia or perdition that awaits the human race in the end.*" Therefore, he concluded that German militarism had to be soundly trounced, for world peace was possible only if militarism was purged from the earth. Taking refuge in Wilsonianism, he wrote that "it is precisely because I am a pacifist that I am profoundly pro-Ally." When the United States declared war on Germany, Herron was convinced, as many were, that it was a war to end wars. America "has taken up arms in order to destroy the need of arms," he said. "She has made herself the militant exponent of the millennial peace of the Apocalypse." When Wilson announced his peace aims, Herron bubbled with enthusiasm, especially for the League of Nations. Wilson had no more dedicated supporter than the former denouncer of most established American institutions. In fact, because of his loyalty and European connections, he was given a quasi-official position in Switzerland and charged with making contact with friends in the Central Powers to convince them of the sincerity of Wilson's peace proposals. In his effort to make the Germans "believe in Wilson," Herron turned his energies on Wilson himself, imploring the president not to yield in his efforts to secure the league. "Let the League of Nations be now, Mr. President," he wrote, for "unto you it is divinely given, and unto you only, to speak the word that shall bring the World-Society into being." William Allen White reported that Herron, "the kind of a man who would attract Wilson," saw the president four or five times at Versailles in order to press his plea on Wilson.[61] Herron's World War I experience, then, restored his faith in America. For the first time since he had exiled himself in 1901, the missionary apostle was fully optimistic about the divine role of his country.

The rejection of the league by the Senate in 1919, however, shattered his tenuously restored patriotism. Herron's disillusionment, shared by many intellectuals, was bitter and permanent. He dedicated a sad little book, *Defeat in Victory*, "to all who, deep in the shadow of The Great Dissappointment [*sic*] . . . still hopefully strive for the redemption of the nations." Wilson, he wrote, was in a line of "political prophets, from Moses to Mazzini," yet, like Mazzini, had been betrayed. To Morris Hillquit he wrote that the failure of Wilson's program was one of the most devastating events of his life. He told Hillquit that he was pessimistic about international socialism and was "entirely convinced that we are in the beginnings of the disintegration of our present civilisation." Grasping for hope, he added that perhaps disintegration was good, for "the time has come when God will sweep the floor of the world clean in order to build anew."[62]

Herron's dream of the kingdom of God seemed ever to be eluding his grasp. "I really believed . . . that America would . . . become a Messianic nation," he wrote six months before his death, "and would establish a new world in which war would be forever ended and in which there would be a new human order that would be at least an approach to the kingdom of heaven. . . . Instead of the kingdom of heaven we have something nearer the kingdom of hell." Alienated from America for some seventeen years, he had returned to Wilsonian idealism for a few months between 1917 and 1919. When even these ideals were betrayed, his alienation returned in a final embittering disillusionment. But if America had failed him, there was still Mazzini's Italy, to which he turned again in the 1920s. He wrote to King Victor Emmanuel III that no nation was as well equipped to effect the social and political regeneration of the world as Italy. The land of "the matchless prophet Mazzini" would, he wrote, lead the family of man to the "fulfillment of the kingdom of heaven on earth." Political changes in Italy did nothing to deter his irrepressible enthusiasm. In 1923 he told Vida Scudder that Mussolini's Fascist government, of all the governments in Europe, was "the only thing that really promises an element of redemption to Europe." He was the true believer to the end.[63]

Herron was, as William Allen White observed, "one of God's pedestal dwellers, always moving about in bronze or marble. I often used to wonder . . . if he made love in paragraphs, pages, or chapters." An impressionable and intemperate man, he adopted Mazzini's messianic role for himself and spread the message in an avalanche of words. His disillusionment was a consequence not only of his excessive words and controversial life but also of his persistent expectations of an imminent reign of peace and justice.

"There is something provokingly illusive about millenniums," a friend wrote to him in 1920, a comment full of insight into Herron's own predicament.[64] Rauschenbusch, however, avoided Herron's excesses and was spared his disenchantment, partly because he differed from Herron in origins and temperament, partly because he succeeded in his personal and professional life, and partly because he believed that his own deeds had contributed to social progress. He interpreted this progress as evidence that the coming of the kingdom of heaven, an organic, developmental process, had begun. For Rauschenbusch the kingdom was already here; for Herron it was always at hand. These are fitting epitaphs.

6

POETS OF BROTHERHOOD AND LOVE: EDWIN MARKHAM AND ERNEST CROSBY

This is my Holy Church, my Sacred Shrine:
In this high place are voiced the mighty themes
Of those who have strength to perish for their dreams—
Love, Labor, Loyalty—the saving trine.

MARKHAM *

Believe me, these partners in creation live; I have seen them—
the apostles of manhood, of justice, of simplicity, of love. . . .
Our children will build the monuments of Tolstoi, and George,
and the rest;
But how will they treat their own prophets?
Happy the land that knoweth its prophets before they die!

CROSBY †

THE DEATH of Walter Rauschenbusch in 1918 moved a poet, Edwin Markham, to mourn his death in verse. He called Rauschenbusch "our social prophet, Our John the Baptist Crying in the Wilderness," and proclaimed anew his dream of the kingdom.

How shall I name you, valiant and so wise?
Shall I not call you conscript of the Christ,
Son of his dream of earth imparadist?
You saw his Comrade Kingdom must arise,
The Kingdom so long hid from mortal eyes,
The truth for which he lived, for which he died,
The Brother Truth the ages have denied,
The Truth the Lyric Heaven forever cries.

For Edwin Markham, however, Rauschenbusch's death was not an occasion for sorrow, but for celebration: in death he gained immortality, joining "Mazzini, Lamennais, and all the heroes of our mortal way."[1] Markham shared Rauschenbusch's dream of the brotherhood of the kingdom, as did another poet of the new religious movement, Ernest Howard Crosby. Both had absorbed religious and humanitarian goals in their youth, yet, like Howells, the full expression of these goals lay dormant until stimulated to the surface by the ethical inspiration of American and European social prophets. Both suffered over their inability to match deeds with words, though Crosby's distress was more openly expressed than Markham's. Both shared Herron's and Bliss's dream of unity among Christian reformers and were prepared to respond favorably to their pleas.

At a series of meetings in New York in January 1901, organized by Crosby, Markham, Bliss, Heber Newton, and Henry George, Jr., a nonpartisan Civic Council was created to coordinate the activities of some one hundred reform organizations. Crosby, who was connected with both the Christian socialist groups represented by Bliss and Newton and the individualist single tax groups represented by George, was elected president of the council. The first task undertaken by the new organization was to invite Herron to New York. Consequently, in April 1901, five months before his flight into exile, Herron brought his social crusade from Chicago to New York; he also brought, not surprisingly, the opprobrium of his divorce. A dinner reception in his honor was canceled as former associates denounced him and refused to attend. According to an Iowa newspaper, only Crosby and Markham among New York reformers defended Herron and indicated that they would attend the dinner. In accepting his invitation, Crosby said that Herron was "one of the best men in the country, the latchet of whose shoes these gentlemen who are criticizing him are unworthy to unloose. . . . I shall be proud to appear on the platform with him." Markham declared his conviction that Herron was blameless in the divorce controversy and called him "a man whose whole life is based on the highest ethical ideals." The uproar over the dinner did not prevent the crusaders from going ahead with their efforts. Markham and Crosby presided at two public meetings where they warmly welcomed Herron and his social crusaders to New York. A number of evenings of fellowship were enjoyed by Herron, Markham, Crosby, and Bliss, as together they sought to unite the reformers in New York into a spiritual socialist crusade. As usual, however, other than fellowship, little came of it, and the Civic Council soon perished.[2]

In 1894 both Markham and Crosby were unknown in eastern reform circles. Crosby was a prosperous, successful international judge in Alexandria, Egypt, and Markham was a school principal and part-time poet in Oakland, California. It went unnoticed that on May 1, 1894, Markham sent a letter to the editor of a West Coast weekly defending the plight of unemployed laborers and Coxey's Army. "The labor problem is only a phase of the religious question," he wrote, urging that "the final solution . . . involves the practical application of the Golden Rule."[3] It also went unnoticed that in that same month Crosby was rededicating his life to the law of love as a result of reading Tolstoy. By 1900, however, Markham and Crosby had become the poet laureates of the new religious crusade. Their poems, letters, articles, and speeches appeared with regularity in several reform journals. Their acceptance by reformers and radicals of a variety of political and ideological beliefs was testimony to their meteoric rise to a position of respect—and sometimes reverence—within the movement. It was also an indication of their emphasis on the idealistic goals of reform, with which most reformers agreed, and of their ambiguity on specific tactics and means, about which reformers usually quarreled.

Markham was a vague Mazzinian socialist, and his poems and speeches were full of proclamations of brotherhood, the dignity of labor, and the "Comrade Kingdom." Crosby, by contrast, was a devoted disciple of Tolstoyan individualism and George's single tax, and wrote poems of love, peace, and the kingdom within. These ideals were shared by individuals and collectivists alike, and Crosby and Markham moved back and forth in both schools, touching both with the elevated mysticism, vision, and idealism of their poetry. Crosby, the individualist, "was exalted almost to Brotherhood of the Kingdom sainthood" by the Christian socialists at Marlborough, and in 1897 Rauschenbusch sought in vain to persuade him to run for mayor of New York. Markham, the collectivist, was hailed as the "laureate of the new socialism" by the editor of a little "Magazine of Individuality" and was praised as "the best beloved poet of our day" by the editor of the *Single Tax Review*. Crosby was particularly difficult to define. At a conference attended by many in the movement at Lake George in the summer of 1897, he was described as "a very lovable fellow," respected by everyone. No one doubted his intentions, "but few knew exactly what those intentions are and I doubt if he knows himself. He sees good in almost every one and every thing. He is a mystic. He wraps things in a warm, tender, beautiful, but vague mist."[4] Similarly, Markham was known and beloved as a mystic, but he wrapped his ideals (and his purposes) in an even vaguer mist than Crosby. His poem "The Man with the Hoe" meant many things to many reformers, and nonreformers as well, and was applauded by Americans representing the entire spectrum of political thought. Both poets eventually were too mystically idealistic to be of much help to the reform movement, or even to themselves. Two contrasting processes of self-failure is the story told here.

Edwin Markham

Benjamin Flower described Edwin Markham as "the reflector of the mighty spiritual undercurrent of our age. He represents the new conscience and the broadening spiritual ideals of our wonderful age." As usual, Flower overstated his case: Markham's road to this position of respect was a difficult one, marked as much by selfish ambitions for wealth and fame as by unselfish commitments to social and spiritual ideals. His ambivalent wavering between these two purposes was the underlying motif of his life.[5]

He was born to a family of rugged pioneers in Oregon City, Oregon, in 1852, soon after a long trek from Michigan. His father was a wagon master, hunter-trapper, and farmer. Markham told Flower that his father had "a deeply religious nature with a dash of mysticism," but the influence of father on son must have been slight: Markham's parents separated and were divorced soon after he was born. After the separation, Edwin—or Charley, as he was known then—went with his mother to Suisun City, California, where he helped in her store and read the Bible and poetry while tending sheep and cattle in the foothills of the Sierras. Markham's mother was a cold, miserly, hard-working, God-fearing, fanatical devotee of the Campbellite sect of Methodism and an ardent Lincoln Republican. His recollection of her alternated between fond memories of her "sweet and tender nature" and the recognition that she was cold and unloving: "Mother could have led armies, but she couldn't lead children." Louis Filler, who examined the relationship in great detail, concluded that "her essential attitude toward him was that of a jailer." This, perhaps, is an excessive judgment, for there were bonds of loyalty and devotion (though little love or joy) mixed with struggle and conflict in their relationship.[6]

What is important here is that there were books in the home, though not enough for young Edwin's curious mind, and that early in his life he had a passion for reading, especially poets. His mother, a versifier of sorts herself, tried to discourage his interests, for books cost money, their work was demanding, and she believed, as Markham told Flower, that a boy's life was "not to be wasted on books or frittered away in idealistic dreams."[7] Once, however, she brought back some books he had requested from a shopping trip to San Francisco, though she purchased them with money he had earned himself. By all accounts, his thirst for poetry and learning was unquenchable; in spite of his mother's opposition he read widely and attended school. His earliest and continuing ambitions were to be a poet and teacher. With the encouragement of two teachers, he left his mother to attend the Normal School in San Jose, where he graduated in 1872. He taught school for a year near San Luis Obispo and attended the Campbellite-oriented

Christian College in Santa Rosa in 1873–1874. For the next twenty-five years, before he splashed into national prominence with his Hoe-poem in 1899, Markham led three lives: one public, one private, and one mixed. All three were part of a search for his identity and for justification of his dual, conflicting purposes in life.

His public life was as a teacher, headmaster, and principal of schools throughout northern California, ending up in Oakland in the 1890s. He even won an election and served a term as a Republican county superintendent of schools in Coloma, and was an officer of an anti-Chinese committee in Placerville. His private life centered around some losing speculative financial ventures (a pattern that continued right through the 1930s) and his various relationships with his mother, mother-surrogates, mistresses, and three wives. The most significant of Markham's lives in this period (with both public and private dimensions) was the development of his social and religious philosophy and its relationship to his ambitions as a poet. The primary influence on him in his quest was the mystical, Swedenborgian, socially utopian California poet, Thomas Lake Harris, whom he first encountered in 1876. Harris claimed to have had a number of supernatural contacts, or visions, and developed a mystical cult full of unconventional theories about death, sexual relations, private property, and communal life. Markham read Harris's books, absorbed with joy his message, and visited his colony of disciples in Santa Rosa. His influence on Markham—"nothing short of a blinding inspiration," Filler calls it—was enormous. First, he freed him from the Campbellite Methodism of his youth so that he could finally repudiate the institution of the church and begin to develop his own religious belief centered around the ethical teachings of Jesus; second, Harris's sexual theories gave Markham some arguments and courage with which to move toward the termination of a loveless marriage; and third, Harris's communitarian, anticapitalistic radicalism supported and furthered Markham's earlier commitments in that direction derived from his reading of Hugo and Fourier.[8]

Markham's discovery of a radical Harrisite philosophy, combined with his own lifelong struggles and hardships, led him to identify with the laboring masses and to conceive of himself as a poet of the suffering and downcast poor. He compiled a notebook full of rebel poems which he hoped to publish, titled variously as the "Song of the Labor Muse" or "Song of the New Humanity" or "In Earth's Shadow." Yet, as Filler points out, it was not these poems that he submitted to eastern editors, but rather poems about the Sierras and nature and ideal love, the kind that might be accepted. Even after his acceptance as a poet of note in the West and the beginnings of recognition in the East, he continued for the most part to submit light romantic poems to editors rather than his "book of darkness," as he now called it. In fact, long after his national reputation had been secured, he refused to issue the various volumes of rebel poems or the book on Harris or on Jesus as a radical that he kept promising. Instead, he cultivated genteel editors and eastern contacts, developed a mythicized story of his past, and ambitiously pursued a secure image as a respectable and conventional (but not too conventional) bard. He did not even conceive of "The Man with the Hoe," which established his reputation with both the literary establishment and the reformers of the new religious movement, as a rebellious poem, for he intended to submit it to elitist *Scribner's Magazine*. The Hoe-poem was rushed into print by no less a conventional figure than the editor of the *San Francisco Examiner*, and when it was published as the title poem of his first volume of verses, the book was dedicated to no less an arbiter of decency and genteel taste than Edmund Clarence Stedman.

And yet, despite his conventional ambitions and restraints, Markham was a significant figure in the reform movement, and it was important to him that he be respected not only by such political and literary conservatives as Stedman and the women who attended his $200 lectures but also by such reformers as Flower, Crosby, Herron, and Debs. And therein lay his essential conflict and source of self-doubts: he pursued both his private literary ambitions, as reflected in published poems, and his public social duties, as reflected in private notebooks full of rebel poems. The two were constantly overlapping, for he did occasionally publish work from his "book of darkness," such as "The Song of the Workers" in 1886 in memory of "the martyrs of the Commune" and a story in 1893 that preached the single tax. After 1899 he jeopardized his carefully cultivated poetic reputation by writing articles for reform journals and by appearing at gatherings of radicals, by his unpopular defenses of the marital practices of Herron and Maxim

Gorky, and by the publication of such dark and somber poems as "Virgilia" and the "Ballad of the Gallows-Bird." Torn between his conflicting purposes and self-images, Markham nevertheless committed himself—but only part of himself—to the reform movement.

His role in the movement was, like Flower's, that of an ethical enthusiast, an interpreter of uplifting and inspiring social messages to other intellectual reformers like himself. During his lengthy life, Markham was often called upon to enumerate the influences on his life and poetry. Certain names invariably appeared, publicly and privately. Other names—most notably Thomas Lake Harris, whose cultist sexual theories involved him in numerous scandals—were conspicuously absent from Markham's public lists. His lists, of which there were many, generally were of three kinds. The first were lists of poets, especially those he judged to be socially significant. He admitted in 1899 that poetry no longer influenced him as it had in his youth, but listed Milton, Shelley, Tennyson, and Browning as among the more lasting influences. But Tennyson's poetry was too socially timid for Markham, and Browning was excessively concerned with individual, not social man. The loftiest of all poets, he said, was Shelley, who "saw the social injustice everywhere around him, and . . . uttered his cry for the rights of the stooped, silent toilers." The era of poets ended in 1830, Markham said, after which the great writers of humanity were the prose poets, who cried the need for social justice, inspiring men to a social crusade. Markham increasingly preferred these prose poets, whose leaders he listed as "Thomas Carlyle, the prophet; John Ruskin, the dreamer; Victor Hugo, the humanitarian; [and] Joseph Mazzini, the liberator."[9]

Markham's third list was of individual books that had influenced his social thought. Invariably, he mentioned the familiar texts of the new religious movement, starting with the Gospels, "the most original and radical writing ever given to mankind." In 1899 he was asked if the views expressed in the Hoe-poem were his own, and he replied that they were not. Rather, he said, they were "embodied in the Sermon on the Mount, in the life and teachings of St. Francis of Assisi, in the aspirations of Savonarola and Cromwell. In modern times they appear in the utterances of such men as Mazzini and Ruskin and Herron. Mazzini's 'the Duties of Man' and Herron's 'Between Caesar and Jesus' should be read by every man who wishes to know the deep, the sublime, meaning of the Christianity of Christ. These two books are great political bibles." Markham had just read *Between Caesar and Jesus* and was attracted by Herron's "powerful appeal for the application of the practical principle of Christianity to our political and industrial life." The poet was attracted to other writers who voiced the same appeal. In 1923 he wrote odes, which he did not publish, to "my four great historic devotions—Savonarola, Lamennais, Mazzini, Victor Hugo. I see in these men four of the greatest souls of all time."[10] What these four—and his other enthusiasms—shared in common was a commitment to his central social concept: the "Comrade Kingdom."

The original inspiration for the "Comrade Kingdom" was the teaching of Jesus. In 1928 he replied to an inquisitive correspondent that "the greatest inspiration in my life has been the great poets, especially the poet Jesus. . . . He confronted a hostile world with a daring social message." Markham first interpreted Jesus' message as social, or so he liked to recall, while tending sheep as a boy of sixteen. The emphasis on the kingdom of heaven in the Sermon on the Mount particularly impressed him. He told his laudatory biographer, William Stidger, that he realized then that the kingdom "referred to a new order of life in the world for men and women. That was my first gleam of the Comrade Dream. That was my baptism into the new social order. Ever since that hour I have looked upon the Gospels as the greatest political and social document in the world." He convinced himself, with the help of Harris, that Jesus' dream of love and brotherhood in a new social order and his own were identical. "I have dreamed that a reformation of the industrial world would do something for human happiness," Markham wrote in 1884, believing that "some such dreams filled the deep, soft, lovable soul of Christ."[11]

At the age of seventeen Markham read Hugo's *The Man Who Laughs*, a romance about a young boy who had been kidnapped and mutilated so that his mouth was cut into a perpetual laugh. Hugo's message of social democracy was evident: the boy, the heir to an English fortune, renounced his wealth and ordered its dispersal to the poor and hungry whom he had known while on a journey after his kidnapping. The romance "sang into my soul," Markham said, "and made vital and real the gospel of the Christ whose whisper I heard in my earlier youth." Years later he inscribed in the front of this volume that it had come to him "at the psychological moment, at the time when all the energies of my mind were bubbling hot in their crater. The huge humanity of Victor Hugo was the fortunate mold into which the fluid emotions ran, cooled, and took form for the labor of a life-time." He retained a lasting admiration for the humanitarianism of Hugo's romances. "The pity and the wonder of them touched my heart, and I was never again the same." At about the age of twenty, before discovering Harris, Markham read Fourier's *Introduction to Social Theory*, an outline of his communal utopianism. He saw "that Jesus in his vision of the Comrade Kingdom, that Victor Hugo in his impassioned defense of the struggling millions, and that Charles Fourier in his vast conceptions of our social possibilities, were all three moving toward the same great ends of life." He turned again to the Gospels and noted that Jesus mentioned the church only three times, but referred to the kingdom of heaven 122 times. This observation convinced Markham that the kingdom meant a new social and industrial order in which all men would be "consecrated comrades."[12] To the extent that this late-in-life explanation of the origins of his thought was accurate—and I believe it to be—he was more than spiritually prepared for the blinding inspiration of Thomas Lake Harris's message, which he experienced shortly thereafter.

The next influences on Markham's social thought were Mazzini and Lamennais. His son, Virgil, said that "father was quite smitten by the nineteenth century liberals, especially Mazzini and Hugo, and used to talk about them a great deal, especially Mazzini." Markham owned the six-volume set *The Life and Writings of Joseph Mazzini*, published in London in 1890, and his copies were abundantly marked with marginal comments. Next to Mazzini's statement that the poet was a divine lawgiver, for example, Markham wrote that the "two things of value in life [were] poetry and unselfish service; these hold the fire of God." The comment is a fascinating revelation of his dual goals. In a margin in the *Duties of Man*, he wrote: "Rights the basis of Democracy: duties the basis of Social Democracy." He recommended the six volumes to a friend, praising in particular Mazzini's essay on Lamennais. The French priest's social philosophy, Markham rightly observed, was almost identical to Mazzini's. Markham's lengthy odes to the two prophets were strikingly repetitive, celebrating their vision of social democracy, their lonely apostolates, and their self-sacrifices. Each had the same dreams. Each fought kings and popes. Each died a martyr's death. Each was in heaven with Dante, Milton, Cromwell, Savonarola, and Shelley. Markham implored each to descend to earth "to lead us in the comrade fight." The work of each continued on earth, for as Markham wrote in the Mazzini ode, his inspiration still led others to

> March to the battles that are yet to be—
> On to the waiting kingdom of the free,
> Your deeds still teach us how to live and die,
> Your faith still helps to build the comrade shrine,
> Your words still feed us with the bread and wine,
> Your valorous soul still leads with startling cry
> On every battle-line.

In both poems Markham expressed his frequently reiterated desire that he might join the two in heaven, for he had sought "the same immortal goals" and had, like them, been involved in

> . . . the same long struggle for the Dream;
> And so I pray that I, the least in grace,
> May sometime humbly stand before your face—
> That there among your battle-sons supreme,
> I too may have a place.[13]

Whether he deserved such a place was another question.

Markham was also inspired by Ruskin and Carlyle, though not as profoundly as by the others. During an illness in the winter of 1883–1884, he read Ruskin's works of social criticism. He was enchanted with them; finding Ruskin's soul to be "all Sweetness and Light," as he wrote to a friend: "His 'Letters to the Workingmen' —what admirable philosophy with its noble scorn of mere luxury! I find it hard to speak of him in terms that will not sound extravagant." He preferred Ruskin to Carlyle because he was a more constructive thinker. Carlyle inveighed against all that was wrong with nineteenth-century political and economic life and thought, but "never saw

Men drawn together in the Comrade Law,
Made one at last in Love's Fraternal State.
Men are not battling bandits: they are friends:
You failed to call them to their social ends.

Ruskin, on the other hand, at once destroyed the thought of the old order and envisaged the new.[14] Few of Markham's lists of favorite books were without at least one of Ruskin's works and his library contains well-marked, multivolume sets of the works of both English critics.

Markham's list of written inspirations was completed by the utopias of Howells and the novels of Tolstoy. Howells's vision of an Altrurian utopia, despite the pastoral agrarian emphasis, was similar to Markham's concept of the comrade dream. Moreover, the poet felt personal affection for Howells, whom he sought out on his triumphant visit to the East Coast after the publication of "The Man with the Hoe" in 1899. He regularly sent published volumes of his poems to the respected critic and just as regularly received warm responses. In a letter to Markham soon after the appearance of the Hoe-poem, Howells said: "I know your work only from your poem on the Angelus of Millet. I think that so very great and noble a poem, that I hope some day to read all you have written." Howells's admiration for Markham increased. The words of the "Hoe-poem," he said later, "pour a lava-tide of scorching questions from the soul of humanity upon the self-complacency of society." In appreciation of many years of friendship, Markham dedicated a volume of poetry, *Gates of Paradise*, to Howells in 1920, shortly before the critic's death. The dedicatory statement was unintentionally ironic, proclaiming Howells as "That Lover of Justice and Brotherhood Who had the Courage to Take Unprofitable Risks." The irony extended to Markham himself, who took unprofitable risks only in financial ventures, not political or literary ones. His volume dedicated to Howells was filled with sad love poems, songs to the "divine Mother," celebrations of victory in World War I, explorations of immortality, and poems about "memorable men," which included not only Father McGlynn but also Alexander Graham Bell. The copy sent to Howells was inscribed: "My dear William Dean Howells: I wish that this little volume were worthier of your great name," a rare, if mild, admission of his personal inadequacies.[15]

Markham respected Howells's master, Tolstoy, as a disciple of the ethics of Jesus and servant of humanity, but neither revered him as did Howells nor reviled him as did Herron. Deeply impressed with *Resurrection*, Markham wrote to Tolstoy in 1899 and sent him a volume of *The Man with the Hoe and Other Poems*, which the Russian kindly, though briefly, acknowledged. In 1907 Markham wrote again to his "Venerable and Revered Brother" and congratulated him on his "distinguished service to humanity." In the manuscript of a speech written several years later, Markham contrasted Tolstoy with Nietzsche. Tolstoy, Markham wrote, was a prophet of self-renunciation, while Nietzsche was a prophet of egotism. Tolstoy had a democratic love for the poor and adhered to the ethics of Jesus; Nietzsche had an aristocratic disdain for the masses and bitterly repudiated Jesus' ethics. Markham clearly preferred the Russian and yet mourned him as a tragic figure. The sad Russian, Markham said, was unable to resolve the conflict between his own comfort and the burdensome condition of men's lives. In still another unpublished poem, which offers an insight into Markham's own troubled inner conflicts, he wrote of Tolstoy that "he saw the hell rooted in all our strife, saw discord even in his secret soul."[16] These, then, were the primary inspirations on Markham's life and thought. All except Herron and Tolstoy had already influenced him when he saw Millet's painting at an exhibition in San Francisco in December 1898 and decided to finish a poem begun twelve years earlier.

Markham had seen a picture of the "Angelus" in *Scribner's Magazine* in 1886 and at that time wrote the first four lines of his poem:

> Bowed by the weight of centuries he leans
> Upon his hoe and gazes on the ground,
> The emptiness of ages in his face,
> And on his back the burden of the world.

The poem remained unfinished until Markham saw the original and was stirred to complete his masterpiece. On that day, as he explained later, he sat for an hour looking at the painting, "absorbing the majesty of its despair, the suggestion of its injustice, the tremendous import of its admonition." The Hoe-man, he said, represented all the toilers of the world, including not only the burdened farmer but also the worker in a New York City sweatshop, the miner in a West Virginia coal mine, and the boatman on the Volga. Markham went home from the exhibition "like a man under a spell" and within a week had finished the poem. In an interview for the *Oakland Tribune*, he explained that his poem was a protest against the degradation of labor in which a man's life was made hideous, hopeless, and beneath that even of the noble savage. Markham's answer to the question posed by the poem—"How will you ever straighten up this shape?"—was, he said, to "reverse the process by which he was degraded. Let the lords and masters get off his back, so that he may straighten up. Let the Hoe-man keep his hoe, but do not grind him down with trusts and combines and infamous monopolies." The toiler's dignity and freedom would return, the poet said, when the golden rule and cooperation were made operative in the industrial order.[17]

In an interview for the *Christian Herald* in 1900, Markham reiterated his conviction that cooperation, labor organization and unity, and an "appeal through the ballot box" were proper means to improve the Hoe-man's opportunities. He deplored strikes as harmful, yet at times as cruel necessities, and urged the creation of a cabinet level department of labor. When pressed for specific proposals which would "straighten" the Hoe-man, he advocated compulsory arbitration, reduced working hours, public works projects for the unemployed, government ownership of railroads, telephone, and telegraph, municipal ownership of public utilities, and equal rights for women. When asked to describe the kind of leadership necessary for the labor movement, he cited men such as Francis of Assissi, Ruskin, and Mazzini.[18] It is revealing that he did not name Debs, or Gompers, or even some local New York labor leader, an indication of the elevation of his thought and his remoteness from the immediacy of the labor movement. It was safer to appeal to some distant and deceased prophet like Mazzini than to embroil himself in controversy by mentioning a contemporary leader.

The publication of "The Man with the Hoe" catapulted the soon-to-be ex-school teacher and principal into national and international reknown. He desired closer contact with the inner circles of the literary (and reformist) establishment, as well as access to a wider audience, and therefore moved in 1899 to the East Coast, living first in Brooklyn and finally on Staten Island. He continued to live his dual role as conventional poet, publishing nonrebellious poems on Lincoln and other acceptable themes, and as committed reformer, revealing his rebel poems and eulogistic celebrations of Mazzini and the "Radical from Nazareth" only to close friends. He lived on Staten Island for the remaining forty years of his life, writing poems, lecturing widely to all kinds of audiences, and delivering addresses or reading poems for ceremonial or dedicatory events, many of them celebrating Markham himself. Rauschenbusch predicted in 1901 that Markham "is going to be a great power for socialism,"[19] but this forecast seems overly zealous in light of Markham's inner conflicts and relative aloofness from the daily struggles of the laboring and socialist reformers he privately admired so much. What concerns us here, however, is the social philosophy he projected at the turn of the century that could elicit such a prediction and his personal restraints that contradicted it.

The principles of Markham's social thought began with his faith in the dignity of labor, as reflected by contrast in the Hoe-man. This faith led him to a kind of vague Christian socialism as the social philosophy by which the Hoe-man's degradation might best be reversed. These were not new ideas for Markham. Their origins lay in his youth, reading the Sermon on the Mount and Hugo's romances while tending sheep in the California hills. As early as 1877 he wrote, "I shall dream dreams & weave visions—of *what might have been*—of *what yet may be*." In 1883 he wrote a poem saying:

> I would be one of those
> Among the noble brotherhood of song
> That sing the starless sorrows of the Poor
> Their passion & their pathos & their wrong.

He almost joined the socialist international in 1886. In an unfinished letter that indicated he was enclosing his application and fees, he wrote that "for many years I have been deeply, passionately interested in Social problems. Ours is certainly a sick world, and I can see no human help for it but in International Revolutionary Socialism." He never sent the letter, however, and never joined any socialist party. Markham's brand of socialism was far from revolutionary. Like Howells, he preferred the gradual approach of the ballot box to violent upheaval. Furthermore, no political label could be pinned to him, and he usually prefaced his declarations of political preference by explaining that he was "not a politician but a literary man." With this qualification, he announced his support in 1900 for Bryan, not Debs.[20] He did not, however, consistently vote Democratic, but supported individual candidates regardless of party. For example, he supported Samuel Jones's nonpartisan mayoral and gubernatorial campaigns in Ohio in 1899, Morris Hillquit's Socialist party campaign for mayor of New York in 1906, and Theodore Roosevelt's and Robert La Follette's Progressive presidential bids in 1912 and 1924.

Markham's socialism was not militant and revolutionary, moreover, because like the other knights he believed that religious and social questions were identical and therefore sought, like Vida Scudder, to infuse socialism with an ethical spirit. Social problems had always appealed to Markham from an ethical point of view, a position he first acquired from Harris and Fourier. The socialists were wrong, he said in 1902, when they placed all their "stress on economic interest. . . . It seems to me that the ethical impulse is as strong as the economic impulse." But neither was the church doing enough for the worker, Markham realized, for it sought to save individual souls rather than to usher in the kingdom by ameliorating industrial conditions. In a response to Samuel Batten, who had sent him some pamphlets of the Brotherhood of the Kingdom, Markham urged that the "coming Industrial Republic" depended upon each church preaching the social message of "Christ the Artisan." In a conversation with Flower in 1909, he declared: "I want to see Christ enthroned in the industrial world. . . . I want to see applied Christianity take the place of churchianity. I want to see religion secularized, industrialized, socialized. . . . Christ is not ecclesiastical: He is social and humanitarian."[21] These beliefs were summed up by his vision of the "Kingdom of Comrades."

Like Herron and Rauschenbusch, Markham believed that the kingdom of heaven on earth was the central concept of Jesus, a belief that began in his youth when he counted the number of references to the kingdom in the Gospels. There were in fact two kingdoms, he wrote, "*one within man, waiting to come forth in character; another above man, waiting to descend in institutions.*" It was the second kingdom, the "comrade dream" he called it, that most concerned him, although his poetry was often directed at the first. In an article in 1907 in an obscure Christian socialist journal and titled "What Would Jesus Be Doing if He Were Here?" Markham concluded that he "would disturb us" by preaching an "*industrial* as well as devotional" message, by seeking to "build His social Gospel into fact," and by allying himself with the college settlement movement, the labor churches, and organized socialism. It is revealing to compare this somewhat strong and threatening Jesus with the public poetic version of the same theme, titled "If He Should Come." In the poem, published in a volume for Doubleday in 1932 in celebration of Markham's eightieth birthday, he did not assert what Jesus would do, but asked, rather weakly, what Jesus' relationship with rich men and churchmen would be, suggesting that he would no doubt disapprove. It is also interesting that in this poem Jesus was the "Workman from Nazareth," but in the unpublished "Church of Rebels," penned three years earlier, he was the "Radical from Nazareth." In general, the Jesus who appears in Markham's notebooks or in small circulation journals of the reform movement is a daring, activist social radical, but the Jesus who appears in his poems published for the Doubleday volumes would not offend the staunchest of orthodox, anti-Social Gospel clergymen.[22]

Still, as poet laureate of the new religious movement, Markham's duty was to promulgate the "comrade dream," however vaguely outlined. In describing the precise form of the kingdom that Jesus would build, he was no more specific than suggesting that the Sermon on the Mount would be its "Constitution," an idea he probably picked up from Herron. Within the sermon, he argued, were the social and industrial principles of the new order. He interpreted each of the Beatitudes and many of the passages in the sermon from a social point of view. Thus, the injunction against mammonism meant that the rich should renounce their worldly wealth for the good of all, the "Our Father" of the Lord's Prayer was a declaration of brotherhood, and "daily bread" referred to economic justice and equality. Above all other requirements, however, the golden rule was "the supreme law in the Kingdom of Comrades." The application of this rule of love, he said in 1899, would solve problems of monopoly, injustice, concentration of wealth, and international disputes. Its application would abolish the rule of gold and would usher in "the Cooperative Commonwealth. . . . After eighteen centuries we have committed the Golden Rule to memory; let us now commit it to life."[23] He was never much more specific than this, even in nonpublished statements.

Edwin Markham's well-known poem "Brotherhood," which he read at the Buffalo conference in 1899 and which was subsequently published in both reformist and conventional magazines, was typical of his elevated vagueness:

> Come, clear the way, then, clear the way:
> Blind creeds and kings have had their day.
> Break the dead branches from the path:
> Our hope is in the aftermath—
> Our hope is in heroic men,
> Star-led to build the world again.
> To this Event the ages ran:
> Make way for Brotherhood—make way for Man.

He realized that these lofty ideals were only words and were of little use unless practically applied. In a letter in 1920 he wrote of brotherhood that it "must not hang in air: it must not be a floating bubble. Brotherhood must descend into the shops and the industries: it must have economic foundation." But recognizing the point was not the same as doing something about it; the poet himself had not descended at all. The only practical work that he performed, other than appearing occasionally to speak on behalf of various reform candidates, was to work for the abolition of child labor. In a series for the muckraking *Cosmopolitan* magazine in 1906–1907, entitled "The Hoe-Man in the Making," he exposed the evils of child labor in mills, factories, mines, and sweatshops. His study, based on official statistics and his own travels and observations, was an immense effort, expressed in language intended to turn the coldest conservative into the most dedicated opponent of child labor in the land. In addition, he frequently made direct appeals for the alleviation of child suffering and spent many hours observing in factories for the National Child Labor Committee. His work was important and should not be underestimated, yet it was his only direct involvement in social problems.[24]

Markham often excused his aloofness from the world of practical reform by calling himself a poet-prophet, not a political economist. As Joseph Miller said in a review of Markham, "poetry may condemn social wrongs, it may point the way of justice, but it cannot furnish a code of political conduct. It can only indicate broad ethical questions; it cannot furnish a social catechism." This was a view with which Markham concurred. He was a poet, and his responsibility, as he told Flower, was to prophesy a religious awakening, "quickening the social passion in man, quickening the comrade love in man." Working to realize the vision he presaged was the responsibility of others; they would find their self-realization in their service as he found his in poetry. The poet's home, he wrote, "is on the heights" above the battle and he had a role to serve:

> The toils of prophecy are his,
> To hail the coming centuries—
> To ease the steps and lift the load
> Of souls that falter on the road.

Yet it can be asked how much solace he brought to those below the heights, to those engaged in daily struggles for the rights of workers, or tenement house reform, or even the abolition of child labor. It is questionable whether the "toils of prophecy" were at all as burdensome as the toils of production and poverty. Markham was proud to report in 1925 that no plowman or workingman had ever misunderstood the Hoe-man poem.[25] That may be so, but one wonders how many read it, and even for those who did, how much bread that reading placed on their table. Markham received encomiums from literary critics like Howells, reform journalists like Flower, and prominent ministers like Rauschenbusch. It is, however, one thing to lift the load and ease the steps of middle-class intellectual reformers like himself, but quite another to bolster those who cared less about the "coming centuries" than they did about next week's paycheck or eviction notice. Markham himself spent his life after 1900 living "on the heights" of Staten Island, engaging in losing speculative ventures, lecturing to women's groups, and reading his poems at exalted national ceremonies like the dedication of the Lincoln Memorial.

It is difficult—and dangerous—to determine to what extent Markham was psychically bothered by his continued dual role as both conventional poet and committed reformer. In 1898 he settled upon a personal motto, which he later made into his bookplate inscription, exhorting, "Come, let us live the poetry we sing!" But which poetry? His inner conflicts and duality were always present, even in poems he chose for publication. His first collection, which included the Hoe-poem and "Brotherhood," mostly contained sentimental poems of love and nature, of crickets and butterflies. In one poem he summons "heroic men . . . to build the world again," while in another he describes his own life idyllically as a dream, climbing clouds and fading with the stars. In *The Shoes of Happiness* he lauds Mazzini, Lamennais, and other "Conscripts of the Dream" for "doing the deed that others pray," yet fills the volume with poems about jugglers, cobblers, and recollections of his California pastoral youth. In one poem he asserts "the right of a man to labor and his right to labor in joy" and in another calls for "love's hero-world" to replace the law of tooth and claw with brotherhood and freedom; yet, for himself, he wishes for a life of "green rafters and quiet hills" where he can stretch out on the grass with a good book to forget the "clamors of the past" and the "broken dream."[26] And so it went in his other published volumes: condemn evils, exhort men in the name of Jesus, Mazzini, and a host of others to redeem the world, and yet seek for himself some quiet, grassy place above the battles. But was this not the role of the poet? Had he not fought enough battles of his own?

Exactly. I believe that Markham almost believed that he was fulfilling his social mission, that writing some socially significant poetry was performing unselfish service to others. In a revealing statement in the late 1890s, probably to his new bride, he explored his goals and sought to justify them to her: "Keats is right: we need the 'heart-easing things.' But what have we in our hearts to ease? . . . We have our private griefs and joys and these are proper themes of song. But must we stop with them? Is there not a larger grief—the Social Joy? . . . If you knew me better you would not grieve that I feel this Social Passion, for it is the best and most unselfish thing in my life."[27] It was precisely the poetic treatment of his Social Passion, he believed, that represented the best and most unselfish part of him, that is, made him feel good. But not only that, for it offered him relief from his own personal sorrows as well. He comes close here (and elsewhere) to seeking Christlike martyrdom by taking the grief of the world as his own. To embody Social Passion in one's poetry is penance and suffering enough; one does not also need to join picket lines or barricades. Moreover, writing poetry exhorting men to share his dream in the coming Comrade Kingdom was, he believed, selfless service enough. He is not only justified by his works but also sanctified by his faith. Thomas Lake Harris and the intervening years had not, it seems, completely eradicated his mother's early Methodist-Campbellite influence.

This revealing passage is not an isolated one. A few years later in 1905, in "Virgilia," the protagonist, "I," concludes a heartbreaking personal adventure in unconventional love by returning to God's work.

> I will go back to the pains and the pities
> That break the heart of the world with moan;
> I will forget in the grief of the cities
> The burden of my own
>
> There in the world-grief my own grief humbles. . . .[28]

Markham again atones for his sins and escapes his own immediate sorrows by taking on the more remote ones of the world.

Throughout his life Markham was fascinated by the symbolism of the cross and had an abiding faith in immortality. His collection of letters in the 1870s and 1880s, while still a young man, is filled with those sent to the friends and relatives of a deceased person in which he expressed his faith in a spiritual life after death. His belief in immortality, however, went beyond the appropriate words of sympathy. Harris had introduced him early in his life to Swedenborg's belief that there was contact between the living and the dead and that, indeed, death did not really exist. Jesus also promised everlasting life:

> we never choose the better part,
> Until we set the Cross up in the heart.
> I know I can not live until I die—
> Till I am nailed upon wild and high,
> And sleep in the tomb for a full three days dead,
> With angels at the feet and at the head.
> But then in a great brightness I shall rise
> To walk with stiller feet below the skies.

And in 1920, while in a hospital in Jersey City, he composed six scrawled pages of searching questions on "How I Think of a Spiritual World." He was obsessed with the question of whether loved ones live after death and if so, "where is their abode & how passes it with them?" Following a sometimes incoherent and mystical analysis of the apostle Paul and Swedenborg, he concluded that matter, even physical being, had no life whatsoever and that "spirit sub. is the only life." In 1926 he published another poem he always regarded as one of his best, the "Ballad of the Gallows-Bird." In it a murderer ("I") who has been hanged but does not die takes a long journey to the kingdom of the dead, bearing his foul victim with him. He encounters ugly, defiled, beastly, dead/live people and "ruined Babylons." He returns at last to the gallows to see ravens picking at the remains of a body only to realize in horror that it was his own, that he really had died: "God of my soul! I was *dead* . . . and *damned*." The poem revealed an intensely troubled man: was he immortal or not? He hoped, though he was not sure, that his rightful place was on the Cross, not the gallows.[29]

In his repetitiously eulogistic poems to his martyred heroes he consistently conceived of a heaven wherein they all resided together. Mazzini, Shelley, and Jesus were all "heroes of the martyrdom" who feared not death and perished for their dreams, as he wrote in 1929 in "The Church of Rebels." His own compelling desire was to join these martyrs in heaven. Had he not suffered enough, both personal sorrows and the "world-grief"? His ode to Mazzini was particularly revealing. After eulogizing Mazzini's sacrificial life, he details the thoughts of the Italian patriot in his hour of death and asks him whether all the loneliness, homelessness, and sorrows of his life were worthwhile.

> Answer our cry, for we would know how seems
> From your high place the worth of Love's great themes—
> Would know the worth of man's heroic quest,
> The worth of all his dreams.

Then, after imploring Mazzini to "descend to lead us in the comrade fight," Markham provides an answer to his question. It is a mixture of hopefulness and self-doubt: for those "who seek with you the same immortal goals, and join the same long struggle for the Dream," the sorrows, burdens, and estrangement of life's struggles will be rewarded.

And so I pray that I, the least in grace,
May sometime humbly stand before your face—
That there among your battle-sons supreme,
I too may have a place.[30]

Markham here seems almost convinced that the reward comes from painting dreams and thinking noble thoughts alone. It did not matter what one did but what one thought and wrote, almost as if he expected that if he wrote enough panegyric poems to Mazzini and Lamennais and Jesus he would earn a place with them in heaven.

But perhaps he protested too much. He continued to reveal his self-doubts and inner conflicts, wavering between unworthiness and conviction that he had earned his seat in the heavenly "church of rebels." The "Ballad of the Gallows-Bird," with its terrifying doubts about immortality, followed the Mazzini ode by three years. In an inscription under a portrait sent to a friend in the month of his eightieth birthday in 1932, he wrote that it "portrays a spirit in me, a spirit hidden, a shadow of the Man of Sorrows." Also in 1932 he wrote a poem deploring depression life in America, a poem that he chose not to include in the volume of verse prepared especially for the gala birthday celebration held for him in Carnegie Hall on April 24, featuring scores of dignitaries, foreign representatives, and even a letter from President Herbert Hoover. The poem was titled "At Eighty Years" and said in part:

I see mothers giving birth
To babes unfit to fill the earth.
I see long lines of hungry men
Gaunt as grey wolves in lonely den.
Even in a country filled with bread
Men go unsheltered and unfed.
I can but flash a sword of song
Against this anarchy and wrong.
I feel more tenderly the tears
Of all the world at eighty years.

He concluded optimistically, however, expressing his expectation that despite the "despairing cries, I have a faith that never dies." Although "the sons of Satan throw their weight, God's sons are also at the gate." Contrast this with one of the poems he did include in his birthday volume, which proclaimed that he was "tired of the battling city and her devastating roar" and desired to "escape to the freedom of fields and the pageant of marching peaks."[31] And thus the ambivalence continued.

Five months later Markham was again sure that he was one of God's sons:

> My life, what is it? All a long revolt,
> A fierce revolt against this world of men,
> This battle for self the slaves of time exalt—
> This battle that is darkness and the den.
> I'm not with them, but with God's noble sons,
> With the great few who left the trampling herd—
> With Shelley and Mazzini, star-toucht ones,
> Who knew the upward look and the Winged Word.[32]

He lived for eight more years, suffering from many psychic disorders, and died in 1940. One hopes that he found his place next to Mazzini and the other "battle-sons supreme." His own "battle sword," as he wrote in the final stanza of the ode to Mazzini, was his "love-song." He had no other.

Ernest Crosby

Edwin Markham's inner conflicts and self-doubts were submerged, surfacing only in an occasional poem. His "comrade" poet, Ernest Crosby, explored his self-doubts and frustrations more openly. Markham was usually optimistic about the coming of the comrade dream to American society; Crosby was more often pessimistic both about his society and about himself. Both poets preached love, brotherhood, the dignity of labor, and the application of the golden rule to society in order to effect the kingdom of heaven on earth. But Markham stressed collectivism and cooperation, the comrade dream, while Crosby emphasized individualism and personal liberty, the kingdom within. Markham leaned toward socialism, Crosby toward philosophical anarchism. Significantly, Markham referred to Jesus as an artisan, while Crosby argued that Jesus was a farmer.[33] Markham preached the subordination of self to the public good; Crosby, who doubted that the public could be good, preached individual self-assertion and denounced the state. His concept of subordination was, like Tolstoy's, the renunciation of material belongings and sensual pleasures, but never of freedom. Markham ambitiously pursued fame and wealth; Crosby, who had wealth, tried, without much success, to get rid of it. In Crosby's many failures and honest self-doubts are revealed not only the frustrations of the intellectual reformer but also the profound difficulties of the self-examined, principled life. In his story we see much in ourselves.

There was little in Ernest Crosby's origins or early life that suggested he would later become a co-worker with anarchists and socialists, remembered by one admirer as "the knight-errant, championing the cause of those who could not help themselves."[34] The Crosby family roots went back to a Puritan immigrant to Boston in 1635 and included rich farmers, revolutionary patriots, physicians, educators, land speculators, and philanthropists. Ernest was born in New York City in 1856, the son of Howard Crosby, pastor of the prestigious Fourth Avenue Presbyterian Church from 1863 to 1891 and for eleven years the chancellor of the University of the City of New York. The senior Crosby was a theological liberal, defending Darwinism against its many critics, but a social conservative, denouncing the Social Gospel and the labor movement. In an article in the *Forum* in 1887 he castigated Henry George's United Labor party and the single tax, arguing that the causes of poverty were not wealth and oppression but laziness and sinful living. "At the bottom of the Henry George movement" and behind the Edward McGlynns and other poverty warriors, he insisted, was envy. The younger Crosby, therefore, absorbed a mixture of enlightened and conventional wisdom from his father.[35]

Whereas Markham had to struggle to find books to read and attended one-room rural California schools, Crosby was given an education befitting a son of the elite: Mohegan Lake school in Westchester County, New York University, graduating with honors in 1876, and Columbia Law School (honors, 1878). He practiced law for ten years, protecting his family's extensive real estate holdings in New York, and was a major in the National Guard. In 1887 he succeeded Theodore Roosevelt as a Republican assemblyman in the New York legislature, where he established his reputation and party loyalty as the promoter of a bill placing a high excise tax on licenses for the sale of alcoholic beverages. In recognition of his growing prominence Crosby was selected in 1888 to deliver an address to the graduating class of the Law Department of the University of the City of New York. His speech was a curious mixture of typical commencement oratory and the germs of radical views he would later develop more fully. Quoting Matthew Arnold, he enjoined the graduates to adhere to their responsibilities as guardians of culture and humanity in their professional careers. This, certainly, was respectable enough. But then he warned them against the excessive materialism, social complacency, and patriotism which threatened, he said, to undermine America. The lesson of the current labor unrest was "that men who live by the sweat of others' brows owe a return to the public," a striking departure from the views of his father. Finally, Crosby offered the graduates some rather typical, if not trite, advice: "You must all grow from within, and be yourselves first and last and at any cost. . . . Do your duty to yourselves and your duty to society will not remain undone."[36] But unlike many commencement orators, Crosby soon took his own advice, attempting to apply these seemingly conventional principles—self-duty and the obligations of the rich—in radical, unconventional ways.

In 1889 President Harrison appointed Crosby to an international judgeship in Egypt. One day five years later he picked up Tolstoy's *My Life*, the Russian's account of his conversion from a life of dissipation and landholding to one of living by the ethical teachings of Jesus, whereby he renounced his wealth in order to share the food, dress, and fieldwork of the Russian peasant. Crosby called *My Life* "as profound an exposition of man's condition and obligations as had ever been written." He read it to the end one Sunday in 1894 and was converted to the Tolstoyan philosophy and way of life. "Nor was the change merely temporary," Crosby wrote ten years later, "for since that day the world has never looked to me quite as it used to." In *Young Man Luther*, Erik Erikson wrote that "in some periods of his history, and in some phases of his life cycle, man needs . . . a new ideological orientation as surely and as sorely as he must have air and food." Identity crises, he explained, are not confined to youth but occur at each successive stage of a person's life. At some point well beyond the various crises of puberty, a person inevitably goes through what Erikson calls "the crisis of generativity." This occurs when he reviews the accomplishments and failures of his life, a process which either "gives him some sense of being on the side of a few angels or makes him feel stagnant." Crosby had been going through such a crisis when he read Tolstoy's book and felt not only his stagnation but his hypocrisy as well.[37]

When he came across *My Life*, the thirty-eight-year-old judge had been intensely unhappy, troubled by self-doubts and a crisis of religious unbelief. In a poem written in 1900 referring to his earlier life he admitted that he had done unloving things which had given him pain. As an attorney, he had foreclosed a mortgage; as a cavalry recruit, he had burned a poor man's house; as a landlord, he had raised rents; and as a judge, he had condemned a man to hang. In Egypt he observed luxury in the midst of abject poverty and cruelty. He was doubly disturbed by heartless English and French imperialism and warfare in Egypt and the Sudan in the mid-1890s. Moreover, he increasingly doubted his right to sit in judgment on other men. While in the throes of this spiritual travail he happened upon Tolstoy's book and discovered a new way of living. The revelation in Tolstoy's book dictated:

> 'Love others; love them calmly, strongly, profoundly,
> And you will find your immortal soul.'
> I leaned back in my arm-chair, letting my hand fall
> with the volume in my lap,
> And with closed eyes and half a smile on my face
> I made the experiment and tried to love.

Crosby's experiment with love made him feel that he had actually "risen to a loftier plane, and that there was something immortal within me." Realizing that he could not love others while at the same time judging them under the aegis of an elevated position and salary, Crosby renounced his $10,000-a-year judgeship and went immediately on a pilgrimage to Tolstoy's home at Yasnaya Polyana.[38] Crosby had read Tolstoy earlier, but he had not then been as psychically prepared for conversion as he was in 1894. In 1892 he had initiated a correspondence with Tolstoy's family by sending some money for the relief of famine-stricken peasants in response to Countess Tolstoy's public request. "Here was an opportunity," Crosby wrote, "to put myself into direct relations with the family of the man whom of all living men I most desired to know." Admitting that his motives were mixed, he sent some funds and began the correspondence which prevented him from being a total stranger when he made up his mind to visit Tolstoy in 1894. When Crosby arrived at Yasnaya Polyana in May, his admiration for the Russian was so great that he had fully prepared himself for the shattering of his preconceptions. He doubted whether Tolstoy's life was conducted according to the prevailing legend, and he was sure that the count's principles were not being carried out in practice. To his delight, his fears were unjustified. He found Tolstoy "just as his photographs depict him," clad in peasant gown and living in "Spartan simplicity." Tolstoy did, in fact, shun all meats, dairy products, and stimulants. "There are very few even of the poorest in America," Crosby estimated, "who live as poorly as he does." Contrary to the charge made by many of Tolstoy's American critics, he had not "the least semblance of a crank" and was a thoroughly natural and unaffected man. This was indeed a life worth emulating.[39]

In their long walks and conversations, Tolstoy talked about his principles of nonresistance and about the ideas of Henry George and William Lloyd Garrison, who became important secondary influences on Crosby's life. Tolstoy's reverence for George made a dedicated single-taxer of the impressionable ex-judge, and from Garrison and Tolstoy, Crosby developed his conviction that the principle of nonresistance was the only legitimate tactic for achieving social change. Later, he wrote a book on Garrison in which he embraced nonresistance to the point of arguing that the South should have been allowed to secede so that slavery could have died a natural death rather than by northern bayonets. The only others with any discernible impact on Crosby's thought were Walt Whitman and Edward Carpenter, an English mystical poet, who, like Whitman, celebrated democracy, nature, menial labor, and "homogenic love," as he called it, in his writings. Carpenter lived a solitary Tolstoyan life of simplicity and manual labor in the English countryside and traveled twice to the United States, in 1877 and 1884, specifically to visit Whitman. Crosby admired both poet-prophets, but especially Carpenter. He wrote a short biography of the Englishman, made up mostly of quotations from Carpenter's *Toward Democracy*, and in 1905 dedicated a volume of poems to him. However much he admired Carpenter, Whitman, George, and

Garrison, Crosby's premier inspiration was Tolstoy, and it was to Tolstoyan principles that he dedicated his reborn life after 1894.[40]

With his spiritual crisis resolved and his faith in Tolstoy confirmed, Crosby returned to the United States in the summer of 1894 talking to all he knew about Tolstoy. He went immediately to a meeting of the Brotherhood of the Kingdom where, as one participant recalled, he spread his "fascinating interpretations of the Russian prophet's views" and was remembered as "a thoroughgoing, consistent, pure-minded pacifist." He surpassed even Howells in devotional ardor and the extent to which he sought to live according to Tolstoy's stringent credo. Leighton Williams, a member of the brotherhood who knew Crosby well both during his years as a young lawyer and after his return to America, noticed that Crosby was a remarkably changed man after 1894; he concluded that Tolstoy had converted an aristocrat into a democrat. The inspiration of Tolstoy, Williams said, "meant to [Crosby] the changed career, the parting of the ways." Crosby himself wrote:

> I take my place in the lower classes.
> I renounce the title of gentleman be-
> cause it has become intolerable to me.
> Dear Master, I understand now why you too
> took your place in the lower classes,
> And why you refused to be a gentleman.

He abandoned his promising political career, renounced his wealthy friends and legal associates in New York, and moved with his wife and mother to a large rural estate near Rhinebeck, ninety miles north of New York and not far from "Rauschenbusch's Assisi" at Marlborough. At Rhinebeck—"Crosbyside" he called it—he farmed and wrote on social themes, living in Tolstoyan simplicity and austerity. Farming, Crosby wrote, was the "genuine life of man between the sun and the soil. The heart of the farm is the true heart of society." He joined the New York Vegetarian Society and, like Tolstoy, renounced meat and tobacco. He was fascinated by sexual theories and was constantly torn between his inclination (which he did not follow) to attempt a life of chastity like Christian ascetics and Tolstoy, and his allegiance to the free love and experimental doctrines of some of his anarchist friends and Carpenter. Although recognizing that Carpenter's sexual theories were "full of originality and suggestion," he could not recommend them and admitted that he could not, for himself, settle "these troublesome questions of sex."[41]

Of more importance than his new interests in vegetarianism and sexual theories, however, Crosby acquired from Tolstoy and Carpenter an abiding commitment to a trinity of principles: love, nonresistance, and the dignity of labor. He wrote about love constantly, but rarely defined what he meant by it with any precision, not clarifying whether it was an altruistic personal guide for human relationships, a nonresistant tactic of the reformer, or a model form of social living. At various times it meant all of these, but most often as a nonresistant tactic, "the only sound basis for reform." In surprisingly violent metaphor, typical however of his poetry, he wrote that the only way to rid the world of evil men of violence and greed was that

> With love we shall dislodge them from their posts of
> vantage.
> They will have to love us in self-defense, for love
> is hell-fire to the unloving.
> We can mine and countermine their strongholds with love,
> for love is the dynamite of heaven.
> Love the oppressors and tyrants!
> It is the only way to get rid of them.

Only through love, he wrote, could the institutions and laws of "ages of hate" be abolished. "Love is the true Revolution, for Love alone strikes at the very root of ill."[42] Translated into political and social action, love dictated nonresistance, the second of Crosby's primary principles inspired by Tolstoy.

Crosby's clearest exposition of this influence was in his book *Tolstoy and His Message*, published in 1904.[43] In an advance review of the book, Walt Whitman's friend Horace Traubel wrote that "the best interpretation of Tolstoy is Tolstoy, but if you don't have time for Tolstoy then read Crosby." His treatment of the Russian was "reverent without being slavish," Traubel wrote, and would "do you good." The slender volume was a short biography of Tolstoy's life and thought, with an emphasis on his spiritual crisis and rebirth, similar to Crosby's own. The foundations of Tolstoy's reborn ethical beliefs were the injunctions of Jesus in the Sermon on the Mount, especially the appeal to nonresistance, "the real keystone of Tolstoy's ethics." According to the ardent disciple, the nonresistance exemplified by Tolstoy was neither impractical nor cowardly. In Crosby's pacifist writings "Peace" was usually represented as "a brawny, bearded man of might" with a "kindly look in his eyes," while "War" was a "headstrong boy, rushing, red-faced, blundering, blustering, with impetuous arms, hither and thither." To the charge made by many Americans, including Howells, that Tolstoy's extreme views of nonresistance were a result of his Russian environment and therefore impractical in America, Crosby's usual response was that Garrison, too, "while quite innocent of Russian environment, became as staunch a nonresistant as Tolstoy." He did not say that it was Civil War violence, not Garrison's nonresistant societies, that abolished slavery. Peaceful nonresistance, Crosby argued somewhat overzealously, was a more effective means of attaining the kingdom of God than all the governments, judges, armies, sheriffs, and prisons of the world. "The man who will not strike back is the only man who cannot be conquered, and the treatment of him becomes an insoluble problem for the tyrant. It is the non-resistant alone who can overcome superior power."[44]

The third Tolstoyan principle to which Crosby dedicated his life after 1894 was that of the dignity of labor, a requirement following from loving one's neighbor:

> How shall I love my fellow men?
> With ineffectual talk?
> By dropping honey from my pen,
> And sighing as I walk?
>
> Nay, rather love thy neighbor
> By working hard and well,
> For in the house of labor
> It pleaseth love to dwell.

His intentions were sincere, but Crosby's temperament inclined him more to ineffectual talk and honeyed writing than to manual labor, as a short story with the same title, "Love and Labor," illustrated. Like the poem, the story was no literary masterpiece, yet was conveyed with Crosby's characteristic directness and simplicity. A wealthy landowner watched from the comfort of his veranda as his hired hands worked. Guilt forced him into the yard to help. He was a nuisance, however, and caused his employees more work by his ineptness. Finally, exhausted by his feeble efforts, he returned to his veranda, not to attempt manual labor again.[45]

It was one thing to espouse Tolstoyan principles but quite another to live by them, and there is much of Crosby in this story. Crosbyside was, in fact, the second most noted Rhinebeck estate, a large red brick house built in 1773 by General Richard Montgomery. The surrounding property encompassed over 700 acres of broad green lawns, large stands of locust trees, and verdant hills rolling down to the Hudson River. Crosby was master of no less an estate than that held by Tolstoy at Yasnaya Polyana. The contrast between his compulsion to do manual work and the fact of his position as landholding baron caused him not a little concern. A thinly disguised poetic portrait of life at Crosbyside, "Farm Pictures," revealed his guilt. In one sketch he contrasted the life of a farmhand, "in his stained red shirt-sleeves and top-boots covered with manure," with that of the rich owner of the estate, "fresh and clean in the best of riding-clothes." They pass each other at the end of the day and the employer pays his workman without as much as thanking him "for his month of hard toil." The rich man thinks that he, not the hand, is "the loafer" and that he should be working for the other. The workman's "days are as full, as mine are empty, of usefulness. I ought to be ashamed to masquerade through life as his superior." In another sketch Crosby contrasted those playing a game of golf on his estate (himself included) with a plowman working an adjacent field. The plowman's labor, he said, will feed fifty loafers, while he ekes out "a bare living for himself." "Knowing this," Crosby wrote, "how can I look the plowman in the face, cleek in hand, without blushing?"[46]

Guilt was not enough, however, to prompt Crosby to spend much time working with his hired hands. He was plainly not suited to a life of menial toil, in part because he was temperamentally unable to do the work and in part because he had other fields to plow. He wrote Lloyd in 1898 to praise *Wealth against Commonwealth*, which he had been reading, and in the letter indicated his eagerness to involve himself more actively in the reform movement. "I have been digging potatoes this morning, but really that field is not big enough for me. I should like to do a little of that and at the same time be building the bones and nerves of the future society."[47] This was a pattern he had already worked out. He did not spend all his time at Crosbyside but spent half of his time in New York, joining many reform groups and living in a modest apartment on the East Side. A friend, Leonard Abbott, observed that Crosby's life was summarized by the ease with which he made the transition from the quietude of his Rhinebeck estate to the stormy debates among radical reformers in East Side meeting halls.

Crosby's participation in New York in a variety of organizations —strange behavior for an anarchist—reflected the broad range of his reform interests. He was concerned with the improvement of organized labor and the living conditions of the poor. Consequently, he belonged to the Brooklyn and New York Central Labor unions, the East Side Civic Club, the Church Association for the Advancement of the Interests of Labor, and the University Settlements Association. His commitment to individualism and the single tax caused him to join numerous single-tax clubs and the Henry George League. His literary enthusiasms were fulfilled by participation in the Whitman Fellowship and the Emerson Club. He was the first president of the New York Reform Club, organized in November 1894 after his return from the visit with Tolstoy. He lectured often at the East Side Anarchist Club, where on one occasion he defended virtually alone in a debate his principle of nonresistance. Anarchism, he said, was a noble ideal but must be won by love rather than by force. He eagerly debated both anarchists and socialists, questioning many of their doctrines. Once Emma Goldman asked him to write a letter to Andrew Carnegie in hopes of freeing Alexander Berkman from prison; he did so, less out of allegiance to Goldman and Berkman than because of his principled opposition to prisons.[48]

Crosby's major commitments after 1898 were to pacifism, anti-imperialism, and ethnic integrity. He espoused an unrestricted immigration policy, arguing against exclusionists and restrictionists that the immigrants, with their greater capacity than Anglo-Saxons for art, culture, laughter, and uninhibited joy of life, were not a threat to American society but a positive blessing. He vigorously opposed Anglo-Saxon pretensions of superiority, asserting instead that "we are the Goths and Vandals of the day." He was an active supporter of neighborhood efforts to resist the Americanization process and therefore to preserve ethnic and national identity. He joined the Italian Immigration Society, the Filipino Progress Association, and the Friends of Russian Freedom. He was instrumental in securing American financial support for the emigration to Canada of the Doukhobors, a pacific pietist sect persecuted in Russia. Lillian Wald recalled that one day a peasant appeared at her Henry Street settlement house in New York and, speaking no recognizable language, presented a card upon which was written only "Kropotkin, Crosby, Wald." An interpreter was found who told her that he was trying to find his way to the Doukhobors; all he knew about America was that Crosby's devotion to Tolstoy and Wald's belief in the Doukhobor cause would help him reach his destination.[49]

The Spanish-American War and American imperialism in the Caribbean and Asia aroused Crosby's deepest concern. He was active in the American Peace Society and both the American and New York Anti-Imperialist leagues, serving as president of the latter. With Bishop Potter of New York, Howells, and a number of single-taxers, he wrote "A Declaration of Peace" in response to Congress's declaration of war with Spain in April 1898. The peace declaration was addressed "To the Workers of America," invoking their support for reason and arbitration in settling a senseless war in which American workmen would be called upon to shoot Spanish workmen. As a sympathizer with the Georgia Christian Commonwealth colony, Crosby was deeply hurt when the spokesmen for the colony equivocated on the war and extended their support for its alleged humanitarian motives. Crosby wrote an article charging that "there should be no 'buts' and 'ifs' for the Christian in this matter of war. War means hate: Christianity means love, and there can be no truce between them." The war in Cuba, he wrote, was "a mad orgy of slaughter, it is a grand national 'drunk.' " For any Christian to support the war in any way was as much a mockery of the "Prince of Peace" as attaching "chaplains to lynching parties." He later expanded these hastily written but stinging indictments into a pamphlet for the American Peace Society. He declared again that "Christian war is as impossible as a Christian murder" and castigated American clergymen for their support of American foreign policy. The church, Crosby said, condemned arson, adultery, rape, murder, lying, and theft, yet supported wars, which included them all.[50]

War not only was not Christian; it was also absurd, "a reversion to the infancy of the race." In January 1901 Crosby addressed a meeting of the American Peace Society in Boston on the subject of "The Absurdities of Militarism." He mocked the fatuity of military dress and manners, the senseless rivalry between army and navy, and the inane hero-worship of military figures. Recalling his own days as a major in the New York National Guard, strutting down Fifth Avenue in a parade with cocked hat and feather, he said that "there is nothing but vanity at the bottom of the whole business." He concluded by vowing to write a book that would "ring down the curtain upon the profession of the soldier."[51] Within a year he published his book, but the War Department's play went on.

Crosby's somewhat infantile novel *Captain Jinks, Hero*, satirized the absurdities of militarism, particularly in its imperialistic manifestations. The novel makes better entertainment than propaganda. The military mold of Sam Jinks's life was cast when as a child he was given a set of lead soldiers. He went through the banal hazing rituals at "East Point" and as a young man sang in church:

> Onward, Christian soldiers,
> 'Gainst the heathen crew!
> In the name of Jesus
> Let us run them through.

He had his first enjoyable taste of war in the slaughtering of "Cubapines," defending "Old Gory" in suppressing the insurrection of "Gomaldo." He served as a censor for the new imperial government in "Havilla" and ordered the Declaration of Independence to be burned, thus reflecting a common anti-imperialist argument that the annexation of the Philippines was a flagrant violation of the principle of consent of the governed. In the army Captain Jinks was taught that it was immoral for a man in the right ("and of course we always are") to fight against a larger, stronger foe, for this gave the wrong an opportunity to win. In order to assure the triumph of "truth" and "right," a man must always fight a weaker foe. "And its just the same way with nations." When he returned to the United States, Captain Jinks was a celebrated hero, but soon went insane because he did not think he was an ideal soldier. If ordered to do so he could imagine killing his mother and father but not his girl friend (the ultimate test) and therefore felt that he was a failure as a soldier. The military creed, Crosby pointed out, was that to every command, no matter how irrational or senseless, a soldier's habitual response was: "I do not think. I obey orders." The novel ends, mercifully, with Jinks in an asylum playing again with lead soldiers.[52]

Crosby brought a satirical wit to the literature of anti-imperialism, similar but inferior to Mark Twain's, which pointed out the ironies of patriotism, militarism, and the belief in Anglo-Saxon, Christian superiority. In addition to his novel, he wrote two books of poems, *War Echoes* (1898) and *Swords and Plowshares* (1902). Both volumes were filled with poems showing Crosby's revulsion against war and imperialism, often expressed with as much blood and violence as the practices he condemned. Samuel Jones chided Crosby once that in his pacifist poems "there are times that you say things so strongly that it really sounds like war itself." For example, in "War and Hell," reminiscent of Twain's "War Prayer," Crosby wrote:

> There is 'great rejoicing at the nation's capital.'
>   So says the morning's paper.
> The enemy's fleet has been annihilated.
> Mothers are delighted because other mothers have lost
>   sons just like their own;
> Wives and daughters smile at the thought of new-made
>   widows and orphans;
> Strong men are full of glee because other strong men
>   are either slain or doomed to rot alive in torments;
> Small boys are delirious with pride and joy as they
>   fancy themselves thrusting swords into soft
>   flesh, and burning and laying waste such homes
>   as they themselves inhabit;
> Another capital is cast down with mourning and
>   humiliation, just in proportion as ours is
>   raised up, and that is the very spice of
>   our triumph.

All this was rationalized, Crosby said, by the fallacious doctrine of Anglo-Saxon superiority, about which he jibed: "Hail to the Anglo-American alliance for the vulgarization of the world! . . . Let us plant innumerable Jersey Cities in the isles of the sea."[53]

His best-known poem was a parody of Kipling's "White Man's Burden."

Take up the White Man's burden.
    Send forth your sturdy kin,
And load them down with Bibles
    And cannon-balls and gin.
Throw in a few diseases
    To spread the tropic climes,
For there the healthy niggers
    Are quite behind the times.

The real "white man's burden," Crosby continued, would mean burdening heretofore happy people with factories, iron mills, wars, twelve-hour working days, mortgages, and exorbitant rents, interests, and taxes. He continued:

Give them electrocution chairs,
    And prisons, too, galore,
And if they seem inclined to kick
    Then spill their heathen gore.

They need our labor question, too,
    And politics and fraud—
We've made a pretty mess at home,
    Let's make a mess abroad.

Crosby wrote scores of poems like these, ridiculing the iniquities and false priorities of American civilization both at home and abroad. "The dictates of Christianity, statesmanship and common sense alike," he wrote, "call upon us to set our own house in order before we attempt to teach house-keeping to the world."[54]

Our own house, he believed, was in need of much reordering. The economic question was most pressing. The gross inequalities of wealth in the United States, he wrote, were the result of monopolies. The laborer, farmer, and consumer alike suffered from the low wages and high prices caused by industrial, banking, railroad, and, worst of all, land monopolies.[55] His poems portrayed the suffering lives of the poor, usually contrasted to the hypocritical and affluent lives of their oppressors, much like his own self-castigation in "Farm Pictures." Thus, the coal miner toiled "at the bottom . . . of the moist black hole" and went home at night to find his children "asleep in a tangled heap, three or four in a single bed," while the owners of the mine lived "like kings of old," caring little "how their wage-slaves fare, so long as they get their gold!"

Similarly, the coal stoker's life in the hold of a passenger liner was contrasted to those who "yawn over . . . novels in the long row of steamer-chairs aligned on . . . the upper deck." The cotton mill, filled with "palefaced children," slumped over their dreary, hateful work, was nothing less than "slavery raised from the dead!"[56]

It was one thing to point out the contradictions in American society but quite another to propose appropriate solutions. He once said that it was time for honest citizens to "turn the waters of a pure public spirit into the corrupt pools of private interests and wash the offensive accumulations away." But how? He was not sanguine that much pure public spirit could be found in Washington, for national political life was as infested with corruption as economic life. He had no confidence whatever in either the president (he called Roosevelt as much a tyrant as the Russian czar) or the Senate, which he called a "plutocratic club." Socialism was no better than capitalism: "socialists in power would be no better masters than the plutocrats of to-day, and many of them would be worse, as the tyrannical behavior of their party often demonstrates." He admitted having a "feeling of friendliness" for many socialists, but denounced their lack of respect for individual freedom. In fact, "the *odium socialisticum*," he wrote, was as tyrannical and distrustful of human freedom as "the *odium theologicum* in its worst form." Socialism was an "imaginary Frankenstein monster which neither hears nor sees nor feels, but on whose altar the individual must be sacrificed"; besides, the solution to domestic problems demanded not more, but less government.[57]

Of the many panaceas for socioeconomic ills at the turn of the century, Crosby placed his greatest confidence in Henry George's single tax on the unearned increment of landlords living off the labor of others. The adoption of the single tax would best enable government to curtail its functions while at the same time redistributing wealth more equitably. He totally underestimated the bureaucratic requirements of administering the tax, a need that even George came to recognize. Crosby frequently corresponded with Tolstoy about the progress of and possibilities for the single tax in Russia and the United States. In 1905 Tolstoy wrote that he was trying to persuade the czar to enact the tax. Crosby hoped that if this were done, the czar might then convince Roosevelt to do the same, as he had already persuaded the president of the efficacy of arbitration of international disputes. To prepare the American people for the single tax, Crosby compiled a set of readings for every day of the year "on the rights of man to the earth," which were published monthly in the *National Single Taxer* in 1900 and later made into a book. The readings were derived from 180 authors, but Crosby quoted most often from Tolstoy's novel *Resurrection*, in which the Russian squarely confronted the land question by advocating the single tax. In an editorial for the *Single Tax Review*, a quarterly successor to the *National Single Taxer*, Crosby argued that, unlike socialists, single-taxers did not wish to change the "natural laws of labor and exchange." The tax, therefore, was a "short-cut to the Promised Land."[58]

As the language suggests, Crosby's ultimate solutions were religious, despite his discouragement with the silence of organized religion on social issues and the complicity of the church in war and economic oppression. By owning tenement properties in New York, he charged, the church took "an active and official part in grinding the faces of the poor." Socialists, single-taxers, and "even the mad anarchist" had more concern for the teachings of Jesus than did the church. "I find more real religion at a base-ball match," he wrote, "than in a Fifth Avenue church." Unlike the advocates of the kingdom movement at Grinnell and Marlborough, Crosby's conception of the kingdom of heaven was personal, not social. He agreed that the kingdom was not "a faraway singing of psalms and harping of harps," but neither was it "a new order here on earth introduced by act of legislature, and enforced by Courts and policemen." The kingdom, he maintained, was as Tolstoy had said, "within you," in the awareness of the "divine consciousness" within each individual as expressed in love for others.[59]

Moreover, the kingdom of heaven could not be achieved institutionally, but only by the actions of individuals. The ethic of Jesus, Crosby wrote, urged individuals "to act towards all men with love and to abstain from force." This meant that government, an aggregation of individuals, was as compelled to abstain from force as were individuals, even in defense of the traditional rights of life, liberty, and property. If life or liberty were threatened, nonresistance was the only legitimate Christian response. As for private property, it should be renounced altogether. The duty of men was, like Francis of Assisi and Tolstoy, to embrace poverty voluntarily.

Ultimately, the ethic of Jesus implied that government should be stripped of all its coercive functions. It should not resist invasions, or perform judicial functions, or maintain police forces and prisons. This would take time, he realized, and the way to encourage others to accept this seemingly impractical ethic was by individual example and inspiration, that is, by Tolstoy's method.[60]

Crosby's philosophical anarchism led him to spurn politics and parties. He believed in working outside of politics and found solace in the fact that Tolstoy and Carpenter had not joined any party. For several years he refused, on principle, to vote. In his earlier poems he expressed a hope that the ballot box would someday become unnecessary along with the policeman's club, the soldier's rifle, and the teacher's birch-rod. In the last years of his life, however, he developed a renewed appreciation for the ballot. In 1900 he voted for Bryan, mainly on anti-imperialist grounds, and Abbott reported with sadness that in 1904 Crosby voted for Alton B. Parker, probably because of his dislike for Roosevelt.[61] At the time of his death in 1907, Crosby was writing a series of editorials for the *Cosmopolitan* in favor of direct election of senators.

Crosby's exploration of various remedies for social and economic problems had found them all deficient. He had little hope in either organized religion or political parties. Socialism denied individual freedom, as did labor unions. Anarchists respected freedom but were tainted by violence. Communitarians were too isolated from society and therefore ineffective. He was left with positive adherence to a curious mixture of strategies for change: individual example, the single tax, and direct election of senators. This was hardly a program to usher in an era of peace, love, and freedom!

Crosby's dilemmas were, in part, in the nature of the intellectual as would-be reformer. Once an intellectual of principle and honesty—and Crosby had both—subjects various reformist theories and their practice to principled examination, he inevitably will find doctrinal inconsistencies or hypocritical behavior. The effect of this is to paralyze his ability to commit himself wholeheartedly to any single theory, or even, given a tentative commitment, to action. Emerson said of intellectual reformers in the 1840s that the "genius of the day does not incline to a deed, but to a beholding. It is not that men do not wish to act; they pine to be employed, but are paralyzed by the uncertainty what they should do. . . . This happens to the best."[62] It happened to Crosby. This incapacity for action leads the intellectual to take the high road of individual example to probable oblivion while others, as Mr. Dooley observed, take the low road to success. Moreover, the intellectual takes refuge in a commitment to vague idealistic goals of justice, freedom, peace, and love. Crosby thought these lofty aims could be fulfilled best by the single tax. But when he looked away from the principles of reformers to their performance, he found even single-taxers morally deficient, for they were as guilty of hypocritical behavior as others:

> We Single Taxers, who denounce landlords, and yet pocket
> gladly the unearned ground-rent ourselves;
> We socialist lecturers, who say, 'Competition is of the
> devil, but so long as you permit it we shall continue
> to profit by it';
> We anarchists, who go on judging and condemning, and
> suing and being sued—
>
> . . . . .
>
> How do we differ from the abolitionist slaveholder,
> or the drunken temperance preacher,
> or any other moral monster?
> Who are we, to throw stones at our brother
> hypocrites of respectability?

Because Crosby was unable to identify wholly with anarchists or socialists, or even single-taxers, and because he had renounced his promising earlier career as a politician, he "stood absolutely isolated" and had "few intimate friends." He was always on the periphery of reform groups, acutely sensitive to their hypocrisy and—more disturbing—to his own.[63]

Despite an occasional expression of cautious optimism, Crosby was afflicted with increasing pessimism and despair. In 1905 he published one of his most despairing poems, "Moods." In it he revealed an uncharacteristic revulsion for humanity, wishing that men were trees, which "never spit nor sweat" nor, when they are cut open, have "ghastly secrets to reveal." Even his faith in human dignity was severely shaken. The crowd of people on Broadway, he wrote, was as "gruesome as the wind-swept clouds of Shades in Hades . . . [and] enough to make your hair stand on end and your voice stick in your throat." Had years of frustration brought him to this? Is there not in most intellectual reformers a latent revulsion, born in limited contact and fear, toward the oppressed peoples they theoretically defend? But this was certainly not the case with Crosby; he had contact, albeit limited, with the farmhands at Crosbyside and with the immigrants of the East Side of New York. In the poem he found men "revolting in their decay," yet he could not have been worrying about his own physical decay; he was strong and healthy—"an Apollo in physique," one observer noted. His death, two years later, was totally unexpected, the result of acute pneumonia. Perhaps Crosby was worrying about another kind of decay, for the poem began with a statement of his own weariness and self-revulsion, an insight into the dilemmas of the principled intellect:

> I am tired of thinking.
> All things are true and so are their opposites.
> I believe every philosophy, but not that it
> contains all.
> I adopt all religions, while I remain the universal heretic.
> I agree with all men, but I see the other side
> which they do not see.
> I sympathize with every fad and also with the
> blind hater of fads.
> But what a weary vacuity this breadth of mine is![64]

The problem of any seer, ultimately, is that he sees too much. His genius leads him, as Emerson said, to "a beholding," but not to deeds, and certainly not to happiness.

Such was the source of Crosby's sadness. Finding all philosophies, religions, and political panaceas wanting, he took refuge in himself. "Where is the answer to all the contradictions?" he asked in 1901; his answer was Whitmanesque:

> There is but one living answer.
> I am that answer;—
> I, with my free will bound up in destiny;
> I, with my prodigality and thrift;
> I, so stormy on the surface and yet with unsounded
> depths of calm beneath;
> I, with my sorrow and joy, my love and hate, my
> sympathy and my cruelty;
> I, going down to death and yet for ever living;

> I, with right and wrong fighting their endless
> duel within me.
> In me the contradictions are reconciled.
> Yes; I, who transcend all philosophies, who refuse
> to be imprisoned by theories and systems, who
> elude all logic, and have no bounds but Eternity.
> I am the answer.

But he found even himself hypocritical and imprisoned, not liberated, by his self-contradictions. He was, as Leonard Abbott wrote, "enslaved by his possessions." He owned land yet could not give it up. "This ought not to belong to me," he told Abbott one day waving his arm over his Rhinebeck estate, "and yet what can one do? Would it accomplish any real, any enduring good to distribute it among the people here?"[65] He believed, like Tolstoy, in a life of menial labor, yet realized, as he wrote to Jones, that to "become a farm-hand is to avoid the social problem & not to answer it." He had been a judge, and was a judge of society, yet doubted his right to do so:

> I judge you?
> Who made me to be a judge over you?
> What do I know about you?
> What do I know about myself?

He preached a doctrine of love, yet realized that in erotic love "one love will devour the other," and that in brotherly love "egoism and altruism" were at work together. Even Jesus, in his belief that he was the Son of God, was guilty of egoism and pride overtaking his altruism. Crosby wrote pacifist poems which themselves showed "warlike proclivities," as Jones had pointed out, and recognized, as he wrote Jones, that "when I hit at the war-spirit . . . I am hitting at something which I find in my own heart too." He dreamed, ultimately, of living the perfect life of principle, but knew he could not:

> Why, Christ Himself could not do it.
> At every step that He took on the dear Bethany road
> He crushed to death a thousand wondrous, life-
> loving insects.
> Can I do more than He?

"Can I do more than He?" No, certainly not.[66]

Ernest Crosby was clearly out of place in human society, as he realized: "I am here by some sad cosmic mistake," he wrote, "and I am homesick," homesick for an ideal land of perfect freedom and love that he feared he would never see. His last published poem, an "Afterthought" to the *Broad-Cast* collection, revealed that even the attainment of his dreams would be unrewarding and unsatisfying:

> When these new ideas of ours become trite,—
> When they pass glibly current from mouth to mouth
> without conviction or comprehension,—
> When the clean-cut edge of the mintage is rubbed off
> and the impression half obliterated,—
> Then there will be a shade of sadness
> even in victory;—
> Then we shall have to pray for the advent of new truths
> and new heretics.

He died on January 3, 1907; he was fifty-one. Leo Tolstoy wrote immediately to an American friend to say that Crosby's death was a very great sorrow for him, adding, "I hope Ernest Crosby did not estimate me more than I loved and estimated him." A finer tribute from master to disciple is difficult to imagine. Yet there was a finer one: in another letter Tolstoy wrote, "It is a great and very rare happiness to possess such a friend, of whom one can be sure that he understands you fully, and whose leading innermost force of life is quite the same as your own." Crosby would have liked that.[67]

Crosby's death came as a tragic shock to those who knew and loved him. The editors of the *Cosmopolitan*, for whom he had been writing at the time of his death, continued to print his series of exposures and predicted (erroneously) that "his influence will grow, and a decade hence he will be known as one of the great prophets of political and social reform." The editors of the *Single Tax Review* bemoaned his death "at the very zenith of his great intellectual powers" and made plans to devote the spring issue of the quarterly to him. When the memorial issue appeared, editor Joseph Dana Miller contrasted the lack of interest by the daily newspapers in Crosby's death to the great interest shown for similar moral leaders in the days of Thoreau and Emerson. The lesson he drew from this was that in the present era "generous impulses and high purposes have been allowed to slumber." Crosby's message, Miller concluded, "comes as the language of a foreign tongue, wholly unintelligible."[68] In 1899 Crosby had written, "Happy the land that knoweth its prophets before they die!" He knew that his children would build monuments to Tolstoy and George; he himself had begun them. "But how will they treat their own prophets?" He should have known. Isolated and alone during his years as a reformer, he was celebrated briefly in death—and then forgotten.

Two months after his death, a memorial meeting was held at Cooper Union in New York. The Crosby Memorial Committee, which organized the meeting, was an impressive group, reading like a roster of the most notable intellectual reformers of the first years of the twentieth century. Men and women as distinguished and diverse as Jane Addams, William James, Clarence Darrow, Hamlin Garland, Samuel Gompers, Booker T. Washington, William Jennings Bryan, and Leo Tolstoy himself were on the list. Lesser known yet still prominent reformers including Abram Cahan, Felix Adler, Lillian Wald, Edwin Mead, E. W. Bemis, Tom Johnson, the sons of Henry George and William Lloyd Garrison, and many others were also represented, as were Crosby's religious crusaders, Bliss, Howells, and Markham. It does not matter that noted figures like these often let their names be used on committees of this sort, or that not all those whose names appeared on the committee attended the meeting. It does matter, however, that reformers as prominent and diverse as these recognized something in Ernest Crosby worth memorializing with their names and testimonies.

What these men and women in their many tributes saw in Crosby was his attempted life of principle, his ability to match his words with deeds, though he himself doubted that he had. The tributes were filled with such words as sincerity, honesty, simplicity, modesty, and purity. Almost all mentioned his individualism, his devotion to the oppressed, and his loneliness. Almost all pointed to the dramatic change which Tolstoy had effected in Crosby's life. Bryan, who like Crosby had walked and talked with Tolstoy at Yasnaya Polyana, praised him as "a rare and loving spirit, whose life was a blessing and whose loss will be severely felt." In the *Arena* in March 1907, Benjamin Flower wrote a typically long and gushy eulogy which claimed that of all men Crosby "most perfectly embodied the spirit of the great Nazarene in life, deed and message." Hamlin Garland stressed Crosby's massive sympathy for the poor, and called him "conscience articulate."[69] But whose conscience? These were strange words coming from a man like Garland who had abandoned (like some of the others) his commitment to reform several years earlier. Perhaps it was his own conscience he had in mind. Crosby's death reminded men of their own potential for a life of principle. To be reminded of one's own most humane possibilities is worth paying tribute to, but one does not dwell on the thought, for it implies self-doubt and guilt. Better to pay one's respects, say all the nice things that one would like to have said about oneself, and move on to less troubling points. And so, the speakers at the memorial meeting took the occasion as an opportunity to do a little intramovement politicking.

The speeches at the memorial gathering illustrated the fractionalized character of the reform movement in the early twentieth century; each tribute to Crosby saw him not only as a principled man but also as an advocate of one's own principles. All acknowledged him as among the foremost pacifists and anti-imperialists of the era; this was easy enough to do, for these reformers were all anti-imperialists, and by 1907 it was no longer an issue. But Garland, Garrison, and John Crosby, all single-taxers, emphasized Crosby's discipleship of Henry George. A trade unionist pointed to his love of factory laborers, and others recalled his East Side sympathies with immigrants and anarchists. Abram Cahan and Markham (who read another ode) took issue with the claim that Crosby was wholly a single-taxer and pointed to his socialist tendencies. In the rather subdued debate over Crosby's ideological leanings, which would have pained him had he been there, the single-taxers had the better argument. Garrison, however, quite rightly pointed out elsewhere that Crosby "was free from the narrowness of many reformers whose wisdom is confined to a special object."[70] He did not, however, say that this was precisely the cause of much of Crosby's frustration and sadness.

Crosby's freedom from any single dogma was indeed the source both of his respect and of his failure as a reformer. He was, as he once said, a dreamer, a quixotic knight, ever searching for an elusive truth. "He used to say," a friend said, "that it was his personal ambition to unite all the 'isms' that the right one might not escape him." This quest lifted him above the petty political squabbling among reformers that he regretted; it also guaranteed his aloneness and ineffectiveness. The attempted life of principle, however noble, does not put bread on the tables of the hungry, as Crosby realized (and Markham did not). What was missing in the memorial tributes to Crosby were those from the Rhinebeck farmer struggling for a decent existence within the shadow of Crosbyside, or from the evicted East Side tenement dweller who could not find work, or from the children in the Gastonia, North Carolina, cotton mill which Crosby visited while on a lecture tour. Of what use to these suffering citizens were his anti-imperialist barbs and misty, mystical declarations of love and nonresistance in books and journals read by other intellectual reformers like himself? Leonard Abbott did not often say anything unkind about his friend, but he did admit once that Crosby "did not always reach the masses," adding that he did reach "a certain spiritual stratum everywhere," which meant nothing.[71] The best that can be said for intellectual reformers like Crosby is that, like prophets, they define the issues that threaten to disrupt the moral order of their society but are not practically effective in applying themselves to positive programs.

But if a lack of practicality is regrettable, what of the principled life? Ernest Crosby can hardly be faulted for his human frailties. Unlike Markham, he knew himself—weaknesses and all. Like Vida Scudder, he struggled against the waves, suffering the consequences of "too much intellect." In his brief thirteen years as an aspiring reformer, Crosby renounced a highly promising career in conventional politics and tried to renounce his wealth. He experimented with an individualistic life-style involving both ascetic social withdrawal and active social commitment. He called the United States to reorder its priorities and advocated the principle of nonviolence as a tactical weapon of change. He condemned the institutional manifestations and perpetuation of poverty and ethnic discrimination and sought to make cities more livable. He agitated against what he called barbaric American imperialism in Asia and mocked the absurdities of militarism. Above all, he tried to live a life of love and principle. Yet, for all this, no Crosby cult developed. No tradition or group emerged dedicated to the unique principles he represented. No permanent memorial was erected in his name. He is all but forgotten today. "Happy the land that knoweth its prophets before they die!" Or even after.

Edwin Markham's ode to Crosby read at the memorial meeting could easily have been an ode to himself. As he did so often, Markham offered a "love-song" to one who had died and gone to heaven, taking his place next to Markham's panoply of heroic, crusading knights and comrades.

Comrade, why did you leave us?
We needed you here in the fight.
Why did the high gods bereave us?
We needed your bold arm, believe us,
To carry the torch in the night.

They sounded recall and you started,
And now you are There upon guard;
In the band of the heroes departed,
Still fighting our battle, high-hearted,
Our captain, our brother, our bard.

You went as a knight goes a-faring,
To join the brave comrades above,
To rally where Lincoln and Waring,
Mazzini and all of the daring
Still fight in the battle of love.

Born within a few years of each other in the mid-1850s, both poets came together at the turn of the century as poet laureates of a crusade of Christian intellectuals seeking to infuse their society with principles of peace, equality, dignified labor, and brotherly love. One poet had been born to hardship and struggle in the hills of California and the other to wealth and gentlemanly breeding in the elite circles of New York. In a sense, the merging of Markham and Crosby was itself a testimony to the society they so often condemned. Despite their totally different origins, both poets, as Markham said in his ode, spoke "for the humble" and called the world "to choose between Mammon and God." Crosby's path to reform, unlike Markham's, was not the result of his ambition but of his renunciation of ambition, as Markham realized:

From purple and pomp, you elected
To walk in the gray common road:
To keep your free soul, high-erected,
You joined the despised, the rejected,
To lift at the terrible load.

It matters not that Crosby had not really lifted any "terrible load," except in himself, or that Markham erroneously thought that he had. What matters is what was next, as the lofty poet knew:

> And now that your errand is ended,
> And now that your steps go afar,
> What strong soul will catch up the splendid
> High dream that your spirit attended—
> The purpose of God for our star?[72]

Who, indeed, would capture the dream and assume the burden? Both Crosby and Markham, like the other knights of the golden rule, "went as a knight goes a-faring" with their vision of a "splendid high dream." But that was all. And that was their problem.

The gap between the world as it was and their vision of what it ought to be could not be closed by the splendid high dream alone. This is not to say that one ought not to dream—and dream big—for certainly one should, lest the people perish as Isaiah prophesied. One should, however, do something with one's dreams, not just to effect the kinds of significant change that one talked about (though this should be enough), but also to avoid personal suffering. There was, after all, little comfort in the anguish of Howells, or the "intolerable stabbing pain" of Vida Scudder, or the elusive fulfillment of Bliss and Herron, or the neurotic death wishes of Markham, or the profound and lonely homesickness of Crosby. The various forms of unhappiness suffered by these knights without armor was rooted in the formidable magnitude of their self-appointed tasks, in the breadth of the gap between the society they envisaged and the one in which they lived. Their pain was compounded, moreover, by the troublesome demands of their self-appointed roles, in the depth of the chasm between the reformer as he wanted to be and the person as he was. Ultimately, to be truly free and potentially effective as a reformer, one must know and accept oneself as one is. Fortunately, there were men and women in America who fully accepted their aspirations and limitations and who were therefore more successful at rendering the ideal more practical. They dreamed the same splendid high dream as other knights, yet were able to count their achievements as well. One such person, to whom these intellectual reformers responded with reverence and enthusiasm, was a small businessman who in 1897 became mayor of Toledo, Ohio, Samuel "Golden Rule" Jones.

7

THE GOLDEN RULE IN ACTION: SAMUEL M. JONES

It is better to lift your whole city up an inch than to pull yourself up to the skies.

JONES*

IN THE late spring of 1904 the Common Council of Toledo, Ohio, extended the franchise of a private street railway company for twenty-five years. The mayor of Toledo, Samuel Milton Jones, who had opposed the extension, promptly vetoed the action. For several years Jones had advocated a public street railway system, and this last of many skirmishes with the city council and the private interest groups of the city was bitterly contested. Five councilmen were on the railway company's payroll in 1903 and the general manager of the *Toledo Times* spent $75,000 to combat the mayor's influence. On the night of July 12, Jones died; the next day the railway company's stock rose twenty-four points.[1] What other reformer in this study could claim such an immediate and practical impact of his death, much less his life? Samuel Jones put the golden rule into action. In death, as in life, he had a singular influence on the people and events of his age.

On the same day as the railway stock was rising, an estimated 55,000 persons filed past Jones's coffin. His funeral on July 15 was equally impressive. Some 15,000 mourners gathered in front of Jones's home to hear a eulogy delivered by his friend and successor as mayor, Brand Whitlock. "I know not how many thousands were there," Whitlock recalled, for "they were standing on the lawns in a mass that extended across the street and into the yards on the farther side. Down to the corner, and into the side streets, they were packed, and they stood in long lines all the way out to the cemetery." Of more significance than the numbers, however, was the diverse character of those who attended Jones's funeral: "In that crowd there were all sorts of that one sort he knew as humanity without distinction,—judges, and women of prominence and women he alone would have included in humanity, there were thieves, and prizefighters,—and they all stood there with the tears streaming down their faces." Whitlock spoke eloquently of Jones's massive sympathy for the poor, the oppressed, and the outcast. Affectionately called "the Golden Rule man" by his many friends, Jones "saw that in the gentleness of love lay the mightiest power in the world." Although accused of being a dreamer by friends and enemies alike, which indeed he was, Jones's aspirations for a society founded on love, equality, brotherhood, and dignity were—in his Toledo environment—partly fulfilled. "With him religion, politics, business and life were one," Whitlock said, and "he could not separate them nor distinguish them." As Whitlock and many others understood, in Jones the dream and deed were one.[2]

Jones was a rare kind of intellectual reformer. He read widely in European and American literature and philosophy, but the knowledge and insights he acquired were used not to torment his own soul but to improve others' lives. He quoted texts, not in obscure little journals, but in city parks, Polish halls, and police courts. He wrote books, pamphlets, poetry, and songs, not for other intellectuals, but for factory and oil field workers. Because Jones applied his intellectual ideals and dreams to his life and deeds as businessman and mayor, he suffered less guilt and fewer self-doubts than the other reformers in the new religious movement. He was influenced by the same sources as they, notably Tolstoy, Mazzini, Whitman, and Emerson, but did not, like so many others, take refuge in the comforts of idealism. These inspirations caused Jones to dream, with the other knights, of the Altrurian millennium. But he knew well that until he put himself "into just relation with my fellow-men," as he wrote in his annual Christmas message to his workers in 1902, it would be "absolutely impossible for me to know perfect happiness." He therefore took small, concrete steps, an approach that enabled him to see the practical accomplishments of his work. In 1894 he "resolved to make an effort to apply the Golden Rule as a rule of conduct," and in 1897 proudly reported that "after nearly three years of a test I am pleased to say the golden rule works."[3] He not only yearned for a world as he believed it ought to be but also was able to understand and deal with it as it was. Rather than engaging in self-reproach for failing to be the reformer he thought he ought to be, he generally accepted himself for the man that he was.

Unlike the other members of the new religious movement, Jones was not bothered by any conflict between collectivist institutions and individual freedom. On the one hand, he recognized, like Bellamy and Lloyd, that since "the trust is here, and here to stay," the only way to overcome it was to own it; "we must all be in the trust . . . whereby through the organized love of the municipality, state, and nation, we can minister to one another better than we can in our individual capacity." But on the other hand, like his good friend Ernest Crosby, he revered the freedom of the individual. He told a crowded hall of immigrants in Toledo: "I don't want to rule anybody. . . . Nobody has a right to rule anybody else. Each individual must rule himself." The apparent contradiction of achieving self-rule within a collective people's trust did not trouble him, nor did an inconsistency of political beliefs. In his Fifth Annual Message to the Common Council of Toledo, he called for municipal ownership of all public utilities and for expanded municipal responsibilities at the same time as he asserted that "they are governed best who are governed least." His constituency, he once said, was "the whole human family." He believed in the "unity of the entire race" and was "content to be one in the mass." Like Emerson, whom he admired, his reverence for both the "one" and the "mass" was thoroughly consistent.[4]

Nor was Jones bothered by a conflict between the principle of widespread democratic participation and the need for bringing exceptional talents to bear on social problems. "The idea that a few of us are endowed with the 'divine right of kings,' and are especially fitted to govern or rule what we have called the lower classes, is undemocratic, as well as unchristian and of course unbrotherly. . . . If we are a democracy, we must believe in the people; there is no escape from that conclusion." And yet, his whole later life was one of using his privileged positions as employer and mayor to do good, as he interpreted it, for the people of his city. Despite his prominence, however, there was absolutely no pretense or intellectual elitism about him. When a visitor chided him for taking off his hat to a scrubwoman in the Toledo City Hall, he commented that "if I should not take off my hat . . . to a scrubwoman who does the dirty work that I don't want to do, then I will not take it off to any one." Whitlock wrote that Jones was "always going down to the city prisons, or to the workhouses, and talking to the poor devils there, quite as if he were one of them, which indeed he felt he was." Jones himself wrote: "I like the 'common people' because they are most democratic. They believe in one another. They are neighborly and helpful. The rich man has no neighbors—only rivals and parasites."[5] Jones trusted the average citizen to rule himself and sought only to remove artificial obstacles to his freedom and happiness. There were no rules in his factory except the golden rule. He loved the workers in his factory and oil fields, and the tramps, vagrants, and prostitutes of Toledo. They returned his love with loyalty to his business, with votes in his four mayoralty campaigns, and with tears at his funeral.

Samuel Jones was born in a humble cottage in North Wales in 1846. At the age of three he came to the United States in steerage with his family, settling near Utica, New York, where his father was a tenant farmer. In his youth Sam worked successively as a farm laborer, in a stone quarry, in a sawmill, and as a wiper and greaser on a steamship. He recalled in 1899 that he had had less than thirty months of formal schooling in his life. At the age of eighteen he traveled with fifteen cents in his pocket to the new oil fields near Titusville, Pennsylvania. He struggled for several years in the fields as a tool sharpener and dresser, pipe liner, pumper, and driller. Gradually, he acquired enough savings to go into business for himself, as did so many others in the early years of the oil boom in the United States. In 1886 Jones moved to Lima, Ohio, where he drilled the first large oil well in Ohio, and became one of the original incorporators of the Ohio Oil Company. Shortly thereafter, however, he sold out to Rockefeller's Standard Oil. He never criticized Rockefeller's business practices, for Jones rarely, if ever, blamed individuals for evils which he believed intrinsic to a corrupt system. "Our trouble is not with the bosses, with the aristocrats, with the corporations or the Standard Oil Company," he wrote, "but with a system that denies brotherhood and makes a weaker brother the legitimate prey of every strong man." Although lacking the predator instinct, Jones continued to prove that he was a strong man in the oil business. He formed the Acme Oil Company, which drilled oil in new fields in northwest Ohio, and in 1892 and 1893 he invented a number of labor-saving devices for oil wells. For the manufacture of his many inventions, Jones opened the Acme Sucker Rod Company in Toledo in the depression year of 1894. As the owner of a factory and oil wells for the next ten years until his death, and as mayor of Toledo for seven of those years, he consistently embodied, as Brand Whitlock said, "the greatest original practical example" of the golden rule in action.[6]

The awakening of Jones's social conscience coincided with the launching of his career as a factory owner. As Jones began in 1894 to manufacture clasp joint couplings, pull-rods, clamp stirrups, sucker rods, and other oil-well appliances, he also discovered his social obligations for improving the quality of life for others. He had felt some sympathy for the degraded human condition before 1894, but he was shocked by the sight of unemployed men begging for work during the depression. "I never had seen anything like it. Their piteous appeals and the very pathos of the looks of many of them stirred the very deepest sentiments of compassion within me." That same year he read George Herron's "Philosophy of the Lord's Prayer," which made a lasting impression on his understanding of brotherhood and the duties of man. These insights, his sense of the hopelessness of the socioeconomic situation, directly influenced Jones to apply the golden rule in his business. Three years later he wrote to W. T. Stead, "I have been a close reader of all that George D. Herron has ever written, and believe he is a prophet of a better era." Jones also read *Wealth against Commonwealth* in 1894. At the memorial meeting in Chicago after Lloyd's death, Jones recalled the notable impact that reading and meeting Lloyd in 1894 had had on him. "Lloyd's great idea of a Golden Rule government for America unfolded itself before my vision" and made him, as he said, a "Golden Rule man."[7]

Jones's initial impetus to reform was prompted by Herron and Lloyd and by depression conditions of unemployment and suffering. His social thought continued to be influenced by the familiar inspirational sources of the new religious movement, most significantly the Bible, Whitman, and Tolstoy. Jones was an avid reader, though hardly a sophisticated intellect, and had a remarkable facility for quoting poems and passages from memory. In a statement in 1901 of the intellectual influences on his life, he cited the New Testament, Isaiah, Job, and Psalms as the primary "help to the development of my life." Among poets he named only Whitman, "the greatest poet of democracy"; among other writers, he most admired Emerson, Edward Carpenter, and Tolstoy. In other lists he also mentioned Ruskin, Morris, Mazzini, Francis of Assisi, and Lamennais. Finally, as an integral member of the new religious movement, Jones frequently cited Crosby, Markham, and Howells, as well as Lloyd and Herron, as contributing to his social thought.[8]

His favorite poet-philosophers were Carpenter, Emerson, and Whitman. Under the advice of Ernest Crosby, Jones began reading Carpenter in 1897 and three years later wrote to the Tolstoyan Englishman to praise his books, all of which he owned, as "some of the loftiest and most helpful things that I have thus far read."

Shortly before writing this letter, Jones had officiated at the wedding of two single-taxers. In an unorthodox ceremony, conducted as the couple wished, he read from Genesis and from Carpenter's *Love's Coming of Age*. Emerson's essays in Jones's personal book collection were well marked, particularly "The Over-Soul" and "Self-Reliance." These two essays helped Jones to see the unity of life without having to sacrifice his faith in individual integrity and freedom. Although he never renounced his commitment to self-reliance, Jones gradually inclined, as he wrote to Eugene Debs in 1899, "more and more to Walt Whitman's idea . . . that there is no possible way of saving a fragment of society, but the *whole thing* must be raised altogether." Jones therefore ardently believed both in individual regeneration and in collective salvation.[9]

The primary source for his faith in individual regeneration, other than Emerson, was the ethic of Jesus. Jones's copy of the Bible and a volume of selections from the teachings of Jesus were both abundantly and vigorously underscored. Among the passages which he not only marked but also frequently quoted in his speeches were those on nonresistance to evil, not judging others, being like little children, and the rich man's obligations and difficult path to heaven. After the nonresistance passage, he wrote: "our rule"; elsewhere in the Sermon on the Mount he added in the margin: "all life is one" and "Jesus the Iconoclast." Next to the Bible on his desk in the mayor's office lay a volume of Whitman's *Leaves of Grass*. Whitlock reported that the book was heavily underscored in red and that Jones often was so excited over a Whitman passage that he would call him up to read it to him. Two pictures of Whitman hung in his office, and many visitors to the mayor could not leave until they had consented to listen to him quote from Whitman. Like Jesus and Emerson, Whitman confirmed Jones's understanding of democracy by celebrating both the individual and the individual *en masse*. After praising Emerson, Carpenter, and Mazzini in a letter to a minister in 1900, Jones wrote that "the one who has led me to see further into the meaning of a perfect Democracy than any of the others—perhaps all—is Walt Whitman." Two years earlier, while bedridden with illness for four days, Jones was reading the Gospels, the *Social Gospel*, Howells's *A Traveller from Altruria*, Lloyd's *Labor Copartnership*, and "a whole lot of Walt Whitman." Six months later he wrote Horace Traubel agreeing enthusiastically to join the Walt Whitman Fellowship and said that he would "always wish to be counted as one thoroughly and hopelessly gone in 'Whitmania.'"[10]

Whitman helped Jones develop his concept of democratic politics, which he applied as mayor; John Ruskin and William Morris helped him develop his concept of cooperative economics, which he applied as factory owner. One of Jones's central beliefs was that art was a necessary and pleasurable part of work. In his book, *The New Right*, he quoted no less than four times Ruskin's statement that "the wealth of a nation may be estimated by the number of happy people that are employed in making useful things." Another of Jones's favorite quotations was Morris's conviction that "art is the expression of a man's joy in labor." He owned many volumes of the works of both English reformers and frequently recommended them to his friends. Jones's "letters of labor and love" to his workers were strikingly similar to Ruskin's letters to English workingmen in *Fors Clavigera*. Soon after Ruskin's death in 1900, Jones delivered a talk on him at Golden Rule Hall, reading from Ruskin's *Unto This Last* to his workers on the proper (paternal) relationship of an employer to his employees. Ruskin was, Jones said, "one of the greatest, noblest, and purest men of our generation. . . . He loved the beautiful and artistic, and indeed gave to the world superb, artistic ideals." Jones's response to Ruskin was not only aesthetic but also practical. His conduct as an employer was dedicated to insuring joyful labor for his workers in the making of "useful things." He introduced profit-sharing in his factory and treated his workers with an ambiguous mixture of paternalism and fraternity. Ultimately, the chief object of the Acme Sucker Rod Company, he wrote, was not making money but making men, which was identical with Ruskin's (and Emerson's) definition of wealth.[11]

The influence of Mazzini helped Jones incorporate his personal responsibilities as factory owner and mayor into a larger view of progress toward a collective utopian society. Jones often quoted Mazzini's assertion that "the next great word is 'Association.'" Mazzini's vision of the oneness of humanity, as well as his emphasis on the duties rather than the rights of man, were central to Jones's social thought. He concluded *The New Right* with a distinctly Mazzinian chapter on the Brotherhood of Man, which was prefaced by a long quotation from the Italian. "America's task," Jones wrote, "is to teach larger views of life and duty." After his book was published, he regretted his choice of title, which had been formulated because his depression experiences had convinced him of man's inalienable right to work. This was "the new right" which Jones deemed imperative. But in a letter written a year after publication, he said that there had been "too much about *rights* to the neglect and hurt of *duties*; there are no rights except as they flow from duties performed. So I am more inclined to call attention to the NEW DUTY than to the NEW RIGHT." Two days before writing the letter, Jones had written another indicating that he was thoroughly absorbed in the writings of Mazzini: "I do not know anything loftier . . . than his chapter on the duties of men." Despite his enthusiasm, Jones's admiration for Mazzini was not unqualified. He opposed the Italian's revolutionary militancy. In the margin of a chapter on Mazzini's organization of the "Young Italy" movement, Jones wrote: "1898 I don't believe in this at all. . . . I don't believe in fighting by physical force." He much preferred the gentler, nonresistant doctrines of Francis of Assisi, William Lloyd Garrison, and Tolstoy.[12]

Portraits of Tolstoy were the only ones, other than Whitman's, to hang in two places in Jones's cluttered office. The mayor often wrote to the Russian and adopted many of his ideas. Jones's understanding and literal application of the Sermon on the Mount, his repudiation of institutionalized religion, his relationship with his employees, his pacifism and opposition to the use of force by government, and his yearning for the simple life all bore the imprint of Tolstoy's influence. He apparently knew about him even before his contacts in the mid-1890s with Crosby and other Tolstoy enthusiasts like Whitlock, who wrote that Jones "was full of Tolstoy at that time." In September 1898 Jones wrote to Tolstoy to say that he had been reading his books for many years and that they had been of great help. He told the Russian that as mayor of Toledo he had "tried to hold up the doctrine of overcoming evil with good as the only scientific doctrine that we could tie to and expect anything from." He expressed the hope that he might visit him someday as Crosby and Jane Addams had done. In an excess of enthusiasm he told Tolstoy that his teachings on war "have had much to do" with ending the American war with Spain and signed the letter "with very tender love." Tolstoy expressed appreciation for Jones's friendship and good wishes in his reply, which Jones proudly included next to a letter from Howells in his book *The New Right*.[13]

Jones's library contained most of the works of Tolstoy, and most were copiously underscored and marked with innumerable marginal comments. In *What to Do?*, *Resurrection*, and a collection of Tolstoy's essays, for example, Jones reacted with exclamation points and enthusiastic assents to Tolstoyan statements of love, nonresistance, the evils of the penal system, the responsibilities of the wealthy, and the need to follow literally the commandments of Jesus. After an injunction to obey Jesus' law of love, Jones added "the law of my being." Wherever Tolstoy rationalized his conscience for his inability to assist all the poor who sought his help, Jones responded with pained agreement. In two places, for example, he wrote: "the universal experience" and "as I do." These are only three of scores of appended comments by the ardent reader. The only places he apparently disagreed with the Russian were where Tolstoy indicated a lack of complete trust and faith in the common people. In *What to Do?* Tolstoy remarked that the rural peasants could not survive well in the city, and Jones, himself an ex-ruralite, commented, "not altogether true." Where Tolstoy asserted that all workingmen could not appreciate high culture, Jones added, "almost all." These, however, were rare qualifications.

By 1899, with the English publication of *Resurrection*, Tolstoy's novel condemning capital punishment and penal practices, Jones's indebtedness to him was unqualified. The mayor talked more and more about Tolstoy in his letters. He wrote to Washington Gladden in April 1900, saying that if the current rumor that Admiral Dewey was going to run for president as an anti-imperialist were true, he would surely support him. Jones compared Dewey to Tolstoy, who had also been a soldier he pointed out, before his great change in middle age. In the early years of the new century, Tolstoy's name appeared with regularity in Jones's lists of "the best minds of today" with whom he agreed on the subjects of war, nonresistance, penal reform, love, and simplicity. In July 1903 Jones arranged to have a picture done of Tolstoy, painted for his office by an artist from Hull House. Beneath the painting, as Jones requested, was an inscription from *Resurrection*: "Men think there are circumstances when one may deal with human beings without love, and there are no such circumstances. One may deal with things without love, one may cut down trees, make bucks, hammer iron, without love, but you cannot deal with men without it."[14] The selection was an appropriate one. For almost ten years Jones had been dealing with people with love. His ethic of putting the golden rule to action required no other guide.

Samuel Jones had only one rule—the golden rule law of love—in his oil fields and factory. As owner of the Acme Oil Company and the Acme Sucker Rod Company, he initiated measures that were far ahead of their time. In 1897 he introduced the eight-hour day for oil well drillers, a first in Ohio, if not the nation, and sought to persuade the Western Oil Men's Association to do the same. His rationale was that to divide the day into three segments of eight hours rather than into two segments of twelve hours would be both more humane for the workers and potentially more profitable for employers. He showed how labor-saving devices (made at Acme Sucker Rod), in conjunction with dividing the day, not only enabled more men to work but also increased production. His practice of increasing from four to six the number of men working on each well during each shift in his oil fields, he admitted, had lowered profits; he had, however, hired more men, lightened the work of all, and insured that "the men who did the work got the money." These were, he insisted, more worthy achievements. In his Christmas message to the workers of the Acme Oil Company in 1897, Jones announced that the company "will never go back to the twelve hour plan." While hundreds of oil drillers were having difficulty finding even one hour's work, it made no sense, he said, to ask others to work twelve hours. "The Acme Oil Company has not yet *made any money. We may never make any.* No matter; we will continue to *stand flat* on the Golden Rule."[15]

Jones's factory employees in Toledo fared even better than his oil workers under the same rule. He frequently wrote inspiring, sentimental poems which were set to music for his workers to sing. One of his songs was "Divide the Day," a "practical" solution to the problem of unemployment:

> Divide up the day! divide up the day!
> In more ways than one 'tis a plan that will pay,
> Then all who desire will have work for their hand,

> And the problem is solved that darkens our land.
> With millions of idle in fruitful employ,
> The homes of the workers will echo with joy;
> Then want and distress will flee far away,
> We can bring it about just by splitting the day.

In addition to his poems and songs, he also wrote annual Christmas letters and even weekly "letters of love and labor" for his employees. At the end of the year in 1900 and again in 1901 he compiled the weekly messages into a small book and added a quotation before each letter from authors "whom I believe to be preaching the Christ principle." All the letters were written in plain, simple, yet unpatronizing language. They generally, though not always, followed his commitment to discuss, rather than to preach. "I wish to write as friend to friend; I wish to have with you simple heart to heart talks, as brother to brother." The several topics of the talks touched on specific reforms introduced by Jones into his factory, as well as his beliefs about trade unionism (he approved, but had a contented company union), democracy, liberty, and fellowship. It was fitting that a letter on "Service Brings Its Own Reward," in which Jones mused somewhat vaguely about equality and helping others, was followed by "A Word on Vacations," in which he announced the continuation of a week's paid vacation for all employees of six months or more. Jones often paired a statement of principle with an announced practical reform, which is what the golden rule in action was all about.[16]

In December 1901 Jones took stock by reporting on the progress of the Acme Sucker Rod Company since 1894. His employees worked eight hours instead of ten; they were paid a $2.00 minimum wage per day for eight hours instead of the Toledo average of $1.25 to $1.50 per day for ten hours. They received a week's vacation and enjoyed two company picnics each year with pay. There were no bosses or timekeepers in the factory ("every man his own boss," "every man his own timekeeper"), and there were no lists of rules: "just the Golden Rule—that's all." In the company cafeteria a worker could get a hot lunch for fifteen cents (the "Golden Rule Dinner") which cost the company twenty-one cents to prepare. The rationale for the dinner, Jones explained, was fellowship, good nourishment, and sparing the worker's wife the effort and cost of making an extra lunch. A cooperative insurance program was in effect by which 1 percent of a man's wages would be deducted and matched by the company. And at the end of the year Jones gave each employee a 5 percent Christmas dividend on his total wages for the year. In his annual Christmas message a year later Jones announced a plan by which his employees, if they wished, could exchange their 5 percent dividend for shares in the company. His intent, he said, was to eliminate the distinction between employer and employee and to create a truly cooperative experiment by equal division of all earnings among all members of the company community.[17]

There was more. Jones needed a foundry, but when he acquired the property adjacent to his factory he turned the land into Golden Rule Park instead. The park was made available to his workers and their families. They met there evenings and Sunday afternoons to picnic, listen to speeches, and enjoy concerts performed by the Golden Rule Band. A large room in the factory was converted into a meeting room, Golden Rule Hall, where various factory clubs met and where the workers could hear speakers such as Lloyd, Herron, Gladden, Debs, Jane Addams, and other reformers whom Jones attracted to Toledo. A typical meeting in Golden Rule Hall was held in October 1899, near the completion of Jones's gubernatorial campaign. The hall was filled with workers. The meeting opened with the singing of Jones's "Industrial Freedom" by the Acme Chorus Club:

> With justice done to everyone, then happy shall we be,
> Poverty will disappear, the prisoners will be free;
> The right to work, the right to live, the love of liberty—
> All God's best gifts to the people.

George Herron then spoke for an hour on the new collective economy presaged by Jesus. The Chorus sang "Divide the Day," followed by an address by Jones on "A Golden Rule Government." The meeting concluded with the singing of Jones's "The Man without a Party."[18]

Jones went beyond specific factory reforms by seeking to instill self-respect in his employees. He refused to ask questions about a job applicant's past; he regularly hired ex-criminals, gamblers, and tramps. He fully believed that "every tramp is a good citizen spoiled" by the demoralizing effects of looking for work and that "social conditions at present make it a hundred times easier for a man to do wrong than right." An employee once broke three sets of castings in a week and a foreman asked Jones what to do about him. Jones inquired into how long the man had been working and with how much vacation. Upon learning that he had had five days off in two years, Jones gave him a two-week paid vacation. The absence of rules or time clocks in the factory was an indication of Jones's trust in his workers. He encouraged criticisms of his policies and often chided his employees for not using the suggestion box. His innumerable assurances of the equality and dignity of all men and women were confirmed when he told his workers that the death of a nineteen-year-old employee in early October 1901 was to be mourned equally with the death of President McKinley three weeks earlier. When Jones announced the 5 percent Christmas dividend he wrote that "this is not intended as a charitable gift; it is an expression of good will, a recognition of faithful service, and an admission that the present wage system is not scientific, therefore not a just system." He continually reassured his workers that his apparently benevolent reforms were not charity but justice. His will provided for $10,000 worth of stock to be given to trustees elected by the employees of the company to do with as they wished. Jones had a realistic, self-ironic awareness of the relationship between his reforms and his profit margin. "Most manufacturers . . . keep about eight out of every ten dollars which their employees earn for them," he said. "I keep only about seven, and so they call me 'Golden Rule' Jones."[19]

Because he occupied a respectable position in the community as a businessman and because his eccentric views were not yet widely known, Jones was nominated as a compromise Republican candidate for mayor of Toledo in the spring of 1897. The party machine tried to force him to campaign on the issue of abolishing the saloon, but he refused, preferring to establish his own issues. These included municipal ownership of utilities and street railway companies, support for labor and the unemployed, and the application of the golden rule to government as he had already begun to apply it to industry. His victory was a narrow one—518 votes out of some 21,000. In a letter of gratitude to Lloyd for his help in the campaign, Jones noted proudly that the ward surrounding his factory had given McKinley a majority of 132 votes in 1896 but had overwhelmingly voted for him by a majority of 435 votes. "It only goes to show," he wrote, "that the common people are quick to respond to just a little touch of Golden Rule fair play."[20]

In his First Annual Message to the Common Council, Jones announced his program. He would support a publicly owned natural gas plant (an old and controversial issue in Toledo), municipal ownership of lighting, home rule for Ohio cities, more public parks and playgrounds, and free music for the people. In addition, he advocated a day-labor plan rather than the contract system for street improvement workers, a higher wage for shorter hours for all city employees, and the municipal responsibility of caring for tramps by providing them with "a bath, a good bed and wholesome food." These men, Jones said, should be required to work for their food and lodging, thus "restoring their manhood—in many cases well nigh crushed by the hopelessness of the despair into which they have fallen." In his succeeding years as mayor, Jones also endorsed the municipal ownership of all utilities, a merit system for hiring and promotion, complete nonpartisanship in all city offices, free public baths and pools, free public skating rinks and sleigh rides for children, and municipal free vocational education and kindergartens. He did not in any way seek more power for his own office; rather, he endorsed a referendum instead of the mayor's veto on actions of the Common Council. He donated his salary as mayor to charity.[21]

Jones's accomplishments were mixed. He fared best in instituting most of the free public services he wanted, in providing lodging and public works employment for tramps and vagrants, and in improving wages and hours for city employees. He failed in his attempts for home rule and municipal ownership of all utilities. He neither abolished the saloon, as some of his supporters had hoped, nor bowed to the dictates of the local party machine, which was furious with him for his repudiation of traditional patronage appointments. Jones admitted in a letter to Lloyd only seven months into his first term that "we have not done very much that is radical in the way of reform in city government." He realized, however, that "a good deal has been done in the way of reforming public sentiment in Toledo and starting it in the right direction." His style was unique and his enthusiasm was irrepressible. Lincoln Steffens, after visiting with Jones, was so overwhelmed by his ambitious efforts that he exploded to Brand Whitlock: "why, that man's program will take a thousand years!"[22]

The most publicized and controversial practices of Jones's tenure as mayor were in the areas of law enforcement and penal reform. He improved the conditions of Toledo's jails. He took away the policeman's side arms and heavy clubs, replacing them with light canes. "I would be glad," he said once, "to see every revolver and every club in the world go over Niagara Falls, or better still, over the brink of Hell." He was strongly in favor of abolition of capital punishment and told Crosby once how proud he was of the warden of the Ohio penitentiary who had resigned rather than preside over an electrocution. Jones was decisively influenced by Tolstoy's severe indictment of the Russian penal system in *Resurrection.* Like Tolstoy, Jones fully believed that drunkards, gamblers, prostitutes, tramps, and petty thieves were victims of an unjust social order and that only the poor went to jail for drunkenness or gambling. Once fined for contempt of court, he pulled out his checkbook and paid the fine in order to show that "the only crime our civilization punishes is the crime of being poor." His political enemies often charged that his lenient policies encouraged crime in Toledo and made the city a haven for criminals and prostitutes. Although these accusations were untrue, Jones did everything he could to encourage them by his unorthodox behavior as a police magistrate.[23]

On Monday mornings Jones often presided in police court, as the mayor was empowered to do in the absence of the police judge. He and his secretary, Whitlock, competed with each other to see who could dismiss more prisoners arrested during the weekend. Jones once discharged two men arrested for petty larceny after lecturing them—and the many visitors who crowded into the courtroom to watch him—on the inadequate rehabilitation provided at the state penitentiary. One day a drunken tramp in possession of a pistol was arrested. Jones preached on the evils of "hellish" weapons and sentenced the man to smash the pistol to bits with a sledge hammer. He was particularly sympathetic to the prostitute's plight. He told Elbert Hubbard that whenever a woman of the streets was brought before him he fined each man present in the courtroom ten cents and himself a dollar for permitting prostitution to exist. When an irate delegation of Toledo's wealthy and prominent ladies came to his office to demand that he drive the prostitutes out of their city, he gently asked them where he should send them. "Over to Detroit or to Cleveland, or merely out into the country? They have to go somewhere, you know." Then he proposed to them that if each promised to take one prostitute into her home and care for her until she found honest work, he would do the same for two of the most hardened harlots in the city. As Whitlock reported the incident, the ladies "looked at him, then looked at each other, and seeing how utterly hopeless this strange man was, they went away."[24]

In a letter to Crosby, Jones justified his lenient policies as a judge by saying that he had no right to do anything as a judge that he would not do as a man, a principle that Crosby thoroughly understood. "I found no difficulty in disposing of these cases," he wrote, "by the application of the law of love." In Jones's office hung a plaque with the inscription "Judge not that ye be not judged." In a letter to a Toledo newspaper, he said that his actions in court were based on the golden rule. "There are two methods of dealing with people whose liberty makes them a menace to society —on the one hand, prisons, penalties, punishment, hatred and hopeless despair; and on the other, asylums, sympathy, love, help and hope." His method seemed to work. Although the outraged leading citizens of the city charged Jones with encouraging crime, under his merciful policies the number of crimes and arrests in Toledo, a notoriously sinful city, appreciably decreased. By 1902, however, a bill, framed by his opponents in Toledo preventing the mayor from sitting as a police magistrate, was passed by the Ohio state legislature.[25]

Although he had been a reluctant candidate for mayor in 1897, Jones eagerly announced in February 1899 that he was a candidate for reelection as "a Lincoln Republican." His party, however, distressed with his eccentricities and furious with his disregard for the party machine, refused to renominate him. On March 4, therefore, Jones declared that he would run as an independent. The ensuing one-month campaign, according to an Ohio historian, was the "wildest in Toledo's history, and one of the wildest in the country." Jones's quest for reelection was bitterly opposed by both major party machines, business leaders (especially the utility and traction companies), the newspapers, and every minister in the city except two. His enemies called him "Millionaire Jones" and the "Golden Sucker Man." The Toledo Pastors Union arranged for the revivalist Samuel P. Jones to come to Toledo in late March, just prior to the election, ostensibly to preach against the saloon. His real purpose, however, as his revival sermons revealed, was to charge the mayor with abetting crime, prostitution, and drinking by his policies. On the last day of the revival, Samuel P. Jones openly attacked Samuel M. Jones as a "devil mayor" who had instituted a rule of hate rather than of love in Toledo. The revivalist argued that he was for the "Golden Rule up to a certain point and then I want to take up the shotgun and the club." The mayor responded by stating that in his version of Christianity there was no place whatsoever for either the shotgun and the club or anti-Christian revivalism. Despite the organized strength and financial resources of his opposition, Jones won the election in a landslide. He received 70 percent of the votes, four times as many as his nearest competitor, and won every precinct but one. His victory, he said, represented "a great triumph for the common people." He was right; almost no one else had supported him.[26]

No sooner had he won than a movement commenced to elect him governor of Ohio in the fall of 1899. In late August, Jones declared his candidacy as an independent under the banner of "equality of opportunity for all." In many respects, Jones's program was a typically progressive one, similar to Robert La Follette's in Wisconsin at the same time. He called for nonpartisan politics, home rule for cities, referendums and initiatives, public ownership of utilities, improved standards of work for labor, the abolition of the contract system for public works projects, and the relief of unemployment as a positive responsibility of the state. Although running formally on this platform, he campaigned much of the time as an anti-imperialist. He lost the election, carrying only Cleveland and, to his particular happiness, Toledo. In a public statement after the election, he indicated that he was gratified by the more than 100,000 votes he received and interpreted "the non-partisan vote in Ohio . . . as favoring a Christian policy towards the Philippines." Privately, however, he wrote to Lloyd, somewhat despondently, that "I must . . . let others do the fighting." He understood his loss to mean that political justice and social peace could not be won by political action alone, but also needed "an awakened social conscience and an enlightened intellect."[27]

Characteristically, Jones wrote another "Freedom Song" for his gubernatorial campaign, "The Man without a Party," which went in part:

> My party's 'all the people'—their rights I will proclaim.
> Struggling for liberty and freedom;
> I'll cast my vote for principle, not for a party name,
> Struggling for liberty and freedom.

Jones held a distinct distaste for partyism of any kind and scorned all political labels. Before 1899 he had been a Republican, but as he constantly reminded audiences, he had been a Republican like Lincoln, Garrison, and John Brown, and not like Mark Hanna, his bitter foe in Ohio politics. At times he thought he was probably a socialist, but as he wrote to Lloyd in 1897 he believed only in the "kind of socialism that is taught in the new testament." Two years later he wrote that "I think I am a socialist," but was just as willing "to be called a collectivist, mutuelist [*sic*], or Brotherhood man." Throughout the election year of 1900, he refused to commit himself, much to the distress of Bryan and Debs, each of whom expected his support. Jones preferred, as he said, to be "a man without a party, for how can I believe in all of the people, of whom I am one, and belong to a *part* or a party of them?" Debs's response to this was that he, too, was for all the people in theory, but in practice was for workers and the oppressed; he pointedly signed his letter to Jones, "a Man With a Party." Bryan's firm anti-imperialist stand and the influence of Ernest Crosby, however, finally persuaded Jones to support the Democrat. He wrote to Bryan to express sympathy after his defeat, and added that "your ideals are far and away ahead of the time." To his distress, so were his own, as he was increasingly finding out.[28]

Although discouraged with nonpartisan political action, Jones ran again for mayor in 1901 and won, with 56 percent of the total vote, a 14 percent decline in two years. Because of illness and the street railway franchise contest, his last campaign in 1903 was a bitter one. Many of his old followers—tired of his unorthodox leadership—had left him. He was hurt seriously from persecution by churches, civic leaders, and the newspapers, none of which would publish his platform and principles or report on his campaign. He campaigned virtually alone, driving around Toledo in a buggy drawn by an old mare, with his son blowing a saxophone to attract crowds. He won the election, but with only 44 percent of the vote. He fought the renewal of the street railway franchise for most of the next year and died halfway through this fourth and unhappiest term. A few years after Jones's death a general strike paralyzed Toledo. Although the workers in the S. M. Jones Company, as it had been called since 1903, were also on strike, their factory was conspicuously one of the few firms in the city not picketed. When Whitlock asked a labor leader why not, he answered, "Oh well, you know—Mayor Jones. We haven't forgotten him and what he was."[29]

The "Golden Rule Man" was not easily forgotten. For ten years he had put his words into deeds by a practical application of the golden rule to economic and political life in Toledo. His policies had improved the quality of life in concrete ways for the workers in his oil fields and factory: a higher wage, an eight-hour day, job security, safer, happier working conditions, paid vacations, and Christmas dividends. The quality of life for the poorer, outcasted citizens of Toledo had also been enhanced: a job, a new chance, a dismissed arrest, a bath, a meal, and a night's lodging. More importantly, he treated each person he encountered with dignity and respect. His trust and love were returned by those whose lives he had enriched.

Nor was Jones easily forgotten or ignored by the other Christian intellectual reformers in the new religious movement. In 1899 he described his platform, by design, in the broadest terms: "Love is the law of life. Co-operation is the social method of love. Competition is war. Parties are warring armies. Punishment is brutal. You can trust the people. The right to work is inalienable. Art is the expression of pleasure in work." In this statement of principles he expounded with simplicity if not precision the several ideals of the crusade and its intellectual inspirers. With Tolstoy and Crosby he made love the operating law of his life, abhorred war and government by force, and sought to overcome evil by good. With Mazzini, Markham, and Whitman he believed in brotherhood, association, and democratic trust in the people. With Howells and Lloyd he condemned competition as war and argued that the solution to the trust and labor questions was in profit-sharing and cooperation.

With Ruskin and Scudder he believed not only that a person has an inalienable right to work but also that his labor should be pleasurable and aesthetically rewarding. With Bliss and Flower he shared an optimistic faith in the inevitability of progress, believing that the signs of the times pointed to the "coming of a wonderful awakening of the social conscience of the world." With Herron and Rauschenbusch he was convinced that "unless we find heaven here . . . I very much fear we shall not realize a heaven hereafter."[30]

Jones understood that one fulfilled these elevated ideals to the extent that one embodied them in action. He pulled himself up toward the skies by lifting his city up an inch. And yet, in spite of his practical applications, he was not entirely immune to the kinds of self-doubts, guilt, and unhappiness that plagued the other knights of the golden rule. He often quoted Mazzini's comment that "we admire martyrdom but do not adopt it" and was discouraged with his inability to martyr himself in some significant way. He thought, for example, that he should "prove the sincerity of [his] convictions by simply going out and willingly becoming poor, as did Jesus, St. Francis, and many others." And no matter how much good he did, it was never enough. In a letter to Lloyd in 1899 he wrote: "We must all understand the gospel of DO. I know well enough how to practice the Golden Rule; the difficulty comes in my unwillingness to do it entirely, with my half-way doing it." Two years later, after giving a talk at Golden Rule Hall on how genuine Tolstoy was, he wrote to his close friend N. O. Nelson that "the cause of all my soul distress—and I have lots of it, comrade,—might be found in the one fact that I am yet lacking the backbone to go and do as Tolstoi does." At this point in the letter Jones's soul distress over his failures was similar to the guilt and pain that Howells, Crosby, or Scudder felt in their inability to emulate Tolstoy or Ruskin. But Jones went on, as the others did not and could not do: "Still, I am plugging away in that direction, and I . . . may even yet do something that is genuine and that is worth while."[31] In fact, he already had, as the others recognized, if he himself did not.

Jones's determination and success in "plugging away" in Tolstoyan directions distinguished him from the others in the movement. Despite the self-recriminations caused by Mazzini and Tolstoy, he escaped the paralyzing effects of the guilt that so often grieved Howells, Crosby, and Scudder. He was, in short, a free person. Although acknowledging the influence of others, Jones insisted that he was "not a Whitmanite, nor a Tolstoyan. . . . Somehow I want to be free. I do not want to 'belong' to anybody or anything." And because he understood this desire in himself, he was able to understand it in others. False altruism and the worship of saviors, he said, was unjustified, a folly. "Neither Moses nor Jesus nor Lincoln nor any other man or woman ever saved the people. All they could do or did was to live the ideal life that each one must live in order to save himself or to be free."[32] Jones sought similarly not to save others but to live *his* ideal life in order to save himself, that he might be free. He was therefore able to be himself and did not try, like Howells or Crosby, to be someone else. This enabled him to retain the self-respect and psychic freedom which is necessary for a healthy, functioning, effective life, particularly as a reformer.

In his practical accomplishments and self-respect Jones achieved what the other knights sought to achieve and could not, except perhaps for Lloyd. More than to any other person, they pointed to Jones as the embodiment of the golden rule in action and, consequently, as the unofficial hero of the movement, an honor he consistently repudiated. Lloyd, Markham, and Herron all went to Ohio to campaign for him, and Crosby wrote a short, eulogistic biography of him. These four, as well as Howells, Bliss, Flower, and Rauschenbusch, all corresponded with Jones and frequently offered their best wishes and admiration for his achievements. Only Vida Scudder, cloistered at Wellesley and Denison House, seems not to have crossed paths with the Toledo mayor. Jones's relationship with the others illustrates not only his ability to perform deeds, and inversely, their inability, but also reflects again their own respective roles and failures as intellectual reformers. Each reformer, it must be added, performed that function most consistent with his temperament, training, and talents. Each person, after all, is what he is.

William Dean Howells was one of the elder statesmen of the movement, often peripherally connected with it, obligated as he was to fulfill his demanding and prestigious role as the dean of American letters. Many young writers and reformers sought him out for praise and encouragement; Jones, however, was sought out by Howells. In December 1898 he received an unsolicited letter from Howells, commending Jones's Second Annual Message as mayor for its humanity and wishing him long years of service to his city. Jones was delighted with Howells's note, proudly published it in his book, and wrote immediately to his well-wisher to thank him. In the letter Jones praised *A Traveller from Altruria*, which he had been reading, and told Howells that "the question of social reform is, after all, a question of moral reform," a vagueness of position that the Altrurian romanticist understood well. During his last campaign, Jones received another letter of encouragement from Howells, who wrote to bolster Jones's spirits in his most difficult campaign. "You may not be elected," Howells predicted incorrectly, "but I know you cannot be defeated."[33] In these brief exchanges Howells was doing what he did best: encouraging others in their efforts to perform deeds which, to his distress, he knew he could not perform himself. His role was a sad, but necessary one.

The relationship between Jones and Henry Demarest Lloyd, both midwesterners and both more active as reformers than Howells, was much closer. As Jones wrote to Lloyd in 1897, "I know there is very much in common between us." Their correspondence was regular and marked by the frankness of genuine friendship. The two had met as early as 1893, again at a meeting of Social Gospel clergymen in the summer of 1896 at Crosbyside, and six months later at a conference at Hull House. Jones often acknowledged his intellectual debt to Lloyd. He wrote to his friend in 1900 that he was "thoroughly in line with your philosophy" of love and social self-interest in the closing chapters of *Wealth against Commonwealth*. As a solution to social problems, Jones could see "no hope in any other."[34] And in his speech at the Lloyd memorial meeting in 1903, Jones recalled Lloyd's profound influence in making him "a golden rule man."

But Lloyd's relationship to Jones was practical as well as inspirational, reflecting his supportive function to unions and other cooperative efforts. Lloyd often went to Toledo to speak on Jones's behalf, sent him money for his campaigns, offered advice on municipal and corporate problems, and wrote letters upon Jones's request to persons of influence in Toledo who were critical of the mayor. Lloyd was a wise and critical counselor; he frequently chastised his friend for allowing his emotions and eccentricities to interfere with his political wisdom. In the summer of 1899, for example, he was angry with Jones for his excessively "kindly tone" in combating the oil trust and advised him to be more stern. And in August 1899, after Jones declared his candidacy for governor, Lloyd wrote to warn him not to make a martyr of himself unwisely, as he later thought Herron had done in resigning from Iowa College. Quoting the Bible, Lloyd cautioned: "we must not only love [*sic*] as doves, but be as wise as serpents." He charged Jones with wasting too much money in the campaign, and wrote: "Keep yourself well in hand; be as cool in your head as you are hot in your heart. Remember that money is the sinews of war, and that, if you keep possession of the means, you can carry on not only this campaign but a score of campaigns to follow." In a postscript Lloyd noted that he was enclosing, as he said, "a little of the sinews of war." Lloyd even refused to speak in Ohio for his friend during the gubernatorial attempt. As he wrote to Gladden, "it seems to me that the campaign in his [Jones's] hands is so unique that no outside influence could do anything but mar it."[35] Jones had his own unorthodox style and approach to social questions, and as Lloyd implied, his uniqueness both earned the admiration of others in the movement and sometimes drove them away. Above all, however, his singularity was in his practical action, equaled in the movement only, perhaps, by Lloyd himself.

Benjamin Flower saw this same uniqueness in Jones. In an editorial in the *Coming Age* on the significance of Jones's mayoralty election in 1899, Flower asserted that Jones was "living nearer to the Golden Rule than any other public official." His victory, Flower wrote in one of his usual hyperbolic outbursts, was "one of the most important and encouraging events of the closing years of our century. It is a positive step toward a truer democracy than the world has yet known." The correspondence between the two men was largely devoted to letters of support from Flower and requests for articles for his several magazines. Jones said of the *New Time* that it was "one of the best things in the line of progressive literature that we have"; he was, however, generally unreceptive or otherwise engaged to meet Flower's insistent requests for articles. Jones's preference for 5 percent dividends and free public facilities rather than Flower's idealistic monthly discussions of issues suggests the major difference between them.[36]

The correspondence between Jones and William Dwight Porter

Bliss was similar, and it was just as discouraging for Bliss as for Flower that the busy mayor failed to produce articles for his many journalistic ventures. Jones was generally sympathetic with most of Bliss's attempts to effect unity among Christian reformers, though he disagreed vigorously with Bliss's temptation in 1899 to start a new party. Jones attended the Buffalo conference, which he compared to the gathering of early Christians in the upper room, and consented to let Bliss use his name as a vice president of the Social Reform Union. "I am in," Jones wrote abruptly, "God bless you." Bliss returned the favor by reporting regularly on Jones's political campaigns in the *Social Forum* and *Social Unity* and happily announced Jones's mayoralty victory in 1899: "Blessing on Jones! May his tribe increase!" Bliss eventually came around to Jones's position that nonpartisanship was preferable to a new party. He pointed out, however, that Jones's solitary success as a nonpartisan officeholder was an exception to his belief that organization in the form of a national Christian socialist union was essential to the overall success of the reform movement. Jones, of course, dissented. He wrote to Bliss that he served Christian socialist principles more effectively without any labels, badges, or organizational limits on his freedom. He repudiated Bliss's implicit elitism, saying: "The mass is good enough for me. . . . I do not propose to wait for socialism or brotherhood. To the extent of my ability . . . I am practising both now."[37] Again, this was the basic difference between Jones and others such as Bliss and Flower, who seemed content to wait for the millennium. Jones was more effective than they were because his attempted range of practical impact was limited. He was effective in Toledo; when he widened his scope to include state action, he failed. The efforts of Bliss and Flower for national unity and influence were spread too thin, and their failures were as large as their expectations.

George Herron was one of the earliest influences on Jones, whose library contained well-marked copies of Herron's many books. To an injunction by Herron to arise and obey the summons of Jesus to love others, Jones responded: "*I will.*" At the end of the *New Redemption*, which he read in 1897, Jones wrote: "*So may it be* every word of it." He wrote to Herron in October that whatever good he had done for his fellow men and women "is due very largely to the inspiration to activity that came from the study of the books you have written." Two years later he told George Gates that the teachings of Herron and Gates at Grinnell and in the *Kingdom* had helped him to realize that "our only hope for real freedom lies in the application of the Christ philosophy to the affairs of every day life." On June 14, 1899, in the midst of the attempt of the Iowa College trustees to force Herron's resignation, Jones delivered the commencement address at Grinnell, as Lloyd had done four years earlier. In reporting the address the next day a Des Moines newspaper said that Jones's speech "pleased nearly every one. . . . He may be a crank, but if he is there ought to be more of them," kinder words than the paper usually had for Herron.[38]

Jones and Herron gradually moved farther apart, partly because of differences of style and partly for political reasons. As early as February 1898 Jones indicated that he found Herron not constructive enough, a more than valid insight. And they disagreed about the national election of 1900. In October, Jones told Herron that he thought the socialist movement was hopeless and that he was going to campaign for Bryan. Part of Jones's disenchantment with Herron and socialist parties derived from the kind of help Herron gave him during his gubernatorial campaign in 1899. Herron made several speeches for Jones in Ohio, but his controversial dogmatism and increasing militancy, according to an Iowa newspaper, probably hurt rather than helped.[39] As Lloyd had perceptively observed, Jones's uniqueness precluded outside help, especially when provided by the impatient, angry, and tainted Herron.

Walter Rauschenbusch and Jones shared an optimistic confidence in social progress already achieved toward the creation of the kingdom of heaven on earth. They corresponded briefly in 1897, as the New York minister sought Jones's help in persuading Crosby to run for mayor of New York. Rauschenbusch also asked Jones to speak at the summer meeting of the Brotherhood of the Kingdom at Marlborough; Jones planned to speak on "The Golden Rule in Business," but pressures of his work in Toledo prevented him from attending. There is little doubt what he would have said. From his detached and professorial position a few years later, Rauschenbusch commended Jones as a civic leader who courageously fought private municipal interests. In *Christianizing the Social Order* he praised Jones, Henry George, Hazen Pingree of Detroit, and Tom Johnson of Cleveland, all of whom deserved to have a "civic crown on their graves. They fought for us." He particularly admired Jones and Johnson, both rich men, as embodiments of Jesus' message to men of wealth. Both had earned their place in heaven, Rauschenbusch wrote, "by proclaiming their own wealth to be derived from injustice and by leading the people to an assault on the sources of it."[40] Little is known about what Jones thought about Rauschenbusch, since the mayor died before any of the prominent theologian's major books were published.

Besides Lloyd, Jones's closest personal friendships among the members of the new religious movement were with the poets, Markham and Crosby. Beginning in 1899, Edwin Markham and Jones exchanged books and carried on a correspondence lauding each other's work. They shared a faith in spiritual and social man, as well as in the efficacy of the application of the golden rule to social questions. They also shared a gentleness of style missing in their mutual friend, George Herron. When Markham initiated the friendship by sending the mayor a copy of "The Man with the Hoe," Jones replied by telling him that he already had memorized the poem. "I see The Man With the Hoe in every mis-shapen child of God that I meet upon the street," Jones wrote, expressing the hope that he would meet the poet soon. They met within a month at Buffalo. Shortly after their encounter, Jones began using stationery in which Millet's painting and part of Markham's poem appeared in the letterhead. A framed picture of the painting and poem hung in his office. When Markham wrote to praise *The New Right*, which Jones had sent him, Jones replied, "I do not know of any other endorsement that could touch me as yours has." Markham reciprocated Jones's enthusiasm in his work as a poet by taking an interest in Jones's "noble work" as mayor. In two different newspaper articles in August 1899, Markham pointed to Jones as an exemplary man, "seeking for a clew to the secret of social salvation—trying to make the Golden Rule a working principle." That same month the poet wrote Jones, "I stand squarely with you," and followed the letter with a visit to Ohio to campaign for his friend. Markham capped this mutual love affair by telling Jones that he was "a God-quickened man. . . . The work you are doing for human welfare is far larger than the orbit in which you move: it is an object lesson to the world." The noble poet, however, did not indicate how Jones's work was an object lesson for himself.[41]

Jones's good friend Ernest Crosby saw the same distinctive qualities in Jones and yet, unlike Markham, was not afraid to measure his own life's work against Jones's high standard. In his biography of the mayor, Crosby wrote that Jones "never uttered a harsh word against anyone, and he gently expostulated with me for being too inconsiderate." He was a man totally without pretense, pride, or illusions. "Day to day," Crosby wrote, Jones "did the best thing that he saw was practicable." He was so different that Crosby thought of him "as a sort of visitor from some other planet where brotherhood and harmony have been realized in the common life, dropped down here in a semi-barbarous world and calmly taking his place in the midst of its crude and cruel institutions." Alone among reformers, according to Crosby, Jones not only "pointed out the iniquities of our organized social life" but also "was sowing the seed of a new harvest."[42]

The friendship between the two began during the conferences at Crosbyside and Hull House in 1896 when, as Crosby wrote, he was struck with "the open and childlike way in which [Jones] expressed his extreme democratic views to everyone," including a crippled janitor at Hull House whom he befriended. Jones and Crosby shared an intense admiration for Tolstoy, Whitman, and Carpenter, were in accord in their dedicated opposition to war, judicial judgments, and penal injustices, and both repudiated political labels. In a letter to Crosby in 1898 Jones thanked the New Yorker for teaching him that he was, like Garrison and Tolstoy, "truly a non-resistant." Crosby continued the lesson by pointing out in his reply that he preferred not to call his position one of nonresistance, which sounded too negative, but rather one of "overcoming evil with good," a phrase Jones eagerly adopted. Two months later Jones sought out Crosby for Tolstoy's address in order that he might "write to him and tell the dear old man for myself how much good his books have done me." They talked often about Tolstoy, and Crosby found a picture of the Russian for Jones's office. Crosby's influence and the Filipino insurrection were decisive in persuading Jones to support Bryan in 1900. In April of that year Jones wrote to Crosby that he was surprised that his friend was going to support the Democrat rather than Debs. By August he wrote a friend that Crosby was going to vote for Bryan as an anti-imperialist, and that "possibly that may be the best thing for the rest of us to do." Within a month Jones committed himself to Bryan.[43]

Crosby helped his friend with definitions, details, and political decisions; he also helped him in a much more profound and significant way, one that illustrates the fundamental difference between them, and, for that matter, between Jones and the other knights of the golden rule. In the late winter of 1902 Jones wrote to Crosby, as he was increasingly writing to others, that he was tired of his active involvement in the city and yearned for rural quietude. His enormous energy, sapped for years by asthma and catarrh, had begun to diminish. And so also had his spirits. As the bitterness of his battles with the interests of Toledo intensified during his last two terms in office, and as he read more of Tolstoy and Thoreau, Jones increasingly wanted to abandon his factory for the simple life in the fields, hoeing beans and digging potatoes, as he told Crosby in his letter.

Crosby's impassioned reply argued that despite the apparent attractiveness of his own serene life at Crosbyside, Jones's hectic life was by far the more personally satisfying and socially useful. "I have nothing to repent," Crosby wrote, but nevertheless "go on marking time." He advised Jones that "it would be a mistake for you to give up manufacturing for potato-digging. Tolstoy's mistake is in not seeing that machinery may be made a blessing to all men." The major problem of material development, which in the main was fine, he wrote, was "how to wed it to . . . spiritual development." For Jones to give up manufacturing to "become a farmhand is to avoid the social problem & not to answer it." This was the fallacy, Crosby pointed out, in Tolstoy's and his own life. As "a maker of machinery" Jones was in a unique position to "show how wealth-producing can be civilised," as he had already been doing. "Pay yourself only $2. a day if you please," Crosby beseeched, "but don't throw away your position in the producing world,—a position which I envy you."[44]

Jones followed his friend's pleading advice and stayed in the producing world. But it was not easy. He continued to write sad and wistful letters about his weariness and yearnings for the simple rural life. In August 1902 he told Jane Addams, after a month's vacation in northern Michigan, that the simple life of Tolstoy and Thoreau seemed to him the only way to live. In June 1903 he wrote to a friend that he was "tired of books, tired of reading, tired of talk, tired of libraries and lectures, tired of respectability." He desired instead a pure life in the open air, "working with my hands rather than by working my jaw." Two months later he wrote to Nelson that he was more and more inclined to "do as Tolstoi did in effect—die to the ownership of property or things; give it away to those who want to own it."[45] The point here is that despite his desires, Jones renounced neither his factory, nor his wealth (what was left of it after his generous giving), nor his political office. He continued to write the letters, but he also continued to fight the prviate traction company, continued to provide free public services and new opportunities for the citizens of his city, and continued to increase the benefits for the workers in his factory.

Eight months after the exchange with Crosby, Jones announced the profit-sharing experiment in his annual Christmas message to the employees in his factory. But the new proposal seemed almost like an afterthought, following a lengthy and curious discourse on good health, exercise, and outdoor living, including a review of Jones's own medical history and the prescriptions he had been following: "I take lots of fresh air, sleep with windows wide open in all kinds of weather, get up at six o'clock, take ten or fifteen minutes of lively exercise, cold bath, walk two miles to the shop, and I feel best when I do a few hours' real hard work. However, I keep busy until 11:30, when I have a good, keen hunger for the first meal of the day; I eat absolutely nothing before that. During the last two months, I have cut out meat, and I think I notice a marked improvement in my feelings since doing so."[46] Jones thereby combined his personal yearnings for hard work and Tolstoyan simplicity with a continuation of his public service in the producing world, as Crosby had advised. Arguing from his own feelings of unhappiness and guilt over his withdrawal to Crosbyside and his ineffectiveness as a reformer, Crosby had helped to convince his friend to escape his own sad plight. His crucial argument was in helping Jones understand that to salve one's conscience by renouncing the world was really to avoid solving the problems of the world and, worse yet, to act selfishly. Although Jones did not admit it, he understood the message. To flee to green hills and potato-digging, however appealing that life seemed, was an evasion of his responsibilities, and Jones knew it.

What Crosby did not understand about Jones, however, was that his standards of personal behavior and excellence were so high that he was incapable of genuine and complete happiness no matter how much good he accomplished. In the Christmas message in 1902 he admitted that as he acted on the golden rule to enhance the happiness of others he was made even more aware of all those whose happiness he had not enhanced. Moreover, he felt personally responsible for good work undone and therefore believed that he deserved to be miserable: "while I leave undone one thing that is in my power to do to enhance the real happiness of the least or lowest man or woman on the planet, my own claim to happiness is defective, and I shall be miserable and I ought, for the same law that entitles me to share in the happiness that I produce condemns me to share in the unhappiness for which I am responsible, whether it be caused by what I have either done or left undone."[47] With a standard of perfection for personal happiness and self-worth like that, one wonders why Crosby envied Jones so much. The point, however, is that he did.

NOTES

Preface

*Karl Marx and Friedrich Engels, *The Communist Manifesto*, ed. Samuel Beer (New York: Appleton-Century-Crofts, 1955), p. 35.

†Ralph Waldo Emerson, "Lecture on the Times," in *The Complete Works of Ralph Waldo Emerson*, vol. 1: *Nature Addresses and Lectures* (Boston: Houghton Mifflin, 1903), pp. 282–84.

1. Ely to Amos P. Wilder, 27 July 1894, Richard T. Ely Papers, State Historical Society of Wisconsin, Madison. The full story of Ely's trial and subsequent "retreat from reform" is in Benjamin G. Rader, *The Academic Mind and Reform: The Influence of Richard T. Ely in American Life* (Lexington: University of Kentucky Press, 1966), pp. 130–58; and in Mary O. Furner, *Advocacy and Objectivity: A Crisis in the Professionalization of American Social Science, 1865–1905* (Lexington: University Press of Kentucky, 1975), pp. 143–62.

2. Walter Rauschenbusch, "The Brotherhood of the Kingdom," *Brotherhood Leaflets*, no. 2(1893); W. D. P. Bliss, "The Ideals of Professed Believers," and Walter Rauschenbusch, "Ideals of Social Reformers," both in the *Report of the Third Annual Conference of the Brotherhood of the Kingdom* (New York: E. Scott Co., 1895), pp. 24–29; "Minutes of the Brotherhood of the Kingdom," p. 23; all in the Baptist Historical Collection, Colgate-Rochester Divinity School, Rochester, N.Y. For a secondary account, see Charles Hopkins, "Walter Rauschenbusch and the Brotherhood of the Kingdom," *Church History* 7 (1938): 138–56.

3. Frank Norris, *The Octopus* (New York: New American Library, Signet Classics, 1964), pp. 388–89.

4. Finley Peter Dunne, *Mr. Dooley's Opinions* (New York: Harper & Bros., 1906), p. 177; *Plunkitt of Tammany Hall*, recorded by William Riordon (New York: E. P. Dutton, Dutton Paperback, 1963), p. 52.

5. Martin Duberman, *Black Mountain* (Garden City, N.Y.: Doubleday, Anchor Books, 1973), p. 238.

1. Knights Awakened & Inspired

*George Herron, *The Christian Society* (New York: Fleming H. Revell, 1894), p. 35.

1. Henry George, *Social Problems* (New York: Doubleday, Page, 1904), p. 245.

2. Charles Barker, *Henry George* (New York: Oxford University Press, 1955), p. 307. Jacob Riis dated the awakening from 1879 specifically because of the publication of George's book; *Social Problems*, p. 241.

3. Lewis A. Coser, *Men of Ideas: A Sociologist's View* (New York: Free Press, 1965), p. viii; see also *On Intellectuals*, ed. Philip Rieff (Garden City, N.Y.: Doubleday, Anchor Books, 1970), for a rich collection of theoretical and case studies on intellectuals as social critics.

4. Christopher Lasch, *The New Radicalism in America, 1889–1963: The Intellectual as a Social Type* (New York: Vintage Books, 1967), pp. xiv–xv. Daniel Aaron's study of pre-progressive "prophetic agitators," George, Bellamy, Lloyd, Howells, and Veblen, *Men of Good Hope* (New York: Oxford University Press, Galaxy Book, 1961), places their emphasis on the ethical, visionary search for "a discoverable utopia" (p. xiii). Aaron endorsed the need for utopianism and idealism, the loss of which he lamented in the technocratic, pragmatic "New Liberals" of the New and Fair deals; I bemoan the excessive idealism of the progressive reformers precisely because of their lack of realism.

5. Ross E. Paulson, *Radicalism and Reform: The Vrooman Family and American Social Thought, 1837–1937* (Lexington: University of Kentucky Press, 1968), p. xiv.

6. Staughton Lynd, *Intellectual Origins of American Radicalism* (New York: Vintage Books, 1969), p. v.

7. Henry Demarest Lloyd, *Wealth against Commonwealth* (New York: Harper & Bros., 1894), p. 496.

8. Paulson acknowledges this point in his conclusion to *Radicalism and Reform.* He noted that the Vrooman brothers believed "in a democratic exercise of power" and therefore "did not reject *all* the ideals of their society." He thought the point, however, not to be worth making in order to avoid the necessity for using "modifying phrases such as 'social and economic radicals' " or for introducing a " 'degrees of radicalism' concept" (p. 261 n.). I agree with him that either of these necessities would gravely affect sharpness and clarity and precisely for that reason have sought to show clearly that the intellectual reformers studied here were not radicals by any definition.

9. Joseph Mazzini, "The Duties of Man," in *The Duties of Man and Other Essays* (London: J. M. Dent & Sons, 1907), p. 9; "Europe: Its Conditions and Prospects," in *Essays: Selected from the Writings, Political and Religious, of Joseph Mazzini*, ed. William Clarke (London: Walter Scott Publ. Co., 1887), p. 290; and *Joseph Mazzini: His Life, Writings, and Political Principles*, with an introduction by William Lloyd Garrison (New York: Hurd and Houghton, 1872), pp. 199–200. See also Gaetano Salvemini's classic study, *Mazzini*, trans. I. M. Rawson (New York: Crowell-Collier Publ. Co., 1962), first published in 1905.

10. John Ruskin, "Traffic," in *The Crown of Wild Olive* (New York: Thomas Y. Crowell, n.d.), pp. 66, 76; Ruskin to C. E. Norton, 31 July 1859, in *Letters of John Ruskin, 1827–1869*, vol. 36 of *The Works of John Ruskin*, ed. E. T. Cook and Alexander Wedderburn (London: George Allen, 1903–1912), p. 311; Norton to Leslie Stephen, 28 March 1900, in *Letters of Charles Eliot Norton*, ed. Sara Norton and M. A. De Wolfe Howe (Boston: Houghton Mifflin, 1913), 2: 292; *Crown of Wild Olive*, p. 85; and *Works*, 17: 55–56, 430. The best source for Ruskin's thought, other than his own writings, is John D. Rosenberg, *The Darkening Glass: A Portrait of Ruskin's Genius* (New York: Columbia University Press, 1961).

11. Leo Tolstoy, *My Confession*, vol. 17 of *The Works of Lyof N. Tolstoi* (New York: Charles Scribner's Sons, 1922), p. 53; *Anna Karenina* (New York: New American Library, Signet Classics, 1961), p. 106; and *Works*, 17: 200. The two most helpful works on Tolstoy are by Ernest J. Simmons, *Leo Tolstoy*, 2 vols. (New York: Vintage Books, 1960), and Henry Troyat, *Tolstoy* (Garden City, N.Y.: Doubleday, 1967).

12. Lyman Abbott, *Christianity and Social Problems* (Boston: Houghton Mifflin, 1896), p. 194. See also Abbott's *Reminiscences* (Boston: Houghton Mifflin, 1923).

13. Joseph Henry Dorn, *Washington Gladden: Prophet of the Social Gospel* (Columbus: Ohio State University Press, 1967), pp. 184–85, 199; Washington Gladden, *The Church and Modern Life* (London: James Clarke, 1908), p. 57; and Gladden, *Tools and the Man* (Boston: Houghton Mifflin, 1893), p. 281. See also Gladden's *Recollections* (Boston: Houghton Mifflin, 1909).

14. For Ely's life see his autobiography, *Ground under Our Feet* (New York: Macmillan, 1938), and Rader's *The Academic Mind and Reform.* Ely published more than twenty books and scores of articles, but the essence of his social Christianity and his pre-1900 attitudes toward the labor movement and socialism can be found in *The Labor Movement in America* (New York: Thomas Y. Crowell, 1886); *Social Aspects of Christianity and other Essays* (New York: Thomas Y. Crowell, 1889); *Socialism and Social Reform* (New York: Thomas Y. Crowell, 1894), especially the sections on the "Golden Mean, or Practicable Social Reform"; and *The Social Law of Service* (New York: Eaton & Mains, 1896).

15. Eleanor Woods, *Robert A. Woods: Champion of Democracy* (Boston: Houghton Mifflin, 1929), p. 39; Robert A. Woods and Albert J. Kennedy, *The Settlement Horizon* (New York: Russell Sage Foundation, 1922), p. 55; and Robert A. Woods, *English Social Movements* (New York: Charles Scribner's Sons, 1891), p. vi.

16. E. E. Hale to Richard T. Ely, 14 January 1889, Ely Papers; Hale, "Count Leo Tolstoi," *Cosmopolitan* 7 (August 1889): 416–17.

17. Brand Whitlock, *Forty Years of It* (New York: D. Appleton, 1925), pp. 84–85; Clarence Darrow, *Resist Not Evil* (Chicago: Charles H. Kerr, 1903), p. 7; and Darrow, *Story of My Life* (New York: Charles Scribner's Sons, 1934), pp. 53, 210.

18. Brand Whitlock, in an unidentified newspaper clipping in a scrapbook, Box 103, Brand Whitlock Papers, Library of Congress; Whitlock to Darrow, 7 November 1900, in *The Letters and Journal of Brand Whitlock*, ed. Allan Nevins (New York: D. Appleton-Century, 1936), 1:32; and Jack Tager, *The Intellectual as Urban Reformer: Brand Whitlock and the Progressive Movement* (Cleveland, Ohio: Press of Case Western Reserve University, 1968), pp. 52–69.

19. Jane Addams, *Newer Ideals of Peace* (New York: Macmillan, 1907), p. 29; Addams, *Democracy and Social Ethics* (New York: Macmillan, 1907), pp. 6, 273.

20. Jane Addams, *Twenty Years at Hull House* (New York: Macmillan, 1920), pp. 262, 268–77.

21. Vida Scudder, *On Journey* (New York: E. P. Dutton, 1937), p. 83; W. D. Howells, *My Literary Passions* (New York: Harper & Bros., 1895), p. 183; Ernest Howard Crosby, *Tolstoy and His Message* (New York: Funk & Wagnalls, 1904), p. 44; and Herron, in a private letter to Gaetano Salvemini, quoted in Salvemini's *Mazzini*, p. 95.

22. The works that focus on these various forces are extensive: among them are Paulson, *Radicalism and Reform*, pp. xvii-xxiii, 21–53; Stanley M. Elkins, *Slavery: A Problem in American Institutional and Intellectual Life* (New York: Grosset & Dunlap, Universal Library, 1963), pp. 157–64; Seymour Martin Lipset, *Political Man* (Garden City, N.Y.: Doubleday, 1960), chapt. 10; Richard

Hofstadter, *The Age of Reform* (New York: Alfred A. Knopf, 1955), chapt. 4; Silvan Tomkins, "The Psychology of Commitment," in *The Antislavery Vanguard: New Essays on the Abolitionists*, ed. Martin Duberman (Princeton, N. J.: Princeton University Press, 1965), pp. 270–98; Robert K. Merton, *Social Theory and Social Structure* (Glencoe, Ill.: Free Press, 1957), pp. 139–60; Erik Erikson, *Young Man Luther* (New York: W. W. Norton, 1958), and *Gandhi's Truth* (New York: W. W. Norton, 1969); and Robert Jay Lifton, *History and Human Survival* (New York: Vintage Books, 1971), Parts 1, 4.

23. Noman Petit, *The Heart Prepared: Grace and Conversion in Puritan Spiritual Life* (New Haven, Conn.: Yale University Press, 1966), pp. 1–21; William James, *The Varieties of Religious Experience* (New York: Crowell-Collier, 1961), pp. 172–76.

24. Erik Erikson, "The Golden Rule and the Cycle of Life," in *The Study of Lives*, ed. Robert W. White (New York: Atherton Press, 1963), pp. 415–17.

25. In his *Radicalism and Reform*, Paulson also argues that "reform and radicalism are part of the process of self-identification" (pp. xv–xvi). Erikson's *Young Man Luther* and *Gandhi's Truth*, as well as other studies in psychohistory, explore this promising but risky biographical possibility. I am not here suggesting anything matching the depth of Erikson's analysis; rather it seems obvious that many men and women turn to radicalism or reform as part of their quest for identity and that self-doubts are an inevitable part of any reformer's psychological state.

26. Shailer Mathews, in *A Dictionary of Religion and Ethics*, ed. Shailer Mathews and Gerald Smith (New York: Macmillan, 1923), p. 225; Herron, *Christian Society*, p. 35; and Walter Rauschenbusch, *Christianity and the Social Crisis* (New York: Macmillan, 1907), p. 338.

27. W. D. Howells to his sister, Mrs. Achille Frechette, 18 November 1887, in *Life in Letters of William Dean Howells*, ed. Mildred Howells, 2 vols. (Garden City, N.Y.: Doubleday, Doran, 1928), 1:404.

28. A brief analysis of the neglect of the black American in the Social Gospel movement as a whole can be found in David Reimers, *White Protestantism and the Negro* (New York: Oxford University Press, 1965), pp. 53–54, and in Dorn's biography of *Washington Gladden*, pp. 291–94. For the sometimes sentimental and sometimes racist treatment of blacks and immigrants by settlement workers during this same period, see Allen F. Davis, *Spearheads for Reform: The Social Settlements and the Progressive Movement, 1890–1914* (New York: Oxford University Press, 1967), pp. 84–102.

29. An exegesis and exposition of Matt. 7:12 is in *The Interpreter's Bible*, ed. George A. Buttrick (Nashville, Tenn.: Abingdon Press, 1951), 7:329–30; Erik Erikson, "The Golden Rule and the Cycle of Life," pp. 413–14.

30. "Edwin Markham's Comment on the Sermon," The Edwin Markham Collection of Florence Hamilton, Library of Congress; Amos N. Wilder, "The Teaching of Jesus: The Sermon on the Mount," *Interpreter's Bible*, 7:155, 162–63.

31. Frederick Denison Maurice, quoted in Francis G. Peabody, *Jesus Christ and the Social Question* (New York: Macmillan, 1903), p. 21; Rauschenbusch, "Ideals of Social Reformers," *American Journal of Sociology* 2 (September 1896): 203; and Markham, "Christ and the Social State," *Twentieth Century Magazine* 1 (January 1910): 347.

32. Robert T. Handy, "George D. Herron and the Social Gospel in American

Protestantism, 1890–1901" (Ph.D. diss., University of Chicago, 1949), p. 176 and passim. The traditional and best studies of the moderately progressive and more radical wings of the Social Gospel movement, including their impact on American reform, are by Henry F. May, *Protestant Churches and Industrial America* (New York: Harper & Row, 1949), and Charles Hopkins, *The Rise of the Social Gospel in American Protestantism, 1865–1915*, Yale Studies in Religious Education, vol. 14 (New Haven, Conn.: Yale University Press, 1940). Hopkins's assessment of the impact is more positive than May's. Arthur Mann, in his *Yankee Reformers in the Urban Age* (New York: Harper & Row, Torchbooks, 1966), also concluded rather optimistically that the religiously motivated reformers of Boston had a positive impact in creating "a new climate of opinion that stimulated urban dwellers to rally behind the progressive creeds" of Roosevelt and Wilson (p. 240).

Several recent interpretations of twentieth-century reform by New Left historians dissent from the traditional view. These historians take their departure in part from Herbert Marcuse's theories on "repressive tolerance" and the capacity of the liberal corporate state in America to absorb and co-opt reform efforts in order to strengthen the established order, thus making radical change even more difficult, if not impossible. This critical interpretation appears most rigorously for the Progressive era in Gabriel Kolko, *The Triumph of Conservatism: A Reinterpretation of American History, 1900–1916* (Glencoe, Ill.: Free Press, 1963), and in James Weinstein, *The Corporate Ideal in the Liberal State, 1900–1918* (Boston: Beacon Press, 1968). James Dombrowski's *The Early Days of Christian Socialism in America* (New York: Columbia University Press, 1936) is an older, patently Marxist view. My study is the first work to examine the Social Gospel movement generally and the Christian socialists specifically from a quasi-New Left perspective.

33. George, *Social Problems*, p. 242.

2. William Dean Howells & Henry Demarest Lloyd

*W. D. Howells to his father, William C. Howells, 2 February 1890, *Life in Letters of William Dean Howells*, ed. Mildred Howells, 2 vols. (Garden City, N. Y.: Doubeday, Doran, 1928), 2:1.

†H. D. Lloyd, "Is Personal Development the Best Social Policy?" *Mazzini and Other Essays* (New York: G. P. Putnam's Sons, 1910), p. 200. An address before the Browning Society, Boston, 25 February 1902.

1. Caro Lloyd, *Henry Demarest Lloyd*, 2 vols. (New York: G. P. Putnam's Sons, 1912), 1:198–99; also in Josiah Flynt, *My Life* (New York: Outlook Publ. Co., 1908), p. 238. The fourth person Tolstoy wanted to bring to the conference, Flynt thought, was an English clergyman.

2. Tolstoy, quoted in the *Single Tax Review* 1 (October 15, 1901): 16; Barker, *Henry George*, pp. 597–99; and Lloyd, *Lloyd*, 1:198.

3. Howells to Lloyd, 2 November 1894, *Life in Letters*, 2:54; Lloyd, *Lloyd*, 1:281; and Howells to Jessie Bross Lloyd, 4 October 1903, Henry Demarest Lloyd Papers, State Historical Society of Wisconsin, Madison.

4. Notebook 7 (1888), Lloyd Papers.

5. Lloyd, *Lloyd*, 1:94, 97; Chester Destler, *Henry Demarest Lloyd and the Empire of Reform* (Philadelphia, University of Pennsylvania Press, 1963), p. 165.

6. Howells to William C. Howells, 13 November 1887, *Life in Letters*, 1:402; Howells to Pryor, 25 September 1887, and Pryor to Howells, 3 October 1887, *Life in Letters*, 1:393–94; and letter to the *Tribune*, in *Life in Letters*, 1:399.

7. Howells, "A Word for the Dead," quoted in Edwin Cady, *The Realist at War: The Mature Years of William Dean Howells* (Syracuse, N.Y.: Syracuse University Press, 1958), pp. 73–77.

8. Lloyd, *Lloyd*, 1:107.

9. Howells to Francis Browne, 11 November 1887, and Howells to Mrs. Achille Frechette, 18 November 1887, *Life in Letters*, 1:402, 404.

10. Unlike the treatment of the lesser known figures in this study, no attempt is made to deal with the whole life and thought of Howells and Lloyd. Numerous studies have been done on both men, especially Howells, including almost every conceivable aspect of his life and literature. My work focuses on an interpretive analysis of the European and American influences on their social thought and on their role as intellectual reformers.

11. W. D. Howells, *Years of My Youth* (New York: Harper & Bros., 1916), p. 131.

12. Ibid., pp. 119, 159–60.

13. Howells to Charles Eliot Norton, 15 August 1866, Norton Papers, Houghton Library, Harvard University, Cambridge, Mass.; Kenneth S. Lynn, *William Dean Howells: An American Life* (New York: Harcourt Brace Jovanovich, 1971), pp. 190–91; and Howells to William C. Howells, 28 January 1872, *Life in Letters*, 1:166.

14. See Lynn, *Howells*, pp. 197–226, 252–67.

15. Howells to Twain, 4 September 1884, *Mark Twain-Howells Letters*, ed. Henry Nash Smith and William Gibson (Cambridge, Mass.: Belknap Press, 1960), 2:503; Howells to James, 22 August 1884, to John Hay, 7 January 1884, and to William C. Howells, 10 August 1884, all in *Life in Letters*, 1:357–66.

16. Howells to Phelps, 4 March 1910, in William Lyon Phelps, *Autobiography with Letters* (New York: Oxford University Press, 1939), p. 504; Hale, 28 May 1887, in *The Life and Letters of Edward Everett Hale*, ed. E. E. Hale, Jr. (Boston: Little, Brown, 1917), 2:328; and Howells to Mrs. Frechette, 18 November 1887, *Life in Letters*, 1:405.

17. Howells to T. S. Perry, 30 October 1885, *Life in Letters*, 1:373; Cady, *Realist at War*, p. 66; Lynn, *Howells*, pp. 289–90; *Diary and Letters of Rutherford B. Hayes*, ed. Charles R. Williams (Columbus: Ohio State Archaeological and Historical Society, 1925), 4:327; Whitman, 24 December 1888, in Horace Traubel, *With Walt Whitman in Camden* (Boston: Small, Maynard, 1906), 3:371; and Howells, quoted by "G," "Mr. Howells' Socialism," *American Fabian* 4 (February 1898): 2.

18. Howells, "Editor's Study," *Harper's Magazine* 72 (April 1886): 809; Howells, "Lyof Tolstoi," *Harper's Weekly* 31 (April 23, 1887): 299, 300. Unless otherwise indicated, all citations from *Harper's Magazine* are from Howells's monthly column, "Editor's Study."

19. *Harper's Magazine* 78 (December 1888): 159–60; Howells, "Lyof Tolstoi," in *Library of the World's Best Literature*, ed. Charles Dudley Warner, 30 vols. (New York: R. S. Peale and J. A. Hill, Publishers, 1897), 25:14987–88.

20. *Harper's Magazine* 72 (April 1886): 808; *Harper's Magazine* 75 (July 1887): 316–17; and Howells, "Lyof Tolstoi," p. 299.

21. W. D. Howells, *My Literary Passions* (New York: Harper & Bros., 1895), pp. 188, 183–84.

22. *Harper's Magazine* 76 (February 1888): 478. See Louis J. Budd, "William Dean Howells' Debt to Tolstoy," *American Slavic and East European Review* 9 (December 1950): 292, 295.

23. Howells to Mrs. Frechette, 18 November 1887, *Life in Letters*, 1:405. The title of *Annie Kilburn* and many of the themes have obvious similarities to *Anna Karenina*.

24. W. D. Howells, *Annie Kilburn* (New York: Harper & Bros., 1891), pp. 65, 240, 232; Howells to Garland, 6 November 1888, *Life in Letters*, 1:419.

25. Howells, *Annie Kilburn*, pp. 151, 155, 329.

26. Howells to Garland, 15 January 1888, to Hale, 30 August 1888, to Henry James, 10 October 1888, to Hale, 28 October 1888, in *Life in Letters*, 1:408–19.

27. Lynn begins his study of Howells with an account of Howells's anguish over the gap between his Tolstoyan beliefs and his incredibly large income in the early 1890s. He was such a skillful negotiator with publishers and manager of his financial resources that, as Lynn points out, his purchasing power in the 1890s was equal to that of a writer who in 1970 earned $120,000 a year. In Howells, Lynn said, "we feel ourselves in the presence not only of an uneasy conscience, but also of a profoundly disoriented imagination and shattered morale" (p. 9).

28. Howells, *Harper's Magazine* 75 (July 1887): 316; *Harper's Magazine* 75 (August 1887): 478.

29. Howells, *Annie Kilburn*, pp. 323, 265.

30. William Dean Howells, *A Hazard of New Fortunes* (New York: Bantam Books, 1960), pp. 261, 378, 391.

31. Howells to Twain, 11 February 1890, *Twain-Howells Letters*, 2:630.

32. Howells to William C. Howells, 27 April 1890, *Life in Letters*, 2:3. For a detailed study of Howells's two years back in Boston and his relationship to Bliss and Christian socialism, see Clara and Rudolf Kirk, "Howells and the Church of the Carpenter," *New England Quarterly* 32 (June 1959): 185–206.

33. Howells to William C. Howells, 2 February 1890, *Life in Letters*, 2:1.

34. This description of Altruria is from the major speech of Mr. Homos at the conclusion of Howells's *A Traveller from Altruria*, in *A Selected Edition of W. D. Howells*, vol. 20, *The Altrurian Romances*, introduction and notes to text by Clara and Rudolf Kirk (Bloomington: Indiana University Press, 1968), pp. 145–75.

35. Howells, *A Traveller from Altruria*, pp. 41, 23; *Letters of an Altrurian Traveller*, in *A Selected Edition*, 20:192.

36. W. D. Howells, *The World of Chance* (New York: Harper & Bros., 1893), pp. 90, 208, 91.

37. Howells to W. C. Howells, 9 November 1890, *Life in Letters*, 2:8–9; Howells to T. S. Perry, 14 April 1888, *Life in Letters*, 1:414; and Howells to Sylvester Baxter, 27 July 1896, and to W. C. Howells, 10 July 1892, *Life in Letters*, 2:69, 25.

38. Howells to Frank Parsons, 22 May 1897, in Parsons, *The City for the People*, rev. ed. (Philadelphia: C. F. Taylor, 1901), p. 291; Crosby to Howells, 18 November 1895, William Dean Howells MSS, Houghton Library, Harvard University, Cambridge, Mass.; *American Fabian* 4 (July 1898): 2; and *Direct Legislation Record* 6 (July 1899): 48.

39. Howells to Aurelia Howells, 3 April 1898, and to James, 17 April, 31 July 1898, *Life in Letters*, 2:89–90, 95.

40. Quoted in Lynn, *Howells*, p. 306. Sturges told Henry James of his conversation with Howells, and James transcribed it in his notebooks.

41. Howells to Norton, *Life in Letters*, 2:242; Howells to Mrs. Howells, 26 April 1909, *Life in Letters*, 2:266.

42. Howells to Narodnay, 4 December 1910, in the Edwin Markham Papers, Markham Memorial Library, Wagner College, Staten Island, N.Y.; Howells to Twain, 24 June 1906, *Life in Letters*, 2:227.

43. Lloyd, *Wealth against Commonwealth*, p. 534.

44. Lloyd to Henry Keenan, July 1872, in Lloyd, *Lloyd*, 1:39–40; Lloyd to Jessie Bross Lloyd, 5 August, 2 September 1885, Lloyd Papers.

45. Lloyd, *Wealth against Commonwealth*, pp. 2, 504–5.

46. Lloyd, *Lloyd*, 1:xi, and Destler, *Lloyd*, p. 187. The two most complete biographies of Lloyd are those by his brother Caro and by Destler. Destler concluded that Lloyd's social philosophy of welfare democracy is best called "liberal socialism." Daniel Aaron's chapter on Lloyd in *Men of Good Hope* placed him in the middle-class progressive tradition. Aaron said that Lloyd, whom he described as "probably the finest product of the middle class conscience in our history," demonstrated "how a middle position—gradualist, pragmatic, tolerant—can be vital and deeply radical at the same time" (pp. 170–71). What he meant by radical is not clear.

47. Notebook 26 (1894), p. 9, and letter to William Saul, 18 January 1900, in Lloyd Papers; also in Lloyd, *Lloyd*, 1:301.

48. Lloyd to President George Gates of Iowa College, 23 May 1895, Lloyd Papers; "Mazzini—Prophet of Action," *Leader*, no. 11 (March 2, 1889), p. 126; and Lloyd, *Lloyd*, 1:301.

49. Lloyd, *Lloyd*, 2:53–60, 65, 67.

50. Lloyd, "Is Personal Development the Best Social Policy?" *Mazzini and Other Essays*, p. 190; *Wealth against Commonwealth*, p. 527; and H. D. Lloyd, *Man, the Social Creator*, ed. Jane Addams and Anne Withington (London: Harper & Bros., 1906), pp. 50, 273.

51. Lloyd, *Lloyd*, 2:185; Lloyd, *Man, the Social Creator*, p. 174.

52. Lloyd, *Wealth against Commonwealth*, p. 528; Aaron, *Men of Good Hope*, p. 137. See also Destler, *Lloyd*, p. 297, for a discussion of Lloyd's Emersonian preference for influencing middle-class intellectuals.

53. Gates to Mr. Warner, 15 June 1895, Lloyd Papers; Lloyd, "The Scholar in Contemporary Practical Questions," *Mazzini*, pp. 147–53.

54. Lloyd, *Mazzini*, pp. 155, 169–75. See also "The Labour Movement," an address in Chicago, 4 July 1889, in *Men, the Workers* (New York: Doubleday, Page, 1909), p. 26.

55. *Wealth against Commonwealth*, p. 518; "A Day with William Morris," *Mazzini*, p. 70; and Destler, *Lloyd*, p. 123.

56. Lloyd, "The Political Economy of Seventy-three Million Dollars," in H. D. Lloyd, *Lords of Industry* (New York: G. P. Putnam's Sons, 1910), pp. 49, 62, 56; "Lords of Industry," *Lords of Industry*, pp. 146–47.

57. Lloyd, *Man, the Social Creator*, p. 124; Destler, *Lloyd*, p. 207.

58. Notebook 8, pp. 4, 16, Notebook 9, pp. 28, 38, Notebook 11, p. 16, and Notebook 13, p. 7 (1888), Lloyd Papers.

59. Lloyd, "Mazzini: Prophet of Action," in *Mazzini*, pp. 2–4, 7. This speech was first delivered before the Chicago Ethical Culture Society on 17 February

1889 and six days later before the Weekly Economic Conference in Chicago, as reported in the *Leader*, no. 11 (March 2, 1889), pp. 124–26.

60. Lloyd, undated fragment, Box 26, Lloyd Papers; Lloyd, *Lloyd*, 1:174; and *Wealth against Commonwealth*, p. 497.

61. Lloyd, *Man, the Social Creator*, pp. 6, 26; "The Labour Movement," in *Men, the Workers*, p. 16.

62. Lloyd, *Man, the Social Creator*, p. 24; *Wealth against Commonwealth*, pp. 495, 499, 503–4, 522–23.

63. Lloyd's many speeches on Debs and the labor movement are collected in *Men, the Workers*. See, for example, "The Union Forever" (1891), "The Safety of the Future Lies in Organized Labor" (1893), "Strikes and Injunctions" (October 1894), and "Lessons of the Debs Case" (November 1895).

64. Lloyd to Ely, 10 October 1896, Lloyd, *Lloyd*, 1:263–64; Lloyd, *Lloyd*, 2:257. See also Lloyd's bitter analysis, "The Populists at St. Louis," *Review of Reviews* 14 (September 1896): 278–303.

65. Lloyd to Ely, 4 November 1896, Lloyd Papers; Destler, *Lloyd*, p. 386; and Lloyd to George Arnold, 19 November 1897, Lloyd Papers.

66. H. D. Lloyd, *Labor Copartnership* (New York: Harper & Bros., 1899), p. 328. See also H. D. Lloyd, *Newest England: Notes of a Democratic Traveller in New Zealand* (New York: Doubleday, Page, 1901); and H. D. Lloyd, *A Sovereign People: A Study of Swiss Democracy* (New York: Doubleday, Page, 1907).

67. Lloyd, *Lloyd*, 2:255.

68. See Lloyd's "Argument before the Anthracite Strike Commission," 9 February 1903, and his "Speech at the Mitchell, Darrow, Lloyd Reception," 16 February 1903, in *Men, the Workers*. See also his "National Ownership of Anthracite Coal Mines," 12 and 13 March 1903, and "The Failure of Railroad Regulation," 15 May 1903, in *Lords of Industry*.

69. *In Memoriam: Henry Demarest Lloyd*, Chicago, November 29, 1903 (pamphlet), pp. 10, 46, 30, 26, 35, 8.

70. Ibid., p. 21; Lloyd, *Lloyd*, 2:119.

71. Lloyd, "Reception of Eugene V. Debs," *Men, the Workers*, p. 190; "What Washington Would Do To-Day," *Lords of Industry*, p. 165.

72. *Man, the Social Creator*, pp. 232 ff.; *Mazzini*, p. 200.

73. "Factory Law Speech," *Men, the Workers*, p. 130.

74. Lloyd, *Wealth against Commonwealth*, p. 517. A few pages later he wrote that reform was inevitable; only the means were in doubt. "The change will come. With reform, it may come to us. If with force, perhaps not to us. But it will come. The world is too full of amateurs who can play the golden rule as an aria with variations" (p. 521).

75. Whitman, 24–25 January 1889, in Traubel, *With Walt Whitman*, 4:17, 22–23.

76. *In Memoriam*, p. 31.

77. Lloyd, "No Mean City," *Mazzini*, pp. 200–232.

78. Howells, *World of Chance*, p. 92.

3. W. D. P. Bliss & B. O. Flower

*W. D. P. Bliss, *Social Unity* 1 (January 1901): 1.

†B. O. Flower, "The Present," *Arena* 1 (January 1890): 241.

1. Flower to Lloyd, 3 July 1895, Lloyd Papers; Flower, "A Magazine with a

Mission," *Coming Age* 1 (January 1899): 94; and Bliss, "What to Do Now," *Dawn* 2 (July–August 1890): 113–14. Both Bliss and Flower used italics frequently, underscoring the urgency that permeated their writing. Unless otherwise indicated, all italics are theirs.

2. The most complete biographical information on Bliss can be found in Hopkins, *Rise of the Social Gospel*, pp. 173–80; Howard Quint, *The Forging of American Socialism* (Indianapolis, Ind.: Bobbs-Merrill, 1964), pp. 109–26, 240–45, 256–67; Mann, *Yankee Reformers*, pp. 90–97; and Chris Webber, "William Dwight Porter Bliss," *Historical Magazine of the Protestant Episcopal Church* 28 (March 1959): 11–37.

3. Paulson, *Radicalism and Reform*, pp. 67–68.

4. The most complete biographical information on Flower can be found in Mann, *Yankee Reformers*, pp. 163–71; Howard F. Cline, "Benjamin Orange Flower and the Arena, 1889–1909," *Journalism Quarterly* 17 (June 1940): 139–50; and Roy P. Fairfield, "Benjamin Orange Flower: Father of the Muckrakers," *American Literature* 22 (1950): 272–82.

5. *American Sentinel* 1 (December 23, 1880): 1. Found in two letters (25 February and 24 March 1939) included in a "Collection of correspondence in connection with Dr. Howard F. Cline's research on the life of B. O. F." for an unpublished senior honors thesis at Harvard University, deposited in Widener Library. Cline claims that Flower destroyed his personal papers; Mann, *Yankee Reformers*, p. 164.

6. "Declaration of Principles" of the Society of Christian Socialists, adopted on 15 April 1889, *Dawn* 1 (May 15, 1889): 3; "Salutamus" and "The Society of Christian Socialists in Boston," *Dawn* 1 (May 15, 1889): 1, 3; and "What Is Christian Socialism?" *Dawn* 1 (January 15, 1890): 2.

7. "What Is Christian Socialism?" p. 3; *Dawn* 1 (February 1890): 2–3.

8. "Why Am I a Christian Socialist?" *Twentieth Century* 5 (October 2, 1890): 5; "Self-Saving Colonies Condemned," *Social Gospel* 2 (April 1899): 17; and "What Is Christian Socialism?" *Dawn* 1 (January 15, 1890): 2.

9. *Dawn* 1 (August 15, 1889): 5; see also Bliss's lead article, "Nationalism and Christianity," in Bellamy's journal, *Nationalist* 1 (August 1899): 97–99; *Dawn* 1 (November 15, 1889): 4; *Dawn* 1 (June 15, 1889): 4; and "What Christian Socialism Is," *Social Unity* 1 (May 1, 1901): 68.

10. "A Symposium upon the Relation of the State to the Individual," *Dawn* 2 (November 1890): 276–82; Bliss's Introduction to John Stuart Mill, *Socialism*, ed. W. D. P. Bliss (New York: Humboldt Publ. Co., 1891), pp. viii–ix.

11. "What Is Christian Socialism?" *Dawn* 1 (February 1890): 3; Bliss to Ely, 7 December 1891, Richard T. Ely Papers, State Historical Society of Wisconsin, Madison. See also the letters from Bliss to Ely on 19 November and 2 December 1891. Bliss was so upset by Ely's caution that he offered to resign from the Executive Committee of the Christian Social Union.

12. *Dawn* 1 (September 15, 1889): 7; *Dawn* 2 (October 1890): 249; and "Our Library," *Dawn* 1 (May 15, 1889): 8.

13. Bliss's Introduction to *The Communism of John Ruskin*, ed. W. D. P. Bliss (New York: Humboldt Publ. Co., 1891), pp. vii–xi; *American Fabian* 1 (December 1895): 2.

14. Bliss's Preface to James E. Thorold Rogers, *Six Centuries of Work and Wages*, ed. W. D. P. Bliss (New York: Humboldt Publ. Co., 1890), pp. iii–vii; Appendix to *Six Centuries*, p. 135.

15. "Facts for American Socialists," which ran from February 1895 to March 1896, when the *Dawn* ceased publication, was practically the only thing in the *Dawn* during this period; *New Encyclopedia of Social Reform*, ed. W. D. P. Bliss (New York: Funk & Wagnalls, 1908), p. i.

16. *Dawn* 7 (January 1895): 1–2.

17. *American Fabian* 1 (February 1895): 5; *American Fabian* 1 (July–August 1895): 6, 8–9; *American Fabian* 1 (December 1895): 8; and *Publications of the Church Social Union*, no. 32 (December 15, 1896), pp. 18–19.

18. Bliss to Lloyd, 5 November 1896, Lloyd Papers.

19. "Unite or Perish," *American Fabian* 5 (June 1899): 1; also in the *Arena* 22 (July 1899): 78–89.

20. The most complete account of the Buffalo conference, based on Eltweed Pomeroy's detailed minutes, is in the *Direct Legislation Record* 6 (July 1899): 33–64. See also Bliss's own descriptions in the first issues of the *Social Forum* and the *Bulletin of the Social Reform Union* (August 1899—January 1900). The best secondary account of the conference, as well as of the Union Reform League which preceded it, is in Quint, *Forging of American Socialism*, pp. 256–67. Paulson's *Radicalism and Reform*, pp. 141–46, includes an account of the internal dissensions of the College of Social Science.

21. Social Reform Union brochure, reprinted in *Social Forum* 2 (January 1900): 32; *Bulletin of the Social Reform Union* 1 (November 1, 1899): 2.

22. Bemis to Lloyd, 1 July 1901, quoted in Paulson, *Radicalism and Reform*, pp. 167–68.

23. *Social Unity* 1 (January 1, 1901): 5–6; *Social Unity* 1 (March 1, 1901): 41; and "The Faith of a Socialist," *Social Unity* 2 (July 1, 1901): 1–11. The journal folded the following month.

24. *Social Progress: 1906*, ed. Josiah Strong, W. D. P. Bliss, and William Tolman (New York: Baker & Taylor, 1906), pp. 266–67; "The Church and Social Reform Workers," *Outlook* 82 (January 20, 1906): 122; and "How the Other Half Lives," *Studies in the Gospel of the Kingdom* 5 (January 1913): 16.

25. "Some Easter Thoughts," *Studies in the Gospel of the Kingdom* 2 (April 1910): 37; Bliss to Herron, 25 July 1924, George Herron Collection, Hoover Library, Stanford University, Palo Alto, Calif.

26. Lloyd to Thomas Morgan, 11 July 1895, Lloyd Papers; *American Fabian* 3 (October 1897): 5; and Longley, quoted in Quint, *Forging of American Socialism*, p. 126. Bliss's failings and the general weaknesses of the Fabian movement in America are discussed in Thomas P. Jenkin, "The American Fabian Movement," *Western Political Quarterly* 1 (June 1948): 113–23.

27. Flower, *Coming Age* 2 (September 1899): 340.

28. "The New Time and How Its Advent May Be Hastened," *Arena* 9 (April 1894): 695.

29. "The August Present," *Arena* 13 (August 1895): 404–5; "Jesus or Caesar," *Arena* 9 (March 1894): 525–26, 531; "The Present," *Arena* 1 (January 1890), 241–42; and "Vital Thought Centers in Transition Periods," *Coming Age* 2 (November 1899): 551. Flower's ideas of progress, which appear throughout his writing, are especially well developed in Part 1 ("The Nineteenth Century: A Backward Glance") of his autobiographical *Progressive Men, Women, and Movements of the Past Twenty-Five Years* (Boston: New Arena, 1914).

30. B. O. Flower, *How England Averted a Revolution of Force: A Survey of*

the Social Agitation of the First Ten Years of Queen Victoria's Reign (Boston: Sherman, French, 1911), pp. 99, 126–40, 150, and passim. The concluding chapter, "Lessons for the Present," pp. 195–210, was first written for the *Arena* 24 (October 1900): 358–78.

31. "The Dawning Day," *Arena* 5 (January 1892): 272.

32. "The Present," p. 243; Flower to Adams, quoted in the *New Time* 1 (June 1897): 69; "A Magazine with a Mission," *Coming Age* 1 (January 1899): 94; and "The Twentieth Century Magazine and What It Stands For," *Twentieth Century Magazine* 1 (October 1909): 77.

33. Hamlin Garland, *A Son of the Middle Border* (New York: Macmillan, 1928), p. 411; Flower, *Progressive Men*, p. 69; and "Is Socialism Desirable?" *Arena* 3 (May 1891): 761–64.

34. "Four Epochs in the History of Our Republic," *Arena* 16 (November 1896): 928–36; *Progressive Men*, p. 109.

35. *Progressive Men*, p. 23.

36. Roy P. Fairfield, "Benjamin Orange Flower: Father of the Muckrakers," p. 274; B. O. Flower, *Civilization's Inferno: Studies in the Social Cellar* (Boston: Arena Publ. Co., 1893), pp. 38, 138–52, 229, 232–37.

37. "The Highest Function of the Novel," *Arena* 1 (April 1890): 630; B. O. Flower, *Lessons Learned from Other Lives*, 2d ed. (Boston: Arena Publ. Co., 1891), p. 74; "Some Social Ideals Held by Victor Hugo," *Arena* 10 (June 1894): 105; *Lessons Learned*, p. 238; and "Some Social Ideals," pp. 105–9.

38. B. O. Flower, *Gerald Massey: Poet, Prophet and Mystic* (New York: Alliance Publ. Co., 1895), pp. ii–iv; B. O. Flower, *Whittier: Prophet, Seer and Man* (Boston: Arena Publ. Co., 1896), p. 136.

39. "William Morris and Some of His Later Works," *Arena* 17 (December 1896): 52; "Fra Elbertus and the Roycrofters: A Social Study," *Coming Age* 3 (February 1900): 137; and "Edwin Markham and the New Conscience," *Coming Age* 2 (September 1899): 281–84.

40. "John Ruskin: Critic, Philosopher, Prophet, and Philanthropist," *Coming Age* 3 (June 1900): 568.

41. "Conservatism and Sensualism: An Unhallowed Alliance," *Arena* 3 (December 1890): 126; "Tolstoi: Prophet, Illuminator and Seer," *Twentieth Century Magazine* 3 (January 1911): 346; and "Fra Elbertus," pp. 141–42.

42. "A New Prophet in the Choir of Progress," *Coming Age* 3 (January 1900): 52; *Progressive Men*, p. 295; see also "A Civic Leader of the New Time," *Arena* 25 (April 1901): 385–400.

43. "John Ruskin: Critic," p. 568; "John Ruskin: A Type of Twentieth-Century Manhood," *Arena* 18 (July 1897): 71, 77–78.

44. "Giuseppe Mazzini," *Arena* 29 (March 1903): 254, 267–69; "A Nineteenth Century Prophet of Twentieth Century Civilization," *Twentieth Century Magazine* 4 (May 1911): 167–68.

45. H. F. Cline, "Flower and the Arena: Purpose and Content," *Journalism Quarterly* 17 (September 1940): 247.

46. "Union for Practical Progress," *Arena* 8 (June 1893): 81; "Constitution of the National Union for Practical Progress," *Arena* 11 (December 1894): p. xx; and "The New Time and How Its Advent May Be Hastened," *Arena* 9 (April 1894): 686. Cline estimates that there were between sixty and eighty Arena clubs formed ("Flower and the Arena: Purpose and Content," p. 256). On this point, see also William Tolman, ed., *Municipal Reform Movements in the United*

States (New York: Fleming H. Revell, 1895), pp. 161–62, and Paulson, *Radicalism and Reform*, pp. 81–96. Paulson calls the Union for Practical Progress "the most successful social experiment with which the Vrooman brothers were associated" between 1890 and 1895, but this must certainly be a comment on their failures elsewhere.

47. Cline, "Flower and the Arena: Purpose," p. 248.

48. Flower, *Civilization's Inferno*, pp. 217–21.

49. B. O. Flower, *The Patriot's Manual* (Fort Scott, Kans.: Free Press Defense League, 1915); B. O. Flower, *Righting the People's Wrongs: A Lesson from History for Our Own Times* (Cincinnati: Standard Publ. Co., 1917).

4. Vida Scudder

*Vida Scudder, "Socialism and Sacrifice," *Atlantic Monthly* 105 (June 1910): 841–42.

1. "Influence and Independence," *Andover Review* 13 (February 1890): 175.

2. Vida Dutton Scudder, *On Journey* (New York: E. P. Dutton, 1937), pp. 51, 121–22, 51–52.

3. Ibid., pp. 30, 43, 58, 68, 78. The only somewhat detailed treatments of Scudder's life and thought, other than her trustworthy and candid autobiography, are Mann, *Yankee Reformers*, pp. 217–28, and Peter J. Frederick, "Vida Dutton Scudder: The Professor as Social Activist," *New England Quarterly* 43 (September 1970): 407–33.

4. Vida Scudder, "Recollections of Ruskin," *Atlantic Monthly* 85 (April 1900): 568–69. Selected portions of these recollections are in *On Journey*, pp. 79–81.

5. "Recollections of Ruskin," pp. 569–71; *On Journey*, p. 83.

6. *On Journey*, pp. 84, 105–6.

7. Ibid., pp. 161–63; "The Social Conscience in American Churches," *Commonwealth* (February 1927): 41; "The Socialism of Christ," *Dawn* 3 (December 18, 1890): 3–4; and "Socialism and Spiritual Progress," *Publications of the Church Social Union*, no. 10 (January 1, 1896), pp. 3, 23.

8. *On Journey*, pp. 126, 140, 176; "Socialism and Sacrifice," p. 839.

9. *On Journey*, p. 109; Vida Scudder, *An Introduction to the Writings of John Ruskin* (Boston: Leach, Shewell & Sanborn, 1890), pp. 1, 15, 196, 140.

10. Florence Converse, *The Story of Wellesley* (Boston: Little, Brown, 1919), p. 138; *On Journey*, pp. 96, 103, 201. In her early years at Wellesley her written works on English literature, besides those cited in this chapter, included *Prometheus Unbound: A Lyrical Drama by Percy Bysshe Shelley* (Boston: D. C. Heath, 1892); *Life of the Spirit in the Modern English Poets* (Boston: Houghton Mifflin, 1897); *Introduction to the Study of English Literature* (New York: Globe School Book Co., 1901); and numerous articles on Macaulay, Wordsworth, Tennyson, Browning, Arnold, and others.

11. Vida Scudder to Louise Manning Hodgkins, [1890], Wellesley Collection, Wellesley College, Wellesley, Mass.; *On Journey*, pp. 176, 178, 181.

12. *On Journey*, p. 128; Vida Scudder, *Social Ideals in English Letters*, new and enl. edition (Boston: Houghton Mifflin, 1923), pp. 1–3, 231, 275. First published in 1898.

13. *On Journey*, pp. 130–31, 127.

14. *Boston Common*, March 9, 1912, clipping in the Wellesley Collection.

15. Scudder to Ellen Pendleton, President of the Wellesley Board of Trustees, 15 March 1912, Wellesley Collection; Scudder to Walter Rauschenbusch, 9 October 1912, The Dores R. Sharpe Walter Rauschenbusch Collection, Baptist Historical Collection, Colgate-Rochester Divinity School, Rochester, N.Y. Scudder's account of the affair in *On Journey*, in which she makes a strong defense of her actions, is on pages 184–90.

16. Vida Scudder, "The College Settlements Movement," *Smith College Monthly* (May 1900): 447, and *On Journey*, pp. 137–40; *On Journey*, p. 111; "The Place of College Settlements," *Andover Review* 18 (October 1892): 347, 349–50; and "Democracy and Education," *Atlantic Monthly* 89 (June 1902): 822. See also Scudder's article, "A Glimpse into Life," *Wellesley Magazine* 1 (February 18, 1893): 221–32, in which she described the benefits of settlement living in Philadelphia on the college women. She was usually more interested in that side of settlement life rather than in the benefits extended to the neighborhood. In this sense she was a teacher more than a reformer.

17. "A Hidden Weakness in Our Democracy," *Atlantic Monthly* 89 (May 1902): 639, 642–44; "Democracy and Education," p. 817; "Democracy and Society," *Atlantic Monthly* 90 (September 1902): 348–51; and "Democracy and the Church," *Atlantic Monthly* 90 (October 1902): 524, 526–27.

18. *On Journey*, pp. 139–41.

19. Ibid., pp. 143–46, 256–66. See also Vida Scudder, "Work with Italians in Boston," *Survey* 22 (April 3, 1909): 47–51; and Davis, *Spearheads for Reform*, p. 41.

20. *On Journey*, pp. 155–56.

21. Ibid., pp. 178–79, 160.

22. Vida Scudder, *A Listener in Babel* (Boston: Houghton Mifflin, 1903), pp. 11, 44, 252, 267, 316, 320–21.

23. *On Journey*, pp. 140, 143–44.

24. "Christian Simplicity," *Publications of the Christian Social Union*, no. 52 (August 15, 1898), pp. 15–16; *Social Gospel* 2 (August 1899): 15; and *Social Gospel*, no. 24 (January 1900), p. 30.

25. *On Journey*, p. 160.

26. Scudder to Rauschenbusch, 21 September 1912, Rauschenbusch Collection; "Why Join the Party?" *Intercollegiate Socialist* 2 (October–November 1913): 6.

27. Vida Scudder, "The Social Conscience of the Future," *Hibbert Journal* 7 (January 1909): 314–15, 328; "The Social Conscience of the Future: The New Righteousness," *Hibbert Journal* 7 (April 1909): 594–95; and Scudder to Rauschenbusch, 21 September 1912, Rauschenbusch Collection.

28. "Socialism and Sacrifice," *Atlantic Monthly* 105 (June 1910): 836–38, 841, 843.

29. Ibid., pp. 838, 847–48.

30. *On Journey*, pp. 171–72.

31. Ibid., pp. 171–72.

32. Ibid., p. 282; "The Doubting Pacifist," *Yale Review* (1917), quoted in *On Journey*, p. 284; and "Some Signs of Hope," *Intercollegiate Socialist* 3 (April–May 1915): 7.

33. Vida Scudder, *The Church and the Hour* (New York: E. P. Dutton, 1917), pp. 1, 37, 129–30.

34. *On Journey*, pp. 287–92.

35. Ibid., pp. 304–5, 427; *Social Teachings of the Christian Year* (New York: E. P. Dutton, 1921), pp. 4–5; and "Varieties of Christian Experience," *Holy Cross Magazine* (January 1937): 18–19.

36. *On Journey*, p. 425; *Christianity and Property*, ed. Joseph Fletcher (Philadelphia: Westminster Press, 1947); and *My Quest for Reality* (Wellesley, Mass.: privately printed, 1952), pp. 94 and passim.

37. *On Journey*, pp. 155, 63–64.

38. Ibid., pp. 212–14, 220–23, 243.

39. Ibid., pp. 223–25, 65. In Aileen Kraditor's *Ideas of the Woman Suffrage Movement, 1890–1920* (Garden City, N.Y.: Anchor Books, 1971), pp. 50–55, this woman as municipal "housekeeper," as enunciated by Jane Addams, is analyzed as one of the expedient arguments for the suffrage.

40. *On Journey*, pp. 430–32.

41. *An Introduction to Ruskin*, p. 18; Jessie Bernard, *Academic Women* (University Park: Pennsylvania State University Press, 1964), pp. 24, 5; and *On Journey*, pp. 52–53.

42. *On Journey*, p. 117.

5. Walter Rauschenbusch & George Herron

*Walter Rauschenbusch, *For God and the People: Prayers of the Social Awakening* (Boston: Pilgrim Press, 1910), p. 107.

†George Herron, "A Psalm of Brotherhood," in "Psalms upon the Way," George Herron Collection, a collection of miscellanea, Hoover Library, Stanford University, Palo Alto, Calif.

1. Walter Rauschenbusch, in a discussion of monopolies at the Eighth Annual Session of the Baptist Congress for the Discussion of Current Questions, Toronto, 12 November 1889, in *Baptist Congress Proceedings* (New York: Baptist Congress Publ. Co., 1890), pp. 60–61; George Herron, *The Larger Christ* (New York: Fleming H. Revell, 1891), p. 22; and George Herron, *The New Redemption: A Call to the Church to Reconstruct Society according to the Gospel of Christ* (New York: Thomas Y. Crowell, 1893), p. 20.

2. Ray Stannard Baker, "The Spiritual Unrest: A Vision of the New Christianity," *American Magazine* 69 (December 1909): 178. This, and other observations of his trip, are also in *The Spiritual Unrest* (New York: Frederick A. Stokes, 1910).

3. The authorized, and highly eulogistic, biography of Rauschenbusch is by Dores R. Sharpe, *Walter Rauschenbusch* (New York: Macmillan, 1942). Sharpe was his student and confidential secretary for many years and was chosen by Rauschenbusch's widow and the Colgate-Rochester Divinity School to write the biography. In his preface Sharpe said that the book was "written out of a deep sense of duty" and was "an act of love" (p. viii). Still, there is no better source for the details of Rauschenbusch's life. A more scholarly treatment, emphasizing ideas, is Vernon P. Bodein, *The Social Gospel of Walter Rauschenbusch and Its Relation to Religious Education*, Yale Studies in Religious Education, vol. 16 (New Haven, Conn.: Yale University Press, 1944).

There is as yet no full-length biography of Herron. Two sources on his early years are Charles Beardsley, "Professor Herron," *Arena* 15 (April 1896): 784–96, and W. H. Dennison, "Prof. George D. Herron, D.D.: A Sketch of His Life and Character," *Social Gospel* 1 (July 1898): 14–20. Robert T. Handy's

Ph.D. dissertation, "George D. Herron and the Social Gospel in American Protestantism, 1890–1901" (University of Chicago, 1949), is best on Herron's years at Grinnell. Herron's relationship to American socialism is described in Quint, *Forging of American Socialism*, pp. 126–41. The years of his life during World War I are treated most thoroughly by Mitchell P. Briggs, *George D. Herron and the European Settlement*, Stanford University Publications in History, Economics, and Political Science, vol. 3, no. 2 (Stanford, Calif.: Stanford University Press, 1932). The best secondary source on them both is Hopkins, *Rise of the Social Gospel*, chapts. 11, 13.

4. Walter Rauschenbusch, *Christianity and the Social Crisis* (New York: Macmillan, 1907), pp. 316–17; "The Church and the Money Power," Eleventh Annual Session of the Baptist Congress, Augusta, Georgia, 5 December 1893, in *Baptist Congress Proceedings* (New York: Baptist Congress Publ. Co., 1894), p. 10; *Christianity and the Social Crisis*, p. 210; and Herron, "The Opportunity of the Church," *Arena* 15 (December 1895): 42, 45.

5. George Herron, *The Christian Society* (New York: Fleming H. Revell, 1894), p. 43; George Herron, *A Plea for the Gospel* (New York: Thomas Y. Crowell, 1892), p. 41; "The Message of Jesus to Men of Wealth," in *Christian Society*, p. 114; and *Larger Christ*, p. 32. Like Benjamin Flower, Herron wrote with such urgency that he often used italics. All emphases, therefore, are his.

6. Walter Rauschenbusch, *Christianizing the Social Order* (New York: Macmillan, 1912), pp. 156, 321–22, 125.

7. Rauschenbusch to Dr. L. C. Barnes, May 1918, quoted in the *Rochester Theological Seminary Bulletin: Rauschenbusch Number* (November 1918), p. 51.

8. Rauschenbusch, "Henry George," quoted in Bodein, *Social Gospel of Rauschenbusch*, p. 5, and in Sharpe, *Rauschenbusch*, p. 80; *Christianizing the Social Order*, p. 394; and *Rochester Theological Seminary Bulletin*, p. 52.

9. Baker, "The Spiritual Unrest," p. 179; *Christianity and the Social Crisis*, pp. 314–15; *Christianizing the Social Order*, pp. 292–93; and *Christianity and the Social Crisis*, pp. 74–82.

10. "Influence of Mazzini," *Colloquium* (November 1889): 28, quoted in Robert T. Handy, "The Influence of Mazzini on the American Social Gospel," *Journal of Religion* 29 (April 1949): 118.

11. Rauschenbusch to Ely, 19 March 1891, Richard T. Ely Papers, State Historical Society of Wisconsin, Madison.

12. *For the Right* 1 (November 1889), quoted in Bodein, *Social Gospel of Rauschenbusch*, p. 9.

13. From an address in 1913 to the Cleveland Young Men's Christian Association, quoted in Bodein, *Social Gospel of Rauschenbusch*, pp. 7–8, and Sharpe, *Rauschenbusch*, pp. 62–63.

14. Walter Rauschenbusch, "The Brotherhood of the Kingdom," *Brotherhood Leaflets*, no. 2 (1893), and "Minutes of the Brotherhood of the Kingdom," p. 4, a one-volume scrapbook of handwritten and published materials; both in the Baptist Historical Collection, Colgate-Rochester Divinity School, Rochester, N.Y.

15. Walter Rauschenbusch, "The Kingdom of God," *Brotherhood Leaflets*, no. 4 (1894), pp. 2, 4–5, 7–8, Baptist Historical Collection.

16. *Christianity and the Social Crisis*, pp. 59, 62, 65; *Christianizing the Social Order*, p. 66.

17. "Minutes of the Brotherhood of the Kingdom," pp. 39, 47, 52, 62,

Baptist Historical Collection; Mitchell Bronk, "An Adventure in the Kingdom of God," *Crozer Quarterly* (January 1937), pp. 23–24.

18. Rauschenbusch's speech topics included "The Ethics of Jesus" (1893), "The Kingdom and the Church" (1894), "Ideals of Social Reformers" (1895), "The Social Ideas of Paul" (1898), "The Program of Christianity: Social Transformation" (1900), "Socialism by Revolution or by Development" (1902), "The History of the Idea of the Kingdom of God" (1903), "The Kingdom Doctrine in Relation to Christian Life and Thought: Why Has Christianity Never Undertaken the Task of Social Reconstruction?" (1906), which became chapter 4 of *Christianity and the Social Crisis*, and "The Relation of the Brotherhood to Socialism" (1913). This list is derived from the "Minutes of the Brotherhood of the Kingdom" and from various "Reports of the Annual Conferences of the Brotherhood of the Kingdom," in the Baptist Historical Collection.

19. Bodein, *Social Gospel of Rauschenbusch*, p. 25; Rauschenbusch, "Ideals of Social Reformers," "Report of the Third Annual Conference of the Brotherhood of the Kingdom," Marlborough, New York, August 5–9, 1895, pp. 26–28, Baptist Historical Collection. This speech, in an expanded form, is in the *American Journal of Sociology* 2 (September 1896): 202–19.

20. Scudder to Rauschenbusch, 8 August 1912, The Dores R. Sharpe Walter Rauschenbusch Collection, Baptist Historical Collection; *Christianity and the Social Crisis*, pp. 408–9.

21. *Christianizing the Social Order*, pp. 396, 403–5.

22. Rauschenbusch, 20 July 1907, *Kingdom* 1 (September 1907); *Christianizing the Social Order*, p. 9; Bronk, "An Adventure in the Kingdom of God," p. 26; and Walter Rauschenbusch, *A Theology for the Social Gospel* (New York: Macmillan, 1922), p. 2. Originally published in 1917.

23. Quoted in John R. Aiken, "Walter Rauschenbusch and Education for Reform," *Church History* 36 (December 1967): 459–60.

24. Ibid., pp. 456–68. For an analysis of why his father's work for the American Home Missionary and Tract Societies in the 1850s was a means of social control of the lower classes by the elite, see Clifford S. Griffin, "Religious Benevolence as Social Control, 1815–1860," *Mississippi Valley Historical Review* 44 (December 1957): 423–44.

25. *Dare We Be Christians?* (Boston: Pilgrim Press, 1914); *The Social Principles of Jesus* (New York: Association Press, 1916).

26. *A Theology for the Social Gospel*, Foreword, and pp. 23–30, 199.

27. Ibid., pp. 52, 248–59, 99.

28. Ibid., pp. 224–25, 227, 238–39; *For God and the People*, p. 107.

29. Bronk, "An Adventure in the Kingdom of God," p. 25; Bliss, *Dawn* 6 (June 1894): 82–83; and Flower, "A Prophet's Cry to the Church," *Arena* 9 (April 1894): 700.

30. George Herron, "Confession of Faith," pp. 2–4, from the *Burlington* (Iowa) *Hawkeye*, 31 December 1891, in the Herron Collection, Grinnell College, Grinnell, Iowa; Herron to Commendatore Orsini, 12 June 1920, Vol. 6, Doc. 34, p. 2, Herron Papers, "Verbatim copies of original documents" used in conjunction with Mitchell Briggs's *George D. Herron and the European Settlement*, in the Hoover Library, Stanford University, Palo Alto, Calif.

31. Herron, "The Thorn in the Flesh," 5 October 1890, in the George Herron Collection, a collection of miscellanea, Hoover Library, Stanford University. At this point in his career, a Herron scholar has suggested, Herron "was certain

that he had been chosen of God for a spiritual task of great import"; Robert T. Handy, "Herron and the Social Gospel," p. 17.

32. Herron, "Confession of Faith," pp. 12–14, Herron Collection, Grinnell; Herron to Ely, 6 July 1891, Ely Papers. Herron enclosed in his letter a copy of his "Message of Jesus to Men of Wealth" and indicated that he had asked his publisher to send Ely one of his books. He was not above using his contacts to serve his ambitions. When he heard that Mrs. Rand had endowed a chair of Applied Christianity at Iowa College, he wrote Ely to ask him to send a letter and documents to Mrs. Rand on his behalf (2 February 1892, Ely Papers).

33. Herron, "At the Shrine of Mazzini," *Kingdom* 10 (February 24, 1898): 379. This is a different *Kingdom* from that published by the Brotherhood of the Kingdom, although the aims of both were much the same.

34. Herron, private letter to Gaetano Salvemini, quoted in Salvemini's *Mazzini*, trans. I. M. Rawson (New York: Crowell-Collier, 1962), p. 95; Herron *Christian Society*, p. 113; and George Herron, *The Call of the Cross* (New York: Fleming H. Revell, 1892), p. 34.

35. Herron, *New Redemption*, p. 43; George Herron, *The Christian State: A Political Vision of Christ* (New York: Thomas Y. Crowell, 1895), p. 74; and Herron, "Jesus and the Existing Order," an address at Cooper Union, New York, 6 March 1896, in the Henry Demarest Lloyd Papers, State Historical Society of Wisconsin, Madison. These ideas were developed further in Herron's *Between Caesar and Jesus* (New York: Thomas Y. Crowell, 1899).

36. George Herron, *Social Meanings of Religious Experience* (New York: Thomas Y. Crowell, 1896), p. 23; *Christian State*, pp. 48–49, 57; and *Christian Society*, p. 90.

37. *Christian State*, p. 174.

38. J. Stitt Wilson, *Social Crusader* 3 (January 1901): 6; Herron, "Personal Florentine Fragments," *Kingdom* 10 (November 11, 1897): 96.

39. Herron, "At the Shrine of Mazzini," *Kingdom* 10 (February 24, 1898): 379–80.

40. *Christian Society*, pp. 51, 35–40.

41. "List of Books for Reading in Connection with Prof. George D. Herron's Lectures on Christian Sociology," 1893–1894, and brochure distributed by the "Department of Applied Christianity," 1894–1895, Iowa College, Herron Collection, Grinnell; Herron, *A Plea for the Gospel*, p. 82.

42. John S. Nollen, *Grinnell College* (Iowa City: State Historical Society of Iowa, 1953), p. 100. Herron's impact on Grinnell is thoroughly described in Handy, "Herron and the Social Gospel," pp. 57–64.

43. See Handy, "Herron and the Social Gospel," pp. 68–73, for an account of his lecture tour controversies, and the *Kingdom* 8 (June 7, 1895), for a special issue of 20,000 copies devoted specifically to defending Herron's side of the California dispute; *New Redemption*, p. 141.

44. Herron to Ely, 17 February 1892, Ely Papers; "A School for the Kingdom" (brochure), June–July 1894, Herron Collection, Grinnell; and Lloyd to William Salter, 14 July 1895, Lloyd Papers. See also Robert T. Handy, "George D. Herron and the Kingdom Movement," *Church History* 19 (June 1950): 97–115.

45. Destler, *Lloyd*, pp. 376–77.

46. George Gates, "The Movement for the Kingdom," and Herron to William Stiles, 26 March 1894, *Kingdom* 7 (April 20, 1894): 4–5.

47. Herron to Lloyd, 13 January 1896, Lloyd Papers; *Social Gospel* 1 (February 1898): 3, 8; and "The Quality of Revolution," *Social Gospel* 1 (June 1898): 8.

48. *Kingdom* 10 (February 17, 1898): 368; "A Confession of Social Faith," p. 3, an address before the Chicago Single Tax Club, 17 March 1899, Herron Collection, Stanford; "The Socialist Disclosures of Spiritual Sources," pp. 8–9, from the "Cooper Union Lectures," fall of 1900, Herron Collection, Stanford; "The Economic Goal," pp. 14–15, a lecture at Grinnell on 27 December [1897], Herron Collection, Stanford; and Herron to Markham, 24 September 1899, reported in the *National Single Taxer* 8 (December 1899): 11.

49. Handy, "Herron and the Social Gospel," pp. 102, 92–98; "American Imperialism," an address to the National Christian Citizenship League, Chicago, 12 April 1899, *Social Forum* 1 (June 1, 1899): 5; "An Address to the American People," 3 July 1899, Herron Collection, Stanford; and *Between Caesar and Jesus*, p. 24.

50. R. M. Haines to Herron, 23 February 1897, and Herron to Haines and J. M. Chamberlain, President, Board of Trustees, 25 May 1897, Herron Collection, Grinnell.

51. Nollen, *Grinnell College*, p. 101; Handy, "Herron and the Social Gospel," pp. 133–43. Handy treats the entire controversy over Herron's resignation and troubled domestic life, citing several accounts by contemporaries, all of whom agreed that Herron's home life was unhappy, that he was often at the home of the Rands, and that he needed "feminine admiration and adulation to an unusual degree" (p. 141). See particularly Fanny Phelps Johnson, "Some Remarks on Caroline Rand," Herron Collection, Grinnell.

52. Lloyd's letter, as well as the entire Iowa College controversy, was reported in the *Social Gospel* 2 (December 1899): 20; Herron to Lloyd, 15 November 1899, Lloyd Papers.

53. Herron to Lloyd, 9 December 1900, Lloyd Papers; "A Plea for the Unity of American Socialists," *International Socialist Review* 1 (December 1900): 326; and Herron to Bliss, 27 December 1900, *Social Unity* 1 (January 1, 1901): 10.

54. "The New Religious Movement," *Kingdom* 11 (April 20, 1899): 485; *Social Forum* 2 (February 1900): 4; *Social Crusader* 3 (February 1901): 2; and "The New Social Apostolate," a conversation between Herron and C. B. Patterson, *Arena* 25 (May 1901): 490–91. See also Herron's *Why I Am a Socialist*, an address at a mass meeting of the Social Democratic party in Chicago, 29 September 1900, Pocket Library of Socialism, no. 20 (Chicago: Charles H. Kerr, 1900).

55. *A Socialist Wedding—Being the Account of the Marriage of George D. Herron and Carrie Rand* (New York: Knickerbocker Press, n.d.); "The Case of Dr. Herron," *Outlook* 68 (June 15, 1901): 379.

56. Herron, "Letter to Grinnell Church Committee," *International Socialist Review* 2 (1901–1902): 21–23; and *Social Crusader* 3 (June 1901): 18–24; Handy, "Herron and the Social Gospel," pp. 156–57; and "The Case of Dr. Herron," p. 380.

57. Herron, "A Menacing Friendship," *Wilshire's Monthly Magazine* (November 1901), p. 30.

58. "At the Shrine of Mazzini," p. 381; Quint, *Forging of American Socialism*, p. 383; and *Social Crusader* 3 (August 1901): 2.

59. Hillquit, quoted in Handy, "Herron and the Social Gospel," p. 170; Herron to Labadie, quoted in Quint, *Forging of American Socialism*, pp. 140–41. In the *Autobiography of William Allen White* (New York: Macmillan, 1946), White wrote that "wherever Herron and the girl and the mother went, the spotlight played upon them," and there were even "demonstrations in the street," which made Herron "miserable" (p. 561).

60. Rauschenbusch, quoted in Sharpe, *Rauschenbusch*, p. 356; Rauschenbusch to Doctor Woelfkin, quoted in Sharpe, *Rauschenbusch*, pp. 385–86.

61. George D. Herron, *The Menace of Peace* (London: George Allen & Unwin, 1917), pp. 16, 36–37; George D. Herron, *Woodrow Wilson and the World's Peace* (New York: Mitchell Kennerly, 1917), pp. 159, 150; and Herron to President Wilson, 31 May 1918, Vol. 12, Doc. 3, p. 14, and White to Mitchell Briggs, based on an article in White's *Emporia Gazette*, 15 August 1929, in the Herron Papers, Stanford. White, who with Herron was appointed by Wilson to the Prinkipo Conference on Russian settlements in 1919, reported that Herron was "a sort of superspy" with unquestionably talented "diplomatic ability" and an "overwhelming belief in himself" (*Autobiography of William Allen White*, p. 561).

62. George D. Herron, *The Defeat in Victory* (Boston: Christopher Publishing House, 1924), pp. 6, 36; Herron to Hillquit, 11 November 1924, Herron Collection, Stanford.

63. Herron to Joseph Allen, 15 April 1925, Herron Collection, Stanford; Herron to His Majesty Victor Emmanuel III, 20 June 1920, Vol. 6, Doc. 38, pp. 2–6, Herron Papers, Stanford; and Herron to Scudder, 5 March 1923, Herron Collection, Stanford. See also Herron's *Revival of Italy* (London: Geoge Allen & Unwin, 1922).

64. White to Briggs, from *Emporia Gazette*; and Charles Crane to Herron, 18 September 1920, Vol. 12, Doc. 28, Herron Papers, Stanford.

6. Edwin Markham & Ernest Crosby

*Edwin Markham, "The Church of Rebels," June 1929, in a small miscellaneous collection of Markham Papers in the University of Southern California Library, Los Angeles, Calif.

†Ernest H. Crosby, "Happy the Land that Knoweth Its Prophets before They Die," *Plain Talk in Psalm and Parable* (Boston: Small, Maynard, 1899), p. 63.

1. Markham, "Walter Rauschenbusch," unpublished poem in the Edwin Markham Papers, MSS, and Private Book Collection, Markham Memorial Library, Wagner College, Staten Island, N.Y.

2. *Social Unity* 1 (January 1901): 13–14, and 1 (February 1901): 18–26; Crosby and Markham, quoted in the *Dubuque Times* (April 1901), clipping in the Herron Collection, Grinnell College, Grinnell, Iowa; and *Social Crusader* 3 (May 1901): 3–6.

3. Markham to the editor of the *Saturday Press*, 1 May 1894, Markham Papers, 1: 65. The volume numbers refer to three bound volumes of collected letters (1), articles (2), and speeches (3) in the Markham Papers.

4. Mitchell Bronk, "An Adventure in the Kingdom of God," p. 25; Michael Monahan, *Papyrus* 1 (July 1903): 28, and Joseph Dana Miller, *Single Tax Review* 1 (April 15, 1902): 47; and Eltweed Pomeroy, from his diary, 25 June 1897, quoted in Lloyd, *Lloyd*, 2:49.

5. Benjamin O. Flower, *Progressive Men, Women, and Movements of the Past Twenty-five Years* (Boston: New Arena, 1914), p. 225. Unless otherwise indicated, all biographical material on Markham is from Louis Filler, *The Unknown Edwin Markham: His Mystery and Its Significance* (Yellow Springs, Ohio: Antioch Press, 1966); Sophie Shields, *A Short History of Edwin Markham* (Staten Island, N.Y., 1953), printed by Wagner College for the Edwin Markham Memorial Library, of which Shields is curator; and William Stidger, *Edwin Markham* (New York: Abingdon Press, 1933). Stidger's biography was largely dictated by Markham himself and consists of so much quotation that it is essentially an autobiography, spiced by Stidger's laudatory comments. According to Filler, Markham so often falsified and misrepresented his past that the Stidger book is "totally insubstantial." In his own book on Markham, however, Filler grinds axes against the literary establishment in America and what it does to the reputation of writers, against his students and contemporary radicals, and against other professors of American culture. His many asides make good reading in themselves, but the book is marred by the omission of an index, bibliography, the dating and location of manuscripts cited in the narrative, and adequate footnote citation. With all these limitations, however, Filler's is still the best study of Markham. My own analysis more often takes Markham at his word, yet within the cautionary framework Filler suggests. It does not matter to me whether or not Markham lied about his mother's role in his life, or about his early experiences with highwaymen and blacksmiths; it does matter, however, how credible he was when indicating ideological influences and other sources of his commitment to reform, such as it was. Even his misrepresentations are important, for how he wished to appear to others (and to himself) is as much a part of the man as the illusory "real" story.

6. Markham to Ruth Le Prade, 18 April 1936, University of Southern California Library, and Flower, *Progressive Men*, pp. 225–30; Filler, *Unknown Edwin Markham*, p. 12. Filler's analysis of Elizabeth Winchell Markham, her divorce, and her relationship to the young Markham is on pages 4–19. The influence of Elizabeth on Edwin's other relationships with women—and the relationships themselves, of which there were many—can be found on pages 32–37, 46–59, 74–76, and 91–96.

7. Flower, *Progressive Men*, p. 230.

8. Filler, *Unknown Edwin Markham*, pp. 39–43. I am indebted to Filler for the following analysis as well.

9. "Edwin Markham Talks of His Art," an interview in 1899 with the *Tribune* (probably the *Oakland Tribune*), Markham Papers, 2: 109; "Poetry and Social Progress," pp. 6–7, typed essay in the Edwin Markham Collection of Florence Hamilton, Library of Congress, Washington, D.C. Hamilton was a poet and disciple of Markham and was his personal secretary and manuscript organizer in the 1920s and 1930s. See also Markham's "Books and the Light They Have Given Me," *New York Times*, 1 March 1900, Markham Papers, 2: 43, and "What and Why and When to Read," Markham Collection of Hamilton.

10. "The Book That Has Most Influenced Me," from the *Delineator* (n.d.), Markham Papers, 2: 39; "The Dignity of Labor," an interview for the *Oakland Tribune*, 12 April 1899, Markham Papers, 2: 94; Markham interview for the *Philadelphia Record*, 24 September 1899, Markham Papers, 3: 115; and Markham to Albert Bender, 21 December 1923, in a small Markham collection at Mills College, Oakland, Calif.

11. Markham to Vachel Davis, 12 June 1928, Markham Papers, 1: 51; Stidger, *Markham*, p. 130; and Markham, letter to Elizabeth Senter, written in 1884, and quoted in the *Staten Island Advance*, 27 April 1947, Markham Papers, 3: 142.

12. Markham, quoted in Stidger, *Markham*, p. 131; handwritten inscription, dated September 1916, in an 1869 edition of *The Man Who Laughs*, Markham Memorial Library; "The Book That Has Most Influenced Me," Markham Papers, 2: 39; and Markham, quoted in Stidger, *Markham*, p. 132.

13. Virgil Markham, interview at Wagner College, Staten Island, N.Y., 23 March 1964; Markham to Clement Wood, 16 June 1918, Markham Papers; and "Mazzini," Container 3, Markham Collection of Hamilton. In the same collection see also "Lamennais: An Apostle of the People, a Martyr of Social Democracy."

14. Markham to Senter, 1 January 1884, quoted in Jesse Goldstein, "The Life of Edwin Markham" (Ph.D. diss., New York University, 1945), p. 202; "Carlyle," Markham Collection of Hamilton.

15. Howells to Markham, 28 April 1899, Markham Papers, and "Comments on 'The Man with the Hoe,' " Markham Collection of Hamilton; Edwin Markham, *Gates of Paradise and Other Poems* (Garden City, N.Y.: Doubleday, Doran, 1928), originally published in 1920, William Dean Howells Collection, Houghton Library, Harvard University, Cambridge, Mass.

16. Tolstoy to Markham, 5 February 1900, and Markham to Tolstoy, 1 September 1907, in Markham Papers; "Nietzsche," Markham Collection of Hamilton; and "Tolstoy," Container 4, Markham Collection of Hamilton.

17. Edwin Markham, "The Man with the Hoe," *The Man with the Hoe and Other Poems* (Garden City, N.Y.: Doubleday, Doran, 1932), p. 15. Originally published in the *San Francisco Examiner*, 15 January 1899, and by Doubleday in 1899; "How I Wrote 'The Man with the Hoe,' " *Dearborn Independent*, 21 November 1925, Markham Collection of Hamilton; and "The Dignity of Labor," Markham Papers, 2: 91–94.

18. Markham, "What Will the Century Do for Labor?" *Christian Herald*, 31 December 1900, Markham Papers, 2: 35–37.

19. Rauschenbusch notes for a speech in Rochester, 14 February 1901, Dores R. Sharpe Walter Rauschenbusch Collection.

20. Markham to "my dear John," probably an older brother, 14 October 1877, Markham Papers; Notebook 2 (1883), Markham Collection of Hamilton; Markham to "Comrade," 4 September 1886, Markham Papers; and "Why Bryan Will Win," an interview for the *New York World*, January 1900, Markham Papers, 3: 248.

21. Markham, in an interview with Leonard Abbott, "Edwin Markham: Laureate of Labor," *Comrade* 1 (January 1902): 75; Markham to Samuel Batten, 24 April 1897, Markham Papers; and "Christ and the Social State—A Conversation with Edwin Markham," *Twentieth Century Magazine* 1 (January 1910): 345.

22. Markham, "What Would Jesus Be Doing if He Were Here?" *Christian Socialist* 4 (December 15, 1907): 1–2, Container 19, Markham Collection of Hamilton; "If He Should Come," *New Poems: Eighty Songs at Eighty* (Garden City, N.Y.: Doubleday, Doran, 1932), pp. 93–94; and "The Hero of the Cross," *The Shoes of Happiness and Other Poems* (Garden City, N.Y.: Doubleday, Doran, 1915), pp. 175–89.

23. "Edwin Markham's Comment on the Sermon," Container 10, Markham Collection of Hamilton; "The Golden Rule—A Practical Suggestion for a Revo-

lution in the World's Affairs," *New York Journal*, 20 August 1899, Markham Papers, 2: 141–42. See also Markham's "What Life Means to Me," *Cosmopolitan* 41 (June 1906): 186.

24. "Brotherhood," *Man with the Hoe*, p. 21; Markham to Joseph Newton, 4 January 1920, Markham Papers, 1: 263; and Edwin Markham, Benjamin Lindsay, and George Creel, *Children of Bondage* (New York: Hearst's International Library Co., 1914).

25. Joseph Dana Miller, *Single Tax Review* 1 (April 15, 1902): 48; "The Issue: Man or Mammon," *Twentieth Century Magazine* 3 (October 1910): 4; "The Poet," *Man with the Hoe*, p. 30; and "How I Wrote 'The Man with the Hoe,' " Markham Collection of Hamilton.

26. Filler, *Unknown Edwin Markham*, p. 96; "Brotherhood" and "Fay Song," *Man with the Hoe*, pp. 21, 105; and "Conscripts of the Dream," "The Right to Labor in Joy," "Love's Hero-World," and "At Friends with Life," *Shoes of Happiness*, pp. 116–17, 126–27, 138–39, 85–86.

27. Quoted in Filler, *Unknown Edwin Markham*, p. 99.

28. "Virgilia," *Shoes of Happiness*, p. 73. Originally published in 1905 in the *Cosmopolitan*.

29. Markham, "Follow Me," *Man with the Hoe*, p. 88; "How I Think of a Spiritual World," in the Markham Collection at Mills College, Oakland, Calif.; "Ballad of the Gallows-Bird," quoted in Filler, *Unknown Edwin Markham*, pp. 179–83. Filler provides verses not included in the original version published in the *American Mercury* 8 (August 1926): 398–407. The poem, Filler said, was "Markham's masterpiece, and he knew it" (p. 183).

30. "Mazzini," Markham Collection of Hamilton.

31. Markham to Barbara Young, April 1932, University of Southern California Library, Los Angeles; "At Eighty Years," Container 3, Markham Collection of Hamilton; and "The Escape," *New Poems*, p. 99.

32. "My Life," 16 September 1932, Container 3, Markham Collection of Hamilton.

33. Ernest H. Crosby, "Was Jesus a Farmer?" *Papyrus* 5 (December 1905): 20–22.

34. Leonard D. Abbott, "Some Reminiscences of Ernest Crosby," *Mother Earth* 1 (February 1907): 22. Unless otherwise indicated, all biographical material on Crosby is from Abbott's article in *Mother Earth* and his little book containing essentially the same material, *Ernest Howard Crosby: A Valuation and a Tribute* (Westwood, Mass.: Ariel Press, 1907); Louis Filler, *Crusaders for American Liberalism* (New York: Harcourt, Brace, 1939), pp. 62–66; *Social Gospel*, no. 21 (October 1899), pp. 29–30; and the *New Encyclopedia of Social Reform*, ed. W. D. P. Bliss (New York: Funk & Wagnalls, 1908), pp. 342–43. Other than Filler's brief treatment, the first serious recognition of Crosby's significance in the literature on progressive reformers is Peter J. Frederick, "A Life of Principle: Ernest Howard Crosby and the Frustrations of the Intellectual as Reformer," *New York History* 54 (October 1973): 396–423.

35. Ernest Crosby, "The Crosby Family of New York," reprinted from the *New York Genealogical and Biographical Record* (October 1898, January, April, and July 1899), New York State Education Library, Albany; Howard Crosby, "The Forgotten Cause of Poverty," *Forum* 3 (August 1887): 568–77.

36. Ernest H. Crosby, "The Legal Profession and American Progress," New York, 7 June 1888, pp. 12–15 (pamphlet).

37. Crosby, "Count Tolstoi at Seventy," *Coming Age* 1 (February 1899):

172; Ernest Howard Crosby, *Tolstoy and His Message*, p. 44; and Erik Erikson, *Young Man Luther*, pp. 22, 243.

38. Crosby, "Not I," *Social Gospel*, no. 31 (September 1900), pp. 106–7; Crosby, "The Experiment," *Plain Talk in Psalm and Parable*, pp. 134–35; and *Tolstoy and His Message*, p. 44.

39. "Count Tolstoi at Seventy," pp. 174–77; see also a similar account of the visit, "Seventieth Birthday of the Grand Old Man of Russia," *Social Gospel* 1 (September 1898): 14–18.

40. See Ernest Crosby's "Tolstoy and Henry George," *Single Tax Review* 5 (October 15, 1905): 1–5; *Garrison the Non-Resistant* (Chicago: Public Publ. Co., 1905), p. 94; and *Edward Carpenter: Poet and Prophet* (Philadelphia: Conservator, 1901).

41. Mitchell Bronk, "An Adventure in the Kingdom of God," p. 25; Williams, in *Addresses in Memory of Ernest Howard Crosby, 1856–1907*, Cooper Union, New York, 7 March 1907, published by the Ernest Howard Crosby Memorial Committee, p. 2; "Now I Understand," *Plain Talk in Psalm and Parable*, p. 38; "Farm Pictures," *Swords and Plowshares* (New York: Funk & Wagnalls, 1902), p. 108; and *Edward Carpenter*, pp. 45–46.

42. Crosby, "Nature and Reformers," *Social Gospel* 2 (April 1899): 9; "Love the Oppressors," *Swords and Plowshares*, p. 97; and "Love Comes," *Swords and Plowshares*, p. 91.

43. The germs of this book are in two articles by Crosby published in 1896: "Count Tolstoy's Philosophy of Life," *Arena* 15 (January 1896): 277–85; and "Count Tolstoi and Non-Resistance," *Outlook* 54 (July 11, 1896): 52–53. Crosby wrote the article on Tolstoy for W. D. P. Bliss's *Encyclopedia of Social Reform* (New York: Funk & Wagnalls, 1897), pp. 1330–31. On the occasion of Tolstoy's seventieth birthday in 1898, Crosby wrote at least two articles, "Seventieth Birthday of the Grand Old Man of Russia" and "Count Tolstoi at Seventy," and delivered innumerable speeches. See, for example, "In Honor of Tolstoy," *Critic* 33 (October 1898): 282–84. For Crosby's evaluation of Tolstoy's fiction, see "Tolstoy, Novelist and Radical," *Comrade* 3 (October 1903): 7–8; and for his great respect for the Russian's innovative educational theories, see *Tolstoy as a Schoolmaster* (Chicago: Hammersmark Publ. Co., 1903). See also B. O. Flower, "A Conversation with Ernest H. Crosby Embodying Personal Impressions of Count Tolstoy as Philosopher, Prophet, and Man," *Arena* 25 (April 1901): 429–39. From February 1901 to January 1905, Crosby edited a little journal entitled the *Whim*, which advertised itself as "a periodical without a tendency." Nonetheless, it had one tendency, namely, Crosby's (and Tolstoy's) ideas of nonresistance and Christian anarchism.

44. Horace Traubel, *The Conservator* (October 1903): 124; *Tolstoy and His Message*, p. 54; "War and Hell," *Swords and Plowshares*, p. 21; Crosby, 24 December 1897, in a letter to the editors of the *American Fabian* 4 (January 1898): 9; and *Tolstoy and His Message*, pp. 63–65.

45. Crosby, "Love and Labor," *Swords and Plowshares*, pp. 86–87; "Love and Labor," *Comrade* 2 (July 1903): 218–19.

46. See Howard Morse, *Historic Old Rhinebeck* (Published by the Author, 1908), p. 396, and a W. P. A. Federal Writer's Project guidebook, *Dutchess County* (Philadelphia: William Penn Assn., 1937); "Farm Pictures," *Swords and Plowshares*, pp. 115, 120–21.

47. Crosby to Lloyd, 30 September 1898, Henry Demarest Lloyd Papers, State Historical Society of Wisconsin, Madison.

48. Crosby's relationship with anarchists is discussed in Abbott, "Reminiscences of Crosby," pp. 22–23. See also Emma Goldman, *Living My Life*, 2 vols. (New York: Alfred A. Knopf, 1931), 1:233. In another incident, Goldman appeared at a meeting of the Manhattan Liberal Club in the midst of the national panic over anarchism after the assassination of President McKinley. She was recognized and condemned by the audience, one man calling her a "murderess." Goldman recalled that "my old friend, Ernest Crosby," who was speaking to the club at the time, defended her presence and helped to restore order (1:320).

49. Crosby, "The Immigration Bugbear," *Arena* 32 (December 1904): 602; Lillian D. Wald, *The House on Henry Street* (New York: Henry Holt, 1915), pp. 234–35.

50. *National Single Taxer* 7 (April 27, 1898): 6; Crosby, "War and Christianity," *Social Gospel* 1 (July 1898): 5–6; and *War from the Christian Point of View* (Boston: American Peace Society, 1901), p. 11.

51. Crosby, *The Absurdities of Militarism*, an address at Tremont Temple, Boston, 16 January 1901, at a meeting to commemorate the progress of peace in the nineteenth century (Boston: American Peace Society, 1901), pp. 7–11.

52. Ernest H. Crosby, *Captain Jinks, Hero* (New York: Funk & Wagnalls, 1902), pp. 12, 227, 323.

53. Jones to Crosby, 11 November 1898, Samuel Jones Papers, in possession of Professor James H. Rodabaugh, Department of History, Miami University, Oxford, Ohio; "War and Hell," *Swords and Plowshares*, pp. 13–14; and "The Anglo-American Alliance," *Swords and Plowshares*, p. 54.

54. "The Real 'White Man's Burden,'" *Swords and Plowshares*, pp. 33–34; "The Blessings of Civilization," *Social Gospel*, no. 20 (September 1899), p. 5.

55. Ernest Crosby, *Labor and Neighbor* (Chicago: Louis F. Post, 1908), pp. 24–38. This volume, published posthumously, is a collection of published and unpublished articles by Crosby, arranged by Louis Post, a single-taxer, and published originally in the *Public* in the spring of 1908.

56. Crosby, "The Land of the Noonday Night," "The Stoker," and "The Cotton Mill," *Broad-Cast* (New York: Funk & Wagnalls, 1905), pp. 29–35.

57. Crosby, "The Man with the Hose," *Cosmopolitan* 41 (August 1906): 341; *Labor and Neighbor*, p. 65, and "Our Senatorial Grand Dukes," *Cosmopolitan* 41 (June 1906): 121; *Labor and Neighbor*, pp. 126–29; and "Socialism a Reversion," *Single Tax Review* 6 (October 15, 1906): 27.

58. "Tolstoy and Henry George," *Single Tax Review* 5 (October 15, 1905): 5; *The Earth-for-All* (New York: Geo. P. Hampton, 1901); and "The Short-Cut of the Single Tax," *Single Tax Review* 5 (January 15, 1906): 38–39. See also Crosby's "Russia's Great Single-Taxer," *National Single Taxer* 8 (July 1899): 3.

59. Crosby to the editor of the *New York Herald*, 11 December 1894, quoted in Herron, *Christian State*, pp. 155–56; "The Ball-Match," *Plain Talk in Psalm and Parable*, p. 92; and "The Kingdom of God," *Plain Talk in Psalm and Parable*, p. 168.

60. Crosby, "Christ's Teaching on Social Problems," *Kingdom* 8 (July 19, 1895): 213–14.

61. Abbott, "Reminiscences of Crosby," pp. 24–25.

62. Ralph Waldo Emerson, "Lecture on the Times," *The Complete Works of*

Ralph Waldo Emerson, vol. 1: *Nature Addresses and Lectures* (Boston: Houghton Mifflin, 1903), p. 283.

63. "Hypocrites and Hypocrites," *Plain Talk in Psalm and Parable*, p. 43; Abbott, "Reminiscences of Crosby," pp. 26–27.

64. "Moods," *Broad-Cast*, pp. 66, 62–63.

65. "The Living Answer," *Plain Talk in Psalm and Parable*, pp. 162–63; Abbott, "Reminiscences of Crosby," p. 26.

66. Crosby to Jones, 4 March 1902, Toledo Public Library, Toledo, Ohio; "Judge Not," *Broad-Cast*, pp. 78–79; "Love," *Broad-Cast*, pp. 105–6; Crosby to Jones, 14 November 1898, Jones Papers; and "Godward," *Swords and Plowshares*, p. 71.

67. "Homesick," *International Socialist Review* 2 (July 1901): 35; "Afterthought," *Broad-Cast*, p. 126; Tolstoy to Bernard Prieth, quoted in the *Single Tax Review* 6 (April 15, 1907): 10; and Tolstoy letter read at the memorial meeting to Crosby, 7 March 1907, in *Addresses in Memory*, pp. 25–26.

68. *Cosmopolitan* 42 (March 1907): 549; "The Late Ernest Crosby," *Single Tax Review* 6 (April 15, 1907): 10.

69. Bryan, *Addresses in Memory*, p. 26; Flower, "Ernest Howard Crosby: Prophet of Peace and Apostle of Social Righteousness," *Arena* 37 (March 1907): 259; and Garland, *Addresses in Memory*, p. 5; see also Garland, "Ernest Howard Crosby and His Message," *Twentieth Century Magazine* 1 (October 1909): 27–28.

70. W. L. Garrison, "His Hospitality of Mind and His Gifts of the Spirit," *Single Tax Review* 6 (April 15, 1907): 12.

71. James K. Paulding, *Addresses in Memory*, p. 1; Abbott, *Crosby: A Valuation*, p. 40.

72. Markham, "A Comrade Called Back," *Shoes of Happiness*, pp. 129–31; in slightly different form in *Addresses in Memory*, pp. 24–25.

7. Samuel M. Jones

*Samuel M. Jones, quoted in Ernest Crosby, *Golden Rule Jones* (Chicago: Public Publ. Co., 1906), p. 53.

1. James H. Rodabaugh, "Samuel M. Jones—Evangel of Equality," *Historical Society of Northwestern Ohio Quarterly Bulletin* 15 (January 1943): 40–41.

2. Brand Whitlock, *Forty Years of It* (New York: D. Appleton, 1925), p. 139; Whitlock, "Funeral Oration for Sam Jones," 15 July 1904, Brand Whitlock Papers, Box 64, Library of Congress, Washington, D.C. For Jones's funeral see also Rodabaugh, "Jones—Evangel of Equality," p. 42, and Crosby, *Golden Rule Jones*, p. 58.

3. "A Christmas Message from Samuel M. Jones to the Working-Men of the Acme Sucker Rod Co.," Toledo, Ohio, 1902, p. 2 (pamphlet); Samuel M. Jones, *The New Right: A Plea for Fair Play through a More Just Social Order* (New York: Eastern Book Concern, 1899), p. 401; and from an interview in the *Chicago Tribune*, quoted in Eltweed Pomeroy, "Samuel M. Jones—An Appreciation," *American Fabian* 4 (July 1898): 2.

4. Jones, *New Right*, pp. 277–78; Jones, quoted in Frederic C. Howe, *The Confessions of a Reformer* (New York: Charles Scribner's Sons, 1925), p. 187; Mayor Samuel M. Jones, "Fifth Annual Message," for the Year 1901, Toledo, 24 February 1902, pp. 2–4 (pamphlet); and Samuel M. Jones, *Letters of Labor and Love* (Indianapolis: Bobbs-Merrill, 1905), p. 119.

5. Jones, in a conversation with Benjamin Flower, "The Rights and Obligations of the Municipality," *Coming Age* 1 (April 1899): 371; Jones, quoted in Howe, *Confessions of a Reformer*, pp. 186–87; Whitlock, *Forty Years of It*, p. 119; and Jones, *New Right*, p. 451.

6. Jones, *New Right*, p. 58; Brand Whitlock, introduction to Jones's *Letters of Labor and Love*, p. 16. The biographical material on Jones is mostly from his autobiography, written in 1899, included as chapter 2 in *The New Right*, pp. 39–112.

7. Jones, quoted in a campaign advertisement, "Who Is Jones?" written for his gubernatorial campaign in 1899, p. 2 (pamphlet), also in *The New Right*, pp. 61–62; *New Right*, pp. 400–401; Jones to Stead, 11 May 1897, Samuel Jones Papers, in possession of Professor James H. Rodabaugh, Department of History, Miami University, Oxford, Ohio; and Jones, *Conservator* (December 1903), p. 152; an expanded version of his address printed in *In Memoriam: Henry Demarest Lloyd*, Chicago, 29 November 1903, pp. 5–9 (pamphlet).

8. Jones to the Reverend Marion Hyde of Toledo, 7 November 1901, Jones Papers. See also lists of authors in letters from Jones to Dr. Tobey, 27 January 1900, the Reverend D. M. Fisk, 18 July 1900, W. J. Ghent, 11 September 1901, and N. O. Nelson, 15 August 1902, all in Jones Papers.

9. Jones to Carpenter, 15 May 1900, and to Debs, 29 November 1899, in Jones Papers.

10. Whitlock, *Forty Years of It*, pp. 118–19; Jones to the Reverend D. M. Fisk, 18 July 1900, N. O. Nelson, 10 November 1898, and Horace Traubel, 26 May 1899, in Jones Papers. Jones's Bible and many other books from his personal library are in the possession of James H. Rodabaugh, who graciously let me study them when I visited his home in Kent, Ohio, in March 1964. Unless otherwise indicated, references to Jones's books and marginalia are to those held by Rodabaugh.

11. Jones, from the *Toledo Commercial*, 5 February 1900, clipping in a scrapbook in Jones Papers; *New Right*, p. 64.

12. Jones, *New Right*, p. 474; Jones to C. B. Newcomb, 20 July 1900, and to D. M. Fisk, 18 July 1900, Jones Papers. The Mazzini volumes are in the Samuel M. Jones Collection, Toledo Public Library, Toledo, Ohio.

13. Whitlock, *Forty Years of It*, p. 117; Jones to Tolstoy, 8 September 1898, Jones Papers, and *New Right*, pp. 84–85.

14. Jones to Gladden, 5 April 1900, Jones Papers; description of Jones's office in a Toledo newspaper shortly after his death, in a scrapbook in Jones Papers.

15. Jones, "To the Workers of the Acme Oil Co.," Toledo, Christmas 1897 (pamphlet); see also his little seven-page booklet, "The Eight-Hour Day in the Oil Regions," Toledo, 1897.

16. "Freedom Songs" (one-page song sheet); *Letters of Labor and Love*, pp. 28–29. The song sheet and many of the pamphlets cited in this chapter are in my possession.

17. Jones, "Social Betterments," 14 December 1901, *Letters of Labor and Love*, pp. 230–36; "A Christmas Message," 1902, pp. 20–22; and see also Frank Carleton, "The Late Mayor Jones' Contribution toward the Solution of Industrial Problems," *Arena* 32 (October 1904): 408–9.

18. The song is from "Freedom Songs"; the account of the meeting is from the *Toledo Non-Partisan and Saturday Night*, 21 October 1899, "a weekly campaign

paper devoted to the reforms advocated by Mayor Samuel M. Jones," Jones Collection, Toledo Public Library.

19. Jones, *New Right*, p. 124; Crosby, *Golden Rule Jones*, pp. 13–14; Jones, "Death of a Fellow-Workman," 5 October 1901, *Letters of Labor and Love*, pp. 193–99; "Who Is Jones?" p. 4; and Jones, quoted by Allan Nevins in a biographical introduction to *The Letters and Journal of Brand Whitlock*, 1: xxxiv.

20. Jones to Lloyd, 16 April 1897, Lloyd Papers.

21. Mayor Samuel M. Jones, "First Annual Message to the Common Council of Toledo, Ohio," 3 January 1898, p. 11 (pamphlet). For Jones's policies and programs as mayor, see his seven Annual Messages to the Common Council of Toledo, 1898–1904. See also Derrill Hope, "The Golden Rule in Toledo," *Social Gospel*, no. 39 (May 1901), pp. 9–10; Rodabaugh, "Jones—Evangel of Equality," pp. 32–33; Frank Parsons, *The City for the People*, rev. ed. (Philadelphia: C. F. Taylor, 1901), pp. 157, 219–20, 497–98, 554; and Jack Tager, *The Intellectual as Urban Reformer*, chapt. 4, "Samuel 'Golden Rule' Jones and the Politics of Reform," pp. 53–76.

22. Jones to Lloyd, 23 November 1897, Lloyd Papers; Steffens, quoted in Whitlock, *Forty Years of It*, p. 164.

23. Crosby, *Golden Rule Jones*, pp. 30–32; Whitlock, *Forty Years of It*, p. 120.

24. Crosby, *Golden Rule Jones*, pp. 26–28; Felix Shay, *Elbert Hubbard of East Aurora* (New York: Wm. H. Wise, 1926), p. 370; and Whitlock, *Forty Years of It*, pp. 269–70.

25. Jones to Crosby, 26 February 1902, Jones Papers; Jones, quoted in Crosby, *Golden Rule Jones*, p. 30; and Rodabaugh, "Jones—Evangel of Equality," pp. 36, 39; see also Derrill Hope, "The Golden Rule in Toledo," p. 10, in which it is reported that under Jones's administration the number of cases appearing, much less dismissed, in police court decreased by 25 percent.

26. Rodabaugh, "Jones—Evangel of Equality," p. 34; William G. McLoughlin, Jr., *Modern Revivalism* (New York: Ronald Press, 1959), p. 324; and Jones, *New Right*, p. 111.

27. *Toledo Non-Partisan and Saturday Night*, 26 August 1899; *Direct Legislation Record* 6 (September 1899): 70–71; unidentified newspaper clipping in the George D. Herron Collection, Hoover Library, Stanford University, Palo Alto, Calif.; and Jones to Lloyd, 2 December 1899, Lloyd Papers.

28. Jones to Lloyd, 16 April 1897, Lloyd Papers; Jones to Fred Warren, 13 May 1899, Jones Papers; "Letters," written in February and May 1900, in the *Social Gospel*, no. 39 (May 1901), pp. 13–14; Debs to Jones, 8 October 1900, in Waggoner's Scrapbook, Jones Collection, Toledo Public Library; and Jones to Bryan, 8 November 1900, Jones Papers.

29. Whitlock, *Forty Years of It*, pp. 310–11. For the 1903 campaign see ibid., pp. 126–27, 130, and Rodabaugh, "Jones—Evangel of Equality," p. 39.

30. Jones, *New Right*, p. 28; "Equality," 12 March 1900, *Letters of Labor and Love*, p. 33; and Jones to M. B. Ibach, 12 July 1898, Jones Papers.

31. Jones to S. P. Dunlap, 17 May 1898, Jones Papers; Jones to Lloyd, 2 September 1899, Lloyd Papers; and Jones to Nelson, 11 November 1901, Jones Papers.

32. Jones to W. J. Ghent, 11 September 1901, and to Henry Bowers, 28 December 1901, Jones Papers.

33. Howells to Jones, 18 December 1898, *New Right*, pp. 84–85; Jones to

Howells, 21 December 1898, and Howells, quoted in a letter from Jones to J. Edgar Jones, 30 April 1903, Jones Papers.

34. Jones to Lloyd, 15 February 1897, and 2 January 1900, Lloyd Papers.

35. Lloyd, quoted in Lloyd, *Lloyd*, 2:158; Lloyd to Jones, 28 August 1899, and Lloyd to Gladden, 5 October 1899, Lloyd Papers.

36. B. O. Flower, "The Significance of Mayor Jones's Election," *Coming Age* 1 (June 1899): 698; Jones to Frederick U. Adams, Flower's co-editor, 6 August 1898, Jones Papers. Jones did consent on at least three occasions to Flower's requests. See the conversation between Jones and Flower, "The Rights and Obligations of the Municipality," *Coming Age* 1 (April 1899): 367–73; Jones, "Patience and Education," *Arena* 25 (May 1901): 544–46; and Jones, "A Plea for Simpler Living," *Arena* 29 (April 1903): 1–4. See also B. O. Flower, "The Late Mayor Jones: His Life and Ideals," *Arena* 32 (September 1904): 323–24.

37. *Social Forum* 1 (August 1899): 85, and 2 (January 1900): 28; Bliss, *Social Forum* 1 (June 1, 1899): 32; and Jones to Bliss, 24 December 1900, *Social Unity* 1 (January 1, 1901): 9.

38. The Herron volumes are in the Jones Collection, Toledo Public Library; Jones to Herron, 25 October 1897, and Jones to Gates, 17 April 1899, Jones Papers; and *Des Moines Times Republican*, 15 June 1899, clipping in the Herron Collection, Grinnell College, Grinnell, Iowa.

39. Jones to the Reverend Donaldson, 28 February 1898, and Jones to Herron, 12 October 1900, Jones Papers; *Des Moines Times Republican*, 24 November 1899, clipping in Herron Collection.

40. See the letters from Jones to Rauschenbusch, 24 April, 1 May, and 5 August 1897, Jones Papers; Rauschenbusch, *Christianizing the Social Order*, pp. 289, 305.

41. Jones to Markham, 5 June 1899, Jones Papers; Jones to Markham, 6 September 1900, Markham Papers; Edwin Markham, "Christian Doctrine of Property," *San Francisco Examiner*, August 1899, and "The Golden Rule," *New York Journal*, 20 August 1899, in Markham Papers, 2: 65, 139–42; and Markham to Jones, 18 June and 14 August 1899, Jones Papers.

42. Crosby, *Golden Rule Jones*, pp. 59–61.

43. Ibid., p. 7; Jones to Crosby, 15 March 1898; Crosby to Jones, 19 March 1898; Jones to Crosby, 25 May 1898, 30 April 1900; and Jones to F. H. Wentworth, 24 August 1900; all in Jones Papers.

44. Crosby to Jones, 4 March 1902, Jones Collection, Toledo Public Library.

45. Jones to Jane Addams, 15 August 1902, to W. F. Copeland, 3 June 1903, and to Nelson, 4 August 1903, Jones Papers. On a less personal level, these sentiments were expressed in his article, "A Plea for Simpler Living," for the *Arena*.

46. "A Christmas Message from Samuel M. Jones to the Working-Men of the Acme Sucker Rod Co.," Toledo, Ohio, 1902, pp. 12–13.

47. Ibid., p. 3.

SELECTED BIBLIOGRAPHY

1. CHRISTIAN SOCIALISM & THE NEW RELIGIOUS MOVEMENT: CONTEMPORARY SOURCES

For the works that can best be defined as Christian socialist, see those listed under Bliss, Herron, Rauschenbusch, and Scudder in Part 2 of the bibliography. The Richard T. Ely Papers and Henry Demarest Lloyd Papers at the State Historical Society of Wisconsin, Madison, the George D. Herron Collection at Grinnell College, Grinnell, Iowa, and the Baptist Historical Collection and Dores R. Sharpe Walter Rauschenbusch Collection at the Colgate-Rochester Divinity School, Rochester, New York, all contain abundant and diverse materials on the reform movement of the 1890s in general and Christian socialism and the new religious movement in particular. The following is a list of the spate of books written in America during the period from 1880 to 1910 which interpreted Christianity and the teachings of Jesus in terms of the social problems of the day. Some of them are specifically Christian socialist; others are more moderate.

Abbott, Lyman. *Christianity and Social Problems.* Boston: Houghton Mifflin, 1896.

Baker, Ray Stannard. *The Spiritual Unrest.* New York: Frederick A. Stokes, 1910.

Behrends, A. J. F. *Socialism and Christianity.* New York: Baker & Taylor, 1886.

Bellamy, Edward. *Looking Backward.* Boston: Ticknor, 1887.

Bierbower, Austin. *Socialism of Christ.* Chicago: Charles H. Sergel, 1890.

Cadman, Henry W. *The Christian Unity of Capital and Labor.* Philadelphia: American Sunday-School Union, 1888.

Crafts, Wilbur F. *Practical Christian Sociology.* New York: Funk & Wagnalls, 1895.

Ely, Richard T. *Social Aspects of Christianity and Other Essays.* New York: Thomas Y. Crowell, 1889.

———. *Socialism and Social Reform.* New York: Thomas Y. Crowell, 1894.

———. *The Social Law of Service.* New York: Eaton & Mains, 1896.

George, Henry. *Progress and Poverty.* New York: Walter J. Black, 1942. First published in 1879.

———. *Social Problems.* Garden City, N.Y.: Doubleday, Page, 1904. First published in 1883.

Gilman, Nicholas Paine. *Socialism and the American Spirit.* Boston: Houghton Mifflin, 1893.

Gladden, Washington. *The Church and Modern Life.* London: James Clarke, 1908.
———. *Ruling Ideas of the Present Age.* Boston: Houghton Mifflin, 1895.
———. *Social Salvation.* Boston: Houghton Mifflin, 1902.
———. *Tools and the Man.* Boston: Houghton Mifflin, 1893.
———. *Working People and Their Employers.* New York: Funk & Wagnalls, 1888.
King, Henry C. *The Ethics of Jesus.* New York: Macmillan, 1910.
———. *Theology and the Social Consciousness.* New York: Macmillan, 1902.
Mathews, Shailer. *The Social Teaching of Jesus.* New York: Macmillan, 1909.
Monroe, Paul. "English and American Christian Socialism: An Estimate." *American Journal of Sociology* 1 (July 1895): 50–68.
Newton, R. Heber. *Social Studies.* New York: G. P. Putnam's Sons, 1887.
Peabody, Francis. *Jesus Christ and the Social Question.* New York: Macmillan, 1903.
Sheldon, Charles. *In His Steps.* New York: Pyramid Books, 1960. First published in 1896.
Sprague, F. M. *Socialism from Genesis to Revelation.* Boston: Lee and Shepard, 1893.
Stead, William T. *If Christ Came to Chicago!* Chicago: Land & Lee, 1894.
Strong, Josiah. *The New Era.* New York: Baker & Taylor, 1893.

The richest source for understanding the ideas and activities of the new religious social crusade are the several periodicals of the movement, most of them short-lived. Some are more socialistic or individualistic in emphasis than religious, but almost all combine social reform along socialist lines with Christian orientations. Where it is particularly descriptive of the journal, I have added the subtitle or motto.

American Fabian. Edited by Edward Bellamy et al. Boston and New York, vols. 1–5, 1895–1900. "The next great word is Association."
Arena. Edited by Benjamin Flower et al. Boston, vols. 1–41, 1889–1909.
Bulletin and *Publications of the Social Reform Union.* Edited by W. D. P. Bliss. Alhambra, Calif., 1899–1900.
Christian Socialist. Danville & Chicago, vols. 1–13, 1903–1916.
Coming Age. Edited by Benjamin Flower and C. K. Reifsnider. Boston, vols. 1–4, 1899–1900.
Commonwealth. Edited by C. P. Somerby. New York, vols. 1–9, 1893–1902. "A Monthly Magazine and Library of Sociology."
Comrade. Edited by John Spargo. New York, vols. 1–4, 1901–1905. "An Illustrated Socialist Monthly." Merged into the *International Socialist Review.*
Dawn. Edited by W. D. P. Bliss. Boston, vols. 1–8, 1889–1896. Subtitled variously, "A Journal of Christian Socialism," "A Journal of Revolu-

tion toward Practical Christianity," and "Thy Kingdom Come; Thy Will Be Done on Earth."

Direct Legislation Record. Edited by Eltweed Pomeroy. Newark, N.J., vols. 1–10, 1894–1903. "A Non-Partisan Advocate of Pure Democracy."

For the Right. Edited by Walter Rauschenbusch et al. New York and New Haven, 1889–1891.

International Socialist Review. Edited by Algie Simons. Chicago, vols. 1–6, 1900–1906.

Kingdom. Edited by George Gates et al. Minneapolis and Chicago, vols. 7–11, 1894–1899. "A Weekly Exponent of Applied Christianity." An organ of the Grinnell Schools of Applied Christianity. Formerly the *Northwestern Congregationalist*.

Kingdom. Edited by William Gardner. New Haven, 1907–1909. Inspired by the Brotherhood of the Kingdom.

Mother Earth. Edited by Emma Goldman. New York, vols. 1–12, 1906–1917.

Nationalist. Edited by Henry Austin. Boston, vols. 1–3, 1889–1891.

National Single Taxer. Minneapolis and New York, vols. 6–10, 1897–1901. Superseded by the *Single Tax Review*.

New Nation. Edited by Edward Bellamy. Boston, vols. 1–4, 1891–1894. Replaced the *Nationalist*.

New Time. Edited by Benjamin Flower and F. U. Adams. Boston and Chicago, vols. 1–3, 1897–1898. Formerly *New Occasions*; merged into the *Arena*.

Papyrus. Edited by Michael Monahan. Mount Vernon, N.Y., and Somerville, N.J., vols. 1–7, 1903–1907. "A Magazine of Individuality."

Publications of the Christian [*Church*] *Social Union*. Boston and Philadelphia, nos. 1–103, 1895–1903.

Single Tax Review. Edited by Joseph Dana Miller. New York, vols. 1–8, 1901–1908. "A Record of the Progress of Single-Tax and Tax Reform Throughout the World."

Social Crusader. Edited by J. Stitt Wilson et al. Chicago, vols. 1–3, 1898–1901. "A Messenger of Brotherhood and Social Justice."

Social Forum. Edited by W. D. P. Bliss. Chicago, Alhambra, Calif., and New York, vols. 1–2, 1899–1900.

Social Gospel. Edited by Ralph Albertson et al. Commonwealth, Ga., and South Jamesport, N.Y., nos. 1–41, 1898–1901. "A Magazine of constructive Christian thought, applying the Law of Love to social problems."

Socialist Spirit. Edited by Franklin H. Wentworth. Chicago, vols. 1–2, 1901–1903.

Socialist Review [*Bellamy Review*]. Edited by T. C. Easterling and R. H. Eaton. Kearney, Neb., vols. 1–2, 1900–1901.

Social Preparation for the Kingdom of God. Edited by A. L. Byron Curtiss. Geneva, N.Y., vols. 1–11, 1914–1924.

Social Unity. Edited by W. D. P. Bliss. New York, vols. 1–2, 1901.

Studies in the Gospel of the Kingdom. Edited by Josiah Strong. New York, vols. 1–8, 1908–1916.
Twentieth Century Magazine. Edited by Benjamin Flower. Boston, vols. 1–4, 1909–1911. "A Magazine with a Mission."
Whim. Edited by Ernest Crosby. Newark, N.J., vols. 1–8, 1901–1905. Merged into the *Papyrus*.

A useful way of gaining a more personal understanding of the ten knights of the golden rule is by reading the autobiographies, reminiscences, correspondence, and other works written by their friends, many of whom were themselves prominent in the social awakening. Among these kindred Christian reformers were the European inspirers of the movement.

Abbott, Lyman. *Reminiscences*. Boston: Houghton Mifflin, 1923.
Addams, Jane. *Democracy and Social Ethics*. New York: Macmillan, 1907.
———. *Newer Ideals of Peace*. New York: Macmillan, 1907.
———. *Twenty Years at Hull-House*. New York: Macmillan, 1920.
Broome, Isaac. *The Last Days of the Ruskin Co-operative Association*. Chicago: Charles H. Kerr, 1902.
Carpenter, Edward. *Days with Walt Whitman*. London: George Allen & Unwin, 1906.
———. *My Days and Dreams*. London: George Allen & Unwin, 1916.
Commons, John. *Myself*. New York: Macmillan, 1934.
Darrow, Clarence. *An Eye for an Eye*. New York: Fox, Duffield, 1905.
———. *Resist Not Evil*. Chicago: Charles H. Kerr, 1903.
———. *The Story of My Life*. New York: Charles Scribner's Sons, 1934.
Ely, Richard T. *Ground under Our Feet: An Autobiography*. New York: Macmillan, 1938.
———. *The Labor Movement in America*. New York: Thomas Y. Crowell, 1886.
Flynt, Josiah. *My Life*. New York: Outing Publ. Co., 1908.
Garland, Hamlin. *Roadside Meetings*. New York: Macmillan, 1930.
———. *A Son of the Middle Border*. New York: Macmillan, 1928.
Gladden, Washington. *Recollections*. Boston: Houghton Mifflin, 1909.
Goldman, Emma. *Living My Life*. 2 vols. New York: Alfred A. Knopf, 1931.
Hale, Edward E., Jr., ed. *The Life and Letters of Edward Everett Hale*. 2 vols. Boston: Little, Brown, 1917.
Howe, Frederic C. *The Confessions of a Reformer*. New York: Charles Scribner's Sons, 1925.
Johnson, Tom. *My Story*. New York: B. W. Huebsch, 1911.
Mazzini, Joseph. *The Duties of Man and Other Essays*. London: J. M. Dent & Sons, 1907.
———. *Essays: Selected from the Writings, Political and Religious, of Joseph Mazzini*. Edited by William Clarke. London: Walter Scott Publ. Co., 1887.

———. *Joseph Mazzini: His Life, Writings, and Political Principles.* With an introduction by William Lloyd Garrison. New York: Hurd and Houghton, 1872.

Morris, William. *News from Nowhere.* New York: Vanguard Press, 1926.

Norton, Charles Eliot, ed. *Letters of John Ruskin to Charles Eliot Norton.* 2 vols. Boston: Houghton Mifflin, 1905.

Parsons, Frank. *The City for the People.* Rev. ed. Philadelphia: C. F. Taylor, 1901.

Rainsford, W. S. *The Story of a Varied Life: An Autobiography.* Garden City, N.Y.: Doubleday, Page, 1922.

Ruskin, John. *The Crown of Wild Olive.* New York: Thomas Y. Crowell, n.d.

———. *Sesame and Lilies.* Chicago: A. C. McClurg, 1892.

———. *The Works of John Ruskin.* Edited by E. T. Cook and Alexander Wedderburn. 38 vols. London: George Allen, 1903–1912. Of particular value is vol. 17, which includes *Unto This Last* and other writings on political economy.

Shaw, George Bernard, ed. *Fabian Essays.* Jubilee ed. London: George Allen & Unwin, 1948.

Steffens, Lincoln. *Autobiography.* New York: Harcourt, Brace, 1931.

Tolman, William H., ed. *Municipal Reform Movements in the United States.* New York: Fleming H. Revell, 1895.

Tolstoy, Leo. *Anna Karenina.* New York: New American Library, 1961.

———. *The Kingdom of God Is within You.* New York: Noonday Press, 1961.

———. *Resurrection.* New York: New American Library, 1961.

———. *Sebastopol.* With an introduction by W. D. Howells. New York: Harper & Brothers, 1887.

———. *War and Peace.* New York: Modern Library, n.d.

———. *What Men Live By.* New York: Pantheon Books, n.d.

Tolstoy, Leo. *The Works of Lyof N. Tolstoi.* Vol. 17: *My Confession, My Religion, The Gospel in Brief.* New York: Charles Scribner's Sons, 1922.

Traubel, Horace. *With Walt Whitman in Camden.* 4 vols. Boston: Small, Maynard, 1906.

Wald, Lillian D. *The House on Henry Street.* New York: Henry Holt, 1915.

White, William Allen. *The Autobiography of William Allen White.* New York: Macmillan, 1946.

Whitlock, Brand. *Forty Years of It.* New York: D. Appleton, 1925.

———. *The Letters and Journal of Brand Whitlock.* Edited by Allan Nevins. 2 vols. New York: D. Appleton-Century, 1936.

Woods, Robert A., ed. *The City Wilderness: A Settlement Study.* Boston: Houghton Mifflin, 1898.

———. *English Social Movements.* New York: Charles Scribner's Sons, 1891.

2. KNIGHTS OF THE GOLDEN RULE

Bliss, William Dwight Porter

There is no biography of Bliss. Many secondary sources contain brief accounts of his life and thought. The best are Charles Hopkins, *The Rise of the Social Gospel in American Protestantism, 1865–1915*. Yale Studies in Religious Education, vol. 14 (New Haven: Yale University Press, 1940), pp. 173–80; Arthur Mann, *Yankee Reformers in the Urban Age* (New York: Harper & Row, Harper Torchbooks, 1966), pp. 90–97; Howard Quint, *The Forging of American Socialism* (Indianapolis: Bobbs-Merrill, 1964), pp. 109–26, 240–45, 256–67; Chris Webber, "William Dwight Porter Bliss," *Historical Magazine of the Protestant Episcopal Church* 28 (March 1959): 11–37.

The most effective way to understand Bliss's indefatigable crusade for Christian socialism and reform unity is by reading the many journals he edited, usually single-handedly. They are *Dawn*, May 1889–March 1896; *American Fabian*, February 1895–March 1896; *Social Forum* and the various *Bulletins* and *Publications of the Social Reform Union*, 1899–1900; and *Social Unity*, January–August 1901. Two significant articles in other reform journals besides his own are "Why Am I a Christian Socialist?" *Twentieth Century* 5 (October 2, 1890): 5–6, and "Unite or Perish," *Arena* 22 (July 1899): 78–89. The *Direct Legislation Record* 6 (July 1899): 33–64, includes a detailed account of the Bliss-inspired Buffalo conference.

Bliss edited a Social Science Library of selected works from English reformers. In the volumes he provided lengthy introductions, prefaces, and editorial comments; the selections themselves are revealing. The volumes are *The Communism of John Ruskin* (1891), *Six Centuries of Work and Wages* by Thorold Rogers (1890), *Socialism* by John Stuart Mill (1891), and *William Morris: Poet, Artist, Socialist* (1891), all published in New York by the Humboldt Publishing Company. Bliss's penchant for cataloging facts of socialism and social reform is evident in *A Handbook of Socialism* (New York: Charles Scribner's Sons, 1895) and the *Encyclopedia of Social Reform* (New York: Funk & Wagnalls, 1897), revised and enlarged in 1908. The *Encyclopedia* is an essential source and aid for any research in the history of secular and religious reform in the late nineteenth century.

Crosby, Ernest Howard

There is no biography of Crosby, a serious omission in the historical literature on pacifism and anti-imperialism. Robert Beisner's *Twelve against Empire* (New York: McGraw-Hill, 1968), a study of anti-imperialists between 1898 and 1900, fails to mention Crosby at all. Other than a brief recognition of Crosby by Louis Filler in his *Crusaders for American Liberalism* (New York: Harcourt, Brace, 1939), pp. 62–66, the first fairly thorough treatment of Crosby's life and significance in secondary literature is my article, "A Life of Principle: Ernest Howard Crosby and the Frustrations of the Intellectual as Reformer," *New York History* 54 (October 1973): 396–423.

Two of Crosby's friends wrote valuable, though eulogistic, reminiscences of him shortly after his death: Leonard Abbott, "Some Reminiscences of Ernest Crosby," *Mother Earth* 1 (February 1907): 22–27, expanded slightly into a short book, *Ernest Crosby: A Valuation and a Tribute* (Westwood, Mass.: Ariel Press, 1907); and B. O. Flower, "Ernest Howard Crosby: Prophet of Peace and Apostle of Social Righteousness," *Arena* 37 (March 1907): 259–71. Crosby's death was an occasion for other eulogies, many of them containing useful biographical information. See, especially, *Addresses in Memory of Ernest Howard Crosby, 1856–1907*, Cooper Union, New York, March 7, 1907, published by the Ernest Howard Crosby Memorial Committee, and "The Late Ernest Crosby," *Single Tax Review* 6 (April 15, 1907): 7–15.

The following is a fairly complete listing of Crosby's most important published articles and books.

The Absurdities of Militarism. Boston: American Peace Society, 1901.
Broad-Cast. New York: Funk & Wagnalls, 1905.
Captain Jinks, Hero. New York: Funk & Wagnalls, 1902.
"Christ's Teachings on Social Problems." *Kingdom* 8 (July 19, 1895): 213–14.
"Count Tolstoi and Non-Resistance." *Outlook* 54 (July 11, 1896): 52–53.
"Count Tolstoi at Seventy." *Coming Age* 1 (February 1899): 172–77.
"Count Tolstoy's Philosophy of Life." *Arena* 15 (January 1896): 277–85.
"The Crosby Family of New York." Pamphlet reprinted from *New York Genealogical and Biographical Record* (October 1898–July 1899).
"The Czar's Rescript." *Coming Age* 1 (March 1899): 258–60.
Earth for All. New York: Geo. P. Hampton, 1901.
"The Earth-for-All Calendar." *National Single Taxer* 9 (January–December 1900).
Edward Carpenter: Poet and Prophet. Philadelphia: Conservator, 1901.
Garrison the Non-Resistant. Chicago: Public Publ. Co., 1905.
Golden Rule Jones. Chicago: Public Publ. Co., 1906.
"The Immigration Bugbear." *Arena* 32 (December 1904): 602.
Labor and Neighbor. Chicago: Louis F. Post, 1908.
"The Legal Profession and American Progress." New York, June 7, 1888 (pamphlet).
"Love and Labor." *Comrade* 2 (July 1903): 218–19.
"Militarism at Home." *Arena* 31 (January 1904): 70–74.
Plain Talk in Psalm and Parable. Boston: Small, Maynard, 1899.
"The Plea of Labor from the Standpoint of a Russian Peasant." *Arena* 17 (January 1897): 312–22.
"Russia's Great Single Taxer." *National Single Taxer* 8 (July 1899): 1–3.
"Seventieth Birthday of the Grand Old Man of Russia." *Social Gospel* 1 (September 1898): 14–18.

"Shakespeare's Attitude toward the Working Classes." Appendix I, in Leo Tolstoy, *Tolstoy on Shakespeare.* New York: Funk & Wagnalls, 1906. Pp. 127–65.
"The Short-Cut of the Single Tax." *Single Tax Review* 5 (January 15, 1906): 38–39.
"Socialism a Reversion." *Single Tax Review* 6 (October 15, 1906): 26–27.
Swords and Plowshares. New York: Funk & Wagnalls, 1902.
"Tolstoy and Henry George." *Single Tax Review* 5 (October 15, 1905): 1–5.
Tolstoy and His Message. New York: Funk & Wagnalls, 1904.
Tolstoy as a Schoolmaster. Chicago: Hammersmark Publ. Co., 1903.
"Tolstoy, Novelist and Radical." *Comrade* 3 (October 1903): 7–8.
"War and Christianity." *Social Gospel* 1 (July 1898): 5–6.
War Echoes. Philadelphia: Innes & Sons, 1898.
War from the Christian Point of View. Boston: American Peace Society, 1901.
"Why I Am Opposed to Imperialism." *Arena* 28 (July 1902): 10–11.
"Wrongs and Remedies." *Comrade* 3 (May 1904): 175–76.

FLOWER, BENJAMIN ORANGE

The most reliable biographical material on Flower is by Howard F. Cline, "Benjamin Orange Flower and the Arena, 1889–1909," *Journalism Quarterly* 17 (June 1940): 139–50, and "Flower and the Arena: Purpose and Content," *Journalism Quarterly* 17 (September 1940): 247–57. These articles were derived from Cline's senior honors thesis at Harvard in 1939, "The Mechanics of Dissent." In Widener Library at Harvard is a one-box "Collection of correspondence in connection with Dr. Howard F. Cline's research on the life of B. O. Flower." According to Cline, Flower apparently destroyed most of his personal papers. See also David Dickason, "Benjamin Orange Flower: Patron of Realists," *American Literature* 14 (May 1942): 148–56; Roy P. Fairfield, "Benjamin Orange Flower: Father of the Muckrakers," *American Literature* 22 (1950): 272–82; and Louis Filler, *Crusaders for American Liberalism* (New York: Harcourt, Brace, 1939), pp. 39–42.

The best way to study Flower is to wade through the many journals he edited, namely *Arena*, 1889–1909 (with occasional absences); *New Time*, June 1897–December 1898; *Coming Age*, January 1899–1901; and *Twentieth Century Magazine*, October 1909–November 1911.

Flower's published books, many of which appeared first in serial form in the *Arena*, are as follows:

Christian Science as a Religious Belief and a Therapeutic Agent. Boston: Twentieth Century, 1909.
Civilization's Inferno: Studies in the Social Cellar. Boston: Arena Publ. Co., 1893.
Gerald Massey: Poet, Prophet and Mystic. New York: Alliance Publ. Co., 1895.

How England Averted a Revolution of Force. Boston: Sherman, French, 1911.

Lessons Learned from Other Lives. 2d ed. Boston: Arena Publ. Co., 1891.

The Patriot's Manual. Fort Scott, Kans.: Free Press Defense League, 1915.

Persons, Places and Ideas. Boston: Arena Publ. Co., 1896.

Progressive Men, Women, and Movements of the Past Twenty-Five Years. Boston: New Arena, 1914.

Righting the People's Wrongs. Cincinnati: Standard Publ. Co., 1917.

Whittier: Prophet, Seer and Man. Boston: Arena Publ. Co., 1896.

HERRON, GEORGE DAVIS

The Herron MSS Collections in the Hoover War Library at Stanford University, Palo Alto, California, and the Burling Library at Grinnell College, Grinnell, Iowa, are the primary sources for his life and thought. The Grinnell Collection includes an assortment of letters, reminiscences, scrapbooks, brochures, course outlines, and newspaper clippings by and about Herron, especially about his stormy years at the college. The Stanford holdings are in two forms. The Herron Collection is a miscellaneous collection given to the Hoover War Library in 1949 by his third wife. It includes five boxes of MSS, lectures, and essays from the pre-1901 period and sixteen boxes of poems, personal correspondence, newspaper clippings, and a record of Socialist party activities from the period after 1901. The Herron Papers are fourteen volumes of verbatim typescript copies of documents from Herron's quasi-official State Department work in Europe during and after World War I, compiled and organized by Mitchell Briggs in connection with his book *George D. Herron and the European Settlement.*

The following primary and secondary sources, including four personal statements by Herron himself, serve as a complete biographical (and autobiographical) record of Herron's varied career:

Abbott, Leonard. "A Socialist Wedding." *International Socialist Review* 2 (1901–1902): 14–20.

Beardsley, Charles. "Professor Herron." *Arena* 15 (April 1896): 784–96.

Briggs, Mitchell P. *George D. Herron and the European Settlement.* Stanford University Publications: History, Economics, and Political Science, vol. 3. Palo Alto: Stanford University Press, 1932.

Dennison, W. H. "Prof. George D. Herron, D.D.: A Sketch of His Life and Character." *Social Gospel* 1 (July 1898): 14–20.

Dombrowski, James. *The Early Days of Christian Socialism in America,* chapt. 13. New York: Columbia University Press, 1936.

Handy, Robert T. "George D. Herron and the Kingdom Movement." *Church History* 19 (June 1950): 97–115.

———. "George D. Herron and the Social Gospel in American Protestantism, 1890–1901." Ph.D. dissertation, University of Chicago Divinity School, 1949.

Herron, George D. "The Confession of Faith of Rev. George D. Herron." *Burlington* (Iowa) *Hawk-Eye,* 31 December 1891.

Herron, George D. "Dr. Herron's Letter of Resignation." *American Monthly Review of Reviews* 20 (November–December 1899): 714–15.

———. "Letter To Grinnell Church Committee." *International Socialist Review* 2 (1901–1902): 21–28.

———. *Why I Am a Socialist.* Pocket Library of Socialism, no. 20. Chicago: Charles H. Kerr, 1900.

Hopkins, Charles H. *The Rise of the Social Gospel in American Protestantism, 1865–1915.* Yale Studies in Religious Education, vol. 14. New Haven: Yale University Press, 1940. Pp. 184–200.

Nollen, John S. *Grinnell College.* Iowa City: State Historical Society of Iowa, 1953. Pp. 82–103.

Quint, Howard. *The Forging of American Socialism.* Indianapolis: Bobbs-Merrill, 1964. Pp. 126–41.

Herron's published books, most of them collections of his sermons, lectures, and articles, are:

Between Caesar and Jesus. New York: Thomas Y. Crowell, 1899.

The Call of the Cross. New York: Fleming H. Revell, 1892.

The Christian Society. New York: Fleming H. Revell, 1894.

The Christian State. New York: Thomas Y. Crowell, 1895.

The Day of Judgment. Chicago: Charles H. Kerr, 1906.

The Defeat in the Victory. Boston: Christopher Publ. House, 1924.

The Greater War. New York: Mitchell Kennerly, 1919.

The Larger Christ. New York: Fleming H. Revell, 1891.

The Menace of Peace. London: George Allen & Unwin, 1917.

The Message of Jesus to Men of Wealth. New York: Fleming H. Revell, 1891.

The New Redemption. New York: Thomas Y. Crowell, 1893.

A Plea for the Gospel. New York: Thomas Y. Crowell, 1892.

The Revival of Italy. London: George Allen & Unwin, 1922.

Social Meanings of Religious Experience. New York: Thomas Y. Crowell, 1896.

Woodrow Wilson and the World's Peace. New York: Mitchell Kennerly, 1917.

Howells, William Dean

The literature on Howells is immense. Among the works that specifically treat his reform activities and writing after 1886, as well as the influence of Tolstoy on him, are:

Aaron, Daniel. "William Dean Howells: The Gentleman from Altruria," chapt. 6 of *Men of Good Hope.* New York: Oxford University Press, Galaxy Book, 1961.

Budd, Louis J. "William Dean Howells' Debt to Tolstoi." *American Slavic and East European Review* 9 (December 1950): 292–301.

Cady, Edwin. *The Realist at War: The Mature Years of William Dean Howells*. Syracuse: Syracuse University Press, 1958.
Carter, Everett. *Howells and the Age of Realism*. New York: J. B. Lippincott, 1954.
Hough, Robert. *Quiet Rebel: William Dean Howells as a Social Commentator*. Lincoln: University of Nebraska Press, 1959.
Kirk, Clara M. *W. D. Howells, Traveler from Altruria, 1889–1894*. New Brunswick, N.J.: Rutgers University Press, 1962.
Kirk, Clara, and Kirk, Rudolf. "Howells and the Church of the Carpenter." *New England Quarterly* 32 (June 1959): 185–206.
Lynn, Kenneth S. *William Dean Howells: An American Life*. New York: Harcourt Brace Jovanovich, 1971.
Taylor, Walter F. "Origins of Howells' Interest in Economic Reform." *American Literature* 2 (1930): 3–14.
———. "William Dean Howells and the Economic Novel." *American Literature* 4 (May 1932): 103–13.

The literature by Howells is also immense. The William Dean Howells MSS Collection in the Houghton Library at Harvard University, much of which is privileged, was of little use to me. The influence of Tolstoy on Howells is amply documented in more accessible sources. His early life is revealed in the autobiographical *Years of My Youth* (New York: Harper & Brothers, 1916). His post-1886 indebtedness to Tolstoy and anguished self-recriminations are revealed in his personal correspondence and reminiscences. See especially the *Life in Letters of William Dean Howells*, edited by Mildred Howells, 2 vols. (Garden City, N.Y.: Doubleday, Doran, 1928), and W. D. Howells, *My Literary Passions* (New York: Harper & Brothers, 1895). See also the *Mark Twain-Howells Letters*, edited by Henry Nash Smith and William Gibson, 2 vols. (Cambridge, Mass.: Belknap Press, 1960), and George Arms, " 'Ever Devotedly Yours,' The Whitlock-Howells Correspondence," *Journal of the Rutgers University Library* 10 (December 1946): 1–19.

Howells wrote many articles on Tolstoy. A chronological record of the influence of Tolstoy on him can be examined in Howells's monthly editorial chat, the "Editor's Study," in *Harper's Magazine* 72–84 (January 1886–March 1892). These editorials were compiled into a book, *Criticism and Fiction* (New York: Harper & Brothers, 1891). See also two significant articles by Howells, "Lyof Tolstoi," *Harper's Weekly* 31 (April 23, 1887): 299–300, and "Lyof Tolstoi," in the *Library of the World's Best Literature*, edited by Charles Dudley Warner, 30 vols. (New York: R. S. Peale and J. A. Hill, Publishers, 1897), 25: 14985–94.

The novels by Howells which reflect the influence of Tolstoy and his ambivalence as a reformer are *Annie Kilburn* (1891), *A Hazard of New Fortunes* (1889), *The Quality of Mercy* (1892), *The Shadow of a Dream* (1890), *Through the Eye of the Needle* (1907), *A Traveller from Altruria* (1894), and *The World of Chance* (1893), all published in New York by Harper & Brothers.

JONES, SAMUEL MILTON

The Samuel Jones Papers held by Professor James H. Rodabaugh, Department of History, Miami University, Oxford, Ohio (pending deposit in the Ohio State Archaeological and Historical Society in Columbus) is a rich and indispensable source for any study of the mayor. The collection includes voluminous correspondence, pamphlets, scrapbooks, and numerous volumes from Jones's personal library. The Samuel Jones Collection in the Toledo Public Library, Toledo, Ohio, contains miscellaneous scrapbooks, pamphlets, newspaper clippings, letters, and books from Jones's library. The Brand Whitlock Papers at the Library of Congress contain useful letters and speeches on Whitlock's relationship with Samuel Jones as successive mayors of Toledo.

There is one unpublished dissertation on Jones, Harvey S. Ford, "The Life and Times of Golden Rule Jones," University of Michigan, 1953. The many journals of the new religious movement followed his career with interest and enthusiasm, especially the following: *Arena*, 1897–1906; *Direct Legislation Record*, 1897–1903; *Social Forum*, 1899–1900; *Social Gospel*, 1898–1901; and *Social Unity*, 1901. The best account of his life to 1899 is the autobiography Jones included in his book *The New Right*. The following articles and books provide diverse and sketchy biographical information on the "Golden Rule" mayor:

Bremner, Robert. "Civic Revival in Ohio: S. M. Jones." *American Journal of Economics and Sociology* 8 (January 1949): 151–61.

Carlton, Frank. "The Late Mayor Jones' Contribution toward the Solution of Industrial Problems." *Arena* 32 (October 1904): 408–9.

Casson, Herbert. "Draining a Political Economy." *Arena* 21 (June 1899): 768–72.

Crosby, Ernest. *Golden Rule Jones*. Chicago: Public Publ. Co., 1906.

Downes, Randolph. "Jones and Whitlock and the Promotion of Urban Democracy." *Northwest Ohio Quarterly* 28 (Winter 1955–1956): 26–37.

Flower, Benjamin O. "The Late Mayor Jones: His Life and Ideals." *Arena* 32 (September 1904): 323–24.

Gladden, Washington. "Mayor Jones of Toledo." *Outlook* 62 (May 6, 1899): 17–21.

Hope, Derrill. "The Golden Rule in Toledo." *Social Gospel*, no. 39 (May 1901), pp. 7–11.

Howe, Frederic C. *The Confessions of a Reformer*. New York: Charles Scribner's Sons, 1925. Pp. 184–88.

Pomeroy, Eltweed. "Samuel M. Jones—An Appreciation." *American Fabian* 4 (July 1898): 1–3.

Rodabaugh, James H. "Samuel M. Jones—Evangel of Equality." *Historical Society of Northwestern Ohio Quarterly Bulletin* 15 (January 1943): 17–46.

Tager, Jack. *The Intellectual as Urban Reformer: Brand Whitlock and*

the Progressive Movement. Cleveland: Press of Case Western Reserve University, 1968. Pp. 52–76.
Traubel, Horace. "Jones of Toledo." *Conservator*, August 1902, p. 88.
Whitlock, Brand. *Forty Years of It.* New York: D. Appleton, 1925.
———. *The Letters and Journal of Brand Whitlock.* Edited by Allan Nevins. New York: D. Appleton-Century, 1936.

Jones wrote less than the other members of the new religious movement, for obvious and significant reasons. A rather complete record of his published writings is as follows:

"American Workingmen and Religion." *Outlook* 65 (July 14, 1900): 642.
"Annual Christmas Messages to the Workers of the Acme Sucker Rod Co." Toledo, Ohio, 1897–1903 (pamphlets).
"Annual Messages to the Common Council of Toledo." Toledo, Ohio, 1898–1904 (pamphlets).
"The Eight-Hour Day in the Oil Regions." Toledo, Ohio, 1897 (pamphlet).
Letters of Labor and Love. Indianapolis: Bobbs-Merrill, 1905.
"Municipal Expansion." *Arena* 21 (June 1899): 766–67.
"The New Patriotism." *Municipal Affairs* 3 (September 1899): 455–61.
The New Right. New York: Eastern Book Concern, 1899.
"Patience and Education the Demands of the Hour." *Arena* 25 (May 1901): 544–46.
"A Plea for Simpler Living." *Arena* 29 (April 1903): 345–48.
"The Rights and Obligations of the Municipality." *Coming Age* 1 (April 1899): 367–73.
"The Way to Purify Politics." *Independent* 54 (February 27, 1902): 512–13.

LLOYD, HENRY DEMAREST

The Henry Demarest Lloyd Papers in the State Historical Society of Wisconsin in Madison are a voluminous and well-cataloged record of his life and work. This invaluable collection, not only on Lloyd but on other reformers as well, includes sixty-seven MSS boxes and additional volumes of correspondence, notebooks, scrapbooks, public addresses, editorials, articles, and reviews.

Caro Lloyd's two-volume biography, *Henry Demarest Lloyd* (New York: G. P. Putnam's Sons, 1912), is in large part a compilation of Lloyd's letters and is a fine and reliable source. A later, more interpretive biography is Chester M. Destler, *Henry Demarest Lloyd and the Empire of Reform* (Philadelphia: University of Pennsylvania Press, 1963). See also Daniel Aaron's "Henry Demarest Lloyd: The Middle-Class Conscience," chapter 5 of *Men of Good Hope*, and *In Memoriam: Henry Demarest Lloyd*, Chicago, November 29, 1903, a 46-page pamphlet of the speeches delivered at the memorial meeting after Lloyd's death.

Lloyd's published works, many of which were posthumously published collections of his most significant speeches and articles, are:

A Country without Strikes. New York: Doubleday, Page, 1900.
Labor Copartnership. New York: Harper & Brothers, 1899.
Lords of Industry. New York: G. P. Putnam's Sons, 1910.
Man, the Social Creator. Edited by Jane Addams and Anne Withington. London: Harper & Brothers, 1906.
Mazzini and Other Essays. New York: G. P. Putnam's Sons, 1910.
Men, the Workers. New York: Doubleday, Page, 1909.
Newest England: Notes of a Democratic Traveller in New Zealand. New York: Doubleday, Page, 1901.
A Sovereign People: A Study of Swiss Democracy. New York: Doubleday, Page, 1900.
A Strike of Millionaires against Miners. Chicago: Belford-Clarke, 1890.
Wealth against Commonwealth. New York: Harper & Brothers, 1894.

MARKHAM, EDWIN

The Edwin Markham Papers, MSS, and Private Book Collection at the Markham Memorial Library, Wagner College, Staten Island, New York, is extensive and well organized, containing correspondence, unpublished poems, and MSS from Markham's relatively unknown years before 1899, as well as scores of newspaper and journal articles, interviews and speeches from his years of fame after 1899. Also housed there is Markham's personal library of some 9,500 volumes. Sophia Shields, curator of the Markham Papers, has written two works, both privately printed by Wagner College, to assist scholars: *A Short History of Edwin Markham* (Staten Island, N.Y., 1953), and *Edwin Markham: A Bibliography*, Wagner College Publications, no. 2 (Staten Island, N.Y., 1952). The Edwin Markham Collection of Florence Hamilton (his personal secretary in the 1920s and 1930s) at the Library of Congress and the small miscellaneous Markham collections at Mills College in Oakland, California, and the University of Southern California in Los Angeles are helpful for the poet's later life.

The most thorough and reliable biography of Markham, despite its querulous tone, is Louis Filler, *The Unknown Edwin Markham: His Mystery and Its Significance* (Yellow Springs, Ohio: Antioch Press, 1966). William Stidger's earlier biography, *Edwin Markham* (New York: Abingdon Press, 1933), is based on dictated conversations with the poet and is essentially an as-told-to autobiography. The quotations from Markham are revealing; Stidger's passages can be ignored.

Among Markham's published statements which reveal his reformist inclinations are "What Life Means to Me," *Cosmopolitan* 41 (June 1906): 185–88; "What Would Jesus Be Doing if He Were Here?" *Christian Socialist* 4 (December 15, 1907): 1–2; the many newspaper interviews he gave for some twenty-five years on how and why he wrote "The Man with the Hoe"; and his exposure of child labor, "The Hoe-Man in the Making," serialized in the *Cosmopolitan* in 1906–1907 and later published as a book (with chapters by George Creel and Benjamin Lindsay), *Children of Bondage* (New York: Hearst's International Library Co., 1914).

Markham's five collections of carefully selected poems, all published in

Garden City, New York, by Doubleday, are *The Man with the Hoe and Other Poems* (1899), *Lincoln and Other Poems* (1901), *The Shoes of Happiness and Other Poems* (1915), *Gates of Paradise and Other Poems* (1920), and *New Poems: Eighty Songs at Eighty* (1932).

RAUSCHENBUSCH, WALTER

The Ambrose Swasey Library at the Colgate-Rochester Divinity School in Rochester, New York, must be visited for any research on Rauschenbusch. The American Baptist Historical Society is housed there, which contains the complete set of *Baptist Congress Proceedings*—Annual Sessions of the Baptist Congress for the Discussion of Current Questions, 1888–1904, and the Visitor's Book, Minutes, Leaflets, and Miscellaneous Reports and Publications of the annual summer meetings of the Brotherhood of the Kingdom. The Dores R. Sharpe Walter Rauschenbusch Collection, containing correspondence, scrapbooks, MSS, pamphlets, and unpublished sermons and speeches, is also located there. The following sources are also useful in understanding Rauschenbusch's life and thought:

Aiken, John R. "Walter Rauschenbusch and Education for Reform." *Church History* 36 (December 1967): 456–69.

Baker, Ray Stannard. "The Spiritual Unrest: A Vision of the New Christianity." *American Magazine* 69 (December 1909): 176–83.

Bodein, Vernon P. *The Social Gospel of Walter Rauschenbusch and Its Relation to Religious Education.* Yale Studies in Religious Education, vol. 16. New Haven: Yale University Press, 1944.

Bronk, Mitchell. "An Adventure in the Kingdom of God." *Crozer Quarterly* (January 1937), pp. 22–27.

Hopkins, Charles H. *The Rise of the Social Gospel in American Protestantism, 1865–1915*, pp. 215–32.

———. "Walter Rauschenbusch and the Brotherhood of the Kingdom." *Church History* 7 (1938): 138–56.

Moehlman, Conrad. "Walter Rauschenbusch and His Interpreters." *Crozer Quarterly* 23 (January 1946): 34–50.

Rochester Theological Seminary Bulletin: Rauschenbusch Number. Rochester, N.Y., November 1918.

Sharpe, Dores R. *Walter Rauschenbusch.* New York: Macmillan, 1942.

The following is a selected list of Rauschenbusch's published books, pamphlets, and articles:

"The Brotherhood of the Kingdom." *Brotherhood Leaflets*, no. 2, 1893.

Christianity and the Social Crisis. New York: Macmillan, 1907.

Christianizing the Social Order. New York: Macmillan, 1912.

"Christian Socialism." In *A Dictionary of Religion and Ethics.* Edited by Shailer Mathews and Gerald Smith. New York: Macmillan, 1923. Pp. 90–91.

Dare We Be Christians? Boston: Pilgrim Press, 1914.

For God and the People: Prayers of the Social Awakening. Boston: Pilgrim Press, 1910.

"The Ideals of Social Reformers." *American Journal of Sociology* 2 (September 1896): 202–19.
"Influence of Mazzini." *Colloquium* (November 1889), p. 28.
"The Kingdom of God." *Brotherhood Leaflets*, no. 4, 1894.
The Social Principles of Jesus. New York: Association Press, 1916.
A Theology for the Social Gospel. New York: Macmillan, 1917.
"*Unto Me.*" Boston: Pilgrim Press, 1912.

SCUDDER, VIDA DUTTON

In proportion to her significance, voluminous writing, and longevity, there has been little biographical work done on Vida Scudder. The chapter here is an expanded version of my article "Vida Dutton Scudder: The Professor as Social Activist," *New England Quarterly* 43 (September 1970): 407–33. See also Arthur Mann, "British Social Thought and American Reformers of the Progressive Era," *Mississippi Valley Historical Review* 42 (March 1956): 672–92, and Mann's *Yankee Reformers in the Urban Age*, pp. 217–28.

Scudder's remarkably candid and detailed autobiography, *On Journey* (New York: E. P. Dutton, 1937), is so thorough as almost to make a biography unnecessary. But since she has been so self-critical of her life's work, a biography is warranted to balance the historical record. The last years of her life are treated in a privately printed second autobiography written at the age of ninety-one, *My Quest for Reality* (Wellesley, Mass., 1952). A few letters and MSS can be found in the Sophia Smith Collection at Smith College, Northampton, Mass., and the Wellesley Collection at Wellesley College, Wellesley, Mass. Most of her personal papers, according to Arthur Mann, have apparently disappeared.

The following is a fairly complete but by no means exhaustive list of Vida Scudder's voluminous published writings:

"Anglican Thought on Property." In *Christianity and Property.* Edited by Joseph Fletcher. Philadelphia: Westminster Press, 1947. Pp. 124–50.
Brother John: A Tale of the First Franciscans. Boston: Little, Brown, 1927.
The Christian Attitude toward Private Property. New Tracts for New Times, no. 11. Milwaukee: Morehouse Publ. Co., 1934.
"Christian Simplicity." *Publications of the Christian Social Union*, no. 52 (August 15, 1898).
The Church and the Hour. New York: E. P. Dutton, 1917.
"The College Settlements Movement." *Smith College Monthly* (May 1900), pp. 447–54.
"Democracy and Education." *Atlantic Monthly* 89 (June 1902): 816–22.
"Democracy and Society." *Atlantic Monthly* 90 (September 1902): 348–54.
"Democracy and the Church." *Atlantic Monthly* 90 (October 1902): 521–27.

The Disciple of a Saint. New York: E. P. Dutton, 1907.
Father Huntington: Founder of the Order of the Holy Cross. New York: E. P. Dutton, 1940.
"A Flight in the Dark." *Atlantic Monthly* 62 (December 1888): 766–77.
"Footprints of St. Francis." *Outlook* 74 (June 6, 1903): 332–38.
Franciscan Adventure. Toronto: J. M. Dent & Sons, 1931.
"A Glimpse into Life." *Wellesley Magazine* 1 (February 18, 1893): 221–32.
"A Hidden Weakness in Our Democracy." *Atlantic Monthly* 89 (May 1902): 638–44.
"Immortality and Evolution." *New Englander* 43 (September 1884): 707–17.
"Influence and Independence." *Andover Review* 13 (February 1890): 167–81.
Introduction to the Study of English Literature. New York: Globe School Book Co., 1901.
An Introduction to the Writings of John Ruskin. Boston: Leach, Shewell, & Sanborn, 1890.
Life of the Spirit in the Modern English Poets. Boston: Houghton Mifflin, 1897.
A Listener in Babel. Boston: Houghton Mifflin, 1903.
"The Moral Dangers of Musical Devotees." *Andover Review* 7 (January 1887): 46–53.
"The Place of College Settlements." *Andover Review* 18 (October 1892): 339–50.
Prometheus Unbound: A Lyrical Drama by Percy Bysshe Shelley. Boston: D. C. Heath, 1892.
"Recollections of Ruskin." *Atlantic Monthly* 85 (April 1900): 568–71.
Saint Catherine of Siena, as Seen in Her Letters. New York: E. P. Dutton, 1905.
"St. Francis of Assisi." *Holy Cross Magazine* (October 1934), pp. 219–24.
"The Social Conscience in American Churches." *Commonwealth* (February 1927), pp. 41–44.
"The Social Conscience of the Future." *Hibbert Journal* 7 (January 1909): 314–32, and 7 (April 1909): 578–95.
Social Ideals in English Letters. Enl. ed. Boston: Houghton Mifflin, 1923.
Socialism and Character. Boston: Houghton Mifflin, 1912.
"Socialism and Sacrifice." *Atlantic Monthly* 105 (June 1910): 836–49.
"Socialism and Spiritual Progress: A Speculation." *Publications of the Church Social Union*, no. 10 (January 1, 1896).
"The Socialism of Christ." *Dawn* 3 (December 18, 1890): 3–4.
Social Teachings of the Christian Year. New York: E. P. Dutton, 1921.
"Some Signs of Hope." *Intercollegiate Socialist* 3 (April–May 1915): 6–8.
"Varieties of Christian Experience." *Holy Cross Magazine* (January 1937), pp. 18–19.
"War and Religion." *Dial* 60 (April 13, 1916): 379–82.

"Why Join the Party?" *Intercollegiate Socialist* 2 (October–November 1913): 5–7.

The Witness of Denial. New York: E. P. Dutton, 1895.

"Women and Socialism." *Yale Review* (April 1914), pp. 454–70.

"Work with Italians in Boston." *Survey* 22 (April 3, 1909): 47–51.

3. INTELLECTUALS, REFORMERS, & THE NEW RELIGIOUS MOVEMENT: SECONDARY SOURCES

Articles & Theses

Carter, Everett. "The Haymarket Affair in Literature." *American Quarterly* 2 (Fall 1950): 270–78.

Forbes, Allyn B. "The Literary Quest for Utopia, 1880–1900." *Social Forces* 6 (December 1927): 179–89.

Franklin, John Hope. "Edward Bellamy and the Nationalist Movement." *New England Quarterly* 11 (December 1938): 739–72.

Gutman, Herbert. "Protestantism and the American Labor Movement: The Christian Spirit in the Gilded Age." *American Historical Review* 72 (October 1966): 74–101.

Handy, Robert T. "Christianity and Socialism in America, 1900–1920." *Church History* 21 (March 1952): 39–53.

———. "The Influence of Mazzini on the American Social Gospel." *Journal of Religion* 29 (April 1949): 114–23.

Harrington, Fred H. "Literary Aspects of American Anti-Imperialism, 1898–1902." *New England Quarterly* 10 (December 1937): 650–67.

Jenkin, Thomas P. "The American Fabian Movement." *Western Political Quarterly* 1 (June 1948): 113–23.

Latta, Maurice. "The Background for the Social Gospel in American Protestantism." *Church History* 5 (1936): 256–70.

Laubenstein, Paul. "A History of Christian Socialism in America." S.T.M. dissertation, Union Theological Seminary, 1925.

Mann, Arthur. "British Social Thought and American Reformers of the Progressive Era." *Mississippi Valley Historical Review* 42 (March 1956): 672–92.

Smith, J. Allan. "Tolstoy's Fiction in England and America, 1862–1938." Ph.D. dissertation, University of Illinois, 1939.

Tomkins, Silvan. "The Psychology of Commitment." In *The Anti-Slavery Vanguard: New Essays on the Abolitionists*, edited by Martin Duberman. Princeton: Princeton University Press, 1965. Pp. 270–98.

Books

Aaron, Daniel. *Men of Good Hope: A Story of American Progressives.* New York: Oxford University Press, Galaxy Book, 1961.

Abell, Aaron I. *The Urban Impact on American Protestantism, 1865–1900.* Cambridge, Mass.: Harvard University Press, 1943.

Barker, Charles A. *Henry George*. New York: Oxford University Press, 1955.

Bremner, Robert. *From the Depths: The Discovery of Poverty in the United States*. New York: New York University Press, 1956.

Coser, Lewis A. *Men of Ideas: A Sociologist's View*. New York: Free Press, 1965.

David, Henry. *The History of the Haymarket Affair*. New York: Farrar & Rinehart, 1936.

Davis, Allen F. *Spearheads for Reform: Social Settlements and the Progressive Movement, 1890–1914*. New York: Oxford University Press, 1967.

Dombrowski, James. *The Early Days of Christian Socialism in America*. New York: Columbia University Press, 1936.

Dorn, Joseph H. *Washington Gladden: Prophet of the Social Gospel*. Columbus: Ohio State University Press, 1967.

Egbert, Donald, and Persons, Stow. *Socialism and American Life*. 2 vols. Princeton: Princeton University Press, 1952.

Erikson, Erik. *Gandhi's Truth*. New York: W. W. Norton, 1969.

———. *Young Man Luther*. New York: W. W. Norton, 1958.

Filler, Louis. *Crusaders for American Liberalism*. New York: Harcourt, Brace, 1939.

Freemantle, Anne. *This Little Band of Prophets: The British Fabians*. New York: New American Library, 1960.

Furner, Mary O. *Advocacy and Objectivity: A Crisis in the Professionalization of American Social Science, 1865–1905*. Lexington: University Press of Kentucky, 1975.

Goldman, Eric. *Rendezvous with Destiny: A History of Modern American Reform*. New York: Alfred A. Knopf, 1952.

Hofstadter, Richard. *The Age of Reform*. New York: Alfred A. Knopf, 1955.

Hopkins, Charles H. *The Rise of the Social Gospel in American Protestantism, 1865–1915*. Yale Studies in Religious Education, vol. 14. New Haven: Yale University Press, 1940.

Jones, Peter d'A. *The Christian Socialist Revival, 1877–1914: Religion, Class, and Social Conscience in Late-Victorian England*. Princeton: Princeton University Press, 1968.

Kipnis, Ira. *The American Socialist Movement, 1897–1912*. New York: Columbia University Press, 1952.

Lasch, Christopher. *The Agony of the American Left*. New York: Vintage Books, 1969.

———. *The New Radicalism in America, 1889–1963: The Intellectual as a Social Type*. New York: Vintage Books, 1967.

Lynd, Staughton. *Intellectual Origins of American Radicalism*. New York: Vintage Books, 1969.

Mann, Arthur. *Yankee Reformers in the Urban Age*. New York: Harper & Row, Harper Torchbooks, 1966.

May, Henry F. *Protestant Churches and Industrial America.* New York: Harper & Row, 1949.

Morgan, Arthur E. *Edward Bellamy.* New York: Columbia University Press, 1944.

Niebuhr, H. Richard. *The Kingdom of God in America.* New York: Harper & Row, 1937.

Paulson, Ross E. *Radicalism and Reform: The Vrooman Family and American Social Thought, 1837–1937.* Lexington: University of Kentucky Press, 1968.

Quint, Howard H. *The Forging of American Socialism.* Indianapolis: Bobbs-Merrill, 1964.

Rader, Benjamin. *The Academic Mind and Reform: The Influence of Richard T. Ely in American Life.* Lexington: University of Kentucky Press, 1966.

Raybeck, Joseph G. *A History of American Labor.* Glencoe, Ill.: Free Press, 1966.

Rieff, Philip, ed. *On Intellectuals.* Garden City, N.Y.: Doubleday, Anchor Books, 1970.

Rosenberg, John D. *The Darkening Glass: A Portrait of Ruskin's Genius.* New York: Columbia University Press, 1961.

Rossi, Joseph. *The Image of America in Mazzini's Writings.* Madison: University of Wisconsin Press, 1954.

Salvemini, Gaetano. *Mazzini.* Translated by I. M. Rowson. New York: Crowell-Collier Publ. Co., 1962.

Schlesinger, Arthur M. *The American as Reformer.* Cambridge, Mass.: Harvard University Press, 1950.

Simmons, Ernest J. *Leo Tolstoy.* 2 vols. New York: Vintage Books, 1960.

Sproat, John G. *"The Best Men": Liberal Reformers in the Gilded Age.* New York: Oxford University Press, 1968.

Tager, Jack. *The Intellectual as Urban Reformer: Brand Whitlock and the Progressive Movement.* Cleveland: Press of Case Western Reserve University, 1968.

Taylor, Walter Fuller. *The Economic Novel in America, 1865–1900.* Chapel Hill: University of North Carolina Press, 1942.

Troyat, Henri. *Tolstoy.* Garden City, N.Y.: Doubleday, 1967.

Weinstein, James. *The Decline of American Socialism, 1912–1925.* New York: Monthly Review Press, 1967.

Ziff, Larzer. *The American 1890's.* New York: Viking Press, 1966.

INDEX

Composition & printing by Heritage Printers, Inc.
from the design by Jonathan Greene.
The book has been set in Linotype Monticello,
a face designed by C. H. Griffith
for use in Princeton University Press's
monumental *Papers of Thomas Jefferson.*
Caslon Open Face has been used
for display.